Swim Smooth

Swim Smooth

The complete coaching programme for swimmers and triathletes

BY PAUL NEWSOME
AND
ADAM YOUNG

WILEY
John Wiley & Sons Ltd.

This edition first published 2012 by John Wiley & Sons, Ltd

Registered office
John Wiley & Sons Ltd, The Atrium, Southern Gate, Chichester, West Sussex, PO19 8SQ, United Kingdom

Editorial office
John Wiley & Sons Ltd, The Atrium, Southern Gate, Chichester, West Sussex, PO19 8SQ, United Kingdom

For details of our global editorial offices, for customer services and for information about how to apply for permission to reuse the copyright material in this book please see our website at www.wiley.com.

Library of Congress Cataloging-in-Publication Data
Newsome, Paul S., 1978-
Swim smooth : the complete coaching programme for swimmers and triathletes / by Paul Newsome and Adam Young.
p. cm.
Includes index.
ISBN 978-1-119-96319-6
1. Swimming—Coaching. 2. Swimming—Training. I. Young, Adam. II. Title.
GV837.65. N49 2012
797.2'1—dc23 2012008183

ISBN: 978-1-119-96319-6 (pbk) ISBN: 978-1-119-96804-7 (ebk)
ISBN: 978-1-119-96806-1 (ebk) ISBN: 978-1-119-96805-4 (ebk)

A catalogue record for this book is available from the British Library.

Set in 11/13pt Gill Sans Std by MPS Limited, Chennai, India.
Printed in Italy by Printer Trento

Contents

All the images in this book are of genuine swimmers in action. Swim Smooth never show swimmers doing impressions or falsely modifying their strokes.

Foreword

We were delighted to be asked to write the foreword for *Swim Smooth*. As the National Governing Body for the development of triathlon coaching and coaches in Great Britain, our mission is focused on developing a world-leading triathlon coaching system, and indeed world class coaches to support the development of triathletes at all levels, from grassroots to high performance. As part of a recent review of our coach education system, and supporting learning resources, we identified the need to bring in respected specialists in a variety of areas to help us provide the most up-to-date innovative thinking. Swim Smooth was identified to support us on the swim coaching aspect of our education programmes.

We didn't just want a swim expert *per se*, we needed a company that understood triathlon swimming and, crucially, how to coach it in a real context. Swim Smooth has built an impressive international reputation and it is exciting that we can now utilise their experience and skills as part of our coaching programme. Swim Smooth will add significant value to our coaching delivery as the demand for coaches in the fast growing modern Olympic sport of triathlon continues to grow year on year.

Feedback from the coaches has always mentioned how the Swim Smooth section has improved their swim coaching. New and developing coaches have engaged with Swim Smooth coaching methods and new drills. One of Swim Smooth's introductory breathing drills – '*breathe-bubble-bubble-breathe*' – is an excellent example of a simple but highly effective drill any coach can use to make an immediate improvement with any level of athlete. Swim Smooth's methodical step-by-step approach to swim coaching helps remove the clutter which many swimmers report they feel when trying to improve their technique.

We look forward to a long and successful partnership with Swim Smooth, and seeing the benefits and added value for our coaches, athletes and the wider sport.

—Paul Moss,
Coaching Development Manager,
British Triathlon

—Giles O'Brien,
Coach Education Officer,
British Triathlon

Preface

The 11-Year-Old Girl

You are in the pool one day, enjoying being in the water and working on your freestyle swimming. You are pretty happy with the progress you have been making and swimming is definitely becoming easier and a little quicker too – which is really satisfying. You set off for a few more laps and then suddenly in the next lane over a young girl jumps in the water, probably about 11 years old, and comes flying past you like you are barely moving. Before you know it she has executed a perfect tumble turn and comes back past you the other way, a near blur of fast moving, perfectly synchronised arms and legs.

If you are an adult who has been swimming for a little while you have almost certainly had a similar experience to this. It can be quite a shock and even disheartening. 'How can she do that? She is just a kid!'. Don't worry, everyone has been passed by a much faster swimmer at some point in their lives and made to feel a little inadequate. Kids are not as physically strong as adults and don't have the option of muscling their way through the water; instead they must use a good stroke technique – and high levels of aerobic fitness – to propel themselves quickly forwards. The fact that someone so small with very little strength can swim so quickly shows you what amazing potential each of us has in the water if we too can develop these areas of our swimming. Try not to be disheartened by the speed of fast swimmers but instead see them as an inspiration: how a child can swim so well and be so comfortable in the water is an amazing thing and there are many lessons the aspiring adult swimmer can learn from them.

A big hello from one of the Swim Smooth Squads in Perth!

This book is devoted to anyone looking to improve their freestyle swimming. You might be very new to swimming and are trying to become more comfortable in the water. Or perhaps you are a triathlete or open water swimmer looking to improve your speed and efficiency and move up through the field. Or you might be a top-age group or elite swimmer searching for a cutting edge in your races. Whatever your level, we have worked with hundreds of swimmers just like you, both in our coaching base in Perth, Australia and on our international clinic tours. We have developed and improved each and every one of those swimmers and as you will discover in this book, we know how to improve your individual swimming too.

Before we get started on that, let's take a quick look at the background behind Swim Smooth and how our coaching system came into existence.

We Live Swimming

Swim Smooth are based in Perth, Western Australia, and if you've ever been here you'll understand why! We are very lucky to have fantastic outdoor pools, a beautiful ocean and a warm sunny climate to train in. We run coached swim sessions for adult swimmers like you every day, with around 300 swimmers choosing from 15 weekly sessions. Whatever your current ability level you would fit in nicely if you were here! We have beginners starting out who struggle to swim a lap at the moment, intermediate triathletes looking to improve their performances, age-group swimmers challenging themselves with swims of 20 km or more and elite triathletes and swimmers dominating their races. We are very proud of our ability to coach and develop this huge range of swimmers.

Alongside these squads we use advanced video analysis above and below the water to help swimmers understand what is holding them back in their strokes and exactly how to improve their speed and efficiency. We have been at the forefront of this technology for the last twelve years and have conducted thousands of analysis sessions in that time – in fact many of the photos in this book are taken from these video analysis and stroke correction sessions. In Chapter 16 we will show you how to run your own video analysis session at your pool using your own camera in movie-mode. This will give you such a powerful insight into your swimming that we strongly recommend you film yourself if at all possible.

Developing coaches outside of Swim Smooth is also a real passion of ours and we regularly travel to North America and Europe to run advanced level training courses for swimming coaches to further their skills. In 2010 we were appointed by the British Triathlon as coaching consultants for swimming and have re-written the syllabus and training courses for their Coach Education system based on our methods.

Paul and Adam.

We run year-round open water skills sessions (great fun and our favourite sessions of the week) and regularly consult with elite triathletes and open water swimmers from around the world looking to improve their swimming. If that wasn't enough to keep us busy, all of the Swim Smooth coaches are competitive swimmers or triathletes themselves and have been racing for many years.

Working with so many swimmers in such an in-depth way has created an insightful, innovative and unique programme for you to enjoy whatever your level of swimming. No other group in the world has immersed itself in these experiences simultaneously for over ten years – we really do 'live swimming' – and don't we know it when the alarm goes off at 4:15am every morning for squad training!

Becoming 11 Again

Before we get into all the details of stroke technique and how to train, let's consider something possibly even more important: your mental approach to swimming. This might be a key advantage that our 11-year-old swimmer has over you: she swims without inhibition or self-imposed limitation. She doesn't over-analyse, she's not self-conscious and she doesn't doubt herself. She looks forward to getting out of school, jumping in the water and having fun. Fun is a key part of the Swim Smooth philosophy because enjoyment really does have the power to make you a better swimmer. With enjoyment comes motivation and the desire to practice the right things on a consistent basis that will ultimately result in improved performance.

If swimming is currently a bit of a frustrating experience for you, or even a 'necessary evil' for triathlon, then of course you need to improve your stroke technique and possibly your fitness preparation too, which we will show you how to do in this book. But over and above that, a positive 'care-free' mental approach is so important, it could literally make the difference between you achieving your goals in the water or not. From time to time we will challenge you with coordinating an area of your stroke or perhaps undertaking a tough training set. We can't promise you that it will always be easy but if you are ever tempted to think 'I can't!' then take a leaf out of that 11-year-old's book: clear your mind and just go for it! You'll soon be on the way to more comfortable, more efficient and faster swimming as a result. Who knows, you might even show some 11-year-olds a thing or two in the water!

Acknowledgements

Paul Newsome

Paul Newsome

Writing this book has been a dream come true and I guess my Grandma Rose was correct when she told me that one day I'd write a book. About what? I'm not sure she was able to predict given that she sadly passed away before I had even created Swim Smooth in 2004. Still, here we are, almost exactly seven years since we produced the very first Swim Smooth DVD and with a piece of work of which I am extremely proud. However, none of this work would have been possible without the help, guidance and inspiration of quite a few key people in my life.

I was always told by my mum (Linda) at swimming competitions to do my best and that no one else could ever ask any more from me than that. Given that I knew quite a lot of kids with very pushy parents when I was in my pre-teens, this advice certainly helped seal my love for the sport of swimming as a keen interest rather than something I was forced into. My mum's devotion to taking me training every morning and every night and suspending her own interests out of commitment to my own passion was totally selfless and something I can only dream of aspiring to with my children. Thanks Mum – this book is for you.

I read two very inspiring and thought-provoking books just prior to commencing work on this project, which got me thinking about my own development as an athlete and now a coach. The first, *Outliers* by Malcolm Gladwell, says that to excel in any field, one must accumulate at least 10,000 hours of practical experience and sound application of those experiences. When I emigrated to Perth in Western Australia I was fortunate enough to find a hub of swimming activity for all levels, ages and backgrounds far surpassing anywhere else in the world. With more 50m pools per head of population than anywhere else on the planet, and a multitude of fantastic open water swimming venues, I found myself immersed in a swimming Mecca with the demand for professional coaching enough to support a thriving full-time business. Over the years I have been incredibly fortunate to work with such a massively diverse group of swimmers and triathletes. If it weren't for them I would not have been able to formulate the ideas behind our unique Swim Types system. I owe thanks to each and every swimmer who I have ever coached in a 1-2-1, clinic or squad situation for allowing me to analyse their strokes and make sense of what efficiency means, not just scientifically, but on an applied basis in the real world. This book is also dedicated to you all in recognition of the need to sometimes go against convention and discover a more pragmatic way to coach a range of different swimmers.

The mighty Challenge Stadium, Perth as seen in our DVDs.

In the second book, *Bounce* by Matthew Syed, discussion is drawn to the fact that dedicated hard work rather than raw talent and chance encounters with the right people at the right time in your life helps nurture success and cultivate new ideas. Every coach that I have worked with as an athlete has always instilled this idea of hard work and dedication within me and fortunate liaisons, close friendships and training and racing experiences with some of the world's best athletes have all helped form my coaching knowledge, persona and understanding of what it takes to achieve at a high level in both swimming and triathlon. To my coaches: Geoff Edmunds, Tony York, Mike Craven, Mrs Brown and Mrs Greenall who all played a role in getting me started in swimming at my first ever club in Bridlington, East Yorkshire; Eric Elbourne who first suggested to me at the age of ten that video analysis would be a good way to show me what I could be doing better in my own stroke, and Ben Pollard who showed me that swim coaching could be a professional pursuit at the Hull Olympic Club; Martin Mosey who encouraged me (at the time as a triathlete) to join his elite swim programme for solid early morning sessions, and to Maurice Pegg who showed so much passion and enthusiasm for swimming at the Borough of Kirklees Club; my running coach Brian Burgin at the Halifax Harriers who demonstrated how a no-nonsense mindset can drive an athlete far beyond his physical capabilities; David Lyles, Ian Turner and 'Bernie' at the University of Bath who again all encouraged me to swim within an elite programme witnessing first-hand how the best swimmers in the UK and Europe train even as a triathlete when many swim coaches might have scorned my triathlon interests; Richard Hobson who gave such support during my university days and Robin Brew who showed me the technicalities of an efficient open water swimming stroke in a language that could be easily applied; Chris Jones my long-term triathlon coach who took me to excellent results at the World Student Games and European Triathlon Championships whilst demonstrating the need to be analytical and scientific in his coaching approach; and to Billy-Jean Clarke, Roy Shepherdson, Jonathan Aspinall, Andrew Blow, Eliot Chaulifour, Nigel Leighton, Brian Squires, Duncan McKerracher, Simon Lessing, Craig Ball, Julian Jenkinson, Jodie Swallow, Mark Foster, Tim Don, Michelle Dillon, Stuart Hayes, Richard Allen, Peter Robertson, Bill Kirby, Shelley Taylor-Smith, Aaron and Warren Milward, Ceinwen Williams, Yann Rocheteau, Wayne Morris, Paul Downie, Lisa Delaurentis, James Forbes, Amanda Nitschke, Judi Clemie, Natalia Vollrath, Bae Hooper, Lawrence Stubbs, Andrew Hunt and Geoff Wilson I thank you all and hope this book does justice to the many, many training hours we have all invested over the years. I am sure I will have accidentally omitted someone's name in this list, but rest assured, if I've trained with you for any reasonable time I owe something to you too – thanks!

Swimming coaching is notoriously 'system' oriented and the large majority of successful coaches tend to work for local, state or national governing bodies who are able to support and assist with funding and salaries. Unfortunately this approach has never been for me as I have always preferred to have the freedom to do things my way and in a manner that I believe in–devoid of politics and committee decisions. With freedom, though, comes risk as a self-employed coach, and without doubt I have to credit this entrepreneurial spirit to both my dad, Shaun, and my step-dad, Stephen, who have both shown me the organisation, mindful planning, tenacity, will to succeed and, above all, a love for their craft, which has been so important in my development as an independent coach. My dad and my sister Sheryl's love of graphics, animations, text / fonts and visually stimulating displays of colour and motion in their line of work has also arguably had a massive impact on my desire to make Swim Smooth a visually attractive learning tool. After all, if a picture paints a thousand words, imagine what an animation can do!

Many things have led me to where I am at this point in my coaching career but none so interesting as how I came to meet my now business partner, Adam Young, on an internet site no less! Shortly after I released the original Swim Smooth website in December 2004, my attention was brought to a popular triathlon forum in the UK called TriTalk. People write in and discuss various matters pertaining to triathlon, with some of the more hotly 'debated' areas being that of correct swimming technique. Between 2005 and 2007 I had been a regular poster to the site under the 'avatar' of 'Swim Smooth', and aimed to help a wide range of swimmers and triathletes solve their swimming inefficiency woes. On the forum at the same time was someone going by the pseudonym 'Younggun' who posted some excellent advice about cycling and running. We struck up a few conversations via email about training philosophy and our shared interest in photography and after Younggun had attended one of our Swim Smooth Clinics in Windsor, I suggested he come over to Australia for six months and see how we do things 'Oz style'. A great friendship was born and in early 2008 Adam officially became my business partner in Swim Smooth. For the next 15 months we worked feverishly hard building and developing the Mr Smooth animation and the website as we now know it, all with the single-minded goal of helping the world's triathletes and pool and open water swimmers improve their knowledge and understanding of what makes an efficient freestyle stroke for them. Adam's work ethic is incredibly fastidious and together we started releasing the ideas and methods that I had been generating for the last few years in a manner that could be accessed easily by all, most notably the Swim Types system. Without Adam many of these ideas would have stayed just that – thoughts without any substance or practical application. We now blog on a weekly basis to over 52,000 people worldwide (as of November 2011) and would like to believe that we have helped create a movement against there being just a 'one size fits all' approach to swim coaching. We hope that our recently appointed status as coaching consultants to the British Triathlon, and our work with the thousands of coaches worldwide who share our philosophy, will aid this effort further. The world needs better swimming.

Thanks also to Giles O'Brien and Paul Moss at the British Triathlon for seeking our help with the British Triathlon coaching programme and to Miles Kendall, Andrew Kennerley and all the publishing team at John Wiley & Sons Ltd. who have allowed this dream to come to fruition by approaching us to produce this body of work you have in your hands right now.

And, finally, a massive thanks to my wife Michelle and my children Jackson and Isla who have supported me through all of the hard work and devotion to my swim coaching career. I have to sacrifice much on a daily basis to do what I do and I often wonder if a nine-to-five job would be a better pursuit in this respect. However, this just wouldn't be me and I have massive respect for Michelle recognising this within me. Michelle has been there from the very start of Swim Smooth: from the very early days travelling around the UK and Europe in our Swim Smooth camper van trying desperately hard to fill clinic places, to now selling out clinic places around the world within a couple of hours of date release. Michelle has witnessed the rapid growth that Swim Smooth has achieved in the last three years as I partnered with Adam, and, as a well-respected physiotherapist herself, is primarily responsible for my knowledge and desire to know more about the anatomy of the shoulder joint, which helps to prevent and cure shoulder pain in swimmers. Without Michelle, none of this would be possible and I thank her for the love and patience that she continually shows me.

Here's to smoother swimming for everyone!

—Paul Newsome
Perth, Western Australia, November 2011

Adam Young

Adam Young

Whilst trying to avoid this becoming a mutual back-slapping piece between us two authors, I simply have to say that Paul's passion and extreme talent as a swimming coach were obvious to me the first time that I saw him at work on a Swim Smooth Clinic way back in 2007. A few months later when I came to visit his squads in Perth, the latent potential of his coaching methods were so apparent that I felt determined we should take them to the world. Paul, thanks for trusting me and my own ideas, the brilliant insight you offer into swimming, the laughs on the pool deck, the shared journey, and all the 4:15am alarm clocks! Most of all thanks for the chance to work on something important – I wouldn't change anything for the world.

There are many great things about Australia but perhaps the best is how open and welcoming Aussies are to new arrivals. My time in Perth so far has been an absolute pleasure and I would like to extend a special thanks to all my Aussie friends including Jo, Lisa, Jo, Michelle, James, Nikki, Martin, Helen, Lindy, Therese, Mary, Judi and Janet. Thanks for making this Pom so welcome, extending your friendship, sharing many glasses of wine . . . oh, and the use of your spare rooms!

I would also like to thank Seth Godin for the huge difference he has made to my professional life and in many ways my personal life too. Your understanding of the present and vision of the future has been astounding and has given Paul and I the confidence and methods to take our ideas to the world. Thanks so very much for lighting the path for us.

—Adam Young
Perth, Western Australia, November 2011

Getting Started

CHAPTER 1

How to Use This Book

The Swim Smooth Complete Coaching Programme for Swimmers and Triathletes covers the very best methods from the Swim Smooth coaching system and is used as a comprehensive resource to develop your swimming, or that of your swimmers if you are a coach. You can read it from cover to cover or use it as an ongoing reference as your swimming improves and as you work on different areas of your stroke technique and preparation.

As with everything Swim Smooth, we have tried to keep the technical jargon to a minimum and made our programme as easy to understand as possible, keeping things in a form you can easily apply to your stroke. The graphics and pictures have been selected to be engaging and insightful, and lead you through the topics as if we were coaching you face to face. If we start talking about 'smiley faces painted on the palms of your hands' or 'kebab sticks running down the length of your spine', we are doing so as a simple way of translating the complex biomechanics of an efficient freestyle stroke into something you can easily apply to your own swimming.

In the book we make extensive use of such 'visualisations' to simplify areas of the freestyle stroke that many swimmers have historically found quite hard to interpret. Swim Smooth has a very visual coaching style and we know that our swimmers love this approach and find it a refreshing way to learn. Even if you are at an advanced level in your swimming, you will find our approach motivating and you will really benefit from decluttering some of the thought processes involved so that you can become more focused and take your swimming to the next level.

From time to time we will recommend equipment and training aids that we find significantly benefit the swimmers and triathletes that we work with on a daily basis. We have been fortunate enough to have tried most of the swimming products on the market – some great and some not so great – and you can be assured that anything we feature gets our full seal of approval and is well worth considering for your own swimming – see Chapter 3. Please do not feel the need to rush out and buy every product we mention; the tips and techniques in this book will give you significant grounds for improvement in their own right without the assistance of these additional tools.

A Quick Overview

Let's run you through the structure of the book:

- We kick off in Chapter 2 with an introduction to freestyle swimming and cover some of the terminology and conventions we use in this book. If you are new to swimming you will find this extremely useful and it will help you make sense of how swimmers and coaches talk about swimming. We then go on in Chapter 3 and take a look at some of the training equipment you might use and how to select the right tools to assist you in the best way possible.
- Next we will take a look at the Swim Smooth philosophy of 'The Three Keys', which are: 1) Stroke Technique; 2) Swim Specific Fitness Training; 3) Open Water Skills. These Three Keys form the outline structure of this book and as we will explain, working on all three elements of your preparation at the same time will give you the best improvements in your swimming. In fact if you have been swimming for a while and hit a speed and efficiency plateau it is likely you have the balance wrong between these three elements of your preparation.
- Stroke Technique (Key 1) takes a close look at each area of the freestyle stroke and how it should be performed. We will clear up a lot of misconceptions or things you might have read on the internet that date back 15 or 20 years or even earlier! Within this chapter we will show you how to improve each area of your stroke so that you become more comfortable in the water and become faster and more efficient at the same time. If you have primarily focused on reducing drag up until now you will find the section on developing your catch and propulsion particularly fascinating.
- Next we have a dedicated section on developing your stroke rate. This is an area that many intermediate swimmers struggle with and can be key to improving your stroke technique and performing well in open water. Even if you are a relative beginner, developing some rhythm in your stroke can be the key to improving your comfort levels and confidence swimming in the great outdoors.
- Then we move on to our fascinating Swim Types system – showing you the six classic ways in which people swim freestyle, including the distinct personality that each Swim Type tends to have. This is a great way to bring all the sections of the book together into a simple step-by-step process for you to follow (Appendix B) that is highly tailored to your individual needs.
- Before leaving Stroke Technique we will take you through a special feature showing you how to perform a video analysis on your own swimming and how to identify common flaws in your stroke. Referring you to the right section of this book we will highlight how to work on and fix those flaws, making your swimming more comfortable, more efficient and faster too. Very highly recommended!
- Swim Specific Fitness Training (Key 2) shows you how you should best train for distance swimming events such as open water swims and triathlon. Fitness from other sports rarely carries over very well to swimming, and developing your aerobic fitness in the water will make a huge difference to your comfort and speed in the water. It will also help you to sustain a better stroke technique as you swim and so improve your efficiency too. This section works in tandem with Appendix C, which contains hundreds of combinations of training sessions for you to follow.
- To complete the section on training, we examine specific flexibility and conditioning work to improve your swimming posture and also avoid injury. The exercises in this section perfectly complement everything we cover in Keys 1–3 and will be essential if you suffer from any pain or injury during or after swimming.

- Open Water Skills (Key 3) explains how to prepare for open water swimming so as to have a confident, comfortable and fast race! Removing anxiety, drafting techniques, sighting and navigation are all included in detail. You can develop and practise these skills in the pool as well as the open water, in fact there are some advantages to doing so in the pool. Don't leave this until near-race day, you should practise these skills year round, they are that important!

Key 3: Open Water Skills should form a key part of your swimming preparation.

Appendix A contains explanations and pictures of the Swim Smooth drills – showing you exactly how to perform them and which areas of the stroke they develop. You will find this very useful as an ongoing resource as you develop your swimming.

Appendix B covers the stroke correction process for each of the Swim Types in turn. These consolidate all of the information from this book for you into a simple step by step process to follow for your individual Swim Type.

Appendix C contains a library of training sessions for you to follow in the pool as recommended in Key 3. Need a technique session or want to train your aerobic system? No problem – there's 5,100 possible combinations of sessions to follow so you will never get bored!

Other Swim Smooth Resources

This book stands alone as a great resource to develop your swimming, however, it becomes even more effective when used in tandem with Swim Smooth's other coaching resources, many of which are free:

Our Stroke Technique Website: www.swimsmooth.com

The Swim Smooth website contains a wealth of interesting articles about developing your swimming. In relation to this book you will find the animations and video clips very insightful – in fact in some chapters we have given you links to the website to follow for just this reason.

Mr Smooth and Miss Smooth Animations

Available for free at our main website www.swimsmooth.com, our animated swimmers 'Mr Smooth' and 'Miss Smooth' show you two ideal freestyle strokes in action. They demonstrate one of the two ideal Swim Types each, the Smooth (Mr Smooth) and the refined-Swinger (Miss Smooth). These animations are extremely powerful visualisation tools and we highly recommend downloading the free application

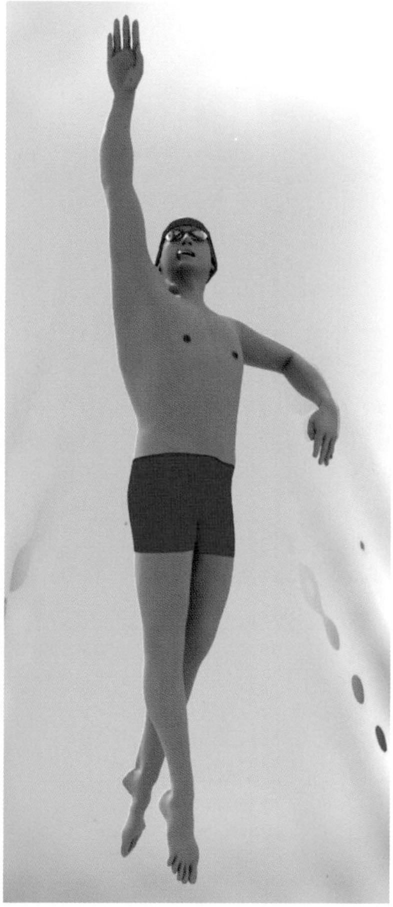

Our animated swimmer 'Mr Smooth' shows us the classic 'Smooth' stroke style in action. You can view him from any angle to gain great insight and understanding.

to your desktop so that you can view them from any angle or at any speed. For best effect, watch them just before you go for a swim and jump in the water and reproduce their strokes! Many swimmers have taken minutes off their times just by doing that.

The Swim Types Website: www.swimtypes.com

Our dedicated website explaining the Swim Type system is well worth viewing in relation to Chapters 17 to 23 of this book as it shows you video clips of each of the Swim Types in action. We hope you benefit from the Swim Type development processes in Appendix B; if you do, consider going on and purchasing the Swim Type Development Guide for your type. This is supplied as a PDF digital download to your computer and contains an even more detailed development process over and above that contained in this book.

Swim Smooth Certified Coaches

At the time of writing Swim Smooth is training hand-picked coaches around the world to pass on our methods and help you to swim faster and more efficiently than ever before. Our network of certified coaches will develop over time – find out if we already have a Certified Coach in your area at: www.swimsmooth.com/certifiedcoaches.

If you are a coach and would like to explore the possibility of becoming a Swim Smooth Certified Coach, then please do so from that web-page. Becoming a Swim Smooth Certified Coach involves a rigorous training process and candidates are selected based upon their education, experience, skill, passion and approach to coaching swimming.

The Swim Smooth Forum: www.swimsmoothforum.com

Want to ask us a question or interact with other swimmers? Then join our forum! It's a great place to share your experiences, find out about other swimmers in your area and get direct access to Head Coaches Paul and Adam, and other Swim Smooth coaches around the world.

Give Us Direct Feedback

As well as posting on our forum, feel free to send us an email at feedback@swimsmooth.com. Tell us how you are getting on with this book or suggest an idea you have that would help you and other swimmers. We get inspired by hearing your stories so please let us know!

Coaching DVDs

If you have enjoyed this book then an excellent accompaniment to it would be one of our coaching DVDs, which cover many of the drills and techniques here but in a visual format. In the DVDs we are able to show you great swimmers (including Olympic champions) in action, and visualising their strokes in the water can be hugely beneficial for your own stroke. At the time of writing we have three DVDs to offer you:

1. The Learn To Swim Programme is a fantastic way to learn freestyle from scratch with no prior swimming experience. We build up your stroke technique and confidence one step at a time, helping you adjust to having your face in the water, developing your breathing technique and constructing your stroke piece by piece. You will be amazed at how quickly you develop and you will soon be swimming your first laps of smooth relaxed freestyle – exhilarating! This DVD covers your first strokes in freestyle in much more depth than we have scope to do in this book.
2. Perfect for intermediate swimmers, The DVD Boxset is actually two DVDs and a CD ROM taking you through all aspects of stroke technique; all the drills you need to improve; open water swimming development and techniques, and a full 25-session training plan to follow in the pool. Featuring Olympic Gold Medallist Bill Kirby who has an extremely smooth stroke for you to watch and recreate yourself.
3. The Catch Masterclass is our latest DVD and features amazing footage from our new 'Hollywood style' filming rig in Perth. Three top-flight swimmers show us the secrets of their catch technique in incredible detail as we explain exactly what they're doing, how to improve your own catch technique and where you might have gone wrong in the past. Five star reviews aplenty!

All these DVDs are available in our store at www.swimsmooth.com/products

CHAPTER 2 Introduction to Freestyle Swimming

The Freestyle swim stroke, often called Front Crawl in many parts of the world, is the fastest of the four competitive strokes and also the one best suited to long distance events. In the elite swimming world it is the only stroke that is raced for distances of 400 m and longer.

Freestyle is unique in that the swimmer has their face in the water for most of the stroke before rotating to the side to breathe very low to the surface. Breathing is a significant challenge when learning freestyle and the struggle to get enough air, without taking on water, is a dominant feature of many beginners' experiences.

The body rotates along the long axis of the spine during the stroke, which helps the swimmer engage their chest, back and core muscles effectively on every stroke. The lack of vertical movement in comparison to butterfly or breaststroke allows good swimmers to sit very high in the water minimising their drag profile. In comparison to backstroke, freestyle has biomechanical advantages, allowing a better propulsive technique in the water. For triathlon and open water swimming, freestyle is a much more compact and 'narrow' stroke than butterfly and breaststroke making it ideal for swimming in close confines to other swimmers and obviously has significant sighting advantages for holding a straight line between points over swimming on your back in backstroke.

As we will see in this book, the exact freestyle technique used by great swimmers varies depending on the race distance, the race environment (e.g. pool vs. open water) and to some extent personal preference. However, the key elements of a great stroke are common between all these great swimmers.

Freestyle is the fastest of the four competition strokes.

ADAM: *If you can swim breaststroke comfortably but are new to freestyle you'll find it a revelation when you get the hang of it. With practice you will be able to feel a real sense of rhythm in the stroke without the stop-go action of breaststroke. It's a bit like breaking out into a run after walking.*

Swimming Terminology

As coaches and swimmers we have names for each area of the stroke and conventions we use for elements like your swimming speed and the length of your stroke as you swim. Don't be put off by this, this 'jargon' is pretty simple and makes a lot of sense when you get the hang of it. The good news is that, for the large part, the terminology used in this book is common all over the world which means you should be able to understand most things written on the internet about swimming and coaching after reading this section.

First, let's take a look at each part of the freestyle stroke cycle and the names we use for each in Figures 2.1 and 2.2. Broadly speaking the arm stroke cycle can be split into two halves: below the water the 'catch', 'pull' and 'push' phases create propulsion to push the swimmer forwards; above the water the arm carries over the surface during the 'recovery' before returning to the front of the stroke with 'hand entry' and 'extension'.

'Body rotation' (or **'Body Roll'**) is also shown in Figure 2.2. This is the rotation movement of the swimmer along the long axis of their spine as they swim, a little like being skewered on a kebab stick (as crude as that sounds!). This roll helps the swimmer generate more power, reduces drag and assists the arms in recovering over the surface. Find out how to develop good rotation in Chapter 11.

'Body Position' refers to how high a swimmer sits in the water, particularly the level of the hips and legs. A low-lying body position creates lots of drag as the frontal profile is much larger. You can find out more about this area of stroke technique in Chapter 8.

'Bilateral Breathing' refers to breathing to both sides when you swim, if not in turn then regularly swapping sides. 'Unilateral Breathing' means the swimmer only ever breathes to a preferred side, either the left or right. Swim Smooth strongly recommend the ability to be able to breathe equally well to both sides, for the benefits of doing so see Chapter 7 and Key 3: Open Water Adaptation.

'The Bow Wave' is the wave formed by your body as you pass through the water; it's a term taken from boating where the wave shape is seen against a boat's bow. The bow wave forms as your head passes through the water with a slight rise in the water's surface in front of the head followed by a dip past the head and neck area, known as the 'trough'. A good freestyle breathing technique takes advantage of the bow wave as the swimmer can keep their head lower and breathe into the trough by their head. This is known as 'Bow-Wave Breathing'.

The bow wave is formed by the head and body passing through the water.

'Feel For The Water' is a term used to describe the sensation of the water on your hands and arms as you swim. When a swimmer is feeling the water well they are timing their stroke movements to create good propulsion resulting in a good feeling of connection with the water. We use drills and visualisations to help you develop this in your own stroke, see Chapter 13.

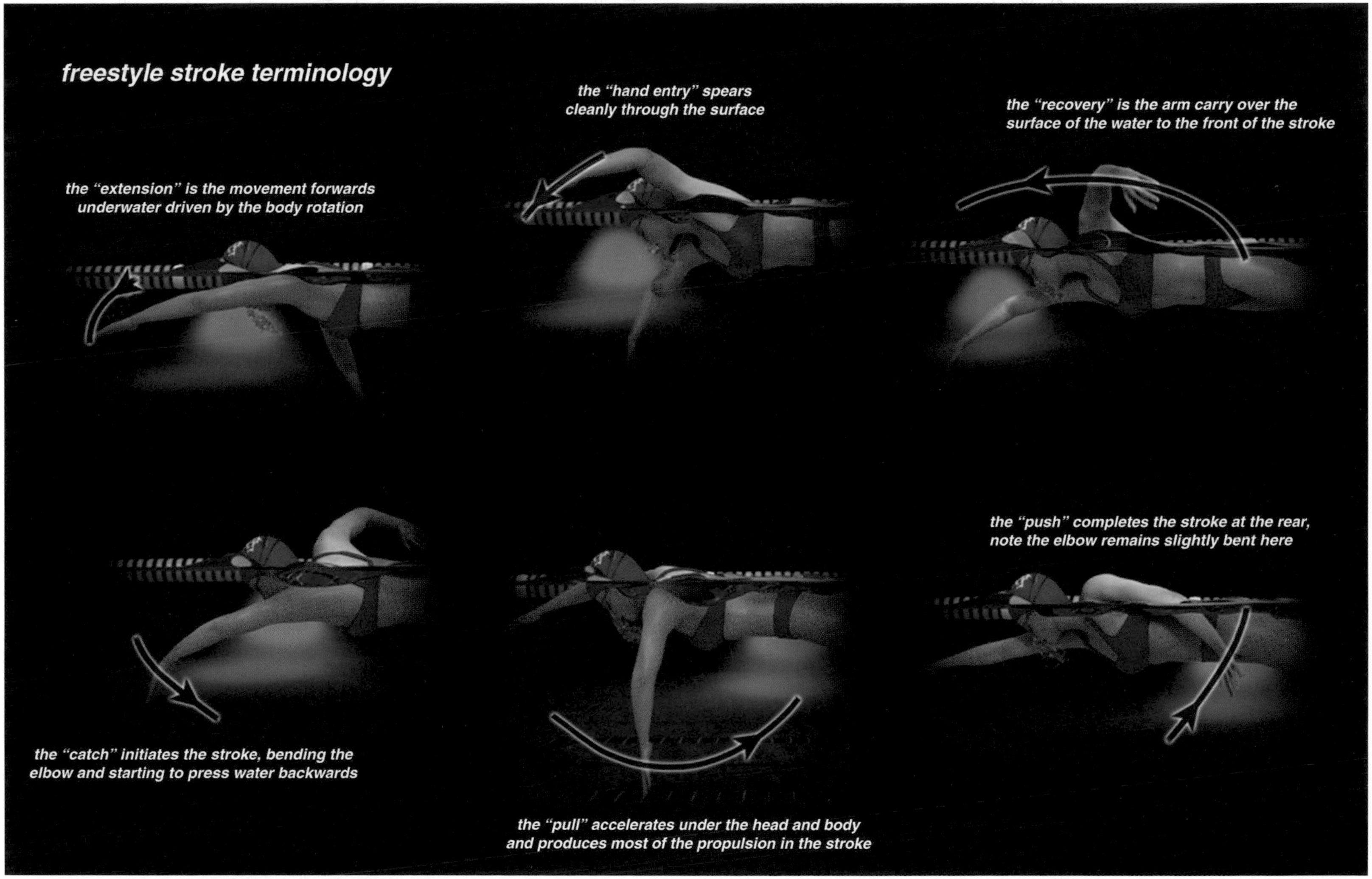

FIGURE 2.1 Freestyle stroke terminology.

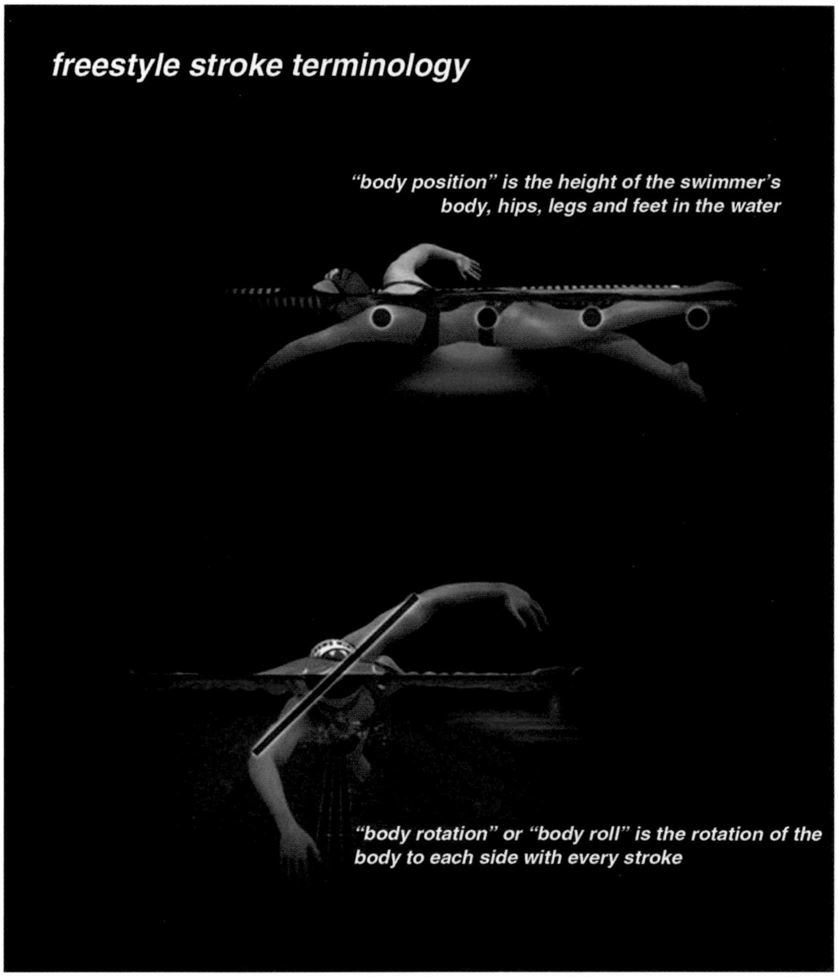
freestyle stroke terminology
"body position" is the height of the swimmer's body, hips, legs and feet in the water
"body rotation" or "body roll" is the rotation of the body to each side with every stroke

FIGURE 2.2 More freestyle stroke terminology.

'Stroke Length' is a commonly discussed area of swimming as we shall see in this book. The normal way to measure it is to count how many strokes you take to swim a length of the pool counting both arms. A lower number indicates a longer stroke. When quoting this figure you should always mention the length of the pool too – e.g. 25 yd, 25 m, 33 m, 50 yd, 50 m. Typical stroke counts in a 25 m pool are between 11 and 30 strokes per length – which you will often see abbreviated to SPL.

'Stroke Rate' (not to be confused with stroke length) is how many strokes you take per minute, counting both arms. This is like cadence on a bicycle except with cadence you only count one leg, not both! The higher your stroke rate, the faster you are turning your arms over. Typical numbers are in the range of 35 to 110 strokes per minute (SPM) with most non-elite swimmers in the 50–65 SPM range.

Traditionally it was very difficult for swimmers to control their stroke rates but with the invention of stroke beepers such as the Wetronome and the Finis Tempo Trainer Pro (see Chapter 3) this has become much easier. These beepers can be set to a given number of strokes per minute and you simply coordinate your strokes to the beep as you swim – controlling your stroke rate in this manner can be extremely beneficial to your stroke technique as we shall see in Chapter 14.

Unlike stroke length, stroke rate can be easily measured in open water and this makes it the key reference for open water swimmers to monitor their strokes. Generally speaking open water swimmers use higher stroke rates with a slightly shorter stroke length than pool swimmers. This helps them punch through waves, chop and the wake from other swimmers. As we will discuss in Chapters 14 and 39 this may be a worthwhile modification to make in your stroke in this environment.

Some references to stroke rate on the internet and in academic papers might refer to stroke cycles per minute – one cycle being the combination of a left and right arm stroke. In this situation 30 cycles per minute is equivalent to 60 strokes per minute. Some sources also refer to cycle time in seconds (a stroke cycle taking 2.0 seconds to complete would also be the equivalent of 60 SPM). What we really like about strokes per minute is a) we are always dealing with whole numbers and not decimals and b) when using a stroke rate beeper the swimmer can coordinate each hand entry into the water with the beep which helps identify issues in symmetry between left and right.

Swimming Speed is normally quoted as the time taken to cover a given distance. This could be time per 400 m or 1000 m but most commonly speed is quoted in time per 100 m swum in minutes and seconds. So 1:30 / 100 m means every 100 m swum is taking you one and a half minutes to complete.

An elite swimmer might sprint at 0:50/100 m and slow down to 1:00–1:05 / 100 m over longer distances (if you can call that slow!). What we call 'advanced' swimmers will fall in the range of 1:10–1:30 / 100 m for continuous swims. 'Intermediate' age-group swimmers will be in the range of 1:30–2:10 / 100 m with beginners taking up to 3:00 / 100 m.

The Pool Pace Clock is a special swimming clock that is well worth learning to use. It does not have a minute hand, just a double second hand coloured red in one direction and black in the other. Elite swimmers do not wear a watch when they swim, instead they use the pace clock to time all their sets – with practice you can learn to time any distance of swim using just the second hands of this clock.

The key to doing this is knowing approximately what time you will swim for any distance. For instance, you might know that you can swim 400 m in close to eight minutes. If you set off when the red hand reaches the 12 o'clock position (jargon 'going on the red top') then you should finish when the red hand is near the top again. So, if you finish with the red hand on 10 seconds you swam 8:10, or on the 45 seconds, you swam 7:45.

This is beneficial because many swimmers find that wearing a standard watch disrupts their 'feel for the water' by disturbing the water flow on your arm. Also, when swimming repetitions you can use the pace clock to set you off. For instance you could swim 100 m repetitions starting every 2:15 and so start the first on 'black top', the second on 'black 15', the third on 'black 30' etc. This is a simple way of swimming sets without having to look at your watch and do lots of mental arithmetic!

A **'Torpedo Push-Off'** or **'Streamline'** is a position adopted by swimmers as they push off from the wall. This position has a very low level of drag, lower than when swimming normally. The quickest way to swim is to push off from the wall and hold this streamlined position until the speed drops to normal swimming speed and then 'breakout' into full stroke. The length of this push-off is normally around 5 m (15 feet) but some elite swimmers can hold the position up to the maximum FINA-legal limit of 15 m (45 feet) and accompany it with a powerful kick. See Chapters 9 and 10 for a discussion of the other benefits of using a good torpedo push-off when you swim.

A pace clock has two opposite second hands – with practice you can time yourself over any distance using it.

In open water swimmers gain an advantage from swimming behind or to the side of other swimmers, a technique known as 'drafting'.

'Short Course' and **'Long Course'** pools are technical terms to describe 25 m and 50 m (or yards) pools respectively. The Olympic Games always uses a long course pool and generally they are slightly slower to swim in than a short course pool as the swimmer turns less often and so loses the speed benefit from a strong push-off from the wall. FINA world championships are swum in both long course and short course pools. Two separate sets of world records are kept for long and short course pools. The Wikipedia page at www.swimsmooth.com/worldrecords has a full and up-to-date listing of these complete records and makes for fascinating reading when comparing it to your own times!

'Hypoxic Breathing' is the process of swimming whilst limiting your supply of oxygen by breathing less frequently than normal, typically every five, seven or nine strokes. Many coaches state that this helps to build lung capacity and aerobic endurance but definitive studies demonstrating this are lacking. At Swim Smooth we use sets of restricted breathing frequency to allow the swimmer to focus on a deeper exhalation in the water rather than holding your breath. When breathing less frequently you should aim to stay calm and to allow yourself time to focus on the symmetry of your stroke.

'Drafting' is the act of swimming behind or to the side of another swimmer to gain an advantage. This is perfectly legal in open water swimming and triathlon and viewed as fair-play with swimmers looking to maximise the benefit they gain when racing. As we shall see in Chapter 36, there are two positions to draft in, either directly behind or to the side and slightly behind another swimmer.

'Sighting' is the act of raising the head above the water's surface to look forward and navigate in open water whilst swimming. Lifting the head places downward pressure on the legs as the body pivots around its centre and this creates extra drag. As we shall see in Chapter 35, a good sighting technique minimises the head lift to minimise additional drag.

Training Session Terminology

Please see Appendix C for special abbreviations and terminology relating to training sessions.

CHAPTER 3

Swimming Equipment

There is a wide variety of swimming equipment and training aids available on the market, which are designed to target specific areas within the freestyle stroke. Whilst some swimmers prefer to train without the use of any pool equipment, at Swim Smooth we are very passionate about using the right tools for your stroke and incorporating them into your programme in the most effective way.

In this review we have categorised a wide range of training aids into 'essentials', 'highly recommended', 'not-essential but nice to have' and 'not recommended' and we aim to show you how each might help you with your swimming. Whilst this is not an exhaustive list of all the pool toys you will find out there, it will give you a very good idea of what to look out for.

Californian swimming technology company Finis is one of the most innovative companies in this area and for this reason we have tried and tested all of its products, our favourite ones of which feature prominently below. Other manufacturers making good swim gear and training aids are Speedo, TYR, Aquasphere, and Arena. Depending upon your location, you may see that some of these brands are more prominent than others.

PAUL: *There will be those swimmers who prefer to keep swimming as simple and pure as they can and will choose to swim with as little gadgetry as possible, but there are those who prefer to use all the latest gear and find this approach to be very enjoyable and in sync with their analytical personalities – each to their own we say! Personally, I'm a bit of a gadget guy but I also love swimming totally free, especially when in the open water.*

Essential Equipment

1. **Bathers/Cossie/Costume/Trunks/Togs/Speedos/Budgie Smugglers** – whatever you call them it's essential to be suitably attired in the swimming pool and ocean! A well fitting swimming costume can make all the difference to how well you slip through the water. Of course you can wear whatever you like to protect your modesty but at Swim Smooth we have a preference towards brightly coloured bathers made by Funky Trunks, Aqua Diva and Speedo as they are a little bit fun and help to brighten up a cold winter's morning!

Goggle clarity in the open water is essential and will make you feel much more comfortable in this environment.

There are many training tools you can use to assist you with your swimming, some useful, some not so useful. For a review of each see the main text.

A mid-length rubber fin (left) is much better for performing drills than a shorter zoomer-style fin (right) due to the extra propulsion and flexibility it offers.

2. **Swimming Cap and Goggles** – silicon swimming caps are our recommendation as they are very durable and don't pull at your hair like the cheaper latex caps tend to. A good cap will also keep your head warm in the open water and help streamline your progress. Caps and goggles are made by a range of manufacturers but our favourite goggles are made by Canadian company 'Sable' (www.sablewateroptics.com) as they provide a great fit, come with a variety of different nose bridges for custom modification and have excellent clarity and anti-fog properties. We recommend that female swimmers with small faces try out junior size goggles for a better fit.
3. **Fins/Flippers** – these are excellent tools to have in your swim kit bag as they help to develop good ankle flexibility and provide extra propulsion when performing technical drills. As long as fins are used correctly and with a purpose you should not consider them as 'cheating' but as an aid to assist you in your swim stroke development. Choose fins that are slightly longer than the shorter 'zoomer' style as they will be more comfortable and encourage a better kicking action for drill work.

   Unfortunately due to health and safety regulations in some swimming pools (especially in the UK) fins are not allowed but it's always worthwhile checking with your local pool to see if they will let you use them. Fins are so beneficial for helping you develop your stroke technique that if it were a choice between two pools with one allowing the use and the other not, always go to the one that does. If you're not fortunate enough to have more than one pool in your local vicinity, enquire with your pool as to whether they might allow fins in a session one night per week.
4. **Pull Buoys** – for those with 'Sinky Leg Syndrome' pull buoys can become a bit of a crux and should not be used to simply mask a low body position or a scissor leg kick. It is generally less challenging aerobically to swim with a pull-buoy and this can lead to de-training if they are overused. On the flip side, they allow you to specifically focus your attention on the catch

phase of the stroke. In our programmes we use pull buoys regularly during sculling drills to build up your 'feel for the water' but you should always remember to emphasise good rotation as everyone has a bit of a tendency to flatten off in their stroke when using one.

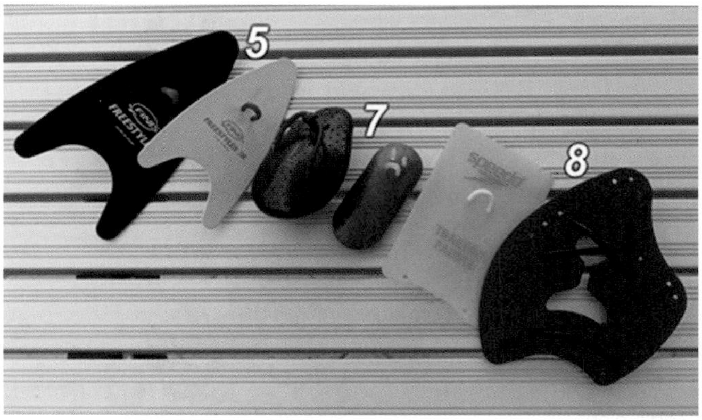

FIGURE 3.3 There is a huge variety of paddles on the market.

Highly Recommended

5. **Finis Freestyler Paddles** – if you only purchase one pair of paddles, our recommendation is for the 'Freestylers' by Finis. These paddles work to improve your hand entry and alignment in the water and are designed to fall off your hand if used incorrectly giving you immediate feedback about your stroke.
6. **Finis Tempo Trainer Pro and Wetronome** – being able to accurately control your stroke rate in the pool and pace yourself well are two key swimming skills that do not come naturally to many swimmers. You programme these small 'beepers' and then put them under your swim cap when you swim; they then beep a target pace per 100 m to you (a beep for every time that you should be at each 25 m marker) or in stroke rate mode, a beep for every single stroke. This sounds very basic but the power of these devices cannot be over-estimated. Firstly, they help to motivate you through training sets and also let you focus on the swimming rather than watching the clock all the time. At the same time they develop your pacing skills, which is a huge advantage in races as nearly every swimmer starts too fast and then slows down – by pacing things correctly you will perform much better overall. In fact you may set some PBs the very first time you swim with one in lap-interval mode for just that reason! In stroke rate mode they give you subtle control over your swimming, allowing you to lift or lower your stroke rate to find the efficiency sweet spots in your stroke. For more information see www.swimsmooth.com/wetronome and www.swimsmooth.com/tempotrainer.

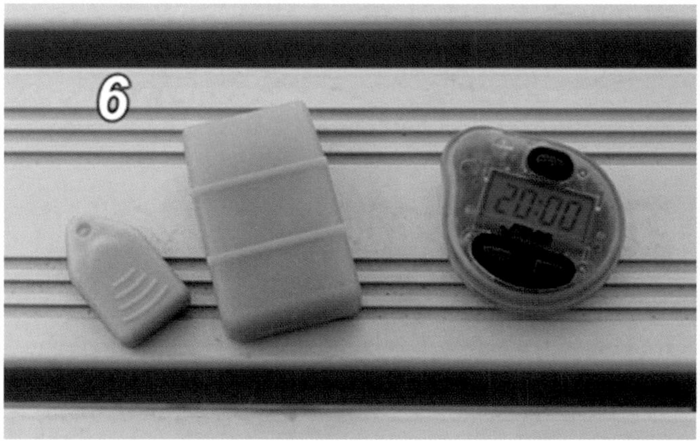

Stroke rate and lap interval beepers by Wetronome and Finis sit under your swimming cap and beep to you a lap-pace or stroke rate as you swim.

Not-Essential but Nice to Have

7. **Finis PT Paddles or Palm Paddles** – conventional paddles work on the assumption that if you create a larger surface area for the hand to work against it will help you develop a greater catch and

feel for the water. However, overuse of large paddles with poor technique can be very troublesome for your shoulders. They might also slow your stroke rate down to an unrealistically low rate and with swimming being limited more by technique than brute strength, the notion that you need to become stronger to swim faster is normally misguided. PT and Palm Paddles work as a direct opposite to a normal paddle in that their convex shape removes the sensation of a good catch and thus encourages you to bend your elbow more under the water to gain a better catch with the forearm. When used for the first time they really feel like your hands are slipping through the water but that is precisely the point – remove the paddle after 50 m to 100 m and your sense of 'feel for the water' is greatly heightened.

8. **Other Conventional Paddles** – there is a huge range of the more conventional style of paddle available on the market, with new designs being created all the time. Conventional paddles still have a place in the kit bag of more advanced swimmers with good stroke technique and certainly the smaller 'finger paddles' (not shown) are great for developing a better initial catch. Avoid overuse of any paddle and be wary of the desire to become stronger by using them – it's usually the stronger athletes, who need a little more finesse in their stroke, who tend to reach for the big dinner-plate paddles before anyone else in the squad.
9. **Finis Snorkel** – snorkels are a good way of taking the breathing action out of the freestyle stroke giving you uninterrupted time to focus on other aspects of your stroke like rotation and your catch. Many swimmers find that they feel quite claustrophobic when using a snorkel because they subtly reduce the air flow and make the process more hypoxic than normal swimming. For this reason it is well worth trying one before investing to see how you get on with them.
10. **Finis Tech Toc** – developing your body rotation can feel like quite an alien concept for those who have swum completely flat for years but the Tech Toc helps you to tune into the rhythm and timing of this essential part of your stroke. The Tech Toc is a hollow cylinder containing a large ball bearing, which sits on your lower back held in place by a waist strap. As you swim it provides an audible click and kinaesthetic sensation as to how well you are rotating. Its name comes from the fact that if you are rotating efficiently you will hear and feel the ball bearing roll to one end of the tube and make a 'toc' sound and then with the next stroke it should roll to the other end and make a 'toc' sound. If you are not rotating well enough it will remain silent!
11. **Swimming watches by Finis, Garmin and Swimovate** – great for gadget lovers everywhere! These sophisticated devices use accelerometers to be able to tell each time you take a stroke, when you reach the end of the pool and when you turn to come back. By recording this data for subsequent review, the swimmer is able to build up a very clear picture of how well they are pacing themselves. All watches contain an algorithm to calculate a 'SWOLF score' which is based on the 'swim golf' idea that if you add the number of strokes taken in a given length to the time in seconds to complete that length, you will have an index of 'efficiency' with the theory being that the lower the score, the more efficient the swimmer.

   As you will read in the rest of this book, SWOLF scores are not always a true indication of actual swimming efficiency and for this reason Swim Smooth tend not to use this measure as it can predispose people to overly lengthening

Specialist swimming watches allow you to review and study every lap you swam in the pool. Great for those who love a bit of analysis!

their strokes. The Garmin 910 XT watch also contains a GPS receiver, which allows you to use the watch in the open water and check how far and how straight you have swum.

Not Recommended

12. **Board Shorts** – many novice male swimmers think that figure hugging bathers should only be worn by more serious 'professional' swimmers but nothing could be further from the truth! Baggy shorts add a huge amount of drag and pull your body position down low in the water – this is the last thing you need when working on your swimming. Switch to some proper swimming bathers and give your stroke an instant lift – literally!
13. **Kick Boards** – we find that kick boards are not effective training aids for most adult swimmers. If you suffer from poor body position and a weak kick, using a buoyant kick board at the front of the stroke is only going to exacerbate this and place you in a very uneconomical position with your front end lifted. We prefer to practise kicking sets without the use of a float and with or without fins in a more specific torpedo or side-lying position in the water.

The training sessions in Appendix C show you examples of how to introduce many of these tools into your training sessions.

The Three Keys to Better Freestyle Swimming

The Swim Smooth coaching philosophy is based on many decades of combined experience of coaching swimmers and triathletes in Perth and around the world. Our coaching team have worked with thousands of swimmers of all ability levels from beginner to elite competitor and developed highly effective coaching methods for every type of swimmer. We also work and interact with hundreds of swimming coaches around the world both in person and through our Coaches Network on the internet. Through all of this coaching experience, one thing has proven to be true time and time again: the swimmers who make the biggest improvements follow a rounded programme covering three critical areas of swimming development:

1. They develop their stroke technique in the pool using drills and visualisations specific to their individual stroke needs.
2. They consistently train their swim specific fitness (with an emphasis on the consistency).
3. They regularly practise their open water skills such as drafting, sighting and rhythm, either in the pool or in open water.

We call these areas The Three Keys and they are so fundamental to the Swim Smooth philosophy that we have structured this whole book around them:

Key 1: Stroke Technique Development – Chapters 5 to 23
Key 2: Swim Training – Chapters 24 to 32
Key 3: Open Water Skills – Chapters 33 to 39

You may immediately appreciate why each of these keys are important to maximise your performance, however you may be tempted to focus on each one at different times of the year (in coaching jargon we call this 'periodisation'). Do not make this mistake. Separating them out into different periods during the year becomes a lot less effective than working on them simultaneously all year round.

Combining the Three Keys

When we first explain to swimmers the concept of working on these three elements at the same time, they are sometimes concerned that this is a complex thing to do or that they might not have time in

PAUL: *We very much follow this philosophy in the Swim Smooth squads in Perth, conducting technique, fitness and open water skills sessions (in the pool and open water) every week. Interestingly, one of the most popular sessions of the week are the harder CSS training sessions that we will explain to you in Chapter 27. We affectionately call them 'Fresh and Fruity' sessions, so called because of the higher intensity required in these sessions and as a way of making light of what are actually quite tough sessions.*

Despite Swim Smooth being renowned locally as a squad focused on developing a swimmer's technical efficiency, these harder fitness sessions are very popular and give each swimmer a great sense of achievement afterwards. Many swimmers join our squads to improve their stroke technique and then really discover the fitness side of swimming too and benefit greatly from the training. They are not afraid of a little bit of hard work and as Captain Matthew Webb, the first man to swim the English Channel in 1875, famously said: 'Nothing great is easy!'

their swimming week. Actually, training in this way is not as complicated or difficult as you might imagine. Instead, the variety of challenges it offers to your brain and body is great fun, really keeping you on your toes and pushing your swimming quickly forward at the same time. You will never get bored or stagnant again!

To help you combine the three keys together in your training week we have developed special weekly 'Skeleton Structures' for you to follow (Chapter 26) and also an extensive set of training sessions to slot into that structure (Appendix C). By following this training routine your swimming technique, efficiency, fitness and race skills will soon be moving forward apace.

How the Three Keys Interact with Each Other

One of the reasons why you need to work on all three of the keys at the same time is that the three areas interact and benefit each other – i.e. they add up to more than the sum of their individual parts. A good example of this is how fitness training benefits your stroke technique development. Many swimmers focus purely on their technique in the pool and avoid any training sets for fear they will harm their stroke technique – we affectionately call this group of swimmers 'Technique Hermits'. Although these swimmers may make some initial progress with their swimming, they soon hit a plateau in performance beyond which they cannot progress. In fact some of these guys are so diligent that they have been repeating the same technique sessions for years with the hope that one day they will break through to better swimming. This is a great shame; such dedicated swimmers deserve much better.

Professional triathlete and Ironman winner Scott Neyedli knows that it takes more than drills and a pretty stroke to allow him to swim 3.8 km in under 45 minutes.

Of course, the opposite is also true: many Masters swimmers focus purely on training and never work on improving their stroke technique. Just as much as the Technique Hermits, this group stands to make some large improvements by following a more balanced approach to their swimming preparation from introducing structured and focused technique sessions.

A second classic example of the interaction between the three keys is how open water skills benefit stroke technique development. If you exclusively focus on stroke technique, the tendency is to develop a long stroke at a slow stroke rate. You may make some progress in the pool by focusing on technique but when summer comes around and you swim in open water you would soon be left behind by swimmers with a slightly shorter faster stroke that is much more suited to this environment. By performing regular open water skills sessions (in the pool in winter) alongside your technique sessions, your stroke technique will naturally develop in the right direction to be efficient in the open water. If you are a triathlete this is especially vital for you.

ADAM: *If you have gone down the technique-only route yourself in the past don't be concerned, by introducing the other two keys (training and open water skills) into your training week you will quickly start to make progress again. If you have held the belief that stroke technique is all important for a long time then it's only natural to feel sceptical at first but judge the results objectively, are you swimming more quickly and more easily with a more balanced preparation?*

Taking Time Out of Your Swim Splits

Another way to explain the importance of the three keys is to look at things in terms of time saving. Let's say you were a triathlete preparing for Olympic Distance races where the swim leg is 1500 m in open water. At the moment you swim around thirty minutes for 1500 m and you set yourself a target of swimming six minutes quicker, what is the best way to go about making this improvement?

Most triathletes in this situation would try to make this improvement by focusing purely on the efficiency of their stroke technique. Of course, this is a worthy goal but you would greatly increase your chances of success by splitting things out and looking to get two minutes each from your technique, fitness and open water skills instead. Or looking at this another way, if you did improve your stroke efficiency to the tune of six minutes you would have left those fitness and open water improvements on the table and you could then be swimming much more quickly still.

A Balanced Approach

With swimming, as with many things in life, a balanced approach works best. Use this book to develop each of these three key areas of your swimming and keep developing them every week, you will get some fantastic results when race season comes around!

KEY

1

Technique

Develop an efficient freestyle stroke technique

What Makes an Efficient Freestyle Stroke?

As someone interested in improving your swimming you've probably watched Olympic swimmers on TV or on YouTube. If you have a good club at your local pool you might have seen some very good junior swimmers up close and if you've been to a large triathlon or open water event you've perhaps watched the elite wave of the race. Comparing all of these great swimmers, all with different builds and all racing in different environments, you will have noticed a large range of stroke styles: some have strong kicks, others nearly no kick, some a high elbow recovery, others a straight arm recovery, some with a short punchy style, others with a long flowing stroke. Yet all of them are swimming extremely quickly. The stroke styles of elite swimmers can look quite different but there are common elements of great stroke technique between them all. Whilst you might never swim quite as quickly as an Olympic champion, just like them you should look to develop your own stroke technique into

ADAM: *Developing a good freestyle stroke technique is essential to swim well in the pool and open water alike. A good stroke technique reduces your drag and increases your propulsion for a given level of effort, meaning you move more quickly or more easily through the water – or both!*

TABLE 5.1 Olympic champions in numbers. Note the range of stroke rates, speeds and recovery styles of all these great swimmers.

Grant Hackett during 1500 m World Record swim: 76 strokes per minute, swimming speed: 0:58 / 100 m, arm recovery style: high elbow, height: 1.97 m (6'5" 1/2")

Ian Thorpe during 400 m World Record swim: 72 strokes per minute, swimming speed: 0:55 / 100 m, arm recovery style: high elbow, height: 1.95 m (6'5")

Michael Phelps during 200 m World Record swim: 77 strokes per minute, swimming speed: 0:51 / 100 m, arm recovery style: high elbow, height: 1.93 m (6'4")

Emma Snowsill during Gold Medal Winning Triathlon at Beijing Olympics: 86 strokes per minute, swimming speed: 1:19 / 100 m (OW 1500 m No Wetsuit), arm recovery style: straight, height: 1.61 m (5'3")

Laure Manadou during Gold Medal Winning 400 m At Athens Olympics: 108 strokes per minute, swimming speed: 1:01 / 100 m, arm recovery style: straight, height: 1.78 m (5'10")

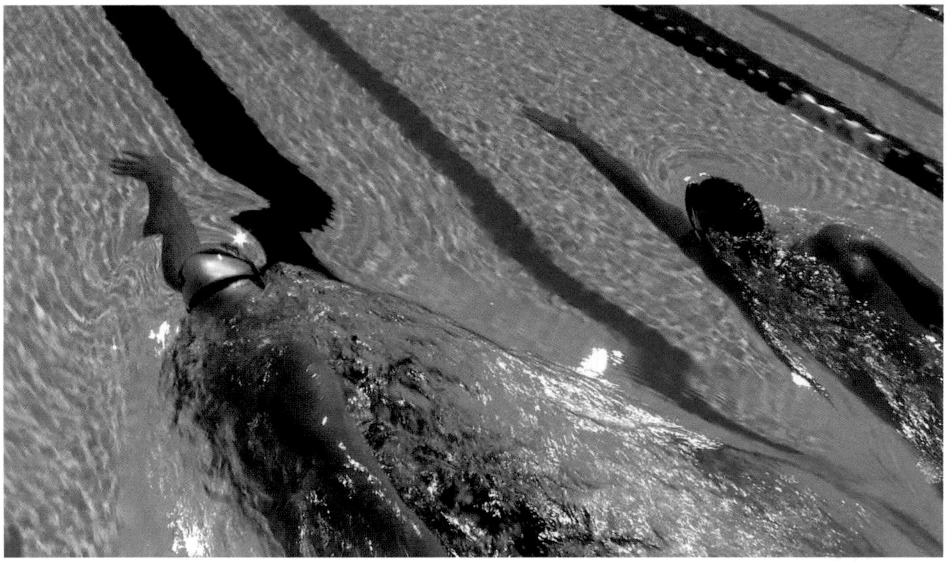

Drills, such as this kicking-on-your-side exercise, are extremely useful to help you develop an improved stroke technique.

one that suits your body type and the environment in which you are racing. Whatever your chosen style, you should share the common elements of good technique with those of the elite swimmers so that you can have low levels of drag and high levels of propulsion in your own stroke.

Shortly we are going to examine each aspect of good freestyle technique in turn, pointing out common flaws and showing you step-by-step methods to remove them from your stroke. We will clear up a few common misconceptions along the way and refer to Appendix A, which contains descriptions of the key drills and visualisations targeting different areas of your stroke technique. These drills are the standard set that we've developed and refined with our large training squads in Perth, Western Australia and also around the world with our popular Swim Smooth Clinic series. They are designed to be used by all levels of swimmer from beginner to elite swimmer – you'll find them very useful to improve your own swimming.

In Chapter 15 we will take a more in-depth scientific look at swimming efficiency, giving a lot of background on the coaching advice we offer to swimmers. If you are technically minded you will find this a very interesting section of the book as we put some classic misconceptions about stroke efficiency to bed.

Later in Chapter 17 we'll take a look at our innovative Swim Types system, which examines the six distinct styles that people use to swim freestyle. When you identify your own Swim Type then we will be able to give you some very specific advice to improve your stroke, referring back to the individual methods in Chapters 7–14 as we do so. This is an extremely powerful way to identify flaws in your stroke if you are not fortunate enough to have a coach watching over you when you swim.

CHAPTER 6

Stroke Flaws – Cause and Effect

A Never-Ending Pursuit

Working on your stroke technique is not just something for swimmers new to freestyle; every swimmer of any ability level should regularly work on their stroke – it's a never-ending pursuit. Nearly all swimmers, even those who are swimming very well, have areas of their technique they could improve on significantly which would make their stroke more efficient, relaxed, faster or offer better endurance. Even an Olympic champion with a fantastic stroke will still spend a significant portion of their weekly training maintaining and reinforcing their technique; without doing so their performances could easily drop off.

Working on your stroke technique does not sound very exciting but it can actually be a lot of fun: it brings variety to your swim training and gives you a different sort of challenge to that offered by fitness training. We will use the Swim Smooth drill set (Appendix A) to assist you in this task; each drill or visualisation is a highly developed tool to help you work on the weaker areas in your stroke technique.

Cause and Effect

Before we start looking at each area of the freestyle stroke, it is important to remember that when you jump in the water to correct your stroke you need to keep things simple at all times. To help you do this, Swim Smooth uses a simple but deceptively powerful coaching philosophy called 'Cause and Effect'.

Cause and Effect says that for every stroke flaw (the effect) there is an underlying cause for it. This is powerful because it helps you get to the root cause of stroke flaws and fix them for good. For instance, a scissor kick where the legs part excessively creating a lot of drag is triggered by a loss of balance from crossing the centre line with the lead hand in front of the head (the cause). By removing the crossover you will fix the scissor kick, without ever thinking about your kick itself. The conventional approach to fixing a scissor kick is lots of kicking technique work and focus on keeping the legs together but ultimately the scissor kick will keep returning as the underlying cause has not been removed.

Note that 'Cause and Effect' also reduces the number of problems that you have to fix in your stroke. You could look at a swimmer and say that they hold their breath underwater and that they have a poor body position with low legs. This is not really two problems though, it is just one: by improving their exhalation the swimmer will reduce the excess buoyancy in their chest and help bring the legs up high. We are sure you are beginning to see the power of this methodology, especially if you have felt a little 'cluttered' in the past by trying to correct multiple aspects of your stroke at the same time.

As we look at each area of freestyle stroke technique in turn we will take a look at the cause of every stroke flaw and provide you with drills and visualisations to remove that underlying cause.

OK, let's get to work!

CHAPTER 7 Breathing

It would not be an overstatement to say that breathing technique is the single most important aspect of freestyle swimming. Good breathing technique is much more challenging in freestyle than the other strokes because the head is in the water at all times and the swimmer must keep their head low and breathe out to the side very near the surface.

Holding your breath underwater will cause a build-up of CO_2 in your lungs and blood stream and make your swimming feel tense.

For swimmers learning freestyle, breathing can be extremely challenging and it's normal to experience high levels of anxiety about getting enough air and not swallowing water! If you feel this way then developing your exhalation into the water and your bow-wave breathing technique is going to be critical to improving your swimming; these are the first two aspects of breathing technique we'll look at here. Don't worry, work on the technique of breathing and you'll soon be feeling much more calm and relaxed when swimming freestyle.

For intermediate level swimmers, brushing up on bow-wave breathing and exhalation into the water is going to be useful for you and will make a real difference to your efficiency and level of relaxation. We also strongly encourage you to learn to breathe bilaterally, which is important as a natural way of keeping your stroke symmetrical and can even help you develop the catch phase of your stroke. Don't worry if you've tried bilateral breathing before and struggled, we'll show you why that was and how to conquer it.

Breathing timing, specifically breathing late, can also be a problem for more advanced swimmers. We'll look at breathing timing in the final part of this section.

Exhalation

PAUL: *If you've ever done any yoga you'll intuitively understand the relationship between breathing technique and relaxation. If you hold your breath you automatically become tense – please never never do this when swimming! Instead focus on exhaling into the water with a long constant stream of bubbles. I ask swimmers I'm coaching to experiment with making sounds into the water as they exhale, for example the 'brrrrrr' sound of a motorboat or motorbike. As simplistic as this sounds it can really make a huge difference to your swimming.*

For all swimmers it's important to constantly exhale whenever you are face down in the water. This rids your lungs and bloodstream of CO_2 and means that when you do rotate to breathe you have more time to inhale as you don't have to exhale first. It also helps to improve your body position as too much buoyancy in the chest lifts your front end up and puts downward pressure on the legs.

Exhaling into the water sounds easy but can be surprisingly hard to learn. For many swimmers it simply doesn't feel like a natural thing to do. To develop good exhalation technique use the Sink Down Exercise in Appendix A. Experiment between exhaling into the water using either your mouth or nose or a mix of both; there's no right or wrong here, see which feels more natural for you and then stick with that method. It should feel like you are sighing and not forcing the air out. Try to be loose and floppy as you sink down to remove all the tension from your body.

Your ability to sink to the bottom of the pool during the Sink Down Exercise is totally determined by how relaxed and efficient your exhalation is into the water. Many swimmers with poor body positions would expect to sink like a stone but often the opposite is true and they find it harder to sink than other swimmers. This is an interesting insight into their swimming as it shows how their tendency to hold onto their breath is actually harming their body position: the excess buoyancy in the chest lifts their front end up but the body then pivots around its centre and so pushes the legs downward.

Once you are able to sink down easily to the bottom of the pool with a nice relaxed exhalation try some easy laps of freestyle

Develop your relaxation in the water using the Sink Down Exercise at the beginning of your training sessions.

PAUL: *Traditionally swimmers were taught to hold their breath as it increases the level of buoyancy in the chest. This is certainly true but most swimmers already have plenty of buoyancy in the upper body, it is in the legs where it is lacking, especially if you are a triathlete with muscular legs. By smoothly exhaling into the water and removing excess buoyancy in the chest, we can counteract this and get your legs higher in the water. This is a classic example of our philosophy of 'Cause and Effect' in swimming.*

swimming. Simply focus on a smooth exhalation into the water using your normal breathing pattern to whichever side you feel most comfortable. For those who normally only breathe to one side, don't be surprised if you notice that you are suddenly able to go from breathing every two strokes to breathing every four strokes and feel more comfortable doing so. Sometimes breathing every two strokes does not physically give you enough time to exhale properly especially if you have a naturally high stroke rate.

Elite swimmer Jono Van Hazel shows us his excellent exhalation technique through the nose.

To really contrast the difference a good exhalation technique makes, trying swimming 100 m straight through as:

25 m exhaling smoothly
25 m holding your breath and exhaling at the last second
25 m exhaling smoothly
25 m holding again

You will really notice the contrast, the difference a good exhalation technique can make is truly amazing!

ADAM: *The key point to remember with exhalation is that as swimmers we are not usually restricted by how much air we can get in but how efficiently we exhale out. Clearing the lungs smoothly before taking a deep breath of air on the next inhalation (without gasping) will really help to keep you more relaxed and aerobic in the water.*

THE BUBBLE BUBBLE BREATHE MANTRA

Now is an excellent time to experiment with some bilateral breathing if you have not done so already – a better exhalation technique will make things much easier for you to go from breathing every two strokes to breathing every three. As we will see when we look at bilateral breathing in a little more depth later on, it is usually the fear that if breathing every two strokes is challenging already, how could you possibly breathe every three? Try this simple mantra:

> Take a breath and then on each of the following two strokes say 'bubble' into the water. Literally speak it into the water to emphasise the exhalation during each stroke! On the third stroke take a breath to that side whilst saying 'breathe' to yourself (not out loud!). Swimming down the lap repeating 'breathe-bubble-bubble-breathe-bubble-bubble-breathe' is a great way to coordinate good exhalation with the timing required to breathe every three strokes (bilateral breathing).

The chances are you might still feel rather strange breathing to your unfamiliar side but with the tips that follow, we will show you how to improve that too.

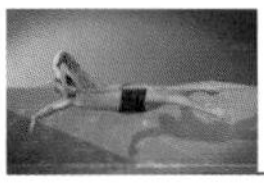

Using the Bow Wave

An efficient stroke technique keeps the head low in the water when breathing. Many swimmers feel that they need to lift their heads to find air but lifting the head excessively causes the whole upper torso to lift and the legs to sink, creating a large amount of drag.

The secret to keeping your head low in the water is to breathe into the trough of air formed by the bow wave created around your head. Every swimmer has a bow wave, it's formed as the head pushes forwards through the water creating a small rise in the water in front of the head and then a trough alongside the chin and neck – a channel of air beneath the main surface level of the water.

The bow wave forms at the top of your head as it travels through the water; it causes a trough of air beside your mouth to breathe into.

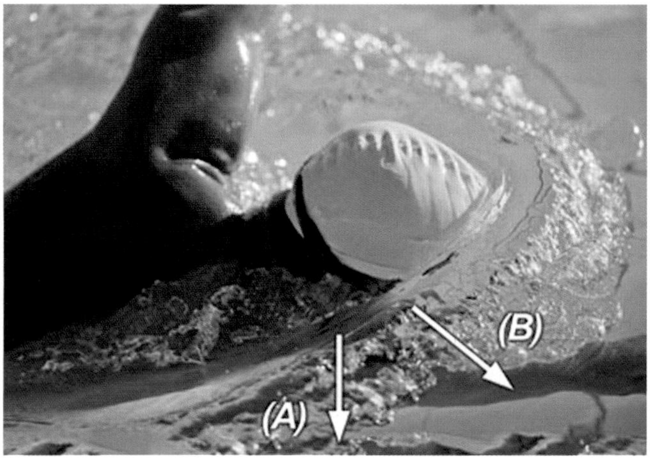

FIGURE 7.4 The ideal breathing angle is (A) where the bow wave is quite deep. If you breathe slightly too far forwards (B) then you will have to crane your head high to reach air.

It's important to appreciate that the bow wave forms off the top of your head and is just deep enough to breathe into by the time it passes the level of your mouth. If you lift your head clear out of the water to breathe then the bow wave will not form off the top of your head and so the trough will not be there for you! This is a very common occurrence for those swimmers who feel they must lift their heads excessively high to keep from swallowing water. Ironically enough, if this instinctive action can be controlled and the head kept lower when breathing, it becomes much easier to get a breath in. Equally though, some swimmers completely bury their heads in the water in an effort to improve body position which, as we will see in Chapter 8, might not be necessary for every swimmer. Furthermore, the act of burying the head may be problematic if it is too deep to cause the bow wave to form cleanly.

When developing a good bow-wave breathing technique think about keeping the top of your head low in the water and try and breathe ever so slightly behind you into area (A) shown in Figure 7.4. If you crane your head forwards (B) then the bow wave isn't as deep, which makes breathing much harder. Many swimmers who spend a lot of time training in the open water often develop position (B) from trying to sight forwards and breathe at the same time, as we will see in Chapter 35 this is something to be avoided.

FIGURE 7.5 Breathing a little too far behind you (position C) can bring your hand across the centre line in front of your head, as we see Serena doing here.

Popeye Breathing: A great way to avoid taking on water when breathing is to angle your mouth to the side like Popeye when he's chewing his spinach! This lets you keep your head a little lower whilst still breathing into the air in the bow-wave trough.

One simple way to make sure you have this position correct is to ask a friend or coach to walk along the side of the pool with you as you swim. Ask them to walk as close to the water's edge as possible and ever so slightly behind the level of your eyes. When you go to breathe, you should be able to see their feet walking alongside you. Avoid turning the head too much to see their whole body, seeing the feet is enough. Experiment with making subtle adjustments to the walker's position relative to you until you find a comfortable breathing point where you are not lifting your head too high or looking too far forward or back. Looking too far back (C) in Figure 7.5 may cause you to bend in the middle and start snaking down the pool or crossing over in front of your head.

SPLIT SCREEN VISUALISATION

When you are working on keeping your head position low in the water, use fins and aim for a *Split Screen View* with the lower goggle beneath the water and the upper goggle above. You should be able to see under and over the water at the same time. This is a useful visualisation to revisit when training or racing and your stroke starts to feel ragged, especially during long distance swims when it can be hard to maintain concentration.

Keep one goggle under the water as you breathe and you will see the split screen view.

PAUL: *Have you ever wondered why elite sprinters breathe so infrequently during a 50m or 100m freestyle race? Even at the pointy end of the field a swimmer's balance and alignment in the water can be thrown off by turning to take a breath, which can make the difference between first and last place in close races. As a result elite sprinters breathe as infrequently as they can. For distances over 100m we need to maintain a much more regular stream of air into the lungs by using a much more frequent breathing pattern: breathing only two or three times per 50m is not an option over longer distances! With regular breathing we need to maintain a close eye on your stroke while you are taking a breath; it's easy to switch your focus completely towards getting the air in, and it is then that things go wrong in your stroke technique. As we get into other areas of stroke technique we'll often be asking you to let the breath take care of itself and maintain an awareness of another part of your stroke.*

Bilateral Breathing

Bilateral breathing is the ability to breathe to the left and the right, swapping sides regularly as you swim. We are big fans of bilateral breathing at Swim Smooth for a very practical reason: it helps keep your stroke symmetrical. Many swimmers find bilateral breathing hard at first, if you have tried and failed before don't worry, we will help you crack it!

Most people think of bilateral breathing as breathing every three strokes. This is certainly the most common way and the one we'd recommend for you to use as it's about the right duration between breaths. However, any breathing pattern where you swap sides regularly is bilateral breathing too, for example:

Breathing 2-3-2-3: This means breathing twice to one side in a row and then performing three strokes to swap to the other side for two breaths in a row. This breathing pattern is used by many elite swimmers when racing.

Breathing 5s: Breathing every five strokes can be useful for those with a fast stroke rate who find that breathing every three comes around too often.

Swapping sides every lap of the pool: This is often done for tactical reasons to keep a close eye on a competitor in another lane, or simply for something different and engaging.

Breathing just to one side is the leading cause of a lopsided stroke, creating issues such as snaking and scissor kicks.

If you are a triathlete or open water swimmer then you should be seriously concerned with the symmetry of your stroke. A lopsided stroke is never a good thing but in the pool you can minimise the harm done by keeping yourself straight with the guidance of the black line and the lane ropes. However in open water a lop-sided stroke is a serious liability as it will cause you to constantly track off course and swim much further than you have to. What is the most natural way to keep your stroke symmetrical? Bilateral breathing of course! Even if you feel you are slightly slower in the pool breathing bilaterally, you'll gain back all this time and much more in open water by swimming much straighter.

How much of your training should you perform breathing bilaterally? If possible, all of it. Some swimmers struggle with hard sets breathing every three strokes; if that is you then we would still encourage you to perform as much as possible breathing to both sides, even if you only think of bilateral breathing as a drill. As long as the majority of your training is bilateral then your stroke should stay symmetrical.

There are certain situations, when racing in the pool or in the open water, when unilateral breathing would be more beneficial than bilateral breathing, which we will discuss further in Chapter 36. Your ability to breathe equally well to either side will be a tactical trump card in racing situations so that you can draft another swimmer closely or keep a close eye on a competitor who might put in a surge at any point. Practicing breathing to both sides in training will give you this ability in races.

PAUL: *Perhaps you're thinking: 'this is all very well but I just can't hold my breath for three strokes!'. But right there lies the problem – you should never hold your breath when you swim! We started this chapter by developing a good exhalation technique and this is the key you need to unlock the door to bilateral breathing. If you hold your breath the* CO_2 *builds up in your lungs and blood stream, and you start to feel very desperate for air. You would never hold your breath when cycling or running and you shouldn't when swimming either. Rid yourself of that* CO_2 *and bilateral breathing becomes a whole lot more achievable.*

The Two-Week Bilateral Hump

If you are lucky you will take easily to bilateral breathing but most swimmers find it a little strange and awkward at first breathing to their less favoured side. That's OK, allow yourself about two weeks (or six sessions) to persevere and keep your discipline with it. We call this the 'two-week bilateral

PAUL: *But what about the argument that bilateral breathing makes you less aerobic when racing? Any breathing pattern will make you less aerobic when you're racing if you're holding your breath under the water; as such good exhalation practice is always essential. The irony is that breathing every two strokes to just one side when racing often doesn't give you enough time to exhale properly and consequently inhalation becomes shallower and more of a gasp. Whatever breathing pattern you ultimately choose – please always remember to exhale!*

hump' after which breathing to both sides should start to feel progressively easier every time you swim. The mistake many swimmers make is to try bilateral breathing for a session or two and then give up – keep your discipline a little longer and you can crack it!

Always bear in mind that if you find bilateral breathing awkward or uncomfortable there is usually something amiss elsewhere within your stroke, which, if fixed, will not only improve your stroke in its own right but also make bilateral breathing easier. A win-win if you're prepared to commit to making the change and becoming a better, more versatile swimmer.

ADAM: *During my eight years as a competitive triathlete I only ever breathed to my right, in fact when swimming a hard set today I still feel a compulsion to breathe just to my right, which I have to resist. Since I joined Swim Smooth in 2008 I've made the effort to transition to bilateral breathing – it took me around six swim sessions to feel comfortable doing it and then another few months of swimming before it felt natural. The interesting thing is that if I switch back to breathing to one side now, within just 50m I start to feel awkward and crabby in my stroke! By 100m I'm starting to veer around in the lane and have to really focus on staying straight.*

Bilateral Breathing and Overgliding

As we'll see in our Swim Types section (starting at Chapter 17), some swimmers have focused on lengthening out their strokes by adding in an extended pause and glide at the front, something we call 'Overgliding'. As we will see, this style of stroke is not only inefficient but it also slows down the stroke so much that it becomes very hard to breathe every third stroke – the time between breaths is simply too long. It's no coincidence then that many Overgliders become very lopsided with their strokes as they are stuck breathing to one side only. In Chapter 21 we will take a close look at Overgliding and show you how to improve the rhythm and timing of your stroke for enhanced efficiency. Lifting your stroke rate into the 'normal' range will allow you to breathe every third stroke and maintain your symmetry much more effectively.

Breathing Timing

The timing of breathing is something that is often overlooked by coaches and swimmers. When the swimmer rotates to breathe, the head should rotate with the body at the same time:

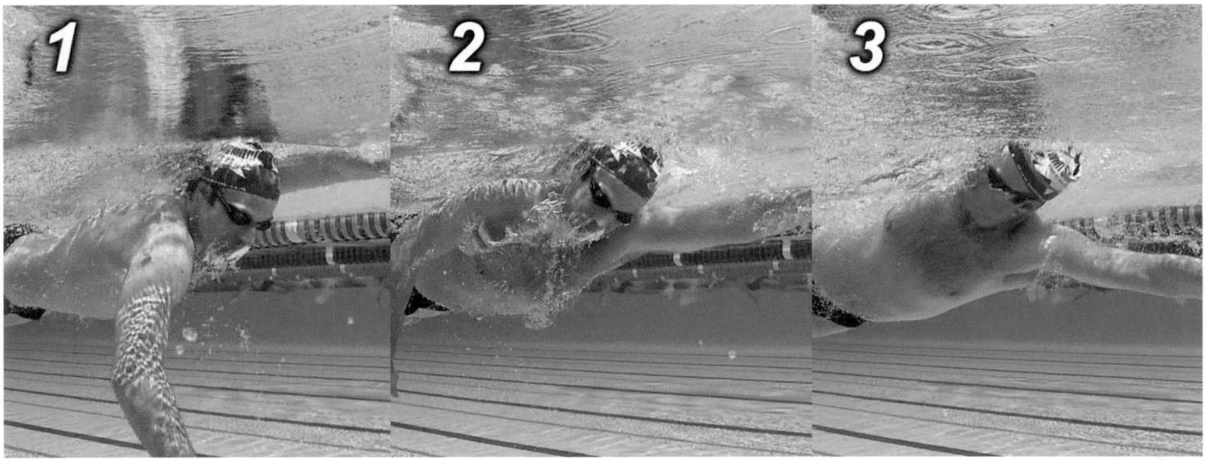

With good breathing timing, the head slightly leads body rotation.

Many swimmers, even some elite swimmers, turn the head a fraction later once the body is already rotated. If breathing to your right for example, the right arm will already be into its recovery phase over the top of the water before you start breathing. When viewed from the side of the pool this can look like the swimmer will knock their nose with their right shoulder as the arm comes over. Late breathing reduces the time available to inhale and makes breathing feel a little tense and hurried.

TURNING YOUR HEAD AWAY FROM YOUR ARM

This is a useful visualisation to help you improve your breathing timing. If you are about to breathe to your left then as your right hand passes your head and extends forwards, turn your head smoothly away from that arm. This should be one fluid motion with the head rotating as the hand enters the water.

If you breathe late, you'll still be trying to inhale as the top arm is about to enter the water.

The top sequence shows classic late breathing with the body rotated (1–2) before breathing high in the air (3). The bottom sequence shows good timing and technique with the head turning away to a low breathing position as the body rotates.

It's common for your breathing timing to be better on one side of your stroke than the other and in fact it is normally your preferred breathing side which has late timing! Although you may feel less comfortable breathing to your un-favoured side you will not have developed any bad habits there and so are likely to have better breathing technique, with better timing and less head lift.

CHAPTER 8

Body Position

A high body position in the water is very important for fast, efficient swimming: the legs, hips and feet should all be in one horizontal line near the surface. A swimmer with low-lying legs in the water creates a huge amount of drag, slowing them down dramatically. If you swim more quickly or more easily with a pull buoy between your legs, or are dramatically quicker in a wetsuit, then this is a strong indication that a low body position is a serious issue in your stroke.

If you have a low body position in the water then you need to work on improving it as an absolute priority for your swimming: it will be the single biggest thing holding you back.

The most common causes of a poor body position are:

- **Holding Your Breath Underwater** (Chapter 7). Holding onto your breath creates excess buoyancy in the chest, which lifts you up at the front and sinks your legs. Work on developing a nice smooth exhalation into the water.

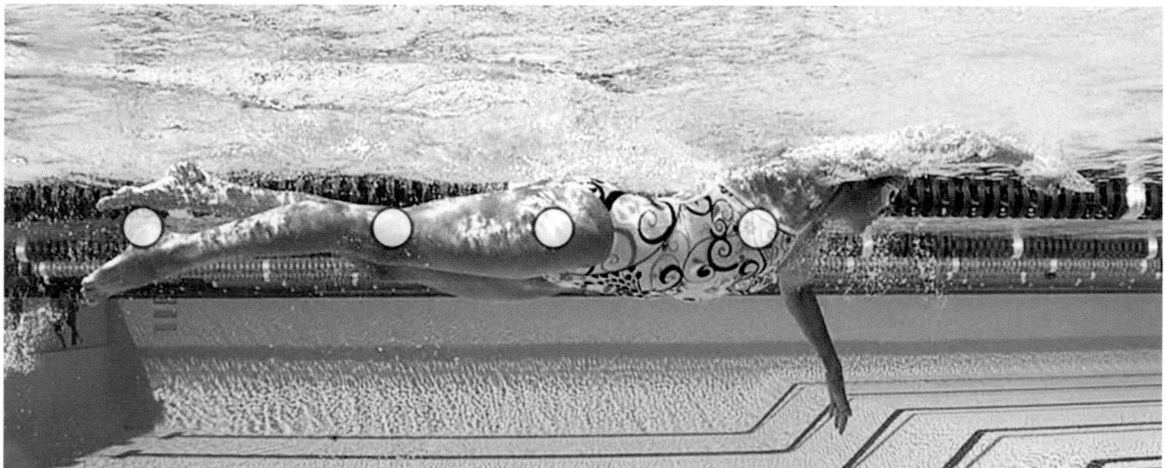

Michelle has a great body position in the water with chest, hips, legs and feet all in a horizontal line.

- **A High-Lifting Head When Breathing** (Chapter 7). In a similar manner to holding your breath, lifting your head high to breathe causes you to pivot at your hips and sink your legs. Developing your bow-wave breathing technique is essential to improving your body position.
- **Looking Too Far Forward in the Water** (this chapter). Many new swimmers with poor natural buoyancy and a feeling of breathing anxiety will swim looking too far forward in the water which in turn can sink the legs at the back.
- **Kicking From The Knee** (Chapter 9). A poor kicking technique with excess knee bend adds a lot of drag and sinks the legs. Work on moving to a kicking technique with a straighter leg driven from the hip.
- **Scissor Kick** (Chapter 9). A scissor kick is normally caused by a crossover of the lead arm in front of the head. This causes a loss of balance and with it an involuntary scissoring of the legs to avoid toppling onto your back. By improving your hand entry and swimming posture (Chapters 10 and 12) you will remove the scissor kick and so improve your body position.
- **Dorsi Flexed Ankles** (Chapter 9). Poor ankle flexibility is a problem for many triathletes with a running or cycling background. Such sports create a lot of stability in the ankle, which harms the swimmer's ability to point their toes. The resultant drag causes the legs to drop down.
- **Under Kicking** (Chapter 9). Swimmers who are focusing on making their stroke very long often try a two-beat kick to further reduce effort. For many swimmers with poor natural buoyancy or poor ankle flexibility this does not produce enough lift and their legs sink downward.
- **Poor Core Stabilisation** (Chapter 10). If you flex through your midsection and aren't sure how to engage your core muscles to hold your backside and legs high then your legs will likely sink.
- **Pressing Down On The Water During The Catch** (Chapter 13). Many swimmers try and overpower the catch phase of the freestyle stroke and end up pressing down on the water with a straight arm. This lifts them up at the front end and sinks their legs at the rear.
- **Poor Hip Flexibility** (Chapter 29). Poor hip flexor flexibility from a lot of sitting at an office desk or lots of cycling (especially on tri-bars) can drag the legs low in the water. Work on a few simple stretches before you swim to promote range of movement around the hips.

Swimmers with very poor body position normally have three or more of these issues in place in their stroke. For this reason there's rarely a silver-bullet solution to improving your body position – it takes an all-round approach across many areas of your stroke. It's important not to become frustrated with

Pressing down during the catch, kicking from the knee and poor hip flexibility is dragging this swimmer's legs low down in the water.

this but be calm and persistent in your approach. From the perspective of our Swim Types system, Arnies are the biggest sufferers of low-lying legs, and for very muscular Arnies it is quite possible that they can never achieve as super-high a body position in the water as some female swimmers can. That's OK, any improvement in body position will reduce drag significantly and is well worth the effort of pursuing.

The term 'swimming downhill' is commonly offered on the internet as a way to help swimmers with 'sinky leg syndrome' to get their legs higher in the water by pushing down with their chest. You should be wary of trying this yourself as it can be very bad for your stroke if you are blessed with a good natural body position. Here Barbara has added significant drag to her frontal profile by being too low at the front.

Head Position and Body Position

Many coaches encourage all swimmers to push their heads down low into the water to help bring their legs upwards, this can be effective for a proportion of swimmers but very bad advice for others. At Swim Smooth we suggest you treat a low head position as a last resort, only using it to improve your body position if all else fails. This is because a very low head position has several disadvantages:

- It reduces your proprioception, or 'body awareness', in front of the head, making the development of a good hand entry and catch harder.
- It makes it hard to see forwards in open water, which damages your navigation and drafting abilities. As we will see in Chapter 36, drafting alone can save you up to 38% of your energy expenditure – a huge reduction that would be unwise to ignore.
- It bends your spine forward and thus harms your swimming posture, making crossovers in front of the head more likely (Chapter 10).

Furthermore, for swimmers with good stroke technique and good natural buoyancy, a low head position can bring their legs too high at the rear and make them feel very unbalanced and unstable in the water. For such swimmers this is exacerbated further when using a wetsuit where the extra buoyancy pushes their legs higher still. Adopting a higher head position is essential for these swimmers to regain their balance and swim well in a wetsuit. We'll discuss this more with regard to Kicktastics in Chapter 20 and also in Chapter 38.

Head technique is a very individual area of stroke technique, something that works for one swimmer will not necessarily work for another.

You can choose from a range of head positions as you swim depending upon your individual stroke correction needs.

Ian Thorpe's Head Position

The legendary Australian swimmer Ian Thorpe won four Olympic gold medals and set numerous world records in the 200 m and 400 m freestyle. Often held up as having one of the most efficient freestyle strokes of all time, as Ian developed his swimming as a junior he found that he needed to keep a very high head position with his eyes just beneath the surface looking forward. With a lower head his legs rose up out of the water and he lost balance in his stroke and the effectiveness of his brilliant kick. Just like Ian, think about how your head position affects your swimming and choose the best position for your individual stroke.

Ian Thorpe used a very high head position when he swam, looking forwards with his goggles just beneath the surface.

Heels Breaking the Surface

The easiest way to check your body position is to ask a coach or friend to check if your heels are lightly breaking the surface as you swim. Make sure you are not doing this by bending excessively at the knee – your heels breaking the surface is only the sign of a good body position if you are achieving this with a good kicking technique, kicking mostly with a straight leg from the hip.

PAUL: *Some swimmers will kick their feet completely out of the water. Whilst this may appear to be very propulsive (especially when sprinting) the reverse is actually true and this action can create a huge amount of additional drag and wasted effort. In fact, an unpublished computational fluid dynamics (CFD) study of Australian sprinter Eamon Sullivan's stroke (Olympic medallist and former holder of 50 m and 100 m world records) in 2010 by Matt Keys and the University of Western Australia [1], found that the only inefficiency in his stroke was that very occasionally his left foot would kick a little too high out of the water. For most of us, addressing this is something that would save us a fraction of a second per length, but when you can swim 50 m in a blistering 21.28 seconds like Eamon, every little counts!*

Reference

1. https://repository.uwa.edu.au/R/-?func=dbin-jump-full&object_id=29616&local_base=GEN01-INS01

CHAPTER 9 Leg Kick

For most swimmers, Swim Smooth recommends using a light flutter kick to keep your legs high in the water. This is called a 6-beat kick by swim coaches as there are six kicks per two arm strokes (a full stroke cycle). If you kick with a nice continuous flutter then you will naturally fall into a 6-beat pattern without too much conscious thought on your behalf.

Leg kick can be seen to have two main purposes: firstly, to bring the legs up high in the water and so reduce drag; secondly, to generate propulsion. As we'll discuss below, generating significant propulsion is something that is more important for elite pool sprinters. For triathletes and distance age-group swimmers, the main purpose of the kick is to balance and bring up the legs as high as possible, with minimum effort on your behalf, it is not to generate propulsion as such:

- Elite swimmers with a powerful 6-beat kick generate only around 10% to 15% of their propulsion with their legs when kicking hard in a race, the other 85% to 90% being generated with their arm stroke [1]. For elite swimmers this small contribution from the kick is worth having as elite races are very close and every fraction of a second gained is critical. However, maximising the leg kick comes at a very high energy cost – for the effort they put in, the propulsion gained is small.
- Elite swimmers also have fantastic flexibility through the ankles, knees and hips, to the point where they nearly look double-jointed. This helps them generate foot angles that push water back behind them as they kick, propelling them forwards. For most age-group swimmers this level of flexibility is

To generate propulsion from the leg kick a high amount of ankle flexibility is required. Elite swimmers are able to flex their feet well beyond straight.

not realistically achievable unless it comes from a significant swimming background acquired during childhood. For triathletes, a very high level of ankle flexibility is undesirable for cycling and running as the lack of stability can easily lead to lower leg injuries such as calf problems and turned ankles.

For these reasons, developing a propulsive leg kick is unrealistic for most age-group swimmers and triathletes who may, at best, only generate 5% of their propulsion from their legs. Over the longer distances raced by these swimmers, the energy saved by reducing kick effort is better utilised with the arm stroke instead, resulting in a faster more efficient stroke overall.

Kicking from the Hip

A good kicking technique is driven from the hip rather than from the knee; the knee itself is loose and relaxed and will bend slightly during the action.

Triathletes are particularly prone to driving the kick from the knee with a lot of knee bend, perhaps as if they are running or cycling in the water. This takes a lot of energy to maintain and creates a lot of drag as the front of the leg is presented to the water flow. Kicking from the knee also uses the large quadriceps and hamstring muscle groups, which burn a lot of oxygen. If you always seem out of breath when you swim, you could well be kicking too much from the knee in this way.

Kicking from the hip with a relaxed straight leg is a much better swimming technique. It takes less energy and keeps the body high in the water resulting in much lower levels of drag. To develop this technique, use the *Ballet Leg Kick* and *Torpedo Kick And Swim Back* drills from Appendix A.

Paula (top) and Michelle (bottom) have contrasting kicking techniques at the same point in their strokes. Paula's kick is driven from the knee, creating a lot of drag and starting to sink her legs downward. Michelle kicks with a much straighter leg driven from the hip, giving her a much higher body position.

The *Ballet Leg Kick Drill* helps you to develop your kick technique from the hip – see Appendix A.

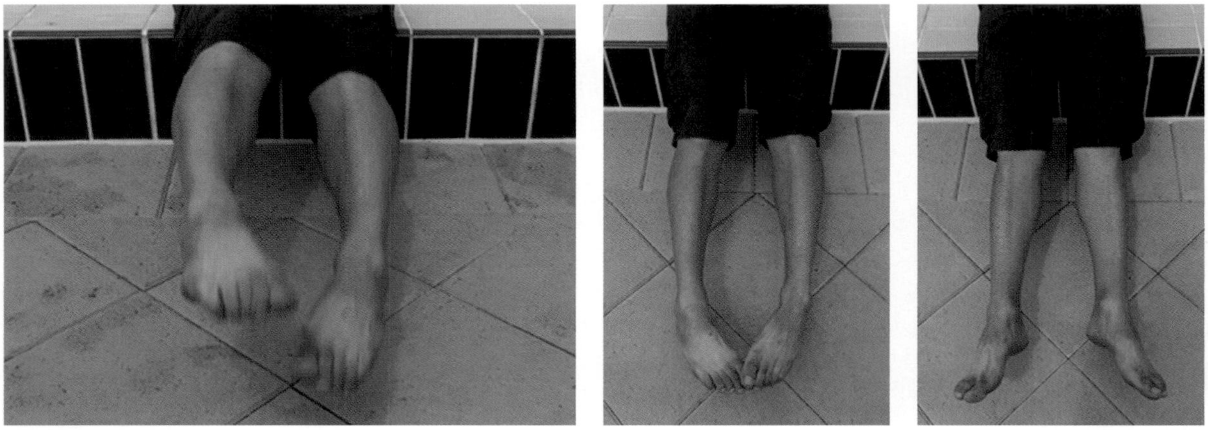

L–R: Toes lightly brushing; which can only be achieved by turning the toes inwards; not turning them outwards.

Turning Your Toes Inwards

An important part of a good kicking technique is to turn your feet inwards slightly so that the big toes brush against each other as they pass. Many swimmers who struggle with their kicking do the opposite and turn their toes outwards. This creates drag and reduces the lift created by the kick. As you swim think about turning your toes in and brush your big toes lightly together as they pass with a tap-tap-tap action. You can practise doing this at any time when you swim, it's particularly useful to try when you get a little tired and you feel like your stroke is becoming ragged – it will often bring things back together for you.

PAUL: *Have you noticed how women tend to be better at kicking than men? Women are often more flexible than men but also have wider hips due to childbirth. The 'Q-angle' created between the hip and knee is more conducive to achieving this slightly pigeon-toed kicking position with the feet. This gives them an anatomical advantage over the guys and turning their toes in feels a lot more natural to them. Men with very narrow hips tend to find themselves kicking hard as their toes tend to do the opposite – turn outwards. So guys, you now have an excuse for why your kick isn't 'all that' but don't let this deter you. Work on turning your toes inwards to improve the effectiveness of your kick.*

Ankle Flexibility

Even though you're not looking for propulsion from your kick, a lack of flexibility in your ankles can still hold you back. Very stiff ankles from field sports, running or cycling make the top of the foot stick out into the water flow. This creates resistance in itself but also pulls the legs downward, harming your body position and creating a lot of drag.

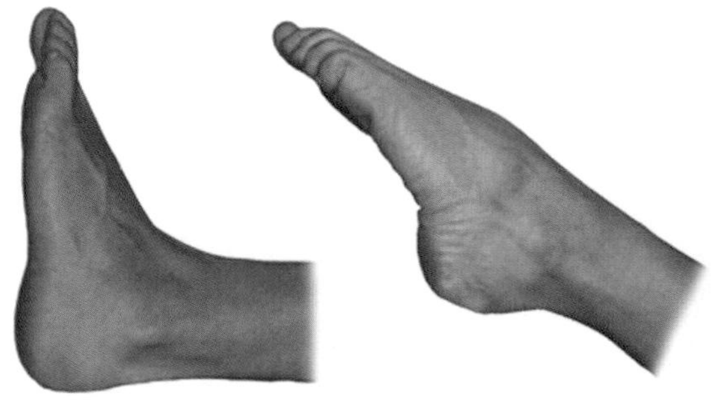

Dorsi flexion (left) and Plantar flexion (right).

THE SEA ANCHORS DRILL

To experience this for yourself, experiment with using the *Sea Anchors Drill*. Using a pull buoy, swim 25 m with your toes pointed behind you (technical term: plantar flexion) as normal. Then bring your ankles to 90° with the toes pointing downward (dorsi flexion). Notice the instant and huge effect this has on your body position, which highlights the difference even small improvements in ankle flexibility can bring to your stroke.

Using a pull buoy, try switching between dorsi and plantar flexed ankles to experience the effect it has on your body position.

If you have very stiff ankles and cannot point your toes straight then we recommend a gentle stretching exercise to loosen off your ankles. You can perform this stretch at any time, perhaps in your office or in front of the TV at home. Don't rush things, it will take many weeks and months to loosen your ankles off by stretching them little and often using the stretches below.

Sitting Ankle Stretch

ADAM: *Many swimmers think that using fins (flippers) in training is cheating in some way. Nothing could be further from the truth – performing drills with a specific purpose using fins is a very important part of developing your stroke technique as they leave you free to focus on the drill rather than on how hard you need to kick to stay afloat! Did you know that fins can also improve your ankle flexibility and kicking technique at the same time? Any time you kick with fins on they place your feet into a plantar flexed position and so gradually stretch your ankles. They also force you to kick with a straighter leg action.*

You don't want to become addicted to swimming with fins but performing a drill set or technique swim of around 400 m will help tune up your leg kick at the same time as you work on other areas of your stroke. Neat!

In a seated position cross one leg over the top of the other and hold the foot firmly with the opposing hand. Gently pull the foot straighter, feeling the stretch across the top of the foot and along the shin. Hold for 30 seconds to a minute and then swap sides. As always when stretching use only light force and progress very gradually to avoid injury.

A scissor kick adds a huge amount of drag, it's like opening up a parachute behind you.

Scissor Kicks

A scissor kick is one of the most common stroke flaws. In fact our records show that approximately 70% of swimmers who attend a Swim Smooth Clinic have a scissor kick in their stroke. Parting the legs like this causes a lot of drag and harms a swimmer's body position in the water.

However, a scissor kick is rarely a problem with the kick itself, instead it's normally caused by an arm crossing the centre line in front of the head or under the body. This 'crossover' causes a loss of balance for the swimmer who parts the legs in a scissoring action to maintain balance, often doing so unknowingly. Fixing the crossover (Chapter 10) will normally remove the scissor kick all by itself, even without any conscious action on behalf of the swimmer.

2-Beat Kicking Technique

A 2-beat kick is used by some elite swimmers racing in the pool and open water. For every two arm strokes, two leg kicks are made. The kicks don't provide much propulsion but they do help drive body rotation, which in turn helps drive the arm stroke.

A 2-beat kick suits swimmers with a faster stroke rate style, such as the Swinger Swim Type. A great 2-beat leg kick is poetry in motion and whilst it looks simple is deceptively difficult to master. Generally speaking we only recommend 2-beat kicks for those swimmers with a refined Swinger style (Chapter 22).

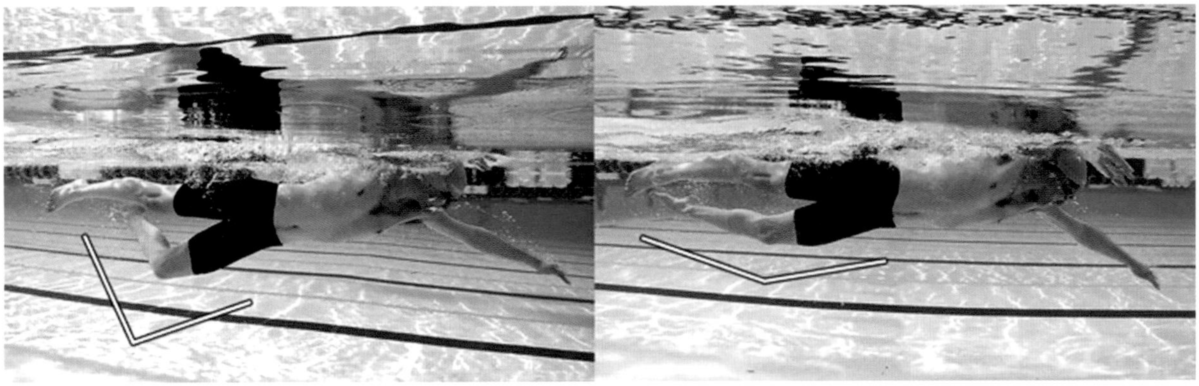

The Classic Overglider (left) uses a large knee bend to kick-start their stroke after the long glide phase. Simply becoming aware of this, and by tuning up his rhythm, has allowed Chris to improve his kicking technique (right).

The timing for the 2-beat kick is much the same as that of the 6-beat kick in that as the right hand enters into the water the left leg should be driving down, and as the left hand enters into the water the right leg should be driving down. Opposite arm to opposite leg. Or, to think of it another way, as the left arm is midway through its propulsive catch phase the left leg should be driving down. The timing of a 6-beat kick is the same as a 2-beat one except that two additional kicks are placed between each kick bringing the total up to six in a stroke cycle. The kicks of a 6-beat kick are more of a flutter and should be smaller than those of a 2-beat.

Sounds a bit complicated? It is, and we have not even hit the water yet!

For most swimmers and triathletes Swim Smooth recommend a light 6-beat kick as the most efficient kicking technique. Some age-group swimmers have tried to combine a very long slow stroke style with a 2-beat kick but this is rarely effective. The tendency here is for the stroke to stall completely during the long pause between arm strokes and kicks, which harms the swimmer's rhythm and timing. These swimmers are often seen from under the water using a substantial kick from the knee to literally kick-start the stroke back into motion after the pause but in doing so add significant drag at the back of the stroke from their knees sitting too deep in the water.

We'll take a closer look at this in the Overglider Swim Type profile and correction processes in Chapter 21.

PAUL: *Back in August 2008 I decided to modify my stroke technique to emulate that of one of my heroes and mentors of open water swimming, seven-time World Marathon Swimming Champion Shelley Taylor-Smith. I already had a reasonable open water technique from my days as an elite triathlete but with my goal of swimming the English Channel in 2011 I wanted to be assured of my ability to maintain the most economical marathon swimming technique for 8–12 hours depending on conditions.*

I was concerned that my strong 6-beat kick and 'longish' stroke (34–35 strokes per 50 m) at a moderate stroke rate of 64 SPM (strokes per minute) might have been OK in events up to 1500 m but could potentially be too fatiguing above this. I was also concerned that this low stroke rate may not have the momentum to carry me through some of the swell and chop that I would encounter in the Channel. It took me over 10 weeks, swimming six sessions per week, before I started to get a true feeling of how this new stroke would work for me.

Converting the 6-beat kick timing to 2-beat was very taxing mentally as I became slower to begin with and for this reason I wouldn't recommend the transition to everyone. The new stroke involved combining a 2-beat kick with a significantly higher stroke rate (80 SPM) but not being concerned about taking more strokes per lap (increasing to 41–43 strokes per 50 m). What I gave away in stroke length I more than made up for in rate and rhythm. Now that I have mastered it, this new stroke is not only faster than the old one at any distance over 400 m (more details in Chapter 27) but is considerably more economical for the type of events I now do – marathon swimming. It doesn't appear quite as smooth or textbook as my old style but in open water there are no points for style, only performance!

If you're interested in seeing how my English Channel swim went, visit www.swimsmooth.com/paulchannel

Reference

1. Toussaint, H. M., Hollander, A. P., de Groot, G., Kahman, R., and van Ingen Schenau, G. J. 1990. Power of leg kicking in front crawl swimming. In N. Berme & A. Capozzo (Eds.), *Biomechanics of Human Movement* (pp. 456–459). Worthington, Ohio: Bertec Corporation.

CHAPTER 10

Posture and Alignment

When thinking about core stability we tend to think about the abdominals, lower back and hip region of the body. This area of the body was the subject of the core stability boom across the sports world in the mid to late 1990s. In swimming terms we would call this the 'lower core' and like in many sports, it plays an important role in the pool as we'll investigate in this chapter. However, the 'upper

ADAM: *One of my roles at Swim Smooth is to manage all of our swimming websites and I spend a lot of time in front of the computer doing this. Working at a computer draws the shoulders and head forwards, shortening the chest muscles and over-stretching between the shoulder blades. As we'll see in this section, if you have an office job yourself this hunched posture could be doing your swimming real harm.*

Poor posture at work (left) can negatively impact your swimming but try to avoid over-exaggerating good posture (right) as this puts pressure on your lower back.

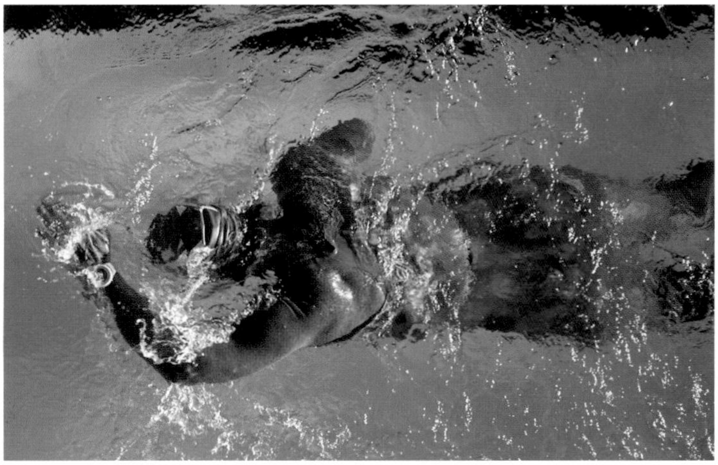

A crossover in front of the head is caused by poor swimming posture.

core' – a swimmer's thoracic spine, their shoulder and scapular region – is thought about much less often but is arguably even more important for good swimming technique.

When we swim we enter the water and extend forwards, the lead hand being controlled by the shoulder, chest and scapular region muscle groups. If your chest muscles are short and the muscles between your scapulae over-stretched, then this tends to draw the lead arm across the centre line of the body causing a crossover in front of the head.

The solution to a crossover is not to think about taking the arm wider. It is commonly said that you should be aiming for your hands to enter at '10 o'clock and 2 o'clock' in order to correct a crossover, the theory being that thinking about going wider will result in you becoming straighter. All this would do though is reduce your body rotation and cause you to swim flatter in the water and over time your arms will have a tendency to move wider and wider!

PAUL: *When you were a child did your parents used to say to you 'stand up tall and proud – shoulders back chest forwards!'? This is exactly what you need to do to improve your swimming posture. At Swim Smooth we call swimming with your shoulders down and back 'swimming proud'!*

Instead of this, the solution to a crossover is to improve your posture by drawing your shoulder blades together and back. We can see in Figure 10.6 how this draws the lead arm straight and also promotes good body rotation. Try this yourself in a standing position.

If you have a crossover in your stroke or you lack body rotation then it's very likely that you need to work on your swimming posture in this way. Improving your posture will also increase the length of your stroke as it helps you extend forward much

FIGURE 10.6 To remove a crossover pull your shoulder blades together and down to pull your arm straight.

straighter, this is of direct benefit to your swimming efficiency. We will take a good look at some exercises and drills in this section to help you tune in to this part of your stroke and we'll recommend some simple stretches to help loosen off your chest and shoulders in Chapter 29.

Transferring Power from Your Rotation to Your Arm Stroke

Hopefully you can see how your upper core helps connect your arm stroke to your body. Swimming with good posture forms a strong connection between the two and lets you utilise the larger muscle groups of the chest and upper back to help drive the arm stroke. Swimming with poor posture tends to overload the weaker shoulder muscle groups, which will quickly fatigue. Having a stable upper core, combined with a good catch and rotation technique will really help you to generate some controlled power in the stroke.

PAUL: *The good news here is that you do not need to be physically strong to swim well, this is one reason why that 11-year-old girl can go zooming past you in the pool with very little upper-body strength. The key is to get in the right positions with a good stroke rhythm and that will produce the necessary power with surprisingly little feeling of force.*

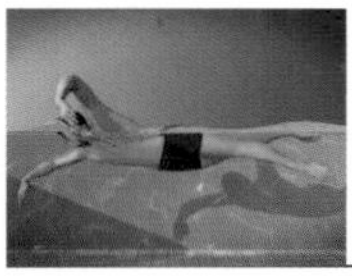

Developing Better Posture in the Pool

At Swim Smooth we like to use drills that involve kicking on your side to improve your posture. Many swimmers have performed similar drills before but normally think of them as rotational drills or something to improve their leg kick. However, the focus here is less about your rotation and more about your posture.

Start off by performing the *Kick On Side Drill* described in Appendix A. Use a pair of fins (flippers) and kick gently to propel you down the pool, extending the lower arm out in front of you. Notice how aligned or otherwise your lead hand is, does it cross the centre line? This is a clear indication of what is happening with that arm in your full freestyle stroke too. Do you find you drift across the lane in the direction of the crossover? Think about bringing this arm straight by drawing your shoulder blades together and down. You should track much straighter when you get this right.

Perform the drill looking straight down past your armpit exhaling in a long stream of bubbles. When you need a breath,

Side kicking with fins is the primary drill for working on your posture: Draw your shoulder blades together and down to bring the lead arm straight.

rotate your head to the side and then return it to the water again. Keep your lead arm perfectly straight while you breathe and do not let it drop down in the water. The other arm should remain relaxed by your side as though your hand was in the front pocket of a pair of jeans.

After 25m swap onto the other side. Repeat the exercise here, working on drawing your arm straight in front of you. It's well worthwhile performing these exercises with a coach or friend watching you from the pool deck to give you feedback on your alignment.

This *Kick On Side Drill* makes you aware of the alignment of your lead hand when you swim and it helps you tune into developing a better swimming posture. When you feel you have got the hang of this you can progress to the *6-1-6 and 6-3-6* drills.

The *6-1-6 Drill* involves kicking on your side again for around six kicks. Then perform one arm stroke to swap sides and kick on that side for six further kicks before swapping back again. This is a more challenging drill because you have got to maintain your posture during an arm stroke. Watch that you don't crossover as you enter into the water and then straighten it up, you're aiming to enter straight in the first place! Again, feedback from an observer is very useful here.

ADAM: *In the Swim Smooth squads in Perth we perform a lot of these side kicking drills. They really help you maintain your stroke, simultaneously working on your posture, and as we will see later, helping you set up for a good catch too. One quick pointer on 6-1-6: make sure you breathe after the stroke not before. You could think of the drill as: 6-1-breathe-6.*

The *6-3-6 Drill* is slightly harder again and involves taking three full arm strokes between side kicking. You should start to feel the power coming into your stroke now as your improved posture helps drive the stroke.

Once you've tried the side kicking exercises perform some full-stroke swimming using the *Middle Finger Visualisation* described in Chapter 12. Focus on entering into the water and extending your middle finger gun-barrel straight down the pool in front of the same shoulder. If you own a pair of the excellent Finis Freestyler Paddles (see Chapter 3) you can also perform some swimming using them. These have a keel on the bottom of the paddle, which gives you kinaesthetic feedback on how straight you are in the water – crossover and you'll feel them trying to spin off to that side!

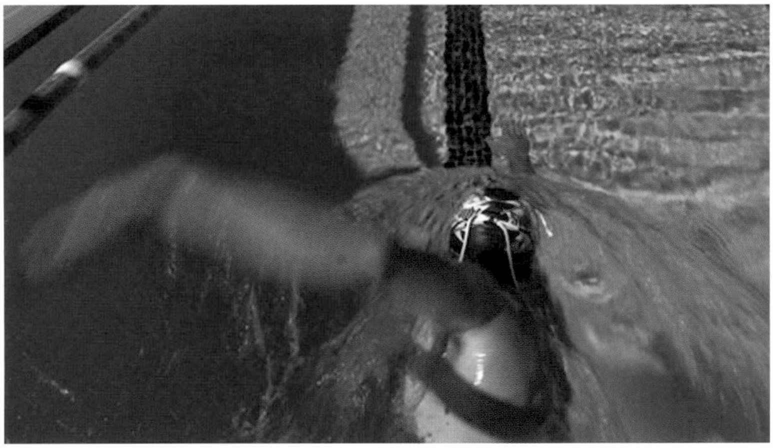

As you introduce arm strokes, maintain a focus on your lead arm staying straight and aligned.

PAUL: *Take the time to carefully read the pointers for these exercises in Appendix A. When you feel like you can perform them quite well, really aim to perfect them with perfect rotation (45° to 60° during the strokes and side kicking at 90°), perfect alignment and a good hand position out in front of you. Stay relaxed and keep exhaling smoothly and continuously into the water.*

THE 1-2-STRAIGHT MANTRA

As you develop your swimming posture you may find that you stay well aligned on normal strokes but on a breathing stroke your crossover returns. This is only natural as during a breathing stroke your focus tends to shift towards 'get that air in'! To help you stay straight whilst breathing repeat to yourself '*1 - 2 - straight - 1 - 2 - straight....*' The *1* and *2* fall on normal strokes and the *straight* on a breathing stroke, which will help keep your focus on that lead hand during the breath.

Other Posture Drills

The Broken Arrow Drill described in Appendix A is ideal for swimmers with tight shoulders and upper backs. The drill has a similar timing to *6-1-6* but the recovering arm is taken vertically and paused there for a second. The elbow is then bent to at least 90° before the hand spears into the water. To perfect the drill, as the arm reaches the vertical position consciously relax the shoulder and feel it sink back down into its socket. This will help you loosen off your upper back and shoulder muscles ready for moving back to full-stroke swimming.

Lower Core Stability

The 'lower core' of your hips, lower back and abdominal area is important in swimming to keep you straight in the water and to help rotate your hips and shoulders together as one. Good core control during swimming has a slightly different feel to it compared to other sports, which can cause some confusion.

The key to developing your lower core control is to feel a stretch between your pelvis and rib cage as you swim. In a sense you are trying to separate out the two as much as possible, raising the chest away from the hips. If you try this you will feel your posture improve at the same time as your chest is pushed out and your shoulders come back – great! Warning: avoid holding your breath when you do this.

Michael Phelps has one of the best streamline positions in the world. See the *Torpedo Kick and Swim Back Drill* in Appendix A to see how to get into this position yourself.

If you suffer from low-lying legs in the water the first benefit you may notice from improving your core control is that your legs are lifted higher so you slip through the water more easily. That's a great sign that you've made a substantial improvement to your stroke!

At Swim Smooth we use several visualisations to help you use your lower core in the right way:

TORPEDO KICK WITH FINS

Kick continuously either on your front or back with your arms above your head in a torpedo position. The streamlined tuck requires you to stabilise your upper back and also stretches your shoulders and chest. Perform 50 m to 100 m at a time with fins on.

Whenever you start any lap of freestyle you are aiming for a nice strong push-off in a streamlined tuck (see Appendix A). This is the perfect time to focus on your lower core using the visualisations below. As you break out in to your freestyle maintain that focus down the lap to integrate the 'core engagement' into your full stroke.

STICK OF LIQUORICE STRETCH

A nice way to think about stretching through the core is to imagine a stick of liquorice that is attached to your pelvis at one end and to your rib cage at the other. As you swim you must keep the liquorice stretched at all times!

BUM CHEEK SQUEEZE!

A slightly crude visualisation this one – imagine that you have a pound or dollar coin between the cheeks of your backside and to keep it there you must lightly squeeze your glute (buttock) muscles! This exercise also helps you kick more from the hip than the knee as the glute muscles are activated.

TILTING PELVIS UPWARDS

Think about rotating your pelvis upwards slightly (technical term: anterior tilt) so that your tail-bone is pulled up a little towards your lower back.

Think about drawing your rib cage away from your hips as you swim by stretching tall through your core.

As essential as good lower core control is to your stroke technique, we can easily forget about it when we swim. An excellent way to remind yourself is to use a good torpedo push-off (also known as a streamline) at the beginning of every length which involves stretching through your core. Doing this will improve the connection between your upper and lower body at the beginning of every length and help remind you to keep that connection and feeling of stretch in place for the whole lap.

PAUL: *Many of the triathletes who swim with us in Perth think that they don't need the discipline of a good torpedo push-off at the beginning of every lap because they don't get to push off in open water. Whilst this is true, they are missing out on developing their core control when swimming which is so essential to avoid fish-tailing (legs sweeping from side to side) and to keep the body high in the water.*

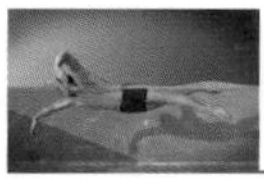

Dry Land Core Conditioning

Most swimmers and triathletes have enough core strength to swim very well, it's more a matter of coordinating and engaging the core muscles in the right way. Unless you have very poor core strength indeed it's not normally necessary to add in additional gym classes to your training routine. Saying that, a strong core has many benefits on dry land so we wouldn't discourage you from a good pilates or yoga class either! Time availability will always be the limiting factor for most non-professional swimmers, so the more specifically you can introduce good core control into your normal swim sessions the better.

PAUL: *Just to prove this point, it's normally the gym junkies who can do hundreds of sit-ups who have the worst core control in the water!*

For more information on dry-land conditioning that you can adopt within your programme in a time efficient way, see Chapters 29 and 30.

CHAPTER 11

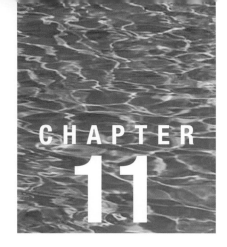

Rotation and Arm Recovery

Body rotation (sometimes simply called 'body roll') is the rotation of the swimmer along the long axis of the spine as they swim. A good freestyle stroke technique has between 45° and 60° of rotation to each side on every stroke, not just when they breathe. This helps the swimmer use the large muscle groups of the core, back and chest to help drive the stroke. A swimmer with poor rotation tends to overuse the small weak shoulder muscles, which soon fatigue.

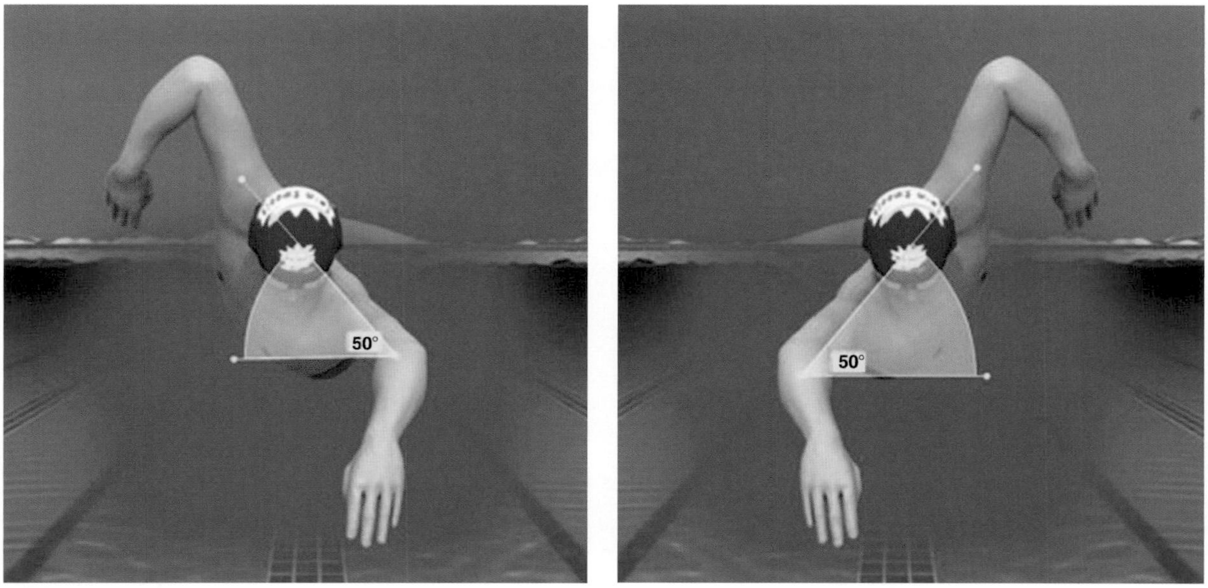

A swimmer should rotate between 45° and 60° on every stroke they take.

THE KEBAB STICK VISUALISATION

Imagine that your body has been skewered on a kebab stick, running through your head and body down to your feet. As the kebab stick is rotated your body rotates as one with the legs, hips and shoulders rotating together.

Rotate 'as one' along your long axis, as if you were skewered on a kebab stick!

Many swimmers feel they should kick vertically at all times when they swim but this misconception can really harm your rotation. Instead you should kick with your rotation:

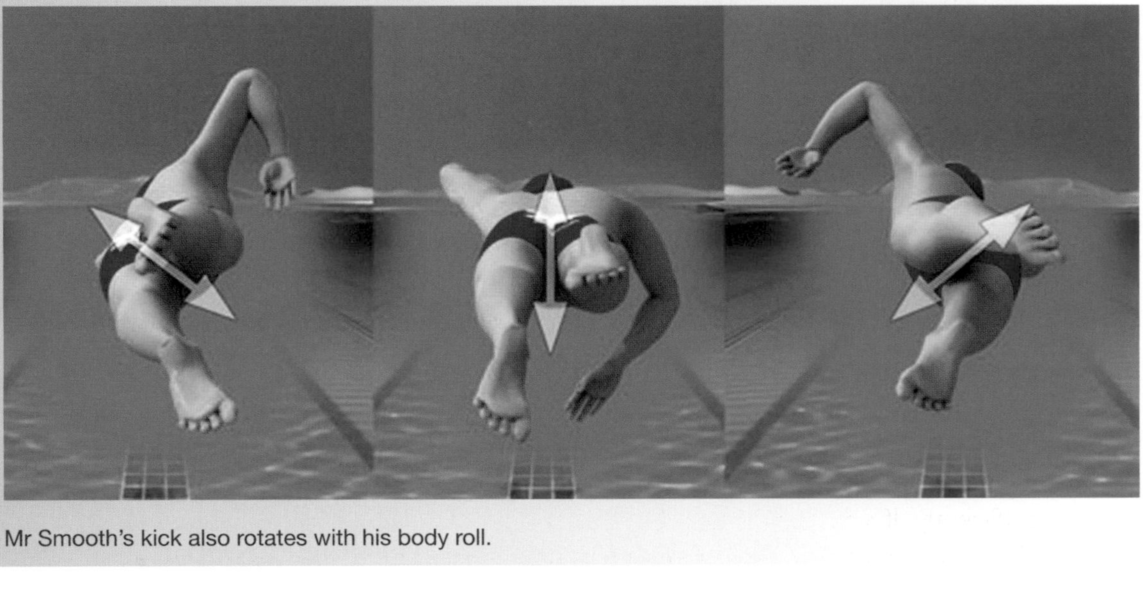

Mr Smooth's kick also rotates with his body roll.

Developing Good Rotation

To develop your rotation use the *Kick-On-Side*, *6-1-6* and *6-3-6* drill sequences from Appendix A as described in Chapter 10 on Swimming Posture. Swimming posture and rotation are heavily related and by swimming with your shoulders back and chest forwards you will naturally drive better rotation into your stroke.

Follow the same process outlined in Chapters 10 and 13 and become accustomed to being on your side, whilst focusing on swimming with good alignment of the lead hand and a good hand position facing downward with the elbow higher than the wrist and the wrist higher than the fingertips. Kicking in this position may feel very strange to you at first but will build your confidence in it. As you move to the *6-1-6* and *6-3-6* drills you will get practice at rotating from one side of the body to the other.

PAUL: *It should be stressed that when the body rotates with each stroke the head should stay stationary and not move with the rotation of the shoulders (with the obvious exception of rotating to breathe). It is very common to see people move their head around on every stroke when they're trying to develop their rotation but this adds drag and may cause dizziness or even nausea, especially in turbulent open water.*

When you are ready, remove the fins and swim some laps of freestyle focusing solely on maintaining that sensation of reaching and rolling with each stroke, always being mindful of maintaining good alignment and not crossing over. Focus on stretching forwards with the lead arm as you press the other hand underneath the water towards the hip, with the sensation of needing to rotate this hip out of the way to allow you to finish the stroke off correctly. We'll revisit this concept of 'timing the rotation to the arm stroke' in Chapter 13, which is about how the catch phase affects your rhythm and timing.

Rotation and Bilateral Breathing

All swimmers rotate a little more on a breathing stroke than a normal stroke. You do this subconsciously to ensure that you get your head in a good position to breathe. Over time this develops a good stroke habit and your rotation becomes good to that side. However, if you only ever breathe to one side (unilateral breathing) then we'll see your rotation become good to that side but poor to the other. This will give you a lopsided stroke and is one of the major reasons why bilateral breathing is so important for maintaining symmetry in your rotation.

The Right Amount of Rotation

A great tool to help you monitor your rotation is the Finis Tech Toc. This neat device sits on your lower back, held by a strap around your waist. The Tech Toc has a large ball bearing in it that slides up and down the tube, making a loud 'click' when it hits the end. The ball bearing will only slide and hit the end of the tube if you are rotating sufficiently. If you're struggling to develop your rotation, the Tech Toc is a very worthwhile investment in your swimming.

The Finis Tech Toc is a great tool to help you develop your body rotation.

Taking Rotation too Far

Whilst good rotation is important, you can take it too far. In the 1990s many swimmers were taught to 'stack their shoulders' by trying to rotate to a full 90° in an effort to swim more 'fish like'; incredibly you will still hear this advice offered in some places on the internet today. In full-stroke freestyle swimming you should avoid rotating to 90° at all costs as it will cause you to lose balance and want to topple onto your back. To regain your balance you will need to part your legs and so create a large amount of drag – like opening a parachute – at the rear of your stroke. Whilst some of the Swim Smooth drills have you kicking in a side-lying position, when you transition into your freestyle stroke you are only ever looking for 45° to 60° of rotation.

ROTATE THE HIP AHEAD OF THE HANDS VISUALISATION

As you swim and your hand comes through and past your chest and stomach, visualise rotating your hip out of the way, maintaining a healthy gap between the two. See Figure 11.7.

Keep the effort in the arm stroke moderate and emphasise the hip rotation instead. This is an excellent visualisation for helping you time the catch, pull and exit phase to your body rotation, which we will discuss more in Chapter 13.

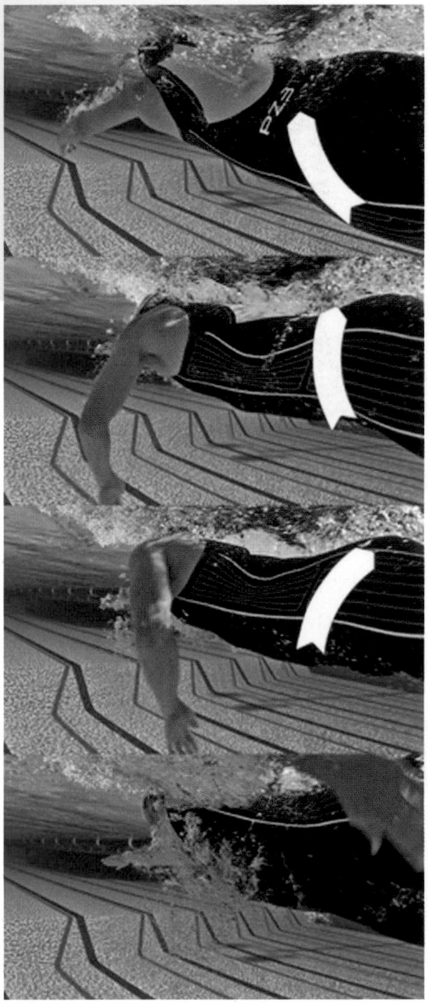

FIGURE 11.7 Rotate the hips out of the way ahead of the stroking arm.

The Importance of Good Rotation in Your Stroke

Good rotation also serves several other purposes:

1. It allows the recovering arms to travel freely over the surface of the water.
2. It reduces the load on the shoulders, lowering the chances of shoulder injury.
3. A rotated body cuts through the water more cleanly, producing less drag than a flat profile.
4. It helps the large muscles of the core, chest and back drive the arm stroke, increasing propulsive power.

You can experience points one and two by lying on your front and then your side on land (Figure 11.8). Start on your front without any rotation and your arms down by your side. Try and recover your arms to the front of the stroke without rotation and see how awkward it feels; even if you are super flexible in the shoulders this will be a real struggle.

FIGURE 11.8 Comparison of arm clearance over the water with poor rotation (top) and very good rotation (bottom).

Now try the same thing from a side-lying position with your lead arm out in front giving you support. Notice how easy it feels now to recover the top arm to the front and how relaxed the shoulder is.

Arm Clearance During the Recovery Phase

An important benefit of good body rotation is that it improves your recovery over the top of the water. When elite pool swimmers perform a classic high elbow recovery, or when elite open water swimmers achieve good clearance with their recovering arm in rough water, they do this with the combination of good shoulder mobility and good body rotation.

If you struggle with an awkward recovery over the water, work on improving your body roll and your recovery will also improve and take some of the load off your shoulders that you may normally experience.

Poor body rotation and stiff shoulders mean an awkward recovery round the side of the body for this swimmer.

Low Awkward Arm Recovery

The classic problem with arm recovery occurs when the swimmer struggles for clearance over the water. This makes the freestyle stroke quite awkward and causes the hand to lead the elbow during the recovery.

A low awkward recovery is caused either by poor posture and shoulder flexibility or a lack of body rotation in the stroke. If you struggle with your arm recovery over the water, work on improving both your swimming posture and rotation (Chapters 10 and 11), the combination of which will make your recovery much easier and more relaxed.

If you struggle with your arm recovery make sure you try the exercise shown in Figure 11.8 to experience the difference better body rotation will make to your swimming.

A Drill to Improve Your Arm Recovery

The Popov Drill is named after the great Russian sprinter Alexander Popov who made this drill famous. Using fins, kick on your side as in *6-1-6* but straight away slowly slide the thumb of the top arm up the side of your body to your armpit. As soon as you reach your armpit slide the thumb back down to your hip before sliding it up again to the armpit and then over into the water, stroking through onto the other side of the body. Repeat this continuously on the other side, swapping sides down the lap. The mantra of the drill is *up-down-up-and-through*. For a full description see Appendix A.

The Popov Drill makes you adopt a relaxed arm recovery with good rotation in the stroke even though you probably won't use such a tight elbow angle in your full stroke.

Differing arm recovery styles from these elite swimmers: Jono Van Hazel on the right with a classic high elbow recovery, Mel Benson on the left with a lower swinging style.

Arm Recovery in Elite Swimmers

In the elite pool swimming world arm recovery styles vary considerably, with some swimmers using a classic high elbow technique while others use varying degrees of straighter arm recoveries. In the open water nearly all swimmers use a straighter arm recovery style which helps increase their arm clearance over waves and chop and also other swimmers in close proximity to them.

Swimmers favouring a higher stroke rate also naturally favour a straighter arm recovery with the arms swinging a little more around the side. As we'll discuss in the Swim Type section of this book, we call this style of stroke The Swinger for exactly that reason. Swingers can be incredibly fast and efficient swimmers even though this style of stroke has traditionally been given a bad press in the swimming world.

PAUL: *When I ask swimmers what is the most important aspect of good freestyle technique many will reply 'high elbows!' As we'll see though this isn't necessarily the case. For swimmers with tight shoulder muscles or those racing in open water, a slightly straighter arm recovery would be a better option.*

Experimenting with a Straighter Arm Recovery

If you are tight in the upper back and shoulders, or you are focused on racing well in open water, then experiment with some laps of freestyle using a slightly straighter arm than you are used to. Simply open out the elbow to different angles and see how it feels. You can expect it to feel strange at first but also notice how relaxed or otherwise the recovery feels.

A straighter arm recovery really comes into its own in open water swims, helping you clear chop and wake from other swimmers.

ADAM: *Swimmers trying a straighter arm recovery for the first time often say that it feels strange and fear that it must look terrible! As a coach I work with swimmers trying this all the time and I can tell you that it doesn't look anywhere near as extreme as it feels at first. Give it a bit of a try out in your own swimming, particularly if you suffer from a low awkward arm recovery.*

If you are a triathlete or open water swimmer racing in a wetsuit you may have found in the past that the restriction of the wetsuit causes your shoulders to become fatigued when swimming. Some go to the extreme of feeling they need to switch to a sleeveless suit (which has more drag) or even hit the weights in the gym to get stronger in the shoulders. But again, a straighter arm recovery may help reduce the fatigue in your shoulders and is well worth experimenting with. If you watch an elite triathlon swim leg you'll see that most elite triathletes use a straighter arm recovery style to great effect.

CHAPTER 12 Hand Entry

How your hands enter into the water at the front of the stroke might not sound important but it can make a large difference to how well you swim and also the chances of you suffering from shoulder injury.

There are three elements to a good hand entry:

1) Hand Angle

The hand should enter into the water at a slight downward angle with the palm facing down towards the water's surface. We call this a 'fingertip-first entry' as the fingertips are the first part of your hand to spear into the water.

This angle of entry pierces through the surface of the water nicely and immediately gets you in a great position for a good catch as you start the stroke at the front. Unfortunately, in some parts of the world you can still find an alternative style of hand entry taught where the palm faces outwards and the thumb enters the water first. This is called a 'thumb-first entry'.

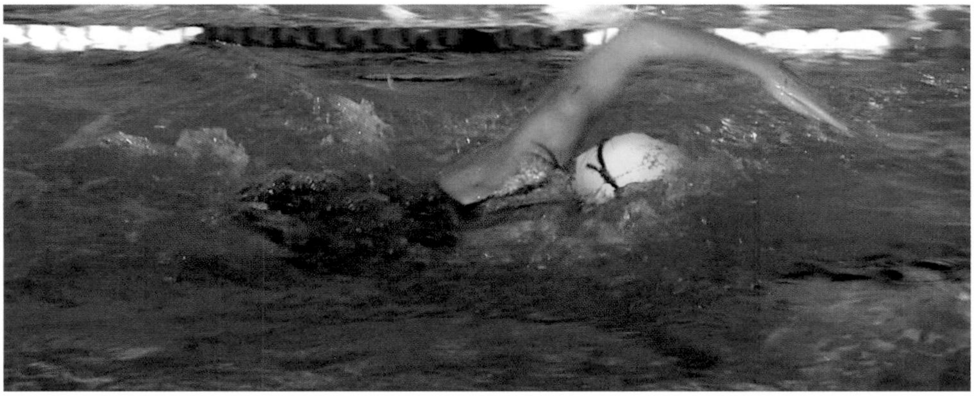

This swimmer displays an excellent fingertip-first entry into the water.

Avoid a thumb-first entry, it is very bad for your shoulders and after entering the water your hand will tend to slice down in the water instead of engaging with it for the catch to follow.

Thumb-First Entry. Warning: this can seriously harm your shoulders!

During the 1970s swimmers were taught to enter into the water thumb first with the palm facing outwards. The idea was to create a cleaner hand entry into the water with less resistance but rotating the hand outwards in this manner internally rotates the shoulder, placing a twisting load on it. Some swimming coaches and websites still recommend using a thumb-first entry but we now understand that because it internally rotates the shoulder, it is the leading cause of shoulder injury in swimming and should be strongly avoided for this reason. If you've had a shoulder injury or are currently suffering from one, you'll find our additional advice on this subject in Chapter 30 very useful.

A thumb-first entry is also less effective in setting you up for a good catch as the hand tends to continue slicing down into the water after it has entered rather than engaging with the water at the front of your stroke.

PAUL: *If you're serious about your swimming performances then you need to take every measure you can to avoid injury. I've been coaching swimmers of all levels for nearly 15 years and in that time it's become very clear to me that consistency in preparation and training is the single most important factor in swimmers achieving their goals. Time out recovering from a shoulder injury will set you back significantly and you will lose the peak of fitness you would otherwise have achieved.*

You may have been swimming for many years and you may not wish to take the time and effort to change from a thumb-first to a fingertip-first hand entry but please understand the very high risk you are taking with the health of your shoulders by not doing so. Changing to a fingertip entry does take some time and persistence but it is so important to guarantee you a long and happy swimming career.

Here are two useful visualisations you can use to help remove a thumb-first entry from your stroke:

- Visualise hiding your palm from someone watching you from the side of the pool, as if someone's written a rude word on it! As your hand recovers over the surface of the water you will have a tendency to turn the hand outwards to create the thumb-first position but this would mean showing your palm to that person on the pool deck, don't do it!
- Visualise carrying a briefcase in your hand as you recover over the water. You cannot turn your hand outwards because that would mean rotating the briefcase – keep it straight as you swim!

2) Hand Entry Point

If you stand and hold one arm straight out in front of you and practise entering with the other, the hand should enter somewhere between the wrist and the elbow of the outstretched arm. This is a good guide for most swimmers but some, particularly elite open water swimmers, like to reach a little further forwards before entering into the water. This can be a useful adaptation to make to your stroke for rougher open water swimming.

Wherever you enter into the water the most important thing is that the hand should spear in cleanly and enter before the elbow. If you overreach and the elbow collapses in first this will harm the catch phase of the stroke that follows.

A good exercise for practising a spearing hand entry is the *Shoulder Tap Drill* shown in Appendix A. With fins on, tap yourself on the shoulder before entering into the water using fingertip-first entry (palm facing down). The shoulder tap slows things down and gives you time to think and to ensure that you are entering from a high position angled downward. As you'll see in the full drill description, breathe on every single stroke (both to the left and right) when performing *Shoulder Tap* and leave the other arm outstretched for balance.

If your other hand was outstretched, the hand should enter somewhere between the distance of your elbow and wrist.

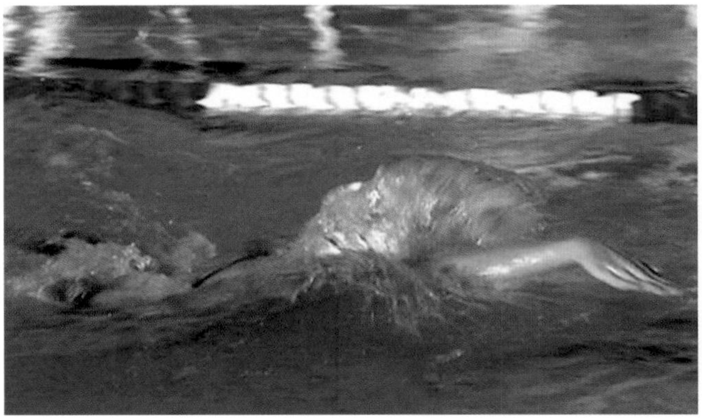

If you overreach on hand entry you will drop your elbow in first.

SPEARING FISH VISUALISATION

To practice a positive hand entry into the water, imagine there's a fish swimming in the water around 30 cm or 1 ft in front of you. As you swim, visualise spearing the fish as your enter the water with your hand like the blade of a spear. Enter with a big splash and you scare the fish away and disrupt the smoothness of your stroke. Enter cleanly, smoothly and stealthily and you will catch that fish! This is a simple but powerful way to focus on a clean hand entry and can be used at any time when you're swimming or racing.

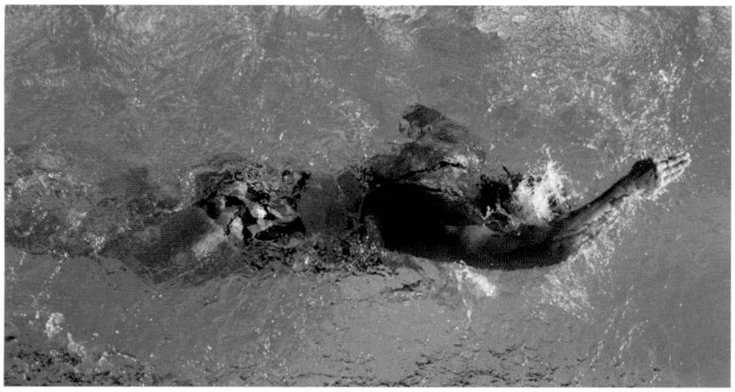

A crossover in front of the head is seen in about 70% of attendees on our Swim Smooth Clinics.

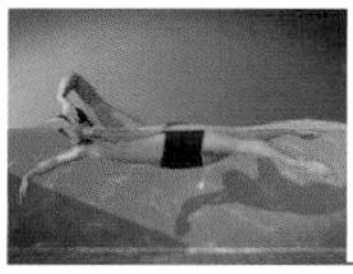

3) Alignment Straight in Front of the Same Shoulder

As your hand enters the water and extends forwards it should be perfectly in line with your shoulder. This keeps you tracking straight and sets you up for a good catch as you start the following stroke. This sounds simple but in reality very few beginner and intermediate level swimmers have good alignment in the water; most cross over the centre line to a greater or lesser extent as their hands enter and extend.

As we saw in Chapter 10 on swimming posture, the key here is to draw your shoulder blades together and back to enter and extend straight forward in front of the same shoulder.

MIDDLE FINGER VISUALISATION

A useful visualisation to improve your alignment on hand entry is to simply focus on the middle finger on each hand as it enters the water and extends forward. Think about that middle finger as you swim and nothing else, extending it straight down the pool as if you are aiming the barrel of a gun.

ADAM: *Entering and extending forward straight in front of the same shoulder sounds easy but it is something that could well be holding you back with your swimming. This is an area of swimming technique where visualisations are very powerful. Memorise how our animated swimmer Mr Smooth looks from the underside angle extending straight and aligned – if you haven't done so already you can download him for free from www.swimsmooth.com. If you have our Catch Masterclass DVD also watch Jono Van Hazel just before you go to the pool and aim to reproduce his stroke in the water. Jono has fantastic alignment and provides a great visual image for you to keep in mind as you swim.*

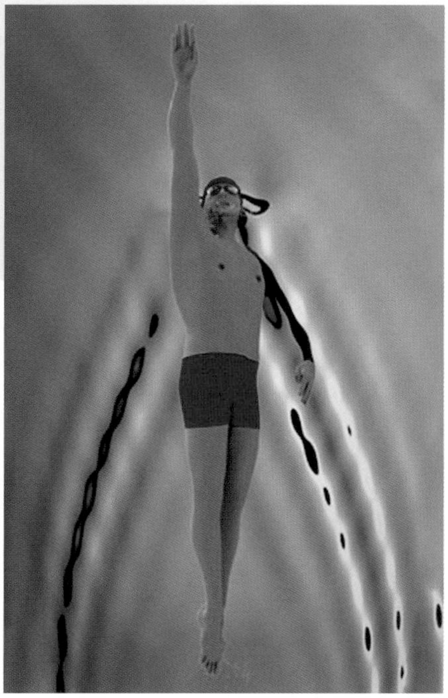

To help overcome a crossover, visualise Mr Smooth extending straight forward in front of the same shoulder as he swims.

PAUL: *Don't underestimate the damage a crossover does to your swimming: it causes you to snake or 'fish tail' down the pool, creates a scissor kick in your stroke and ruins your catch on the water. A crossover can also place stress on your shoulder, increasing the risk of shoulder injury particularly in combination with a thumb-first entry. It will also make swimming straight in the open water very challenging. In summary, a crossover adds a huge amount of drag, ruins your propulsion and could stop you swimming completely through injury – pretty serious! Ask a friend or coach to check if you are crossing over the centre line in front of your head, even momentarily. If you do you should make fixing it an immediate priority.*

Using Paddles to Work on Hand Entry

The added surface area of a pair of paddles can be a great way to feel how you are entering into the water. Any paddle will be useful for this but we highly recommend the Finis Freestyler Paddle as its unique shape (like the blade of a spear) gives you immediate feedback on how straight you are entering. So much so that if you cross over or drop your elbow on entry then you'll have trouble keeping them on your hands!

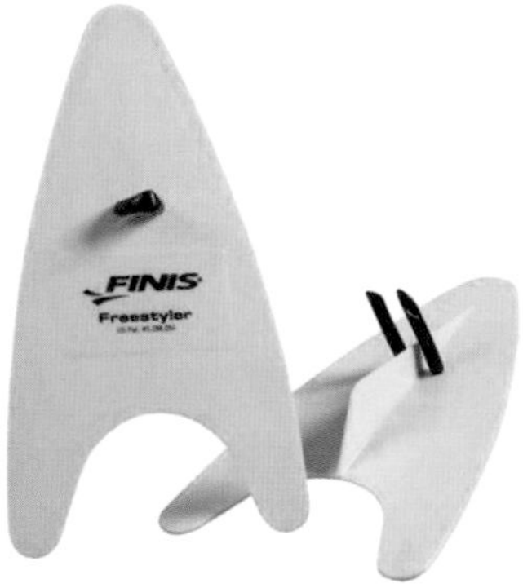

The Finis Freestyler, a great paddle for working on your alignment and catch set-up.

Catch and Pull-Through

The catch and pull-through phases of the freestyle stroke are where a swimmer develops between 85% and 100% of their propulsion. The key to a great catch and pull is to feel the water during the catch phase and engage with it by pressing it in a backwards direction. Pressing the water back produces an opposite force propelling you forwards in the water.

Problems that occur during the catch normally involve the swimmer pushing downward on the water, or sometimes to the side or even forward! Pushing downward on the water during the catch does not create any propulsion, instead it simply lifts the front end of the body upwards and sinks the legs. It's no coincidence that swimmers with very low-lying legs in the water normally push down during the catch phase.

If you suffer from a poor body position in your stroke then by improving your catch mechanics you will create more propulsion and your legs will be higher, lowering your drag. A win-win!

Sam presses down on the water in comparison to elite swimmer Rhys Mainstone who presses the water backward by bending his elbow and tipping his wrist – great technique.

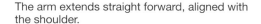

ADAM: *Many swimming coaches consider working on the catch and pull-through to be for advanced level swimmers only. At Swim Smooth we passionately believe that this is not the case! Approached in the right way, making improvements to your catch can be achieved quite easily and these changes will benefit your stroke technique as a whole. As we'll see with our Swim Types system, many beginner swimmers have very poor feel for the water and lack any 'oomph' in their stroke rhythm. If you struggle to feel the water at all at the front of your stroke then developing a better catch is critical to help you progress.*

Let's examine the movements of a good catch and pull-through step by step. By following the advice in the early steps of this chapter you will already have some of these elements in place in your stroke:

The hand enters the water cleanly using a spearing hand entry with the fingertips and palm facing downward.

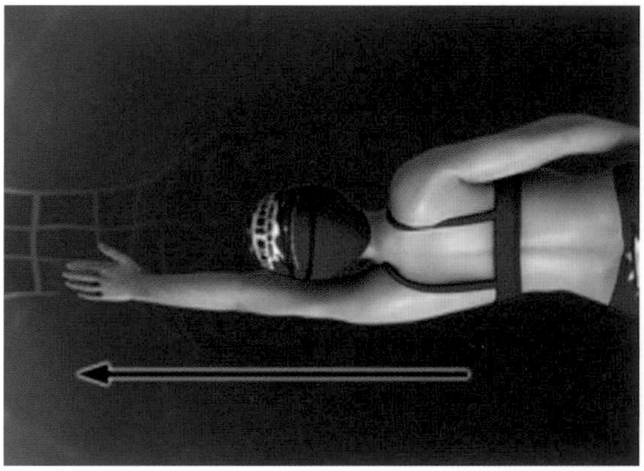

The arm extends straight forward, aligned with the shoulder.

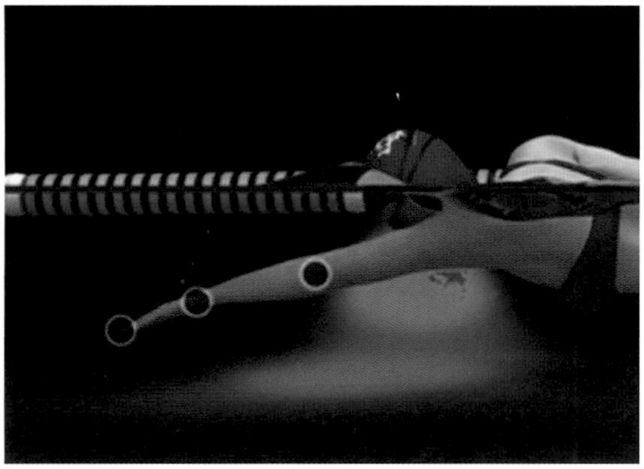

During arm extension the fingertips stay slightly lower than the wrist and the wrist slightly lower than the elbow at all times.

The catch is initiated with a tipping of the wrist. This is momentary and easily missed when looking at video analysis of great swimmers. See Figure 13.9 for examples of this in elite swimmers' strokes.

The elbow bends and the forearm becomes more vertical in the water.

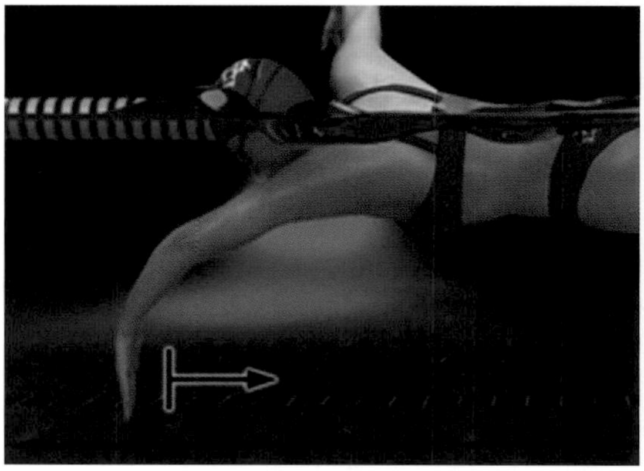

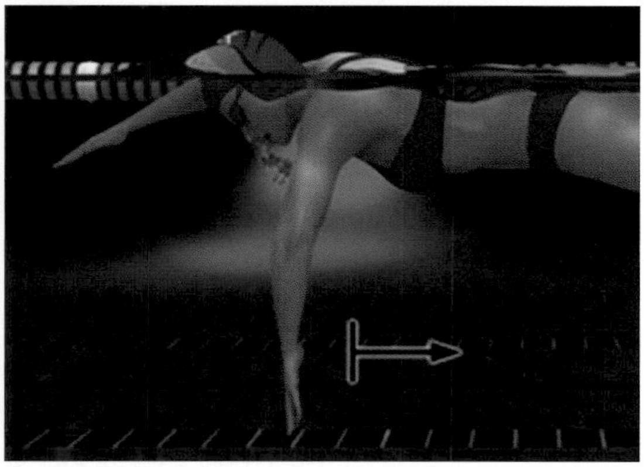

As the hand travels under the head the pull phase is entered, with the hand and forearm now facing directly backwards.

For distance swimming the depth of the pull is such that the elbow is bent somewhere between 100° and 120°. The hand does not cross the centre line or move outside elbow width during the whole stroke action.

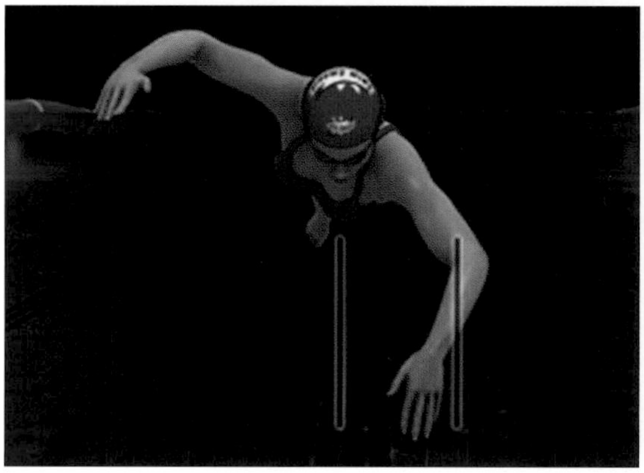

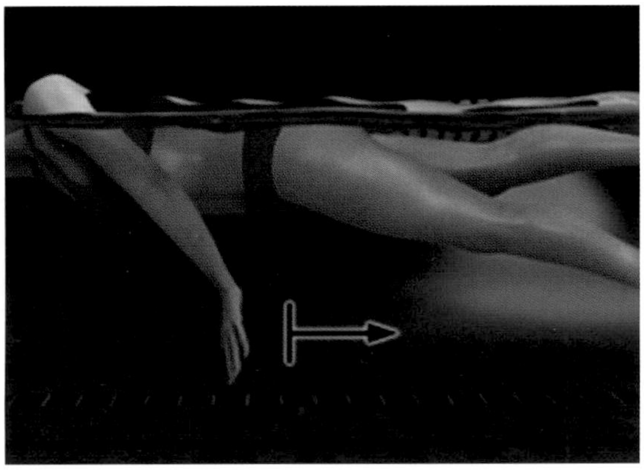

As the hand moves toward the back of the stroke the palm is kept facing straight backwards.

At the rear of the push, the hand is turned slightly inward towards the thigh to finish the stroke as the hip on that side rotates upward.

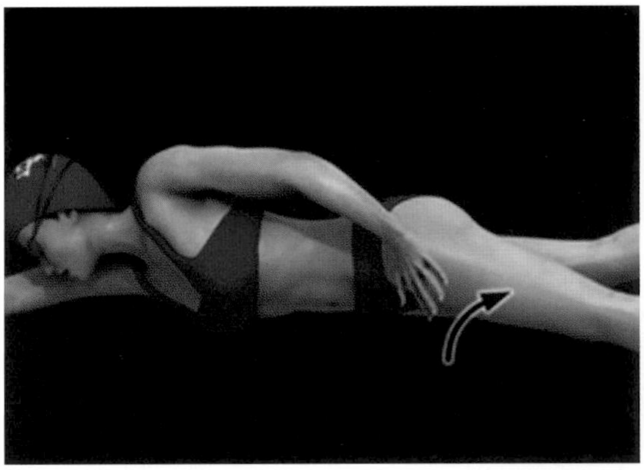

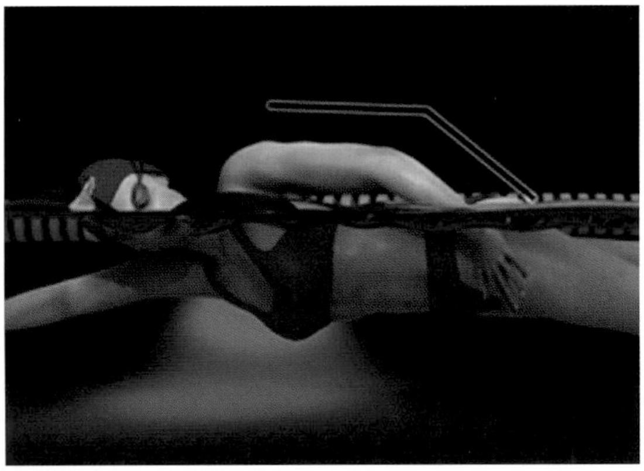

The arm exits once it has extended to around 150° of elbow bend. Note the arm is not fully extended with the elbow locked out.

Don't worry if that seems like a lot of information or even a bit overwhelming! The key thing to remember is that you are trying to press the water back behind you during the catch and pull-through underwater. Using a good mix of key drills and visualisations will help you tune into these movements and get a good feel for them.

As you work on your arm stroke under the water, particularly during the catch, don't become frustrated if it takes a little time to click into place in your stroke. Developing a good catch is challenging and is something that elite swimmers need to constantly work on and maintain in their strokes too. However, even small improvements in your catch technique will have an immediate benefit to your speed and efficiency in the water, which you will notice straight away.

A High Elbow Catch and Pull-Through

You might have heard or been told by a swim coach to 'keep your elbows high' when you swim. Sometimes this comment refers to your arm recovery over the top of the water but as we saw in Chapter 11, a classically high elbow recovery over the water is now considered less important than it used to be in swimming technique. However, during the pull-through under the water a high elbow technique is essential to create good propulsion.

The reason a high elbow technique is important is that it helps you press the water in the right direction – backwards – so that you are propelled forwards. It allows you to do this not only with the hand but your forearm too. This use of the forearm is important as it increases the surface area that you are using as a paddle in the water.

FIGURE 13.9 Examples of wrist tipping by elite swimmers, top-bottom: Mel Benson, Shelley Taylor-Smith, Rhys Mainstone.

Here are some examples of swimmers showing classic flaws in their catch technique. Notice how our animated swimmer maintains a high elbow in all these positions with the elbow higher than the wrist and the wrist higher than the fingertips throughout:

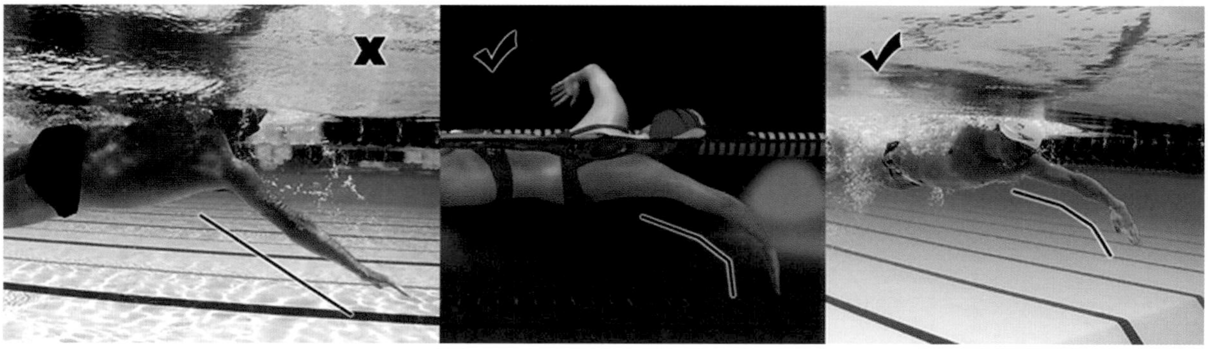

Ron pushes down on the water with a straight arm, this only lifts him up at the front and does not generate any forward propulsion.

Greg crosses the centre line under his body, losing propulsion and his balance at the same time. Notice the scissor kick forming behind him as he has to stabilise himself.

Tim pulls through with a very straight arm under the body. This forces him to press down during the catch phase and overloads the weaker shoulder muscles.

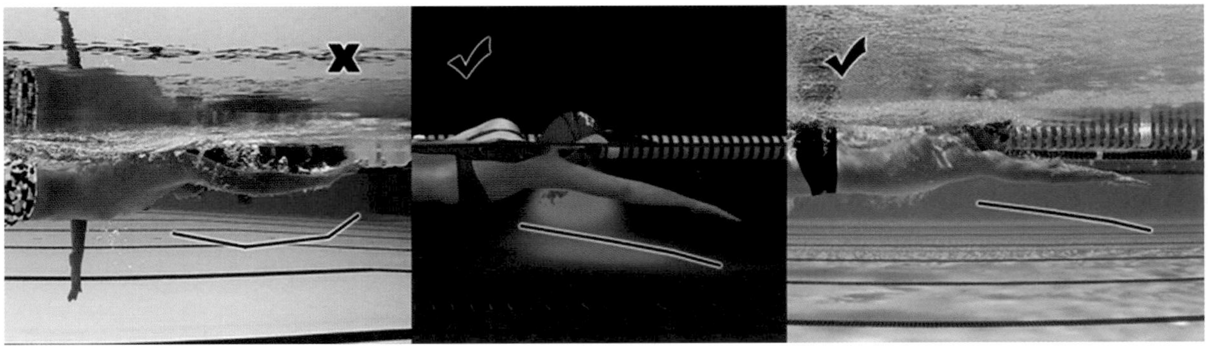

Henry drops his wrist and elbow and shows the palm forwards. Overgliders very often do this as they try to absolutely maximise stroke length.

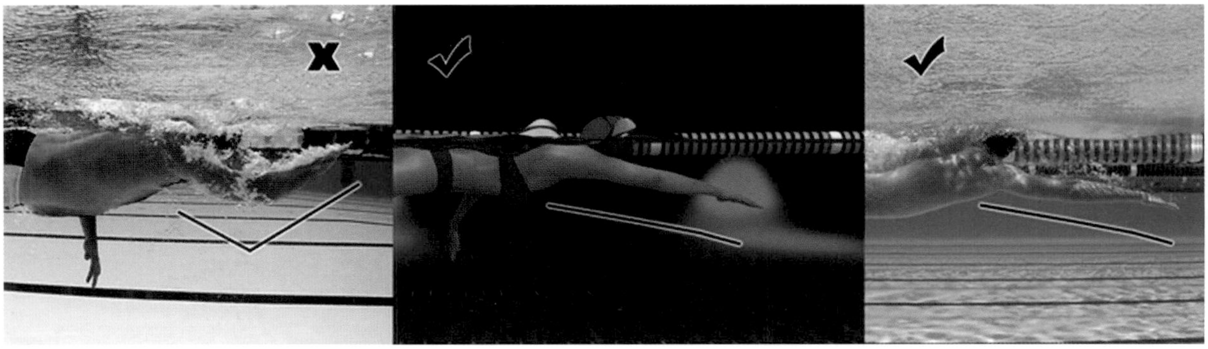

Tim drops his elbow just before the catch, from here he will find it nearly impossible to get his elbow up high for the catch to follow.

The Limits of Flexibility

If you have read a lot of material about swimming on the internet you might have come across the term Early Vertical Forearm or 'EVF' for short. This refers to some elite swimmers' ability to achieve a very vertical forearm position early in the stroke in front of the head. This is technically very difficult to perform and requires a lot of flexibility and stability in the shoulder joint; for adult age-group swimmers and triathletes we recommend a less extreme position at this point in stroke.

See Figure 13.10 for a comparison of these positions, note that the elbow is still higher than the wrist and the wrist higher than the fingertips in a more conventional catching position. The conventional catch still creates a lot of propulsion and allows you to swim very quickly indeed. Olympic swimmer Jono Van Hazel who features in our Catch Masterclass DVD swam sub-50 seconds for 100m using such a catch, so there is no shortage of speed available!

FIGURE 13.10 An extreme 'EVF position' (top) has the arm nearly vertical in front of the head. A conventional catch (bottom) has a less extreme vertical forearm.

FIGURE 13.11 Use a friend or coach to investigate your muscular recruitment in the catch position.

Your Strength and the Catch

Referring to Figure 13.11 try the following practical exercise:

Position 1: Stand square on and face your friend with your arm locked straight out in front of you. Have them support your hand and press down on it hard. Notice how all the effort is coming from your shoulder muscles and how your friend does not struggle to resist you too much. This is not because you are not strong but because all the effort is coming from your shoulders, which are a relatively small, weak muscle group. This position demonstrates a poor catch technique with the swimmer pushing down on the water with a straight arm.

Position 2: Standing in the same position, now bend your elbow and again push down on your friend's hand. Notice how you are now starting to engage your back and chest muscle groups, which are stronger – your friend should notice the increase in force you can create here. However, we know that this position is still not correct as the elbow is dropped and the body is not rotated.

Position 3: Rotate your feet and body to be more side-on to your friend and bend your elbow but keep it high so the elbow is higher than the wrist and the wrist is higher than the fingertips. In this position think about pressing the water back behind you rather than pushing it downward. Notice how you can really engage your chest and back muscles here and easily generate a lot of force. You will see from this position where the term 'reaching over a barrel' comes from.

The key point with this exercise is to show you how a good catching position on the water allows you to use larger more powerful muscle groups. This makes it easy to generate the forces required during the catch. So easy in fact that when they start to get this right swimmers either pull too hard and overpower the catch or it feels too easy and they think it cannot be correct – surely a good catch should feel solid and hard? Actually a good catch is a relatively light connection with the water and should not feel overly forceful or hurried.

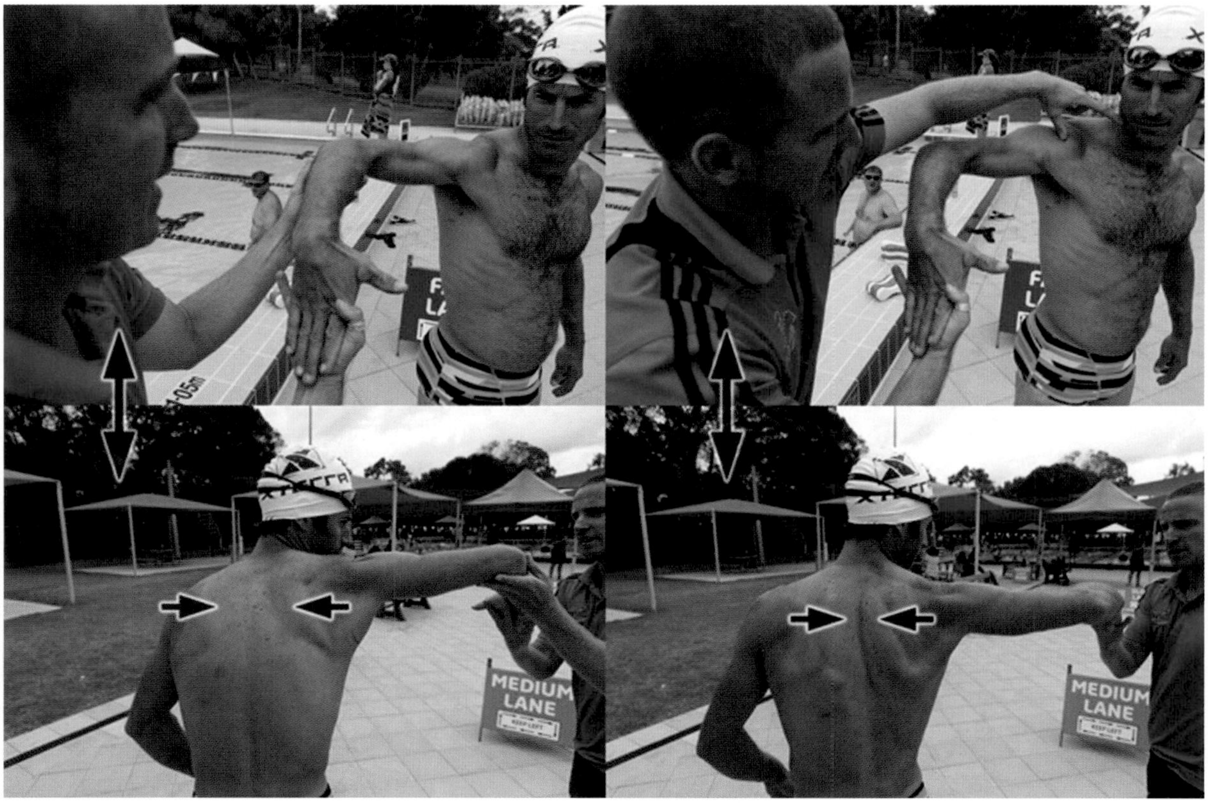

One more thing to perfect this exercise. Did you notice in the third position that your shoulder was rolled inwards as shown in the left hand pictures? As we discussed in Chapter 10 this is poor swimming posture. Whilst in this position think about drawing your shoulder blades together and your shoulders back and down. Notice how this really connects your arm to your body for a great catch!

Developing Your Catch Step 1: Catch Set-up

Alignment and Posture

The first step to developing your catch is to refer back to Chapter 10 where we looked at improving your alignment and posture in the water. Use the steps there to straighten out your stroke and ensure that you are entering the water and extending forward with the hand straight in front of the shoulder. If you cross over the centre line in your stroke then you will find it nearly impossible to catch and pull-through effectively on the following stroke.

Whilst performing the *Kick-On-Side*, *6-1-6* and *6-3-6* drills, introduce a new focus on the position and angle of the lead hand itself. During this exercise, are you dropping the wrist and showing the palm forwards or perhaps facing the palm sideways in a karate chop position? Have you dropped the elbow lower than the wrist and fingertips?

PAUL: *A common mistake that I see many swimmers making is to rush straight to developing their catch mechanics – i.e. the bent elbow pull-through itself. Whilst this is important, if you don't first focus on the stage in your stroke immediately before, developing your catch will be a fruitless and frustrating exercise for you. Take the time to improve your catch set-up using the tips in this section – they can make improvements to your propulsion even without focusing on the catch itself.*

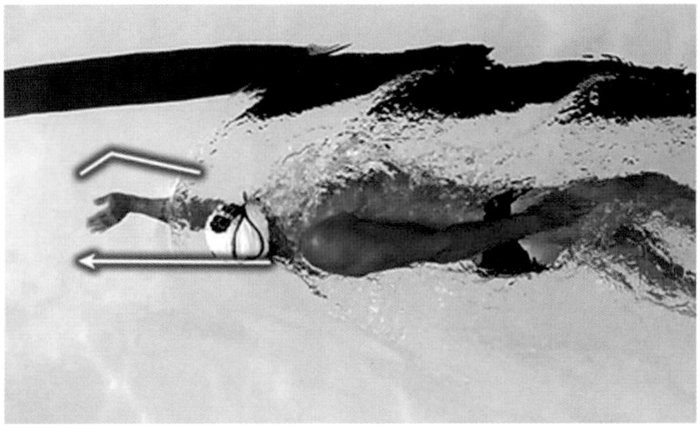

Classic mistakes whilst kicking on your side: crossing over the centre line (left) and dropping the wrist and showing the palm forwards (right).

ADAM: *Many swimmers feel that their hand should be very near the surface of the water in this position but to achieve that they have to drop their elbow or wrist. It is much better to go a touch deeper with the hand to get into a better catch set-up position, you won't lose any stroke length from doing so but you'll gain propulsion from a much more effective catch.*

To generate a good catch we need to get the hand and elbow in a good set-up position at this point in the stroke. As you kick on your side focus on keeping your elbow slightly higher than your wrist and the palm itself facing downward to the bottom of the pool. Create a very slight angle at the wrist so that the whole hand slopes slightly downward.

This slight tipping of the wrist is important as it will help you initiate the catch itself. If you create too much of a downward angle you will feel your hand pull down towards the bottom of the pool. This is a bit like having your hand out of a car window, changing the angle of your hand in the airflow to pull it up and downward. Experiment with the lead hand in the same way when you are kicking on your side in the pool.

By aiming to start his catch from very near the surface of the water, Paul C has unwittingly dropped his elbow and from here will have to press down on the water during the initial catch. Spearing forwards a little lower in the position shown will give Paul a much greater use of the effective arc of his catch.

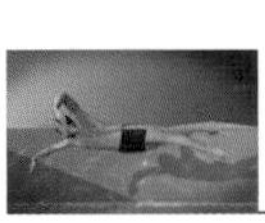

Supporting Yourself while Breathing

A significant benefit of entering the water and extending forward in this position is that it offers you good support and stability at the front of your stroke. In contrast many swimmers' lead arms collapse down when breathing, removing any support offered to them. This causes the head to sink and the mouth to drop below the surface, making breathing a real struggle! If you take on water when you swim then introducing a better catch set-up position in your stroke will give you much more support when breathing.

Clare's arm drops down when breathing, giving her very little support.

You may find, however, that your arm still wants to drop down as the movement has become a habit. To help break this, use the mantra *1 - 2 - Stretch* as you swim, the 1 and 2 on non-breathing strokes and the *Stretch* when breathing to keep you focused on keeping the lead arm extended and offering you support.

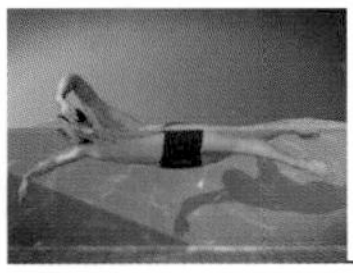

Developing Your Catch Step 2: Catch Mechanics

The key to a great catch and pull through is to press the water backwards using the hand and fore-arm as a paddle. Pushing the water downward or to the side harms the catch and wastes a great deal of energy. To help you develop your catch we are going to use three main drills: *Scull #1*, *Scull #2* and *Doggy Paddle*. Each will help you get a feel for pressing the water backwards in a bent elbow position.

Sculling is a very valuable exercise, which helps to develop your 'feel for the water' – learning how the water should feel to you during the catch and how to time the stroke movements to create good propulsion. Most swimmers find sculling challenging at first but that's OK, follow our pointers carefully and you will soon get better at it.

PAUL: *Any time you struggle to perform a drill I think you should actually look at this as a positive: you've simply uncovered an area of your stroke technique or proprioception that needs work and you stand to benefit greatly from working on it!*

SCULL #1

Referring to the full drill description for *Scull #1* in Appendix A, push off down the lap with a pull buoy between your legs and raise your head above the surface. Start sculling the water left and right in front of you changing the angle of your hand to keep a light water pressure on the palm. Make sure that your elbow is higher than your wrist and your wrist is higher than your fingertips. You may need to exaggerate this and move your hands a little lower in the water to make sure the palm is facing backwards.

Scull #1 practices the position at the initial phase of the catch. Many swimming coaches talk about 'reaching over a barrel' or 'reaching over and hugging a Swiss ball' during the catch in the position you are in here. These can be very useful visualisations whilst performing *Scull #1*, try them out yourself.

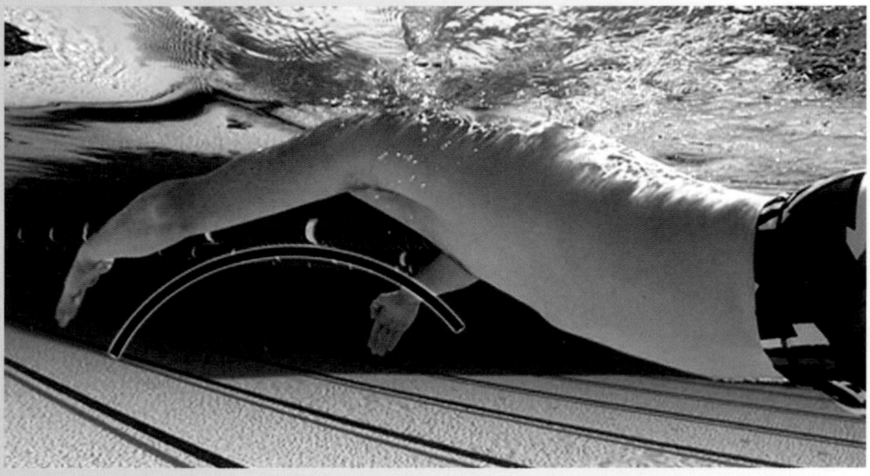

As your perform Scull #1, visualise reaching over a barrel or hugging a Swiss ball. This will help you develop the correct catch position.

Sculling drills are always slow paced but a good sign that you are getting Scull #1 right is when your speed picks up noticeably and you feel your chest rising up a little in the water.

Scull #1 and Overgliding

A fascinating test you can try when performing *Scull #1* is to move from your high elbow position into one where you drop the elbow and wrist so that your palm is facing forwards. If you are a bit of an Overglider you probably do this in your full stroke, dropping the wrist and showing the palm forwards. We call this position 'putting on the brakes'.

Overgliders tend to do this in their strokes without realising it as they strongly emphasise the extension forwards and add a glide to their strokes. You'll notice when dropping the elbow and wrist in this position when sculling that you immediately stop moving forwards and may even start to move backwards! This goes to show how harmful Overgliding is for your stroke efficiency.

You will also feel more water pressure on the palm of the hand in this position, which could make you think that you are getting a good catch in your full stroke. Of course, to be efficient you need to be pressing the water backwards, not forwards and away from you!

DOGGY PADDLE

PAUL: Doggy Paddle *drill is probably the oldest drill in the swimming world, it's something I can recall doing at age six in the pool! It may be a very old drill but it's great for developing your catch technique; in fact it's the perfect drill to use if you have a tendency to catch or pull through with a very straight arm under the water.*

Referring to the description in Appendix A, perform the *Doggy Paddle drill* using a pull buoy starting off with your head above the surface. Imagine there's a rope under the water, which you are moving over about 50cm or 2ft beneath the surface, and as you perform the drill aim to pull straight down that rope. Pull-through all the way to your hip and emphasise your body roll, the drill's mantra is *'reach and roll'*!

Recovering the hands back under the water will feel strange at first, don't worry too much about this, simply bring them through as smoothly as you can with a flat hand, fingers first. The focus of the drill should be in bending your elbow early in front of your head and getting over the top of the movement to press the water backwards using your hand and forearm as paddles. If you struggle with this experiment try moving a little deeper with the hands to help you get over the top of the stroke.

Once you have got underway with *Doggy Paddle* you can drop your head down into the water and watch your movements in action. Keep it smooth and always in motion – either extending forwards, catching the water or pressing it backwards. No dead spots please and no showing the palm of the hand forwards!

Transition into full-stroke swimming and continue the visualisation of pulling down a rope under your body, bend that elbow early in front of your head just like in the drill itself. You should find you pull through with a nice rhythm and tempo to the stroke.

If you are an advanced swimmer you can get up quite a speed with *Doggy Paddle*!

SCULL #2

Similar to *Scull #1*, this drill focuses on a slightly later point in the stroke as you are entering the pull phase under the head. It is ideal for swimmers who pull through with a straight arm under the body as it emphasises a bent elbow position at this point of the stroke.

During *Scull #2*, scull the water lightly by moving the hands slightly wider than the body and on the way in, nearly meeting in the middle. Keep your elbows in a fixed position and perform the sculling motion with a 'mixing' action from the elbows down. This is a harder drill than *Scull #1* as it offers you less support to keep your head up in the water.

When you transition into full-stroke swimming, focus on pulling through smoothly under the head with an elbow bend at approximately 100° to 120°

SMILEY FACE VISUALISATION

The key to a successful catch and pull is to press the water back behind you through the whole arm stroke. Here is a simple way to visualise this as you swim: imagine someone's drawn a smiley face on the palm of your hand and as you swim you've got to show that face back to the wall behind you at all times. This might sound slightly childish but it is a very effective way to focus you on a good pull-through technique.

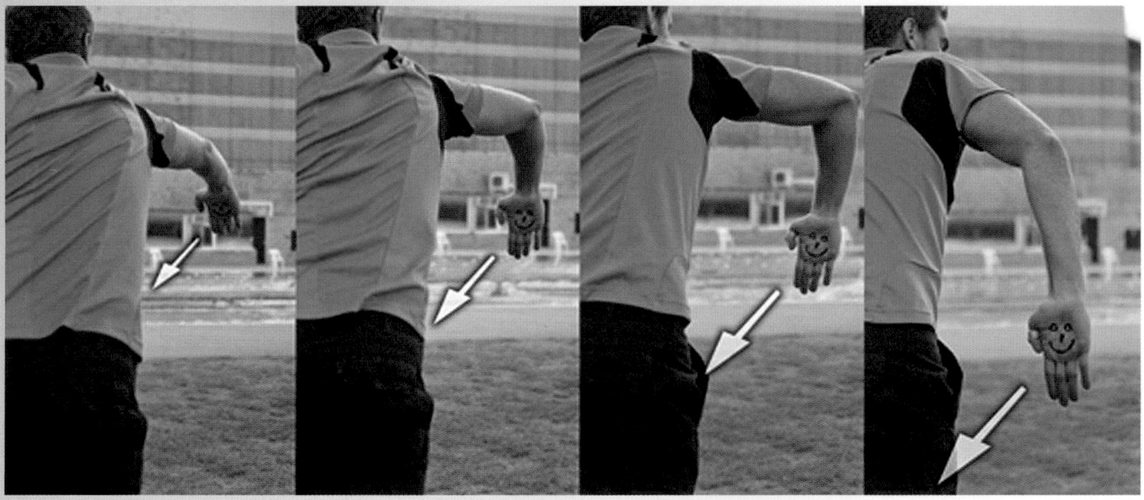

Imagine someone's drawn a smiley face on the palm of your hand and as you swim show the face back to the wall behind you.

Integrating Catch Drills into a Set

Sculling and Doggy Paddle drills are best followed immediately by full-stroke swimming to transfer the movements and 'feel for the water' into your full stroke. We recommend that you swim these drills for around 10–20 m and then transition into full-stroke swimming. For example:

4 × 100 m as 15 m *Scull #1* transitioning into 85 m freestyle
8 × 50 m as 15 m *Scull #2* transitioning into 35 m freestyle
2 × 200 m freestyle with the 0-25 m and 100-125 m *Doggy Paddle*
4 × 100 m as 10 m *Scull #1* into 10 m *Doggy Paddle* into 80 m freestyle

As you transition into freestyle in the above sets use the *Smiley-Face Visualisation* as you swim.

Right Can Feel Wrong!

A key element of a good catch and pull-through is to press the water back behind you at all times. Relative to you, the water is already moving in this direction as you swim through it, so in a sense you are simply helping the water on its way. However, a poor catch and pull-through presses down on the water or shows the palm forwards to push against the flow. Since water is so dense you will feel a significant pressure on the palm of your hand as you do this and it is quite possible you are misinterpreting that pressure as a good catch.

The irony is that as you improve your catch and start pressing the water backwards, you will feel less pressure on the palm as you are no longer changing the water's direction. As you improve your propulsive technique it's easy to feel the reduced pressure on the palm and think 'this can't be right, a good catch should feel strong and solid' and so return to your old stroke technique. This is one of the reasons why developing a good catch is so elusive for many swimmers. A good catch should allow you to feel a firm but not forced connection with the water.

Fingers Spread or Together?

Perhaps the most common question we are asked by swimmers about the catch phase of the stroke is how they should hold their fingers: should they be together or wide apart?

For 95% of swimmers we recommend holding your fingers lightly together with no gaps between them. This is quite easy to coordinate and leaves you able to focus on the more important issues in your stroke technique. Elite swimmers do hold their fingers ever so slightly apart – enough to slip a few sheets of paper between but nothing more. This increases the effective surface area of their hands very slightly, however this is a very fine motor skill. Let the fingers move any wider and water starts slipping through the gaps and a lot of propulsion is lost.

Holding your fingers lightly together will allow you to swim very quickly and efficiently without the risks of slipping by trying to hold them slightly apart.

The Exit at the Rear of the Stroke

The push phase at the back of the stroke by the hip and thigh has been emphasised in many swim programmes around the world. Whilst it's important to avoid finishing the stroke too early, many swimmers feel like they need to lock-out their elbow straight in an effort to really press through at the back of the stroke. The cue that you may have heard is to 'brush the thumb against the thigh'. If the recovery phase of the freestyle stroke starts with the arm locked

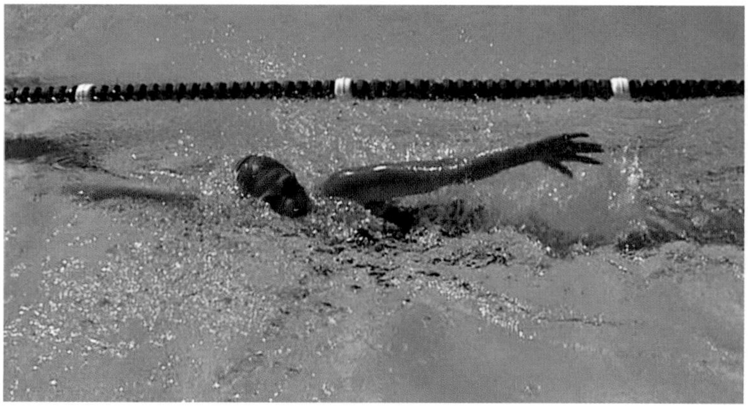

Nic is trying to maximise her stroke length with a distinct push at the back of her stroke – this is placing a lot of stress on her elbow joint and shoulder.

Above and below the water, note how elite swimmer Rhys Mainstone does not lock his arm out straight, he leaves the elbow slightly bent to start his arm recovery smoothly without a flick at the rear.

out straight, it will take place with a very internally rotated shoulder, which is a recipe for shoulder injury (also see Chapter 30).

Whilst less common than shoulder strain, some swimmers experience elbow pain when swimming. This pain is often referred to as 'Golfer's Elbow' or to give it its medical term: medial epicondylitis. We have found from experience that the most common cause of Golfer's Elbow in swimmers is a rapid snapping of the hand against the thigh from trying to really lengthen out the stroke at the back. Swimmers who do this can be seen to flick the water upwards at the rear as the hand comes out of the water with the fingers staying as the highest point during the arm recovery.

To avoid this, focus on the elbow exiting the water at the back of the stroke before the hand does. Aim for around a 150° angle, starting the recovery with the elbow leading.

Feel for the Water

When a swimmer is creating good levels of propulsion they often report feeling 'in tune' with the water; they have a perception of feeling the water well with the hands and forearms. After spending some time out of the water even great swimmers lose this feel slightly as the subtle timing of the stroke is lost. Thankfully it only takes a few swim sessions to regain it.

With your own swimming you too should aim to develop an appreciation and 'feel for the water' during the catch and pull phases of the stroke. The timing of your stroke is critical such that you can feel a smooth consistent pressure on the water as your body rotates rhythmically with the arm stroke. With this in mind we'll look at improving the timing of your stroke in the final part of this chapter.

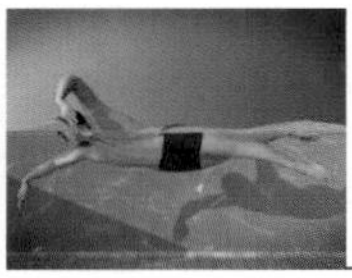

Developing Your Catch Step 3: Rhythm and Timing

The Catch and Rhythm

The catch and pull-through phases of the freestyle stroke have a huge knock-on effect on the stroke rate and rhythm of your stroke. A poor catch takes a long time to initiate as the water is pressed downward, to the side or even forwards. This slows down the stroke as the swimmer is forced to change the water's direction. As you work on improving your catch technique and start to press the water backwards the catch phase takes less time as the water's direction no longer needs to be changed. This lifts the overall tempo of the stroke and gives you a much greater sense of rhythm.

A swimmer with a good catch technique is constantly in motion, either extending forwards, catching the water or pressing it backwards. It's important not to tear at the water by rushing the catch as this will cause the arm to slip through with little purchase. After the arm has finished extending, a good catch starts without delay as this gives the swimmer time to engage with the water in a high elbow position in front of the head. The drills in this section (and *The Doggy Paddle Drill* from the catch mechanics section) are a great way to develop this fluid catch technique.

PAUL: *After following steps 1 and 2 of our catch development process you should already be feeling a much improved level of propulsion in your stroke, perhaps setting some personal bests or swimming much more easily for the same speed. That's fantastic but to really integrate a better catch and pull-through into your stroke we need to pay attention to the rhythm and timing of your movements using some special drills.*

ADAM: *If you like numbers (like me!) here's a quick example to reinforce this point. Say you swim at 55 strokes per minute (SPM) at the moment with a poor catch technique. If you were to improve your catch such that you took just 0.2 seconds less to perform it (less than the blink of an eye!) then your stroke rate would lift to 60 SPM. This is a significant lift in stroke rate and one that would greatly benefit your speed and efficiency*

The good news here is that this wouldn't feel harder to do as you would be working with the water rather than against it. For most swimmers it actually feels easier to swim at a higher tempo once they've improved their catch technique. Check out Chapter 15 for some recent research demonstrating this point.

Overgliding and Catch Timing

As we'll see in Chapter 21, an Overglider is a type of swimmer who tries to swim with an extended glide phase at the front of their stroke. This adds a large dead spot or pause in their stroke timing. Overgliders are normally diligent swimmers who have worked hard on reducing their drag profile in the water but have become frustrated (and often a little confused) by why they are not swimming faster than they are.

The overall timing between an Overglider and an elite swimmer is similar but the elite swimmer does not actually pause as they extend forwards – they are constantly in motion either entering the water, extending forwards or catching the water. By introducing a dead spot to their stroke the Overglider is then forced to hurry their catch to restart their stroke again. This hurried catch makes it very hard to engage with the water without slipping through it. This is the main difference between an Overglider's stroke and a Smooth's stroke (Chapter 23) – other than the fact that the Smooth swims at twice the speed!

If you are an Overglider the path to improving your swimming is to remove the dead spot from your stroke by developing an improved catch technique. This will give you a more fluid stroke and will also lift your stroke rate slightly, giving your swimming a renewed sense of rhythm.

PAUL: *Overgliders have become extremely common around the world as many coaching programmes actively encourage adding a deliberate pause-and-glide into the stroke, often saying the swimmer should be 'patient' with their catch to encourage the pause before starting it. As we'll discuss in Chapter 15 (Science of Swimming) and Chapter 17 (Swim Types), teaching swimmers to overglide is something that myself and the other Swim Smooth coaches fundamentally disagree with as it stops swimmers reaching their true potential in the water.*

UNCO DRILL

The *Unco drill* is described fully in Appendix A and is a one-arm drill performed with the inactive arm resting by the swimmer's side. Using fins is essential to propel you through the water as the active arm recovers over the top. Breathe on every stroke away from the stroking arm.

The key to *Unco* is to emphasise your body rotation, particularly thinking about the shoulder of your inactive arm and dipping it down low into the water as the active arm recovers over the surface. A good mantra for the drill is '*breathe and dip, breathe and dip . . .*' to help you remember to breathe away from the stroking arm and emphasise dipping the inactive shoulder and hip.

PAUL: *Australians are fond of shortening words and Unco is Aussie slang for uncoordinated! It's quite an advanced drill and you may struggle with coordinating it at first, particularly if your stroke timing needs some work. The irony is that when you get this drill right it is anything but uncoordinated as it forces you to time your stroke to your body rotation without the assistance of the recovering arm.*

The transition to full-stroke swimming is important as you will feel an immediate benefit to your stroke's timing. We suggest you swim sets of *Unco* as 100 m continuously:

25 m left arm *Unco* (breathing to the right)
25 m freestyle (only breathing to the right)
25 m right arm *Unco* (breathing to the left)
25 m freestyle (only breathing to the left)

As you transition into the freestyle portions you should feel a nice easy rhythm to your stroke.

ADAM: *In Chapter 10 we discussed how good swimming posture helps connect the arm stroke to the body, allowing your body rotation to assist in driving the stroke. To maximise this transfer of power, the swimmer also needs good timing of the arm stroke in relation to the body roll. As a former Overglider with poor timing* Unco *is personally my favourite drill, it's fantastic for tuning up the timing of my stroke.*

WATERPOLO DRILL

Head-up Waterpolo swimming is a great drill to help upper-intermediate and advanced level swimmers to improve the rhythm of their stroke. It is especially effective for removing dead spots from stroke timing as it is almost impossible to swim head-up with a long pause in the stroke!

As described in Appendix A, the key to the drill is to swim it quickly at near sprint pace to really focus you on a fast stroke rate. Perform it with your chin on the surface for just 25 m at a time. If you struggle to complete the drill well try it with fins to give you more lift and drive.

Perform the drill as 4 × 25 m Waterpolo with about 15 seconds rest between each 25 m. Immediately transition into 100 m of steady paced swimming focusing on an easy rhythm to the stroke.

PULL BUOY AND BANDS

Swimming with a pull buoy between your legs and a rubber band around your ankles is a simple way to force you to focus on the rhythm of your stroke. The band holds your feet together eliminating any kick and adds some drag to the back of the stroke.

The combination of a lack of kick and the extra drag created by the band forces you to keep the tempo of your stroke high, otherwise your legs will sink down low into the water. Focus on removing any dead spots from your stroke and also stretch through your core using the *Liquorice Stretch Visualisation* (Chapter 10) to help keep your legs up high.

If you are lucky enough to be naturally buoyant and find this an easy drill then increase the difficulty by trying it without a pull buoy!

Using a Wetronome or Tempo Trainer to Improve Your Stroke Rhythm

The Finis Tempo Trainer Pro sits under your swim cap and beeps a steady stroke rhythm to you.

Wetronomes and Tempo Trainers are small electronic beepers that sit under your swim cap, which you can hear beeping as you swim. To focus on stroke rhythm the beepers are set to beep at a fixed stroke rate – for example 60 strokes per minute (SPM). As you swim, all you need to do is time your strokes to the beep to control your stroke rate precisely.

These stroke beepers are particularly useful for helping you subtly raise or lower your stroke rate. If you have a tendency to fight the water with a large crossover in your stroke then to help you become straighter and more aligned in the water it's worthwhile lowering your natural stroke rate by 3–5 SPM. For an Overglider who is working on removing the dead spot from their stroke it's more appropriate to lift your stroke rate by 3–5 SPM.

PAUL: *Judging your stroke rate whilst you are swimming can be quite difficult without a Wetronome or Tempo Trainer to refer to. They are fantastic little devices and come highly recommended by the Swim Smooth team. You can find out more about them at www.swimsmooth.com/wetronome and www.swimsmooth.com/tempotrainer*

The Stroke Rate Ramp Test

A ramp test uses a stroke rate beeper to take you through a range of stroke rates in turn. You might start 10 SPM slower than your natural stroke rate and end up 15–20 SPM higher. You will need a friend or coach to help you with the test and record the results as you go, including your strokes per length, your lap times and how hard each stroke rate felt.

The test helps you find sweet-spots in your stroke rate where the movements start to click together into good timing. At these points you will be moving more quickly and easily than you otherwise would. Very often you will find two sweet-spots, one at a steady pace and one at a faster race-pace. We highly recommend running through a ramp test after working on your stroke to help 'bed in' the changes.

Find out how to run the test, how to analyse the results and see a video example at: www.swimsmooth .com/ramptest.

CHAPTER 14 Stroke Rate Development

Balancing Stroke Rate and Stroke Length

This chapter is a special feature on the methods required to increase stroke rate, this is an area that Overgliders need to work on and to some extent Smooths too if they are looking to make a successful transition to racing in open water. However, it is important to emphasise here that not all swimmers need to lift their stroke rate – some need to be lengthening out their stroke instead (e.g. Arnies) and in this case it is often advisable to lower stroke rate a little to help achieve this.

Fundamentally, the speed you move through the water is a combination of the length of your stroke and your stroke rate. We can use a simple equation to show this:

$$\text{swimming speed} = \text{stroke length} \times \text{stroke rate}$$

At either extreme a swimmer becomes inefficient: with a low stroke rate you overglide and lose too much speed; increase stroke rate too high and you start to fight the water. The key to becoming an efficient swimmer is to find the sweet-spot in the middle where your stroke movements and stroke rhythm click into perfect harmony. This exact point varies significantly from swimmer to swimmer depending on your build, fitness and individual stroke style. The Swim Type stroke correction processes in Appendix B are designed to lower or raise your stroke rate as appropriate and find this efficiency 'sweet spot' in your stroke.

ADAM: *Take a look ahead to Figure 14.13 The Swim Smooth Stroke Rate Chart later in this chapter, which highlights how some swimmers are over-revving and fighting the water (the red zone) while others are adding a large dead spot to their timing (the blue zone). For swimmers in the blue zone, raising stroke rate presents a difficult challenge especially if they have a heavily imprinted dead spot in their stroke timing. This chapter is dedicated to helping those swimmers lift their stroke rate.*

Stroke Rate and Open Water Swimming

As we shall discuss later in Chapter 33, swimming in open water is very different from the pool. The disturbed water from waves, chop and the wake from other swimmers means that any dead spots or pauses in your stroke leave you vulnerable to being stalled completely between strokes. For this reason, the trade-off between stroke length and stroke rate is always shifted towards shorter faster strokes in open water. If you feel the need to lift your stroke rate in open water then use the advice in this chapter to do that.

Lifting Stroke Rate

In a nutshell, the way to lift stroke rate is to remove dead spots or pauses from the stroke timing and so get into the catch phase a little sooner. However, many swimmers struggle to raise their stroke rate without significantly increasing their level of effort. There are two main reasons for this:

1. The dead spot in their stroke timing is very imprinted and hard to remove. When trying to lift stroke rate, the swimmer increases the speed of every other movement of the stroke but keeps the dead spot in place. This increases effort levels but does not improve efficiency.
2. The swimmer has a large press downward on the water during the catch phase of the stroke. This acts to lift the front end of the body upwards and sink the legs. As the swimmer tries to increase stroke rate they press down harder on the water and so sink the legs, increasing drag. This increase in drag offsets any gains in efficiency from a more continuous stroke. Such swimmers often feel their swimming is very 'one paced' – increasing effort does not increase their speed very much at all.

Age-group swimmer Paul (top) is about to press down on the water with a straight arm in comparison to elite open water swimmer Mel Benson (bottom) who has bent her elbow and is pressing water backwards.

The key to lifting your stroke rate is twofold:

1. Improve the timing of your stroke so that you remove the glide and dead spot whilst keeping all the other stroke elements the same speed. This will improve efficiency with very little, if any, increase in effort. As you swim the sensation here will be to keep the lead hand constantly in motion, either extending forwards, catching the water or pressing it backwards. Never pausing and gliding!
2. Improve your catch mechanics so that you press the water backwards, not downward. This will be a quicker action as water is heavy and takes time to change its direction. By pressing it backwards you are helping the water in the direction it is already travelling relative to you and this will take less time – thereby increasing stroke rate all by itself. As effort is increased, your stroke rate will lift further as the downward press and resultant drag has been removed.

To develop your catch mechanics and remove your dead spot follow the process in Chapter 13 and also the relevant Swim Type stroke correction process in Appendix B.

You Are Not Looking to Shorten the Stroke

It is very important to appreciate that by lifting stroke rate you are not shortening the stroke at all, you are still starting from the front of the stroke at full extension and finishing at the thigh at the rear. Instead of shortening the stroke you are simply looking to remove the delay pre-catch.

In Figure 14.12 there are some photos of elite open water swimmer Melissa Benson swimming at around 100 strokes per minute – if you have ever used a stroke rate beeper you will know this is a very high stroke rate! Whilst it is unlikely you will want such a high stroke rate yourself, even in this extreme example you can clearly see Mel is not shortening her stroke, she is starting at full reach and completing the stroke at the thigh.

PAUL: *I took a swimmer for a video analysis session in late 2010 who I often refer to when discussing the balance between stroke rate and stroke length, and the perils of overgliding. This swimmer told me that he couldn't understand why he could swim a single 50 m lap in 28 strokes (which he added was 'better than Ian Thorpe') but was not able to break 25 minutes for 1000 m. He also complained of being fatigued at the end of each lap and needing a rest. What was most confusing was that this guy was tall, had a good swimmer's build and had been swimming four times per week for over five years and wasn't seeing any improvement – in fact he told me he was actually getting slower.*

What he didn't appreciate at that point was that whilst his stroke was very long, his stroke rate was an incredibly slow 33 strokes per minute. He paused for over a second at the front of the stroke and said he enjoyed this pause to glide as it was giving him a 'rest'. Unfortunately this 'rest' was causing him to decelerate to a near stop between strokes and so causing him to start to sink in the water. He was shocked when he saw just how badly this was affecting his body position – something he thought must have been OK from all the balance drills he had been working on.

Whilst we often look at swimmers like Ian Thorpe and perceive a long, slow stroke, the reality is that Thorpe swam at 72 to 76 SPM – well over twice that of my extreme Overglider example. Clearly this guy was not better than Ian Thorpe despite his stroke being longer – something we have all been told in the past is the key measure of swimming efficiency. The truth is that stroke length is only part of the full picture and neither stroke length nor stroke rate should ever be taken in isolation.

FIGURE 14.12 Elite swimmer Mel Benson has a very high stroke rate but still uses her full reach from full extension (1) to the finishing at the thigh (2).

TABLE 14.2 Typical results of Overgliders reducing the dead spot in their stroke showing the resultant increase in stroke rate.

	before		**after**	
	stroke rate (strokes per minute - SPM)	length of dead spot (seconds)	target reduction in dead spot (seconds)	resultant stroke rate (SPM)
Slight Overglider:	53	0.3	0.2	58
Classic Overglider:	47	0.5	0.3	53
Extreme Overglider:	38	1.0	0.5	45

Dead spots and Stroke Rate in Numbers

Let's look at the three swimmers who need to lift their stroke rate in Table 14.2. These numbers are very typical and if you are an Overglider yourself, you will have similar figures.

On the left-hand side we see the stroke rate of the swimmers and the length of their dead spot in seconds. The slight Overglider has a dead spot or overglide lasting around 0.3 seconds, the classic Overglider around 0.5 seconds and the extreme Overglider a full second! In comparison a classic Smooth swimmer would have around 0.1–0.15 seconds between one stroke finishing at the rear and the next one starting at the front. A refined Swinger would have zero delay or even an overlap, starting the stroke at the front before the stroke at the rear finishes.

In the right-hand column we show a target reduction in dead spot, this is the initial reduction we might aim for when working with this swimmer in a one-to-one coaching situation. In the far right-hand column we calculate the resultant stroke rate if nothing else changes in the stroke but the shortening of the dead spot. We can see that each of the swimmers gains between five and seven strokes per minute by reducing the dead spot in their strokes alone, a very noticeable improvement which you will feel as a real increase in your stroke rhythm.

Dropping the wrist and elbow and pushing forwards adds a big pause to the stroke, lowering your stroke rate.

ADAM: *If you own a Wetronome or a Finis Tempo Trainer Pro, go through the process of improving your catch technique and reducing the dead spot in your stroke. Then use the beeper to return to your old stroke rate – it is amazing how slow it will feel. When trying this, rehabilitated Overgliders can't believe how they ever swam at such a slow rhythm!*

Slowing Down Stroke Rate

Whilst Overgliders and many Bambinos should look to increase their stroke rate, other swimmers such as classic Arnies and unrefined Swingers may need to lower their stroke rates at least in the short term. This reduction will give them time to remove crossovers from their stroke and lengthen things out.

If you are using a Wetronome or Finis Tempo Trainer Pro you can do this by lowering your stroke rate by 3–5 SPM. This may not sound like a large change but you will immediately notice the extra time this gives you to work on your alignment in the water.

In time you can lift your stroke rate back up again and combine that straighter stroke with a faster stroke rate to gain a real increase in speed.

For more details on this process see the Arnie and Swinger guides in Chapters 18 and 22.

Finding Your Current Stroke Rate

There are several ways to do this. The easiest is to use a Wetronome or Finis Tempo Trainer Pro and adjust it up or down until it feels about normal for you. The second is to have a friend or coach measure your stroke rate using a specialist stop watch such as the Finis 3X-100M; if you are a coach yourself one of these watches is a great investment in your coaching. The third way is to have a friend use a normal stop watch and time how long you take to perform ten strokes (counting both arms), then divide 600 by that number. So if you take 12 seconds for 10 strokes, 600/12 = 50 strokes per minute.

The Swim Smooth Stroke Rate Chart

A useful tool to help you assess your stroke rate is our stroke rate chart, shown in Figure 14.13. The chart shows swimmer speed against stroke rate – it covers the whole range of swimmers from beginners up to elite distance swimmers. The chart was developed from analysing hundreds of swimmers' strokes in comparison to their speed and stroke rate.

The chart contains three zones: the first is the blue zone, which shows where the swimmer's stroke rate is too low – normally the result of an overglide in their stroke timing. The second zone is the red zone where a swimmer is fighting the water, resulting in a short fast stroke. The white zone is the 'sweet spot' indicating a good trade-off between stroke length and rate.

Use the chart to assess your swimming and decide how you need to progress things. You can find an interactive version of the chart on our website at www.swimsmooth.com/strokerate.

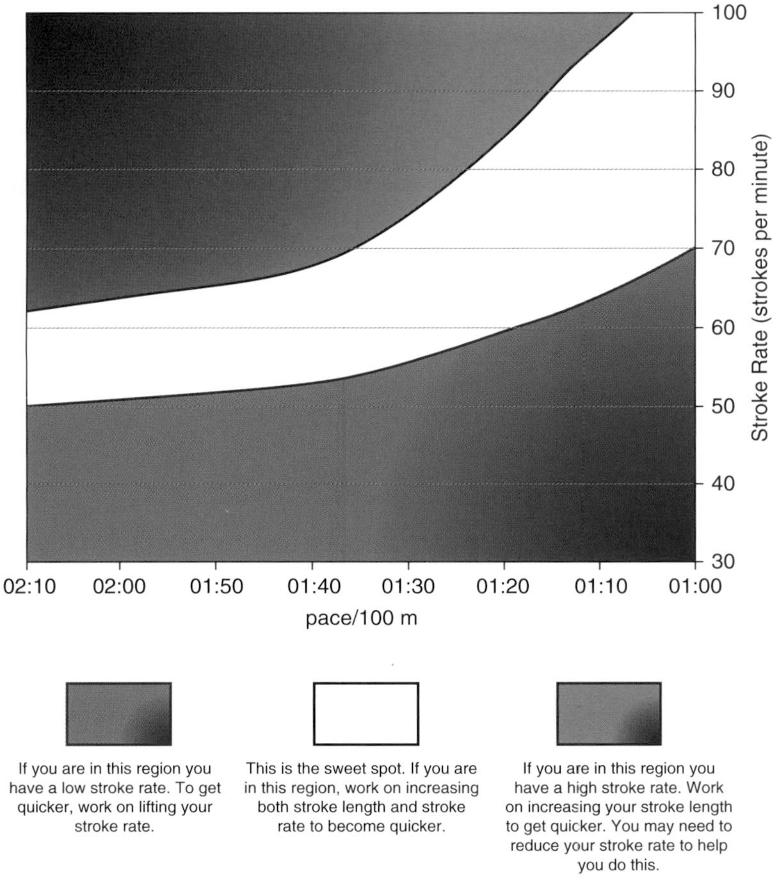
100
90
80
70
60
50
40
30
Stroke Rate (strokes per minute)
02:10
02:00
01:50
01:40
01:30
01:20
01:10
01:00
pace/100 m
If you are in this region you have a low stroke rate. To get quicker, work on lifting your stroke rate.
This is the sweet spot. If you are in this region, work on increasing both stroke length and stroke rate to become quicker.
If you are in this region you have a high stroke rate. Work on increasing your stroke length to get quicker. You may need to reduce your stroke rate to help you do this.

FIGURE 14.13 The Swim Smooth Stroke Rate Chart.

Using a Wetronome or Finis Tempo Trainer

As we have already mentioned in this chapter, using a stroke rate beeper is an extremely useful tool to adjust your stroke rate. They help you really take control of your swimming and double up with a very useful lap-interval mode, which is great for pacing you through training sets.

Find out more about these tools in Chapter 3.

The Science Behind an Efficient Freestyle Stroke

If you have ever visited a swimming or triathlon forum then you will be aware that the internet is full of discussion about swimming technique and how it should be performed. There is a saying that 'Google never forgets' and never was it so true as for swimming advice! Unfortunately by searching for a term such as 'swimming technique' on Google you will find lots of contradictory advice in videos and on discussion forums, some of which is very out of date and badly advised for the majority of swimmers.

In this section we are going to take a close look at the concept of efficiency in swimming, why it is important to be an efficient swimmer and how different aspects of your stroke affect it. We are also going to clear up many of those misconceptions from the internet and other sources along the way.

ADAM: *This section is a little more technical than the rest of the book as we explain the background behind our coaching methods from a scientific perspective. If you enjoy a little technical discussion and analysis then you will find this fascinating but don't worry if you don't – you can safely skip this chapter, it won't harm your swimming to do so.*

Why Efficiency is So Important

Elite pool and open water swimmers have a great stroke technique, which is the dominant reason why they move so quickly through the water. In fact, an elite swimmer's stroke is so effective that when swimming at an easy pace they move more quickly than most 'normal' swimmers can sprint – amazing! What's their secret? It comes down to the efficiency of their strokes.

Elite swimmer Rhys Mainstone has a very efficient and fast stroke which lets him swim around 1:10/100m at a steady pace. How can he move so quickly?

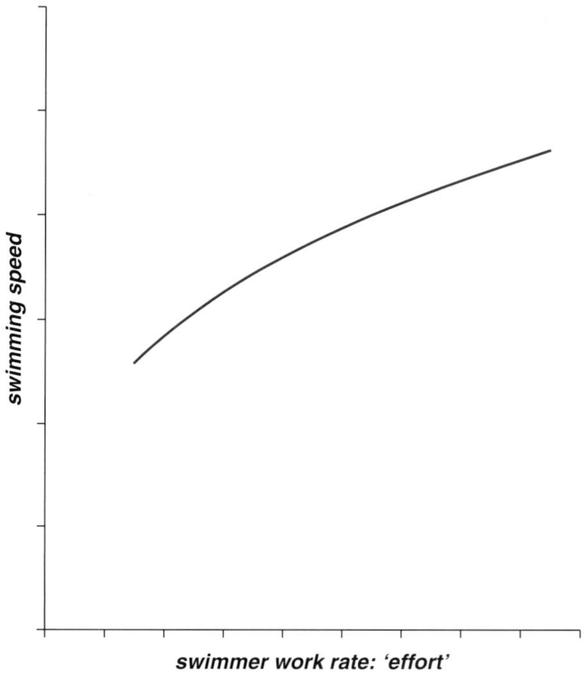

FIGURE 15.14 Efficiency plot for a swimmer of fixed efficiency*.

How fast you move through the water is down to a combination of the efficiency of your stroke and how hard you are working. Let's look at this on an 'efficiency plot' as shown in Figure 15.14. On the x axis we will put your physical effort (we could measure this as oxygen uptake or perhaps heart rate) and on the y axis your speed. Any given swimmer with a fixed level of efficiency will make a distinct curve on the graph. The relationship between effort and speed is fixed for the swimmer; as you increase your effort you move more quickly but it's a case of diminishing returns as drag of the water increases quickly, creating the curved line.

Now let's introduce two other swimmers, one who is less efficient and one who is more, as shown in Figure 15.15.

Our elite swimmer shown with the green line has superior stroke technique whilst the beginner swimmer shown by the red line has a relatively poor stroke. Notice how the efficiency effect works – it moves the whole line up and down, i.e. efficiency benefits you at all speeds whether going at an easy pace,

---

**These efficiency plots are based on the 2.0–2.2 power relationship between velocity and drag at sub 1.4 m/s swimming speed [1]. Above this speed drag increases even more rapidly as wave drag becomes dominant [1]. The plots assume a constant propulsive efficiency for each swimmer across their effort range. In practise propulsive efficiency is known to increase with effort level, which will slightly steepen the relationships shown on the plots. To date no research has quantified this increase and so it is assumed fixed for the purposes of this analysis.*

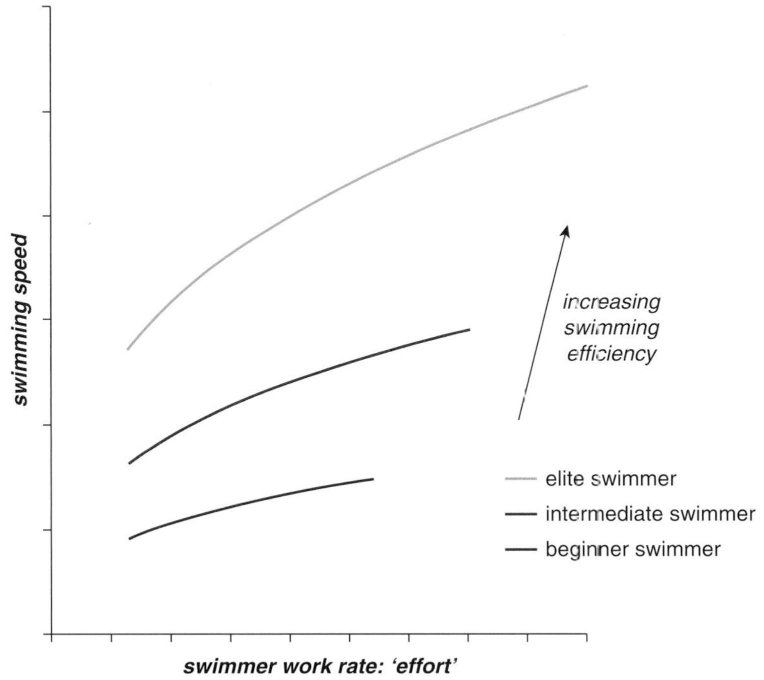

FIGURE 15.15 Efficiency plot of three swimmers of wide ranging ability. Beginner, intermediate and elite swimmers have increasing levels of fitness respectively and so can sustain higher work rates.

moderate or hard. This is an interesting insight all by itself as it tells us that if you are efficient you should also be pretty fast. You cannot be a 'slow but efficient swimmer' as some people believe — really there is no such thing.

If we had two different swimmers with the same stroke efficiency then their lines would be over the top of each other. In a race the fitter swimmer would win as they could sustain a higher level of effort but if they had the same fitness they would swim at the same speed.

ADAM: *Last year I was filming Olympic swimmer Jono Van Hazel and he was zooming up and down the pool very quickly with his super efficient stroke. As an experiment I asked him to slow down from the speed he was doing, around 1:10/100m down to 1:40/100m pace. The fascinating thing was that he actually couldn't swim that speed without disrupting his stroke technique. He had to change his stroke and become less efficient by adding a pause and glide to the stroke. In terms of our efficiency graph, he couldn't slow down enough just by lowering his effort, he had to hurt his stroke technique and so jump down to one of the lower efficiency lines to swim 'as slowly' as 1:40 per 100m!*

PAUL: *Don't worry if you're struggling to understand this graph and the curved lines, this is the most technical we're going to get in this book! The important message to take away from this section is that a good stroke technique makes you an efficient swimmer and that's what we should all be aiming for as it will make your swimming fast and feel much easier too.*

Efficiency and the Three Keys

So if swimming efficiency is so important, does that mean that you should focus on stroke technique development in the pool and nothing else in your swimming preparation? Unfortunately not, for two reasons:

1. As you fatigue you cannot sustain a good stroke technique, the stroke becomes shorter as you tire because you cannot finish the back of the stroke properly. This shorter stroke reduces your body roll and so the arms start to carry lower over the surface giving you that feeling of fighting the water or that your stroke is 'falling apart'. For swimmers with poor fitness this deterioration in efficiency can happen very quickly after only 100 m or 200 m of swimming. To be an efficient swimmer you need to have good swim-specific fitness to sustain good stroke technique.
2. As we shall discuss in Chapter 33, your stroke efficiency is highly dependent on the water conditions you are swimming in. A longer stroke style suffers a large drop in efficiency in open water as it is more prone to being stalled by small waves and chop, after which the swimmer needs to put in additional effort to accelerate again. To race well in open water it's necessary to develop a technique that suits that environment and not simply focus on an efficient pool stroke. To be an efficient swimmer you need to have a stroke that is efficient in your race environment. Navigation and drafting skills are also critical for racing well in open water and need to be given a portion of your training time too.

From the perspective of our efficiency graphs in Figures 15.14 and 15.15, the early onset of fatigue from poor fitness or using a stroke not suited to open water will drop you down onto a lower line. This is the fundamental understanding behind our 'Three Keys', to be an efficient and fast swimmer you need:

Key 1: An efficient stroke technique with low drag and high propulsion levels.
Key 2: Good fitness levels to sustain your swimming effort with good stroke technique.
Key 3: Good open water skills, to adapt your stroke to the open water.

Efficiency and Low Drag

The term 'efficiency' is very commonly discussed by swimmers and triathletes in relation to swimming and most understand that to be a good swimmer you need an efficient stroke technique. However, many swimmers define an efficient stroke to be one that has low levels of drag; whilst this is partly the case it is a long way from the full story and trying to lower their drag at all costs has led many swimmers down a blind alley with their stroke technique.

An efficient freestyle stroke is one that has both low levels of drag and high levels of propulsion. Actually, to be strictly correct we mean high levels of propulsive efficiency because any swimmer can generate more propulsion by lifting their work rate but that doesn't make them more efficient. What we are really interested in is how much forward propulsion you create given how hard you are working physically: if we can increase that propulsive efficiency you will create lots of propulsion from low levels of physical effort and this will lift your overall efficiency dramatically.

We could say that:

$$\text{overall efficiency} = \text{drag profile} \times \text{propulsive efficiency}$$

Let's consider both of these areas:

Low drag is very important to a good stroke technique because water is so dense, 800 times denser than air in fact. Any object moving through water creates drag, which tries to slow it down, but the shape and profile of the object has a large effect on how much drag is created by the water. As a swimmer we are looking to be as streamlined as possible in order to slip easily through it. This means keeping all elements of your stroke as straight and aligned as possible and also keeping your body position (chest-hips-ankles) as horizontal and high in the water as possible.

Propulsive efficiency is about creating as much forward propulsion as possible given how hard you are working. As discussed earlier in Chapter 9, as an adult swimmer you are aiming to generate most of your propulsion from your arm stroke as it's much more efficient than your leg kick, i.e. for any level of physical effort, you create more propulsion with your arm stroke than you would with your kick.

As we saw in Chapter 13, the key to developing good upper-body propulsion is to press the water backwards with good timing, thus sending you forwards. A poor stroke with poor propulsive efficiency pushes the water to the side, downward or even forwards – this is very hard work and results in much less propulsion.

Which is more important, low drag or good propulsion? Neither, they are in fact equally important. If you made a 10% reduction in your drag you would gain the same in overall speed and efficiency as a 10% improvement in propulsive efficiency. In a nutshell, you cannot be a strong swimmer without low drag and good propulsion so you need to work on both areas of your stroke technique.

Which should you develop first? Generally speaking we recommend you develop both at the same time but some swimmers already have low drag and need to work more on their propulsion as a priority and vice versa. In the Swim Types section in Chapters 17 to 23 we'll give you some specific advice on this for your individual swimming.

ADAM: *A good reason to work on your propulsive technique, even as a novice swimmer, is that a poor technique can actually harm your body position and create drag. Many swimmers overly focusing on drag reduction introduce knock-on problems into their stroke technique, which actually increase drag again. There's no need to go to the extremes when you develop your swimming, keep a mix of stroke work focusing on propulsion and lowering drag and you'll be on the best path to developing a very efficient stroke.*

Stroke Length vs. Stroke Rate

The speed at which you move through the water is a combination of the length of your stroke (metres) and the rate of your stroke (strokes per minute):

$$\text{swimming speed} = \text{stroke length} \times \text{stroke rate}$$

In cycling terms, this is equivalent to the gear and cadence you are using – increase either and you move more quickly. To become faster you need to either increase your stroke length or stroke rate, or both. How you should go about doing this is a controversial area of swimming coaching. As we shall see on the next page, Swim Smooth strongly believe that you need to maintain the right trade-off between these two elements to be a fast and efficient swimmer. The exact balance you strike between the two will depend on your build, experience, skill level and natural stroke style.

Efficiency and Stroke Length

In the early 1990s a movement developed in swimming promoting the idea that all swimmers should look to maximise the length of their strokes. This was based on the following observations at the time:

1. Olympic champions often (but not always) have long strokes, taking fewer strokes per length than 'normal' swimmers. For instance, freestyle great Alex Popov taking around 31 strokes per 50 m.
2. Slow inefficient swimmers who fight the water have shorter strokes and take more strokes per length than more capable swimmers.

The conclusion drawn was that to be efficient you need a long stroke and this should be a priority for all swimmers to develop, regardless of whether they were pool or open water swimmers. Swimmers were taught to lengthen out their strokes as much as possible and try and glide down the pool, with the lead hand held out for an extended time creating a distinct pause between strokes. At Swim Smooth we call this style of stroke 'Overgliding'.

Unfortunately this approach was a very over-simplified view of swimming technique and did not take into account the true facts:

1. Many other Olympic champions use a shorter faster stroke very effectively if it suits their natural style. For instance Janet Evans and Laure Manadou taking around 50 strokes per 50 m. These swimmers are examples of the refined Swinger style (see Chapter 22).
2. Great swimmers that were observed with long strokes were not achieving their stroke length through gliding, they were achieving it through low drag and great propulsion (see below). Video analysis of these swimmers shows that the gap between one stroke finishing at the rear and the next starting at the front is between 0 and 0.15 seconds [2]. For Overgliders with an artificial glide, this gap is typically 0.5 to 1.0 seconds.
3. Elite open water swimmers and triathletes use a shorter faster stroke style that helps them punch through disturbed water from other swimmers in close proximity.

Our key message here is that different styles of stroke suit different swimmers – a long stroke may suit you and you will be very efficient performing it, or a slightly shorter punchier style may be more efficient for you. Take an individual approach to your swimming and you stand a much greater chance of swimming success.

Making a Stroke Longer

There are three ways to make a stroke longer:

1. Reduce drag so that you slip through the water more easily.
2. Increase propulsion so that each stroke pushes you further.
3. Introduce an extended glide to elongate each stroke.

The first two are excellent ways to lengthen your stroke – they are the result of good stroke technique having low drag and high levels of propulsive efficiency, which will make you more efficient. The problem with the last way, gliding, is that it is an artificial way to lengthen the stroke and does not make you more efficient for three major reasons:

1. Whilst overgliding you decelerate in the water and then have to re-accelerate on the next stroke, which is hard work.
2. This is a technical one: for a fixed swimming speed, by introducing gliding you have a higher peak speed as you accelerate and decelerate more on every stroke. Because drag in water is very non-linear, the higher peak speed creates a very high level of drag, creating more drag overall than a swimmer moving at a more constant speed.
3. An overglide kills the rhythm in your stroke, which is very unnatural for the body as it prefers to operate in a much more continuous fluid way.
4. An overgliding stroke is very inefficient in open water where waves and chop easily stall you in the long gap between strokes.

The inefficiency of artificially lowering stroke rate was confirmed in a fascinating study in 2010 carried out by the Southwestern University in Georgetown, Texas [3], which demonstrated the inefficiency of lowering stroke rates in the pursuit of an overly long freestyle stroke. The study found that heart rate, oxygen consumption and perceived exertion in swimmers was significantly higher at stroke rates 10% to 20% below their natural stroke rate. The researchers also measured kick rate in response to manipulating the swimmer's stroke rate between ±20% of their natural baseline and determined the higher work rate of the swimmers at lower stroke rates was primarily due to the increase in leg kick required to propel the swimmers through the induced dead spot at the front of the stroke. The study also highlighted that there was no significant increase in effort when stroke rate was elevated by up to 20% above their natural baseline and that the swimmers were able to reduce kicking intensity at these more rhythmical tempos.

This study clearly demonstrates that at fixed swimming speed:

1. Artificially lengthening the stroke reduces efficiency.
2. Stroke rate can be lifted by at least 20% above natural stroke rate without a loss of efficiency.

The latter conclusion is interesting because it highlights the 'headroom' that swimmers have to lift their stroke rates to help them punch through waves and chop in open water, offering them a huge advantage in the process.

Swim-Golf or 'SWOLF' Score

A common test used by coaches is the 'Swim-Golf' or 'SWOLF' test – SWOLF being an abbreviation of Swim-Golf. Here the swimmer is timed over a short distance (e.g. 100 m) and counts their strokes at the same time. They then add the number of strokes taken to the time in seconds to come up with an overall score. For instance, a swimmer taking 110 seconds for 100 m and taking 90 strokes has a score of 200.

The swimmer is then challenged to repeat the swim and lower the score, either by swimming quicker with the same number of strokes taken or by taking fewer strokes at the same speed. The idea being to use a longer stroke and therefore become more efficient. If you have been swimming for a while yourself you have probably tried this test at some point.

At Swim Smooth we dislike using Swim-Golf tests because they encourage swimmers to add glide to their strokes and to kick hard to artificially lengthen them. They also encourage swimmers to simply

PAUL: *When I am coaching I very rarely encourage swimmers to count their strokes or perform Swim-Golf tests. To create a more efficient stroke we need to improve a swimmer's technique by lowering their drag or increasing their propulsive efficiency. The end result is a longer stroke without the swimmer consciously chasing it. Putting the cart before the horse and making the objective a long stroke only encourages swimmers to over-glide and so ironically become less, not more, efficient.*

increase their effort by pushing harder on every stroke to take them further on each stroke.

Stroke Length and Stroke Style

As we will discover in the Swim Types section of this book, there are two distinct styles of stroke used by elite swimmers to great effect. The first is the 'Smooth' style which is what most of us think of as an efficient stroke, being long and silky smooth but still – vitally – maintaining good stroke rhythm. The second is the 'Refined Swinger' style, which is a shorter more punchy style of stroke with a higher stroke rate.

Both of these styles are very efficient. In fact the longer-smoother style tends to be used by sprinters and middle distance athletes whilst the Swinger style is used predominantly by distance swimmers from 800 m and up, especially in the open water. This is the opposite of what most swimmers would think, as they would consider the longer stroke more efficient and therefore more suited to distance swimming. This simply highlights that the refined-Swinger style has been misunderstood (and under-appreciated!) by swimmers and coaches for so long; it is in fact an extremely efficient stroke style and the superior style in open water.

Choosing the Right Trade-Off Between Stroke Length and Stroke Rate

So should you chase a particular stroke count per length? Probably not – it rarely helps to do so. Instead, use the Stroke Technique sections of this book (Key 1) to reduce your drag, increase your propulsion and improve your stroke rhythm. The end result will be the right stroke length for your given build, height, arm length, experience level and natural style.

Once you have developed your stroke you can then refine things a little further using the Stroke Rate Ramp test, which we described at the end of Chapter 13. This will help you determine the right stroke rate for you where all the elements of your stroke 'click' together.

If you feel that you need to increase or decrease your stroke rate, refer to Chapter 14 where we took a close look at the process of doing so.

References

1. Toussaint, H. M. 2010. Biomechanics of drag and propulsion in front crawl swimming. *World Book of Swimming: From Science to Performance.*
2. Swim Smooth Video Analysis Study: http://www.feelforthewater.com/2011/08/our-stroke-analysis-two-best-1500m.html
3. McLean, S.P., Palmer, D., Ice, G., Truijens, M., Smith, J.C. 2010. Oxygen uptake response to stroke rate manipulation in freestyle swimming. *Med Sci Sports Exerc.*, 42(10):1909–13.

CHAPTER 16

Performing Your Own Video Analysis Session

PAUL: *Isn't technology wonderful? I first started using a Sony digital video camera back in 1997 as an easy way to communicate with the swimmer what they were doing in the water and how they might improve their stroke technique. Being able to see what they were doing whilst I simultaneously analysed their stroke had a profound benefit that simple poolside demonstrations could never replicate.*

I vividly recall as a 12-year-old my squad coach telling me that he would bring his huge 1980s Betacam system down to the pool to film me and show me how I might refine my stroke but alas this never happened. However, the idea was sown and as soon as I commenced my Sport and Exercise Science degree course, I was keen to combine my sports biomechanics studies with my love for swimming and coaching through the use of video analysis.

Over the last 14 years I have used a vast range of video recording equipment, computer hardware and analysis software to analyse the strokes of thousands of swimmers around the world but never has it been so easy and relatively inexpensive for you to do this yourself. We are hoping that you will combine the new knowledge gained from this book with the tools you already might have at hand to video yourself swimming and see what you are doing in the water. After identifying what you need to do to improve your stroke you can then select the right Swim Type process to follow and take some big strides forward in your technique.

Our best advice is to seek expert tuition from a good coach but if cost, time and geographical issues prevent you from doing so, conducting your own analysis is the next best thing and will help you avoid the statement that we hear most often from swimmers:

'I know what I should be doing but I don't know what I'm actually doing or how to improve it!'

Please note: in most pools around the world strict regulations make it is essential to have prior permission to use any sort of recording equipment. Always ask permission first, in many cases it may only be possible in a private booking or club session.

Camera Hardware

If you are going to the trouble of filming your stroke we highly recommend using a camera that will allow you to film below the water as well as above. Being able to see what you look like under the water is incredibly beneficial, above the water the distorting properties of the surface can give a very deceptive view. In fact, it is fair to say that the view from above water is normally much more flattering than that seen from below the surface.

Technology is constantly evolving but at the time of writing the following list of camera systems gives you an idea of the options and costs involved (also see Figure 16.16).

1. Compact camera with video capability, with or without waterproof housing: US$75 upwards.
2. Waterproof compact camera with video capability, e.g. Speedo Aquashot (www.speedo.com): US$100 upwards (not shown).
3. Waterproof housing for your smart phone (e.g. LifeProof www.lifeproof.com): Approx US$80.
4. Compact lifestyle video camera with underwater housing e.g. The Flip (www.theflip.com): US$125 upwards (not shown).
5. Underwater housing for large prosumer camera with movie mode (supplied by camera manufacturer): US$200 upwards.
6. Waterproof POV style helmet camera (e.g. VIO POV HD www.vio-pov.com): Approx US$500.

Most of these cameras will have either a removable memory card or have a sync feature to be able to transfer your recorded video images to a computer for playback.

FIGURE 16.16 Underwater video filming options.

Computer Hardware

If you are planning to purchase a video camera specifically for filming your swimming, ensure that your computer is capable of playing the video files that the camera produces. Most computers purchased since 2007 should not have a problem playing files from these types of cameras but it is always worth checking, especially for those cameras with high definition recording capacities. In some cases you may need to install a video codec on your computer but these codecs are normally supplied on a disk with the camera.

Computer Software

Nearly every modern computer will have a basic media player pre-installed that will play your video clips and pause them at interesting points, e.g. Windows Media Player on a PC and QuickTime Player on a Mac. Some media players have more advanced capabilities like slow motion playback or even frame-by-frame motion, which can come in very handy when viewing your video files:

Kinovea (www.kinovea.org) is a great piece of free PC software that allows you to analyse your swim stroke in more detail. It includes advanced features like side-by-side comparisons, angle measurements, stopwatches and frame-by-frame slow motion. At the time of writing, HD video playback is a little stuttery with Kinovea at full speed but the software is constantly being developed and as it is free it is well worth trying on your PC.

Objectus Video (www.objectustech.com) is a great piece of software, which adds similar capability to Kinovea to the Mac platform only. HD playback is smooth on hi-spec machines. US$99.00, free demo version available.

The 'LifeProof' waterproof case for your iPhone is an ideal way of recording how your stroke is progressing. When used with an app like 'Swim Coach Plus' you have a very easy-to-use analysis tool at your disposal.

Filming Your Stroke

Have a friend or coach film you over 200 m whilst you swim at the pace you would use for your chosen race distance. e.g. for Olympic distance triathletes, your 1500 m pace. Try to relax and swim as naturally as possible and do not attempt to try and change your stroke – you want to be picking up on your stroke issues, not hiding them by trying to swim with a 'perfect' stroke.

If you can, swim in a side lane of the pool and if possible capture the following angles, aiming to film at least 10 strokes from each angle:

The Classic Side View (1) helps to identify technique issues during the recovery phase over the water – particularly stiff shoulders, a lack of symmetry and problematic hand entries. e.g. in (1) the thumb-first could potentially cause an injury. Do not shoot from this angle alone as it does not show many stroke flaws.

The Overhead View (2, 3, 4) is perhaps the most confronting view you can see of your stroke as it immediately highlights one of the most common flaws – a mid-line crossover that leads to a scissor kicking of the legs (2), causing significant drag. This angle also examines how your breathing pattern (unilateral or bilateral) affects your stroke's symmetry.

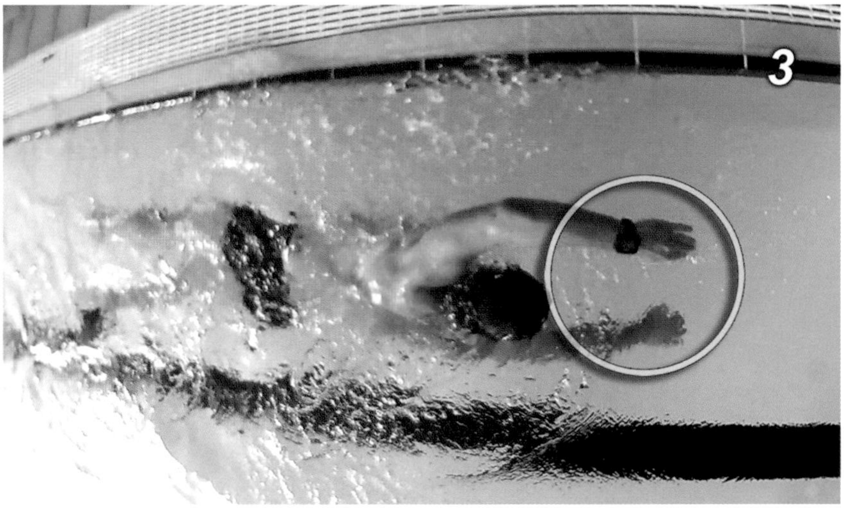

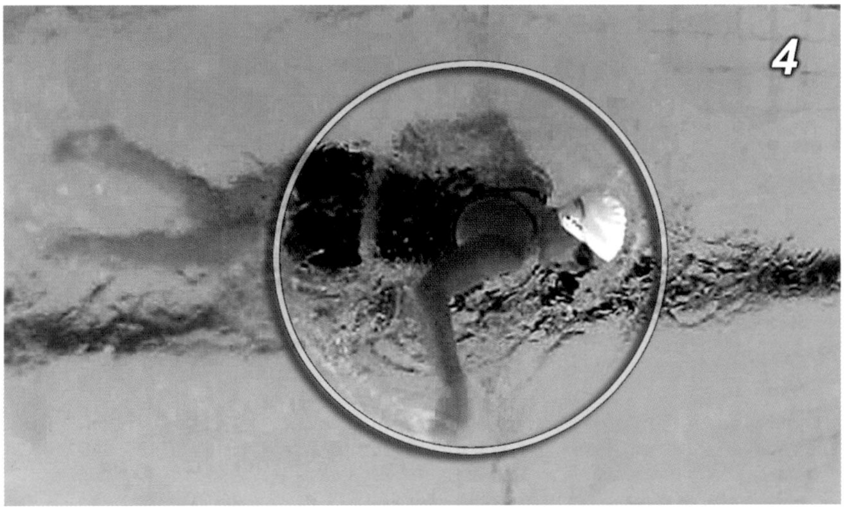

If you are either a Bambino (4) or an Overglider (3) you will be able to see how your stroke timing is affecting your stroke. Overgliders can spot a near catch-up in their stroke and Bambinos will notice their lead hand collapsing down so that they lack any support in front of the head while breathing.

The Perfect Side View (5, 6, 7) is your first glimpse of how your body position may be holding you back in the water and what might be causing this. From above the water it is easy to misinterpret how high your legs sit but from this angle under the water we can easily see how much 'sinky' legs might be holding you back (5). This is also a great angle to see how pressing down at the front of the stroke is one of the primary causes of 'Sinky Leg Syndrome'.

For Overgliders, this is a very powerful image to demonstrate how your catch-up style (6) can lead you to overglide and apply the brakes at the front of your stroke (7). Given that many true Overgliders are intentionally targeting a slow stroke rate, you can see here how applying the brakes would slow your stroke rate down – for this reason putting on the brakes and Overgliding are strongly linked. Use the process in Chapter 13 to develop a better catch technique and your stroke rate will naturally lift, returning a nice sense of rhythm to your stroke.

The Front View (8) shows parts of the catch and pull-through in more detail. If you are a more advanced swimmer you may be wondering how you can improve your catch – this angle will give you a prime insight into that. What is the angle of your elbow bend during the pull-through? Is it greater than 140° or less than 90°? If so your catch probably needs some refining (8). Many swimmers will press down with a straight arm rather than bending the elbow and pressing backwards. You are also looking to examine the amount of bubbles coming off the arms too. If you fight the water you will see a sleeve of bubbles compared to someone with an efficient stroke having a clean pull-through.

Other flaws to watch out for from this angle are crossing over of the centre line under the body (9) and also whether you are holding your breathing underwater – we should see a constant stream of bubbles exiting from either your nose or mouth.

PAUL: *One word of caution when performing your own video analysis: don't become so pedantic about your stroke that you invoke 'paralysis by analysis'. Rome wasn't built in a day, so after breaking your stroke down work on a single aspect at a time, this will be much more productive than trying to change everything at once. As you go along, use the Stroke Technique (Key 1) chapters of this book to recognise the Cause and Effect nature of your stroke flaws and discover what the underlying causes are. Remember: one at a time!*

Should We All Swim The Same?

CHAPTER 17 The Swim Types System

Coaching the Swimmer, Not the Stroke

Since Swim Smooth's creation in 2004, we've talked a lot about the need for an individual approach in swimming; how swimmers needed to work on different aspects of their technique based on their age, height, experience, gender and even personality. In contrast to this, many traditional swimming programmes treat everyone the same and have them repeat the same visualisations and drills constantly with one ideal stroke in mind. This one-dimensional approach has several major disadvantages:

- The vision of a perfect stroke may not suit the swimmer's physical attributes e.g. height, strength, gender, natural buoyancy.
- The starting point of the swimmer is ignored and so the coaching is never tailored to their individual needs. As a consequence their rate of progress is dramatically slowed or stops completely.
- No account is taken of the environment in which the swimmer is racing and the importance of tailoring the swimmer's stroke technique to those conditions. e.g. pool versus open water and wetsuit versus non-wetsuit swimming.

Ceinwen is 1.60 m tall and Andy is 2.00 m. Should these two swimmers adopt the same stroke style?

Our Swim Types system is a way of taking a much more individual approach to your swimming:

- Swim Types gives you the option of two ideal stroke styles to head towards, one of which will suit your physical make-up and personality.

- Your current stroke technique is recognised and a tailored development path is set for you, allowing you to take rapid steps forward.
- The system shows you how differing styles suit different race environments and helps you develop your stroke to excel in those conditions. This is not just about maximum performance, the right stroke style will make things much more comfortable and enjoyable too.

Swim Types has been used internally by Swim Smooth coaches since 2008 but since the website www.swimtypes.com was launched in 2010, it has been used directly by swimmers with hundreds of thousands of followers from around the world visiting the site and using the system.

The Development of Swim Types

The Swim Types system is Paul Newsome's brainchild, here he takes a look back at the thinking behind the system and how it was created:

PAUL: *Coming from a competitive swimming background as a kid growing up in the UK, I always found it fascinating to see how different body types and builds gravitated towards each of the four competitive strokes – butterfly, backstroke, breaststroke and freestyle. The tallest swimmers with great hip flexibility tended to excel at breaststroke; the tall, muscular swimmers with great kicks were strong in the freestyle and backstroke sprint events; and the shorter, stockier swimmers with good upper-body flexibility tended to be good at butterfly. Being a little vertically challenged myself (compared to some of my giant-like rivals!) my best events were the 100 m and 200 m butterfly and the longer distance freestyle events. I could not seem to sprint like the other guys no matter how much speed work I put in but ask me to move along at a moderately fast pace and maintain this for repetition after repetition, well that I could do! Still, there were no prizes for being good at training or having a good work ethic – all that counted was who was first to the touch pads.*

Proudly representing Bridlington Swimming Club aged 9 (centre)

I couldn't change my growth rate or the size of my feet but swimming would have been a lot less frustrating had I been shown how genetics potentially predisposed me to one stroke or distance of event over another. I certainly wouldn't have kept trying to become a super-quick 50 m freestyle specialist against my 1.9 m / 6' 4" rivals! What's more, the recommended stroke style and technique that worked for these guys just didn't seem to work for me.

As a junior I was told by my coaches that my stroke didn't look that pretty and I was often affectionately known as 'Steam Boat Willie' by my friends because of my high stroke rate and a punchy style. Unfortunately, open water swimming wasn't very popular in the late 1980s and early 1990s and at 10 or 11 years of age, very rarely would we be encouraged to swim more than 400 m freestyle at a meet. This is a shame given what we now know about the differences in swimming style and suitability towards different environments and distances.

Unfortunately I didn't progress beyond county (state) representative level in the pool. However I did switch to triathlon at the age of 16 and instantly felt at home, revelling in the new open water environment with my aerobic engine and high revving stroke. I was much more suited to the longer distances in rougher water than to the 50 m or 100 m dash in the pool, and went on to represent Great Britain in triathlon as a Junior and Under-23 between the years of 1997 and 2001. Being one of the fastest swimmers in the field was fantastic and I was thankful for both my swimming background and for being persistent enough to stick with the sport when many of my fellow swimmers 'retired' in their mid-teens.

There was never any doubt in my mind that the one thing that I wanted to do after completing my Sports Science degree at Bath University was to coach swimming and triathlon. I wanted to work primarily with adult age-group athletes of limited swimming experience and put my biomechanics knowledge and video analysis skills to best use by helping these swimmers improve their efficiency in the water. As it turned out everything fell into place a little sooner than I thought it might.

Proudly representing Great Britain in 2000.

Whilst on a backpacking trip in 2002 (complete with long, bleached-blonde hair and hippy clothing) I found myself in sunny Perth and was offered a job as the Head Coach for the largest triathlon club in Western Australia. The Challenge Stadium Aquatic Centre was to be my base and with three 50 m pools all in one giant complex, what a playground this was! Having 24/7 access to some of the world's best swimming facilities, and with a seemingly endless demand for my video analysis and stroke correction services, I started to build up a big library of experience. Whilst being on the receiving end of a bit of banter from the locals for being a 'pommie' teaching Australians to swim, I worked with a huge range of swimmers from those just getting started in the sport to those winning triathlon and open water competitions.

Racing Under-23 Elite in 2001.

When you are fortunate enough to work full-time with thousands of swimmers of varying ability you start to notice trends in the way people move in the water. Being of an inquisitive and scientific mind, I started cross-referencing some of the most major faults within people's strokes against their body-type, build, gender and swimming background. Was there any link between a swimmer's inefficiency in the water and their physical make-up? Was I giving similar instruction to certain types of swimmers but giving differing advice to others – even if this advice seemed to contradict what I was telling the first group?

> **ON SHELLEY TAYLOR-SMITH**
>
> **COACH GRAEME CARROLL:** *Shelley's body shape and swimming technique was forged to be 'the perfect open water swimmer'. I likened her to a Ferrari: built to do the distance at speed. Shelley was able to keep a steady rate of 40–45 [80–90 SPM] in all types of conditions, rough and smooth waters, and varying temperatures.*
>
> *What sums it up best is Shelley coming to me one day in her late 30s when she was still ranked world number one woman, wanting to change her body (in particular her big shoulders) to be more feminine. I replied 'that body is the body of a World Champion and you can mess with it anyway you want when you retire but right now nothing is broken, so we're not changing a thing!'*
>
> *Steven Munatones, Founder www.openwaterswimming.com and former USA Open Water Swimming Team Coach: 'Shelley Taylor-Smith's legacy – in which she beat her male competitors so consistently – led to the international governing body to create equal prize money for both men and women in the sport. Shelley's greatest achievement will live on throughout the waterways of the world.'*

The world view within swimming at this time was that everyone should be taught to fit a single mould, irrespective of physical build or background. One of the strongest notions was that if you could make your stroke as long as is physically possible by reducing the number of strokes you took per lap, then you'd supposedly become ever more efficient. But how long is long, and is this the same number of strokes for everyone irrespective of their height and arm length? Aiming for less than 40 strokes per 50 m seemed to be the hallowed goal of swimmers and coaches; after all Ian Thorpe and Alexander Popov were reputedly taking fewer strokes than any of their contemporaries and looked so graceful in the process. Swimmers would be taught to do endless technique sets in the pool trying to reduce the number of strokes taken per length with those producing the lowest numbers being praised and those over the average being rejected as failing to be efficient, despite how fast they might have been swimming in races.

Most coaches and theoreticians seemed to be looking past those swimmers excelling in events longer than 400 m in the pool and open water when they wrote their manuals on how all of us should aim to swim. Enter Shelley Taylor-Smith, seven times World Cup marathon swimming champion and open water specialist from Perth. In 1991 Shelley was ranked number one in the world for women and men in marathon swimming events and in the same year she won the 25 km open water event at the World Aquatics Championships in the Swan River in Perth. In no other endurance sporting event would a woman out-perform the men and yet here was Shelley doing just that, breaking all the rules.

Not only was Shelley breaking the gender rules, she was also breaking the stroke rules too! At 1.65 m / 5' 5" Shelley wasn't able to swim with less than 40 strokes per 50 m in the pool as most of the guys would do, instead she would take around 52 strokes. Shelley would generate her speed by matching this stroke length with a very fast stroke rate around 90 strokes per minute. For many such a high stroke rate with so many strokes per length would have been laughed off as inefficient but here was one of the world's best ever distance swimmers doing just that, winning world championship after world championship and often beating all the men in the process. Shelley had developed and refined a stroke which was the most optimal style for her, as did Olympic Champion Janet Evans before her and Laure Manadou, David Davies and Lotte Friis (all Olympic Medallists) have done since. Meeting Shelley and seeing her in action was mind-blowing and I was seeing more and more that the consensus in swimming was wrong and there was more than one type of fast and efficient freestyle stroke.

Whilst everything in the printed media and online at this time was still saying 'longer strokes are always better', in practice I was finding that whilst this would work for some, for others this advice was proving totally detrimental if they simply didn't have the physical height and strength to make it work for them. In pursuing a very long stroke, these swimmers were creating as many problems in their technique as they were solving. I coined the phrase 'Overglider' as far back as 2004 after seeing so many swimmers introducing a long glide to their stroke to try and lengthen it out as much as possible. These swimmers had pretty good alignment and body position but were stuck on a performance plateau whilst in pursuit of an ever-longer stroke. With my sports-science background I respect the fact that research and evidence was needed to test hypothesis and the evidence was stacking up here against the 'longer is more efficient' world view.

Thinking back to my own swimming, a long stroke would have been great for the 1.9 m tall giants with powerful kicks to push them through the gap between strokes but I was neither tall nor was I very good at kick! Nor were many of the swimmers that I was coaching and most were training for open water swimming and triathlon where the conditions are much bumpier from swimming in close proximity to other swimmers. One key thing that my sports-science degree taught me was that specificity in training is essential. It's OK to use models of efficiency as a starting point (e.g. our Mr. Smooth animation) but you must have the ability to adapt your stroke to the environment in which you are swimming and, equally, to find a stroke that works for you given your own experience, physical makeup and even your personality.

One of my old coaches at university used to say 'all swimmer's strokes are like fingerprints, no two are the same' and whilst this is true, I was also starting to appreciate how many of these stroke flaws and movement patterns were clustering into 'types' of swimmer. Stronger athletes with limited swimming backgrounds would attack the water like they would the rugby field but would be held back by low sinking legs in the water. Some swimmers would have a strong kick and great body position but slip to the back of the lane when using a pull buoy. The more studious and analytical swimmers could tell me exactly what they should be doing in the water from all their research but then be unable to put this into practice. I could personally identify with another group of swimmers who had a strong swimming background but had developed a complex about the tidiness of their strokes and inability to kick (and sprint!).

It was very obvious to me that all these types of swimmer should be developed and worked with differently. If we could classify them and provide each 'Swim Type' with their own individual pathway for developing their strokes then all swimmers would develop at an optimal rate and into a style of stroke best suited to their makeup. We would be able to move away from a cookie-cutter programme that only works for the lucky few. Working with the other Swim Smooth coaches and sharing experiences and ideas, I formulated this into the full Swim Types system in 2007–08. We used and refined the system and stroke correction processes for a further two years before launching it to the world on www.swimtypes.com in June 2010. I was very excited about the potential of Swim Types but also aware that the system needed to be extremely well thought through and as fool-proof as possible before launching it.

After developing the stroke-style aspect of Swim Types, the area that fascinated me most was how each of the types tended to have a distinct personality. As a coach, one of the most important things I have learned over the last 15 years is that communication and the way you give direction to an athlete is just as important as what you actually say. I have met a wide range of swimmers over the years: some are very direct and want straight-forward answers with no 'fluff', some crave a detailed scientific explanation, some seek minimal guidance but want assistance with motivation and others respond best to a reassuring approach without any technical jargon at all. Swim Types helps you tune into these traits and tailor your communication accordingly. Knowing what to say, when to say it and how to put the message across is the key to successful coaching and this is the area I am most excited about with the Swim Types system.

What you see today is a highly-developed system with thousands of hours of coaching experiences behind it. We've put a lot of effort into making the system easy to understand and memorable using cartoons and some light-hearted humour but don't be fooled into thinking we've thrown it together in a light-hearted way. Quite the opposite, identify your Swim Type and follow your individual stroke correction process and you'll make the same sort of rapid progress with your swimming that you would if we were coaching you in person here in Perth.

ADAM: *If 'typing swimmers' is a new idea to you then you may have some doubts about how a classification system is possible, I had a lot of questions in my mind when Paul first took me through the concept in 2007. Please keep an open mind as you browse through the information of each Swim Type, read the profiles and watch the video clips on our website. I'm absolutely sure you'll start to recognise swimmers that you know, both in how they swim but also in their personalities.*

Since we launched the system we've spoken to many swimming coaches around the world who have told us how they often think about swimmers in types themselves, albeit without having put a proper system around it. If you've already been thinking along these lines yourself, you'll find it fascinating how we've recognised swimmer personality and the 'two ideal stroke types' concept in the system. I hope Swim Types gives you new ideas and thoughts for your own coaching and gives you the confidence to step outside the 'one size fits all' approach we've all been conditioned to use for the last 20 years.

Two 'Ideal' Swim Types

The Swim Type system covers six types of swimmer which we've given caricature names: Arnie, Bambino, Kicktastic, Overglider, Swinger and Smooth. The Smooth type is the long stroke style that everyone traditionally thinks of as being fast and efficient. To see an Olympic level Smooth in the flesh is awe inspiring as they slip through the water with grace and purpose. However, a fascinating aspect of the Swim Type system is that it recognises a second stroke style as also being 'ideal'.

The Swinger – in its refined form – is an exceptionally fast and efficient stroke style too and is often used by elite swimmers and triathletes to great effect. It's a shorter, punchier style that's won many Olympic Gold Medals in the pool, but in rougher open water its natural emphasis on stroke rhythm makes it completely dominant and is used by a significant majority of elite swimmers in this environment. Until now the Swinger stroke style has been much misunderstood and underappreciated in the swimming world as it is not as aesthetically pleasing as the Smooth style, at least not when viewed above the water. When speaking to Swingers, nearly all are under the impression that they don't have a very good stroke and that they are succeeding in swimming despite their technique when actually nothing could be further from the truth.

If you follow professional cycling there's an interesting analogy here. Jan Ullrich and Lance Armstrong were famous for racing head to head in the Tour de France with very different pedalling styles. Jan liked to turn over a very big gear, while Lance would spin a smaller gear at a faster speed. Each worked perfectly for each cyclist as it suited their individual biomechanics, style and physiology. The same is true for swimmers and their natural stroke style – you could say the Swinger is Lance Armstrong to the Smooth's Jan Ullrich.

The Swim Types system highlights the strengths and weaknesses of these two ideal styles and shows you which is the best for you to pursue, depending on your individual build and the environment in which you are going to swim.

Identifying Your Swim Type

We are sure you are dying to discover your own Swim Type! There are three ways to do this:

- By reading the profiles of each type in Chapters 18–23; the chances are you will immediately identify with the experiences and personality of one of the types!
- Using the Swim Type Questionnaire at: www.swimtypes.com/yourtype – this is great fun but be aware that it is not entirely fool-proof and sometimes misdiagnoses your type, it is best used in conjunction with the Swim Type profiles.
- Using the observation sheet at: www.swimtypes.com/observation – this is particularly useful if you are a coach observing swimmers in the pool.

Swim Type Statistics

Since we launched the Swim Type system in 2010 we have been collecting statistics from the questionnaire on the website (www.swimtypes.com) and also from sales of the Swim Type Stroke Correction Guides. From this we're able to gauge the percentage split of each Swim Type:

ADAM: *The most interesting of these statistics to me is the sheer quantity of Overgliders out there! On the Swim Smooth blog and website we talk a lot about the problems of adding too much glide into freestyle and the dead spot it creates. Now you can see why – overgliding has reached epidemic proportions in the swimming world!*

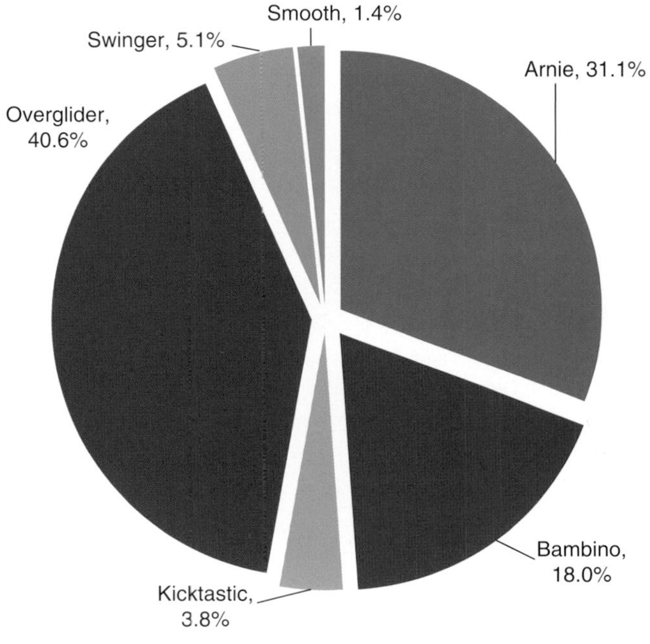

Sales of Swim Type Guide by type.

The Gender Divide

The gender divide amongst the Swim Types is clear to see below with men much more likely to be Arnies and Overgliders, and women much more likely to be Bambinos and Kicktastics. As we'll see, male and female versions of each Swim Type do exist though, for example: strong, athletic females often new to swimming may be known affectionately as 'Arnettes'; Bambino is Italian for young boy but in the case of Swim Types, can be taken to mean anyone very new to swimming, often with a limited general sporting background.

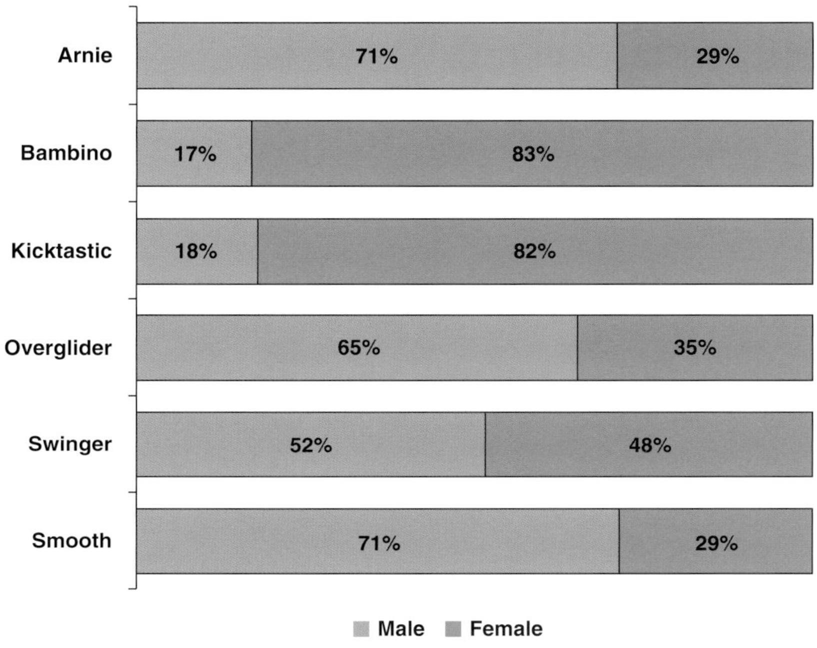

Split of Swim Type Guides by Gender from website sales.

Swim Type 'Cross-Breeds'

The Swim Types describe the six classic ways that people swim. At Swim Smooth we refer to someone who fits their type perfectly as a 'classic Overglider' or 'classic Arnie'. However it would be an exaggeration to say that all swimmers fit a type perfectly. Generally speaking the more coaching a swimmer has had, the more they move towards another Swim Type and many of these swimmers are mid-way between two types.

The most common cross-breed is the Arnie-Overglider. Many Arnies become very frustrated with their swimming and follow common advice to lengthen out their strokes as much as possible by introducing a significant glide. They may still have a poor body position in the water and a tendency to cross over in front of the head, which are relics from their pure-Arnie days.

Another common cross-type is the Bambino-Kicktastic. These are normally Bambinos who never really get to grips with arm propulsion and start to over-kick to compensate.

Lastly, the Kicktastic-Smooth can be seen in the fast lane of many squads. These can either be Kicktastics who have a reasonable catch technique and are on their way to being pure-Smooths or Smooths who have lost some of their feel for the water since their competition days and are over-kicking to compensate.

If you feel that you are a bit of a cross-breed caught between two types then start off by following the stroke development process for the type from which you originally came. For instance, in the case of the Arnie-Overglider you should follow the Arnie guide first and if you still feel Overglider tendencies then follow the Overglider process afterwards.

The Swim Types Website

Swim Smooth operates a dedicated website about the Swim Types system which will also be a very useful resource to you at www.swimtypes.com. You'll find video clips of each Swim Type and also a questionnaire that you can complete to assess your own swimming. The website also sells a full training and development guide of approximately 20 pages in length for each Swim Type. This takes you through each step of your swimming development in greater detail than is possible in this book and shows you the exact steps you need to improve your swimming. If you find the Swim Type system useful for the development of your swimming you will find one of these detailed guides a very useful supplement to the development process provided in this book.

Swim Type Personalities

Perhaps the most fascinating aspect of the Swim Types system is how each type tends towards distinct character traits. Whilst not set in stone, if you recognise your personality in the following Swim Type profiles then you're really quite likely to swim with that distinct style.

ADAM: *As a coach, when meeting a swimmer for the first time it's always good practice to chat to them about their goals and their swimming experiences. This chat, and the insight it offers into their personality, is often enough to have a very good guess about their stroke style using the Swim Type system – more often than not these educated guesses turn out to be correct!*

The classic Swim Type personalities are:

Arnie: Driven and competitive, anxious to get on with things and progress. Arnies are normally talented athletes on land and so find swimming very frustrating. Sometimes this frustration is very apparent and bubbling away just beneath the surface, in fact Arnies often do not enjoy swimming and many treat it is a necessary evil for triathlon.

Bambino: Normally quite anxious and occasionally positively frightened in water. A Bambino's goals are likely to be about health, personal achievement and fulfilment rather than competitive placings. Open and receptive to coaching, they feel very rewarded by every small improvement in their swimming.

Kicktastic: Often quiet and self sufficient, Kicktastics can appear a little disinterested or aloof to their fellow swimmers. Underneath the surface they are as keen to improve as any other swimmer but are susceptible to becoming bored while swimming and need a variety of stimuli to maintain focus.

Overglider: Thoughtful and analytical, this is the swimmer who's reac all the books on swimming and studied all the Youtube videos. Loves to record and analyse data and can normally tell you their times and stroke counts off the top of their heads. Love to use their intellect to improve their swimming but may be susceptible to over-thinking!

Swinger: These guys just love to swim! So much so that they often dislike technique work as they feel it interrupts the flow of their session. Normally the first to arrive on the pool deck for a squad session and impatient to get in the water and get on with it. Outgoing and social, these guys are not afraid to wear bright bathers!

Smooth: Quiet but with an inner self-confidence, these guys know their place in the pool – at the front of the fast lane! However, after many years of training they can feel uninspired – they know they have the ability to be very quick but sometimes lack motivation to train.

CHAPTER 18 The Arnie

Arnies are normally male but female Arnies do exist, we affectionately refer to them as 'Arnettes'. At their heart Arnies have a competitive personality across all walks of life, they tend to be naturally athletic and normally excel at sports. For this reason it can come as a bit of a shock that they don't take to swimming nearly as well; this combined with a driven personality and high expectations can lead to a lot of frustration!

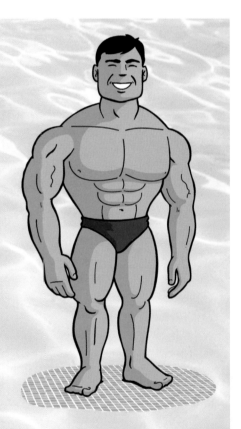

PAUL: *When I'm talking to an Arnie the most common thing they will tell me is 'I just don't understand it, I'm much fitter than these other people and yet they can swim much faster! I have run marathons and yet can't even swim a length of freestyle!'. This frustration is nearly always present with Arnies and in some extreme cases bubbling away just beneath the surface ready to boil over.*

Our cartoon caricature of the Arnie is overtly muscular and whilst this is a bit of fun to emphasise the point, many Arnies do have a strong build with lots of muscle bulk. Don't be distracted by this though, many other Arnies are less heavily built but nearly all have lean (and so 'sinky') muscle mass, which has a direct impact on their swimming. The female Arnette is not bulky but they're athletic and competitive at land-based sports, just as their male counterparts.

the arnie

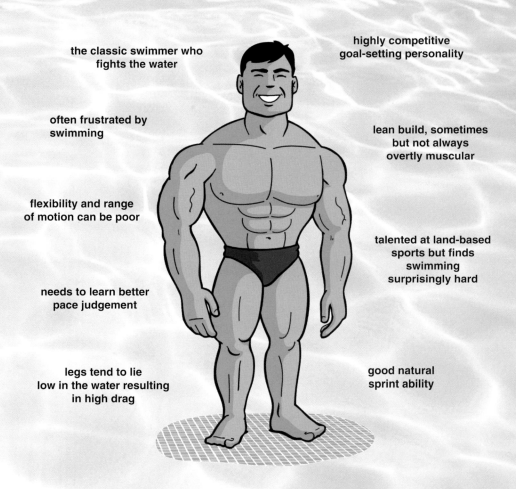

the classic swimmer who fights the water
highly competitive goal-setting personality
often frustrated by swimming
lean build, sometimes but not always overtly muscular
flexibility and range of motion can be poor
talented at land-based sports but finds swimming surprisingly hard
needs to learn better pace judgement
legs tend to lie low in the water resulting in high drag
good natural sprint ability

The Arnie displays a wide variety of stroke flaws in one package and is the classic swimmer we think of who fights the water. A lifting head to breathe, crossing over in front of the head, scissor kicks, kicking from the knee and a low body position are all very much in evidence. If you are an Arnie this may sound like a bad situation to be in but the positive is that innate athleticism of yours. If we can improve your stroke technique so that the effort you are putting in is being used effectively then you stand to make some major strides forwards from where you are now.

In terms of pace, classic Arnies swim 1:50 to 3:00/100 m for continuous swimming but can normally sprint considerably quicker for short distances. As Arnies develop their strokes they can become quicker than 1:50/100 m, albeit they will still be held back by their low body position in the water.

See Arnie video clips at: www.swimtypes.com/arnie

The classic Arnie with low-lying legs in the water.

Arnie Key Stroke Flaws

The single biggest thing holding an Arnie back is their low body position in the water, which is caused by a combination of stroke flaws which each need to be tackled in turn:

- A strong tendency to hold onto their breath underwater which harms relaxation and creates excess buoyancy in the chest, lifting the front end up and pushing the legs downward. Since Arnies tend to have significant lean muscle mass they are always quite 'sinky' in the water and so are more vulnerable to this effect than any other type. Working on a relaxed smooth exhalation into the water is key to improving their body position.
- Kicking from the knee rather than the hip is a key Arnie trait. This adds significant drag, lowering the legs in the water and burns large amounts of oxygen from overly utilising the large quadriceps and hamstring muscle groups.
- Arnies swim flat in the water and miss out on using their body rotation to lengthen the stroke and help

Of all the Swim Types, the Arnie is the most susceptible to crossing over in front of the head.

drive it. This style of swimming overuses the shoulder muscles, which partly explains why many Arnies have poor swimming endurance.

- The lack of body rotation causes the arms to swing around the side of the Arnie with the momentum carrying the hand across the centre line in front of the head. Arnies often have stiff upper backs and shoulders, which, combined with this low swinging arm recovery, can exacerbate crossovers further.

Another classic Arnie trait is a large scissor kick, which drags the legs down low in the water.

- Whilst it's possible for any swimmer to have a scissor kick, the Arnie is the most susceptible because of their tendency to cross over in front of the head. This causes a swimmer to lose their balance slightly and give an involuntary (and often subconscious) scissor kick to regain their balance. Scissor kicks add a large amount of drag and act to sink the legs, worsening the drag profile still further.
- Most Arnies feel a desperate need to get air whilst they swim resulting in a distinct lifting of the head to clear the surface rather than using the bow wave to breathe. This lifting of the head causes the legs to sink downward adding significant drag.
- Poor ankle flexibility is often a hindrance to Arnies as they have an inability to point their foot straight, leaving the top of the foot out in the water flow. This pulls the legs downward and creates a lot of drag. A little-but-often approach to developing some ankle flexibility will really pay dividends for their swimming.
- Arnies have a poor catch technique with a dominant push down on the water at the front of the stroke. This only acts to lift the front end upwards and sink the legs without adding any forward propulsion.
- A straight arm pull-through under the water is common, which overworks the shoulder muscle groups.

Whilst not strictly stroke technique, Arnies are also the worst culprits when it comes to poor pacing with a real tendency to start a swim or training set too fast and then blow up and slow down dramatically. Developing a good sense of pace awareness and control is a critical skill for any swimmer trying to reach their potential. For more information on this see Chapter 28.

For the full Arnie stroke correction process see Appendix B.

CHAPTER 19

The Bambino

Bambinos are often but not always female and would love to be good at swimming, perhaps not in an overtly competitive way but from a healthy self-fulfilling perspective. Fundamentally, Bambinos lack confidence in the water and this is reflected in their stroke style, which lacks positivity and 'oomph'.

ADAM: *If you are a Bambino then don't fear, we'll show you how to tune up your stroke technique and build up your confidence in your swimming. A good positive attitude will go a long way in helping with this; be positive in your thoughts and never put yourself down – you deserve much better than that!*

Bambinos are normally in the speed range between 2:00 and 3:00 per 100 m. A classic Bambino may struggle to complete 25 m of freestyle as they feel like they're sinking and struggle to breathe. Even as they develop their swimming fitness, many have to stop every length to catch their breath.

In terms of developing their strokes, Bambinos defy conventional logic. They only respond slightly to balance and streamlining exercises (the approach for an Arnie for instance) but make much larger improvements by work ng on their catch and stroke rate, which is traditionally left to more advanced swimmers. This is because they have such poor feel for the water and are so lacking in rhythm that they find it very hard to progress without some attention in these areas first.

the bambino

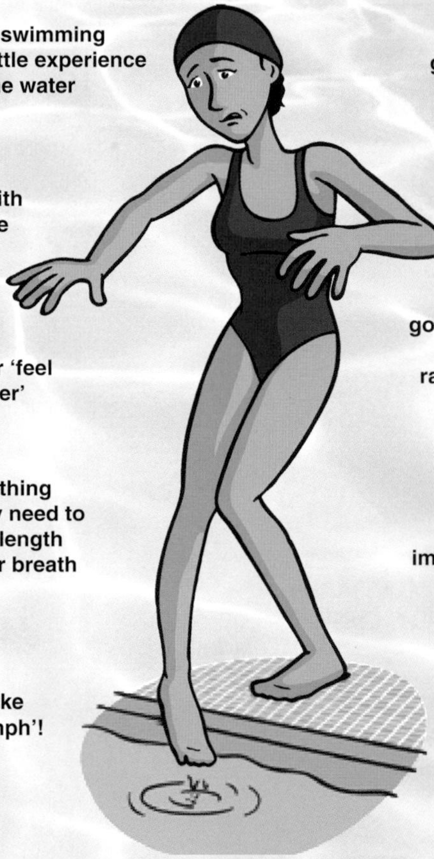
new to swimming with very little experience in the water
normally anxious in the water to a greater or lesser extent, in extreme cases finds putting their face in the water very frightening
may struggle with coordinating the freestyle stroke
goals are normally health and fitness related rather than competitive
has very poor 'feel for the water'
finds breathing hard and may need to stop every length to catch their breath
gets a real buzz from improving their swimming
lower power stroke without much 'oomph'!
friendly and emotionally open personality

Many Bambinos are quite short with small hands and short arms. This means that a long gliding stroke style is unlikely to work well for them. If you are a Bambino be very wary of adding a glide into your stroke as more than any other type you are vulnerable to the inefficiencies of doing so. A faster stroke rate style with more 'oomph' will work for you much more effectively.

PAUL: *If you can find a nice friendly swim group or squad we highly recommend that you join their sessions. Whilst you won't be the fastest swimmer there, having other swimmers around you will push you along and help you achieve things you didn't know you could do! This really will do wonders for your confidence and give you a real buzz of achievement!*

See Bambino video clips at: www.swimtypes.com/bambino

The Bambino's lead arm collapses down in the water whilst breathing, giving very poor support.

Bambino Key Stroke Flaws

The single biggest thing holding a Bambino back is the poor rhythm and timing in their stroke due to a lack of confidence and coordination:

- Bambinos normally hold their breath completely underwater which builds up CO_2 in the lungs and bloodstream, making things feel much more tense and anxious than they need to be. This is a contributing factor to a Bambino's anxiety in the water.
- A slow stroke that lacks rhythm and 'oomph'. The more anxious a Bambino is in the water, the less positivity there is in their stroke movements.
- A poor 'feel for the water' where the arms slip through with very little purchase or propulsion.

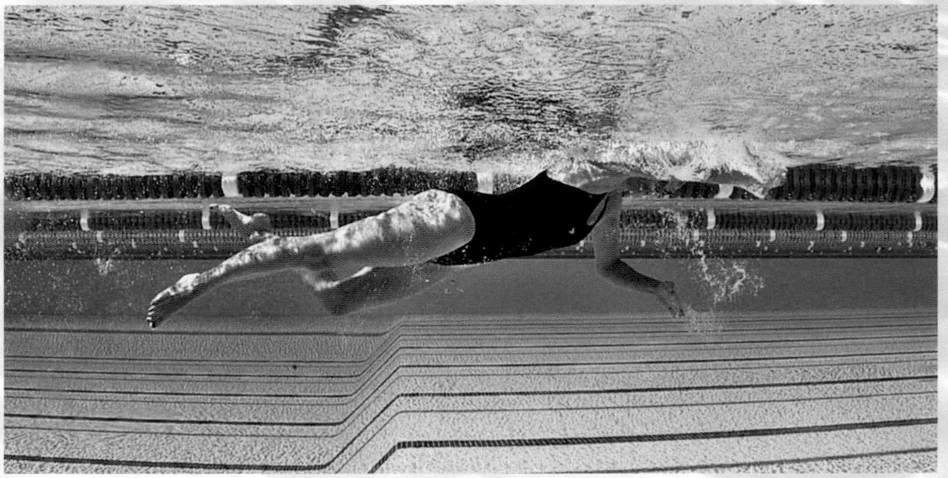

Like Arnies, Bambinos often kick from the knee with a jittery action, which creates a lot of drag and pulls the body low in the water.

- A tendency to cross over in front of the head, which further reduces 'feel for the water'.
- This poor feel means that the lead hand collapses down when breathing offering very little support. This is why breathing feels challenging to many Bambinos and they commonly take on water when trying to breathe.
- Poor kicking technique, often kicking from the knee. This is hard work as it uses the large muscle groups of the quadriceps and hamstrings, and it creates large amounts of drag.
- A tendency to push the water upwards rather than backwards at the rear of the stroke. This upwards push pulls the legs downward and does not create any propulsion.

For the full Bambino stroke correction process see Appendix B.

CHAPTER 20

The Kicktastic

Like Bambinos, Kicktastics are often female but unlike Bambinos, they normally have a background in swimming to a greater or lesser extent. As the name suggests, they have a dominant 6-beat kick which powers them through a relatively poor catch phase of the arm stroke in front of the head. They generate very little propulsion from the front of their stroke and make up for this with a push from the legs.

Many Kicktastics swam as a young child and then stopped swimming in their teens. This is a very common scenario as young kids always swim with a dominant leg kick before they develop the arm length and proprioceptive feel required for good upper-body propulsion. When Kicktastics resume swimming as an adult they carry on where they left off with the trademark Kicktastic style.

PAUL: *The problem with over-kicking is that it's such an inefficient source of propulsion. If we could transfer your propulsion over to your arm stroke you would be swimming much quicker or much easier at the same speed.*

Despite having a very dominant kick, the action is so familiar to Kicktastics that most are unaware of how hard they are kicking. Ironically, many feel their kick is quite weak! In some cases this may be true in terms of propulsion – although all Kicktastics have a vigorous kick, some do not have very good kicking technique and so generate very little propulsion despite the high level of effort.

the kicktastic

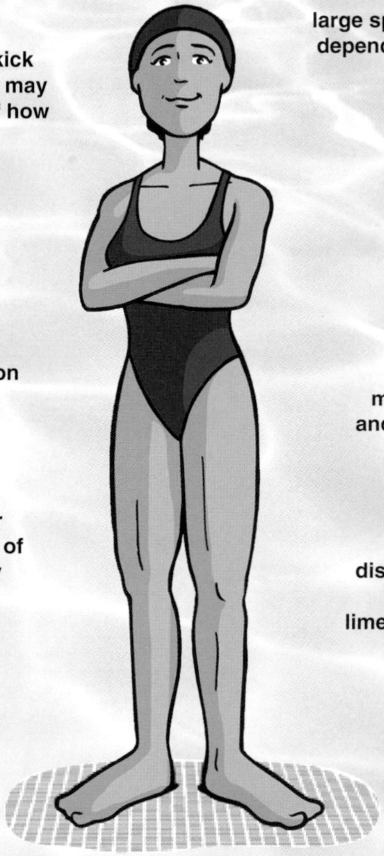
powerful leg kick - although they may not be aware of how powerful
often but not always female
very good body position in the water
competent swimmer with some experience of swimming, normally as a child
poor 'feel for the water' during the catch phase of the stroke
large speed range of swimmers depending on their level of feel for the water
commonly feels short of breath
often tall with long legs
may become bored easily and needs plenty of variety to keep them stimulated
dislikes being the centre of attention and avoids the limelight in group situations
often feel that they only have one swimming pace

Kicktastics like to kick and kick hard!

One disadvantage of working so hard with the legs is that it uses a huge amount of oxygen in the body making many Kicktastics short of breath when they swim. Most are aware of this shortness of breath and assume that there's something wrong with their fitness.

Kicktastics vary hugely in terms of swimming speed, ranging between 2:00 per 100 m to under 1:20 per 100 m depending on their level of arm propulsion and also the effectiveness of their kicking technique. At the very fast end there is a crossover with the Smooth Swim Type who also use a propulsive 6-beat kick, albeit with extremely good arm propulsion too!

ADAM: *A good way to prove that it's the kick causing your shortness of breath is to swim with a pull buoy and keep your legs held straight behind you. Despite potentially being slower as you lose your propulsion from the legs, monitor your breathing and if it feels much easier then that's cast-iron proof you're over-kicking in your stroke.*

For obvious reasons Kicktastics dislike swimming with a pull buoy (with no leg kick) and are normally significantly slower with one than without. Interestingly, they often dislike swimming in wetsuits too as the buoyancy of the suit brings their legs up too high making them feel very unbalanced. They also lose kick propulsion as they start to kick into thin air. If you find this with your own swimming, in the stroke development section we'll show you a stroke adaptation you can make to improve your wetsuit swimming.

The personality of a classic Kicktastic is one of the most fascinating: often quiet and reserved, Kicktastics seem to shy away from attention or standing out from the crowd – they seem to be quite happy slipping under the radar and going their own way with their swimming. However, underneath the surface they are extremely keen swimmers and are as anxious to improve as any of the other Swim Types. They also seem to get bored quite easily in swim sets and benefit from a lot of variety and mini-challenges to keep things interesting.

Tall Male Kicktastics

A little harder to spot than most Kicktastics is the tall male variety. Rather than using a very rapid kick, these swimmers often employ a slower kick, but with a larger amplitude up and down. Although apparently less vigorous, their kick is still very dominant in their stroke and extremely energy-sapping. Their kick may also surge a little more than conventional Kicktastics, a typical rhythm being four hard kicks and then two easy.

See Kicktastic video clips at: www.swimtypes.com/kicktastic

Kicktastic Key Stroke Flaws

The Kicktastic's dominant leg kick comes from a lack of catch and 'feel for the water' at the front of their stroke. By improving your catch the leg kick will naturally drop down to a balanced level with the arm stroke. We're not looking to kill your kick, just bring it under control.

Kicktastics have a strong tendency to pull through underwater with a straight arm.

- A very strong energy-sapping leg kick. Slower Kicktastics may kick excessively from the knee, which produces less propulsion and more drag.
- Poor catch and 'feel for the water', normally pushing down on the water at the front of the stroke with a straight arm rather than bending the elbow and pressing the water backwards.
- Crossovers in front of the head are common with Kicktastics, further harming their 'feel for the water'. Unlike the other classic offender of a crossover (the Arnie), Kicktastics don't typically display a scissor kick due to the rapid continuous movement of the legs smothering this effect.
- Many Kicktastics pull through with a very straight arm under the body, over-working the weaker shoulder muscles, which are not powerful enough to generate much propulsion. A good stroke technique involves bending the elbow so that the larger muscles of the back, chest and core are engaged with the movement.
- Poor body rotation, resulting in the arm recovering round the side of the body rather than over the top. For classic Kicktastics with restricted upper backs this can be very tight and awkward.

For the full Kicktastic stroke correction process see Appendix B.

CHAPTER 21 The Overglider

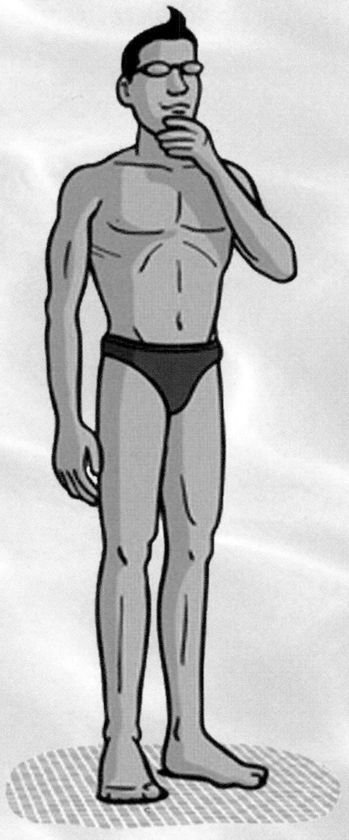

Overgliders are normally swimmers who learned freestyle as adults, they tend to be thoughtful individuals who have studied swimming carefully in books or on the internet. In nearly every case they have latched on to the idea that, to be an efficient swimmer, the freestyle stroke should be long with minimum strokes taken per length. Above the water they can look smooth and relaxed but under the water we see why they are not as efficient (or quick) as they would like to be.

Unfortunately Overgliders have taken the idea of a long freestyle stroke a little too far to the point where they've added a significant glide-phase to their stroke at the front end. Some even report that they like the 'rest' time between strokes without realising the significant deceleration in the momentum of the stroke that this causes. This stop-pause-and-do-nothing rhythm is inefficient because the swimmer slows down significantly between strokes and then has to re-accelerate on the next stroke. In an effort to lengthen out, many Overgliders also drop the elbow and wrist and show the palm of the hand forwards. This harms the catch phase to follow and creates a lot of drag in its own right – we call it 'putting on the brakes'.

ADAM: *I admit it, I used to be an Overglider before I joined Swim Smooth! One of the fascinating things about the Swim Type system is the correlation between stroke styles and personality. Here's an interesting one: nearly all Overgliders work in technical professions such as engineering or IT. What did I used to do before joining Swim Smooth? Funnily enough I was an engineer – doh!*

the overglider

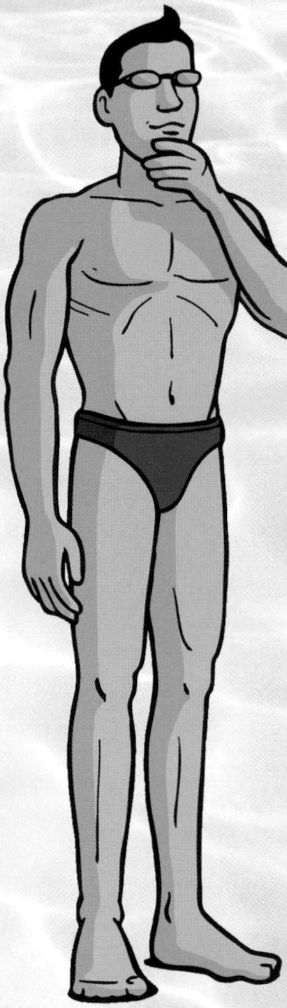
an over-emphasis on the length of the stroke with a long overglide at the front
often but not always male
dilligent approach to swimming, normally read all the books and watched all the videos on youtube
often from technical professions such as IT and engineering
focused on reducing drag in their stroke at the expense of propulsion
may be guilty of overthinking every stroke movement to the detriment of their stroke rhythm
commonly feels short of breath
may try and use a 2-beat kick to further reduce swimming effort
poor catch technique often pushing forwards on the water and 'putting on the brakes'
in extreme cases avoids fitness training fearing that their stroke technique will suffer

An overglide in the stroke creates an additional problem, it slows the stroke rate right down and causes the swimmer to lose touch with their rhythm and timing. The freestyle stroke should be smooth and continuous, moving seamlessly from one phase to another. A dead spot and pause interrupts this rhythm, which quickly becomes imprinted in the stroke timing and can be as hard to remove, or harder, than other stroke flaws. This is ironic as many Overgliders are trying to avoid imprinting bad stroke habits by swimming correctly at all times. A typical Overglider learns freestyle as an adult and makes good initial progress as they diligently improve their body position and rotation in the water. However, they quite quickly reach a speed and efficiency plateau which they can't seem to break through. The speed at which they can swim is normally heavily dependant on their height and arm length with many taller Overgliders reaching around

1:40 per 100 m and shorter swimmers around 2:00 per 100 m before hitting a plateau.

Overgliders often realise they need to lift their tempo and stroke rate to improve their swimming but when they try to do so they keep the glide in place in their stroke and speed up every other movement. If you've tried this yourself you will know it is very hard work, a little like driving down the freeway with the handbrake on! Instead, the key is to remove the glide by improving your catch technique, this naturally lifts up the stroke rate while keeping all other movements at the same speed. When you learn to coordinate a better catch and remove the glide, you will gain a significant increase in speed for little, if any, increase in effort.

See classic Overglider video clips: www.swimtypes.com/overglider

The classic Overglider: head buried low in the water and the elbow and wrist dropped during the over-glide.

Overgliders and Fitness Training

In extreme cases a focus on efficiency above everything else has led some Overgliders to disregard any form of fitness training from their swimming preparation, with those that are triathletes believing that bike or run fitness will carry across into their swimming. Unfortunately this goes against the principal of specificity in training (see Chapter 24) and the resultant de-training can see many of these swimmers becoming slower in their races. If you have neglected your swimming fitness then you stand to make some large gains in speed from getting back into some training using Chapter 27 of this book.

Overgliders and Open Water

As we discuss in Key 3: Open Water Adaptation, open water swimming is distinctly different to pool swimming as waves and chop constantly buffet you. Even in an otherwise flat lake or river, the wake from other swimmers is enough to disturb your progress and interrupt your stroke rhythm.

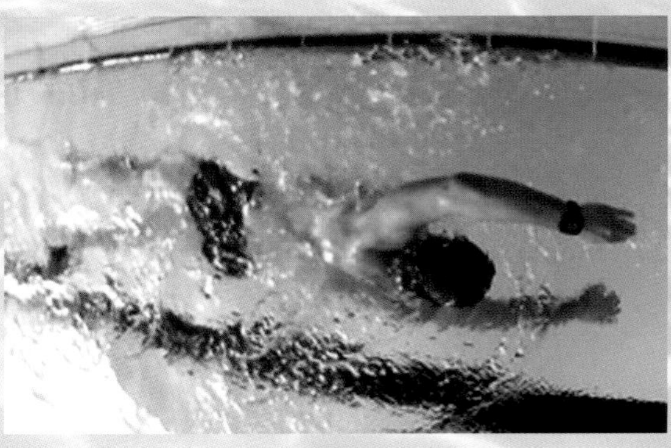

As a result of pausing with the lead hand, Overgliders have a tendency to 'catch-up' and bring both hands together in front of the head.

If you swim in open water with a slow stroke rate and an overglide you will be slowed down and stalled in the gap between strokes by disturbed water. Swimmers with a faster more continuous stroke (e.g. Swingers) cut through open water much more efficiently as the delay between strokes is much smaller or in some cases non-existent. This stroke style is very efficient in open water.

PAUL: *From working with Overgliders I know that many are frustrated with their performances in the open water. This may be partially offset by the added buoyancy and so improved body position offered by a wetsuit but for the effort you are putting in (both intellectual and physical) you deserve to swim much more effectively in this environment.*

Overglider Key Stroke Flaws

The Overglider's dominant stroke flaw is a large dead spot in their stroke timing caused by the introduction of a long glide into their stroke. Working on their catch technique and developing their stroke rhythm will get them off the speed and efficiency plateau they find themselves on.

- A long pause-and-glide is always present at the front of an Overglider's stroke, interrupting their rhythm and causing them to decelerate significantly during the resultant dead spot.
- Many Overgliders' recovering arms 'catch up' at the front giving what is known as 'catch-up timing'. A much better timing is where the hands just pass in front of the head with the stroking arm already into the catch phase as the recovering arm comes past the head.

- A poor catch technique with the elbow dropping and very often the palm of the hand facing forwards 'putting on the brakes'. This is a by-product of trying to swim with a long slow stroke style since the poor catch technique acts to slow the stroke down (see Chapter 13) and so supports the desire to glide.
- After the glide, the swimmer has to rush the catch to get the stroke back underway. A hurried catch action causes the hand to slip backwards with very little purchase on the water.
- It is common to see Overgliders only breathing to one side as they swim, normally this is because their stroke rate is so slow that it's too long between breaths to breathe every three strokes. Over time breathing to one side develops a lopsided stroke with a lack of symmetry, this is particularly a problem for open water swimming where it can cause the swimmer to track off course constantly.

After the long glide phase, Overgliders literally have to kick-start their strokes with a large knee-driven kick.

- A pulsing kick is often used to kick-start the stroke again after the long glide phase. To create the required impetus to restart the stroke the knee is often bent too far during the kick, creating drag and harming the swimmer's body rotation. A light flutter kick is normally much more appropriate for Overgliders as it keeps the body position high and helps maintain stroke rhythm.

For the full Overglider stroke correction process see Appendix B.

CHAPTER 22

The Swinger

PAUL: *If I told you about a swimmer who takes around 50 to 52 strokes per 50m lap of the pool it's unlikely you'd be very impressed, you might think they couldn't be a very good swimmer – they should be taking far fewer strokes per length than that. But what if I told you that swimmer was Frenchwoman Laure Manadou who won Olympic Gold in the 400m freestyle at the 2004 Athens Olympics and also held the world records at 200m and 400m? Laure and swimmers like her defy the conventional swimming logic that you must always swim with a long stroke in order to be efficient. Here lies the Swinger: fast and efficient but unappreciated and unloved – until now! See Laure swim here: www.swimsmooth.com/manadou*

Swingers are nearly always experienced swimmers with many years of swimming behind them, often from a young age. Classic Swingers have a shorter stroke than many other swimmers but make up for it with a fast stroke rate; this distinctive 'punchy' style is very natural to them, they find it very hard and quite alien to swim in any other way. The good news is that it's not necessary to change that style at all, by refining it and working to their natural strengths of great rhythm and momentum they can become exceptionally fast swimmers both in the pool and in open water.

the swinger

experienced swimmer, normally with a competitive swimming background

a fast choppy stroke style that oozes rhythm

many elite swimmers are swingers, particularly open water swimmers and professional triathletes

a natural disposition to distance swimming and dislikes sprinting

most commonly found in Masters swim squads

may have received unfavourable comments about their stroke in the past in comparison to smoother swimmers

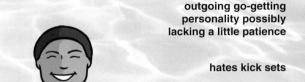

outgoing go-getting personality possibly lacking a little patience

hates kick sets

often found in unrefined form with crossovers and a poor catch

faster stroke rate style naturally suits a 2-beat kick

classic swingers love to get on and swim with minimum stoppages or distractions such as drills

likes to wear bright bathers!

The fast stroke rate used by a Swinger means that they roll their body to a slightly lesser extent than the Smooth Swim Type. This means that their arms come a little more around the sides rather than over the top of the body, in doing so they use a straighter arm recovery. This swinging recovery style of a classic Swinger is where they get their name.

ADAM: *Swingers tend to look quite choppy and unrefined from above the water, which has given them a bad press in swimming circles over the years. Since the invention of underwater video technology we now get to see the beautiful part of their stroke: under the water. Here a refined Swinger's stroke mechanics are poetry in motion: a great catch and perfect rhythm and timing all working together in perfect harmony!*

Swimming legend Shelley Taylor-Smith shows the refined Swinger style: bent elbow catch underwater and the recovering arm swinging around the side.

In terms of speed, Swingers cover a very large range depending on the level of refinement in their strokes. Unrefined Swingers may swim 1:45/100m, while an elite level Swinger with a refined stroke can swim sub 1:00/100m pace – matching Smooth types over distances of 400m and over. Swingers have a natural disposition towards distance swimming and normally dislike sprint training. Their personality is very go-getting and they like to get on with things without waiting around or thinking about it too much!

Whilst there are examples of Swingers performing well with a 6-beat kick, a classic Swinger really comes into their own with a 2-beat kick. A refined Swinger uses their kick with great timing, using it to drive their body rotation from one side to the other, which in turn drives the arm stroke. Whilst they may not achieve much propulsion directly from their kick, they use it to drive the arm stroke which is a much more efficient use of the kick effort. To achieve really high stroke rates a Swinger needs to use a 2-beat kick, a 6-beat kick simply becomes too rapid at these stroke rates to keep up with (see Chapter 9 on the various kicking styles).

PAUL: *When I ask an Overglider what they think of when they swim, they can list off several parts of their stroke they are thinking about at any one time! But ask a Swinger the same question and you tend to get a blank look or an answer like 'nothing really!'. A Swinger's ability (and preference) to switch off their brain and just swim is a strength in many ways. Focused stroke technique development has an important place in swimming (and Swingers may well be guilty of skipping over this part of their preparation) but at other times it's very important to stop analysing and just swim, which is when the Swinger's 'stop talking and let me get on with it' personality really comes into its own!*

Unrefined Swingers may have stroke faults such as crossovers, scissor kicks and a hurried catch but the fundamental punch and rhythm is always in place. If you are a Swinger whose stroke has become a little ragged over the years you need to take some time out to work on some refinements in your stroke technique. You'll polish up quite quickly and will soon be back to what you love best – swimming long sets and swimming them fast!

Swingers and Open Water Swimming

Open water swimming is a natural strength of Swingers and they really become a dominant force in this environment. Their faster stroke rate style helps punch through chop and wake from other swimmers and the longer distance races suit their natural disposition towards endurance events. Where they may lose out to some talented swimmers with long smooth strokes in the pool, they are able to turn the tables on them in open water.

Becoming a Swinger

In many ways there are two types of Swinger, those who naturally adopt this style ('classic Swingers') and those who have developed their strokes towards this style out of necessity. Many swimmers who are short in height or with short arms are forced to use a shorter faster stroke style to swim quickly and efficiently, and so gravitate towards the Swinger style as they develop their strokes. Others are looking to race well in longer distance open water events or triathlon, so even though they are capable of swimming with the Smooth style they choose to adopt the Swinger route to be more efficient in this environment. Very often such swimmers are able to switch between the two stroke styles at will.

Be wary of drawing the conclusion that those with long arms suit a Smooth stroke style and those with shorter arms the Swinger style. Whilst the latter may be true, the former isn't. There are many swimmers with long arms who swim naturally – and extremely quickly – with a Swinger style, Laure Manadou and Shelley Taylor-Smith being prime examples.

Unrefined Swinger – Classic Stroke Flaws

Swingers are accomplished swimmers and for this reason their strokes don't need a major overhaul. Instead, they are likely to need a tune-up in a few areas, removing any crossovers, tuning up their catch technique and possibly formalising a 2-beat kick.

- A common flaw in unrefined Swingers is a crossover in front of the head on hand entry or crossing over the centre line under the body. Over the years this may have gradually crept in as flexibility and posture has worsened since their days as a junior swimmer.
- A thumb-first entry into the water is another common flaw seen. In some cases this feels like a natural way of entering to the swimmer while in other cases they were coached to enter thumb first as junior swimmers. In either case this needs to be rectified because of the high risk of shoulder injury from a thumb-first entry – in fact many Swingers already suffer from shoulder pain for this reason.

Sam shows us three common Swinger flaws in one photo: holding breath, thumb-first entry and crossing the centre line underwater.

- A hurried catch phase results from a Swinger's desire to get on and swim at a high tempo. Taking a little longer over the catch will allow the swimmer to get into a better high-elbow catch position and gain a better purchase on the water.
- Many Swingers have become a little too flat in the water over the years and need to stretch out just a little more in their strokes. The right balance always needs to be struck between stroke length and stroke rate – whilst a Swinger definitely sits towards the shorter faster end of this spectrum it's possible to take this a little too far and 'over-rev'. In these cases adding a touch more stroke length is recommended.
- Despite their experience as swimmers, Swingers can be some of the worst culprits when it comes to holding their breath under water. By improving their exhalation technique Swingers should be able to breathe bilaterally quite easily; in fact with their fast stroke rate breathing every five strokes may be an option.

For the full Swinger stroke correction process see Appendix B.

CHAPTER 23 The Smooth

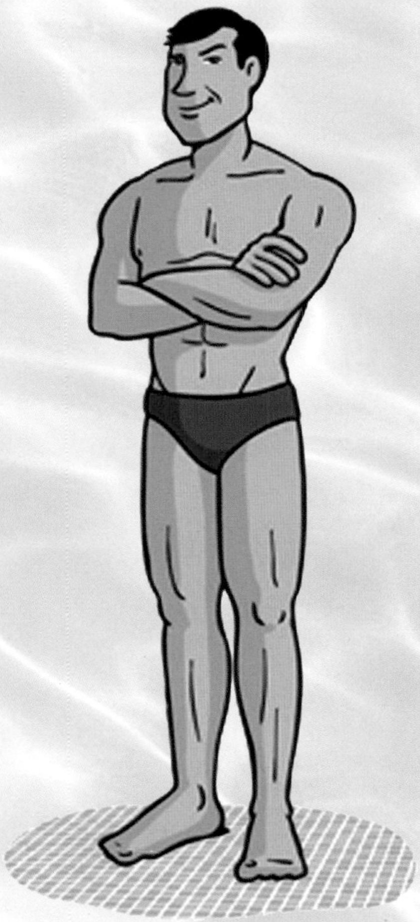

The Smooth Swim Type is what everybody thinks of when they imagine a long efficient stroke style. They are the envy of the pool with their relaxed style moving them seemingly effortlessly through the water accompanied by a 6-beat kick. They are strong technically in all areas with great turns and starts, and they are normally competitive at backstroke, breaststroke and butterfly as well as freestyle. Most elite pool swimmers are Smooths, with all time greats such as Ian Thorpe and Alexander Popov typifying this category. Although many observers believe this style of stroke is very efficient and therefore well suited to distance swimming, in practice the opposite is true, most elite Smooths excel as sprinters and middle distance (200 m / 400 m) freestylers.

Nearly all Smooths have a significant childhood swimming background, very few adults have been able to develop their strokes to this level without such a background, although it is possible. Smooths are talented athletes with excellent technical skills, coordination and awareness of their body movements in the water. When making modifications to their stroke Smooths are able to do so quickly and easily once they understand what they need to do.

The Smooth stroke style is certainly efficient but that does not make it 'effortless' as many other swimmers might believe. A Smooth will tell you how hard they are actually

the smooth

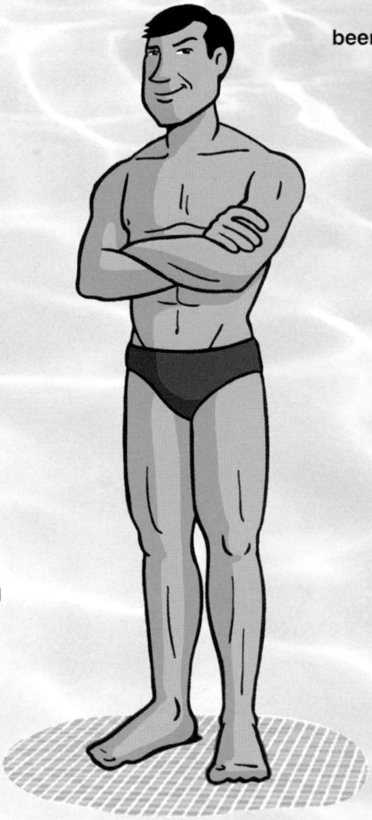

accomplished swimmer with a competitve swimming background, only found in the top lane of squads

silky smooth style, moving apparently effortlessly through the water (this is normally an illusion)

excellent catch and 'feel for the water'

6-beat kick that becomes more powerful when racing

a natural sprinter

very good levels of flexibility and stability

been there, seen it, done it! May be a little burnt out from swimming and struggles for motivation

confident in their ability but modest and often reserved

needs new goals and challenges to motivate them - open water?

technically strong all round with great starts and turns

normally excellent understanding of swimming and stroke technique

Olympian Jono Van Hazel shows us his classical high elbow recovery.

working when they swim, it's their huge control and technical ability that makes the stroke appear effortless from the outside. Think of their movements as being like those of an Olympic gymnast or ballet dancer – they have tremendous grace and poise but to do so they are using strength and control.

This is an important distinction to understand as many swimmers aspiring to the Smooth stroke style try and introduce the concept of 'effortless swimming' into their own strokes, which results in a slow stroke with poor rhythm and timing – anything but efficient. Although Smooths can look as though they have a slow stroke rate this is an illusion brought about by the sheer speed at which they are moving relative to their stroke rate. Smooths operate in the 65–75 strokes per minute range at a steady pace, 75–85 strokes per minute at race pace and even higher when sprinting 50 m. In contrast most Overgliders (who very much aspire to be Smooths) are swimming at 50 strokes per minute and below, slowed down by the imprinted pause-and-glide in their strokes.

As adults, Smooths often suffer from a lack of motivation. Whilst they are normally quiet and modest characters, they are also very confident in their own abilities in the water and they know that if they put the effort back into training they could become an extremely fast swimmer again. This is not an issue, the real question is can they conquer their motivational demons and get inspired again?

PAUL: *I see a surprisingly large number of Smooths in Perth, which might be because of the sheer number of adults in Australia who have swum competitively as kids. A lack of motivation is a common theme for them, and I find the key to inspiring them is to change the environment. Many Smooths have developed severe 'black-line-fever' from childhood and dislike hard training in the pool as it brings back too many bad memories! The solution to this is to set yourself some new challenges by moving to the open water – either pure swimming events or by getting into triathlon. As we'll see later, you might have to make some modifications to your stroke to reach your potential in the great outdoors!*

Smooths and Open Water

Compared to Swingers, Smooths have a longer stroke with a slower stroke rate. Whilst they don't pause and glide in their stroke like an Overglider, this lower stroke rate is still a disadvantage in open water and can cause them to be stalled slightly as they are buffeted by chop and wake from other swimmers. It can come as quite a nasty shock that some of those Swingers – who you can gap with a devastating turn of pace in the pool – are suddenly right with you in open water or even pulling ahead. Fortunately there is a solution to this problem, with a few modifications to your stroke we can make you much more efficient in open water and leave you fresh to unleash that sprint finish at the end of the race.

Experimenting with a straighter arm recovery is important for Smooths in open water as their classical high elbow and low trailing hands can clash with waves and chop as they travel over the water. Getting into the catch a little sooner in the stroke will lift the stroke rate and help drive you through that disturbed water much more effectively. We're not going to turn you into a high-revving Swinger – that simply wouldn't suit you – but we do need to shorten your stroke slightly and turn it over a touch quicker. If you're a triathlete you'll understand the analogy of using a smaller gear, you're moving the same speed with a slightly higher cadence but each stroke is slightly easier in itself.

As a Smooth you are going to have a nice symmetrical stroke which will help you track straight in open water but developing your drafting, sighting and navigation skills is also going to be critical to take on the open water specialists who are very strong in these areas. As a Smooth transitioning to the open water, you'll really find the advice in Key 3 very beneficial and hopefully it will add a renewed enthusiasm to your swimming.

Smooth Stroke Flaws

ADAM: *A Smooth's stroke flaws? You might be thinking this could be a short section! But actually without good coaching feedback since their competitive swimming days a Smooth's stroke will tend to deteriorate slightly and they probably have one or two small areas of their stroke they need to work on, most commonly their catch technique. You will still look good in the water but might well have started to over-kick to compensate for a slight loss in your arm stroke propulsion. If you have been out of the water for a few years you'll soon brush up and you may be surprised at how quickly you can swim again, perhaps even breaking some old PBs in the process.*

- Pressing down on the water slightly with a straight arm during the catch is the most common stroke flaw seen with Smooths. You'll still be generating reasonable propulsion with your arm stroke but pressing downward wastes energy and will harm your stroke's rhythm.
- Over-kicking slightly (perhaps becoming a little Kicktastic) is another common flaw with Smooths and is related to that slight deterioration in arm stroke propulsion. When you restore your catch and 'feel for the water' to its former glory this leg kick will fall away naturally and you'll notice the reduced oxygen demand from a less vigorous kick.

Michelle is a classic Smooth who's been out of the water for a while. Her kicking technique and exhalation is still in good order but she's just overreaching a little and dropping her elbow a touch. This will harm her 'feel for the water'.

Professional triathlete Guy Crawford is a Smooth who needs a little tune-up with his catch technique. He's about to bend his elbow to catch the water but he needs to do this a little sooner – we should already start to see the elbow bend in this shot.

- A slight overglide with the wrist dropping on arm extension is another common flaw if the Smooth has been trying to emphasise the length of their stroke. With so much literature on the internet focusing on this aspect of swimming technique it's little wonder some Smooths are influenced by it and introduce a small glide into their stroke timing.
- Holding onto your breath is something that is taught to many sprinters, which by definition includes most Smooths! With a powerful sprint kick, the extra buoyancy in the chest does not cause the swimmer's legs to sink and effective breathing is not critical over sprint distances. However for distance freestyle it's very important to use a constant smooth exhalation whenever your face is in the water.
- Late breathing timing is a surprisingly common flaw seen in Smooths. This occurs where the rotation of the head to breathe is a little late, following after the rotation of the body when it should in fact be simultaneous. This reduces the time available to inhale and makes breathing feel quite hurried – work on fixing this and you'll notice a major improvement in your level of relaxation.

For the full Smooth stroke correction process see Appendix B.

KEY

2

Training

Specific fitness training for swimming

CHAPTER 24

The Importance of Fitness Training

The sport of triathlon has seen a huge boom in the last 10 to 15 years and with it a large influx of people with little or no swimming background taking up the sport for the first time. More recently, open water swimming events have experienced a similar boom allowing those enthusiastic swimmers who have previously been stuck within the confines of their local pool to appreciate the freedom of swimming in some amazing open water locations. Whilst the challenge of training for the three sports of triathlon might be unattainable for those with busy professional and family lives, training for open water swimming is much more achievable and equally rewarding.

At Swim Smooth we are passionate about open water swimming and are very excited about the growing number of open water events and challenges available for swimmers around the world.

Even if you don't view yourself as being a super-competitive person and are more interested in achievements and self-fulfilment than competitive placings, you still stand to gain a lot from learning how to train your fitness levels according to the race distance and type of event you have ahead. Balancing your stroke technique development with the right fitness work is essential.

Training consistently in the pool is one of the keys to improving your swimming.

The training methods we will recommend in this section will put a new lease of life into the idea of fitness training for distance swimmers and triathletes, and will help you discard some myths about what this type of training entails. We will show you how to integrate the stroke technique development work covered earlier (Key 1) and ensure that the work that you put into your fitness sessions pays dividends for your chosen event and general swimming proficiency.

PAUL: *You might be reading this and thinking 'I don't ever plan to do a competitive swimming event' and that's absolutely fine. However, you will still gain greater enjoyment and variety from your swimming by implementing some of what we are about to suggest. Equally though, I'd personally love to see you sign up for your first event and take a brave step forward towards your first pool or open water competition. Completing such an event is hugely satisfying and from my own experience I know that having a goal to work towards can be very motivating indeed. Getting out of bed at 'stupid-o'clock' to swim before work is much easier when you have something to focus on!*

My boyhood dream was always to swim the English Channel. As a child I was a competitive pool swimmer and this just seemed to be the event that all British pool swimmers would eventually gravitate towards. In 2006 I was surprised to see that my 'comedy hero' David Walliams from the British comedy show 'Little Britain' would be attempting the Channel. The level of interest in swimming within the UK that David's successful crossing raised has been nothing short of amazing, so much so that I often hear from people with no swimming background at all who have set swimming the Channel as their personal goal. Whilst tackling the Channel is still no mean feat, David's crossing has helped show people that they really can get out there and do it. For the sport of swimming this is just fantastic and in September 2011 not only did I get to achieve my lifelong dream of swimming the Channel, I also got to meet and swim with David Walliams on the second day of his epic eight-day swim down the River Thames for Sport Relief. Good things really can happen when you set your mind to it!

Our local race in Perth, Western Australia: the 19.7 km Rottnest Channel Swim is the world's biggest mass participation channel swim with over 3,000 participants. A fantastic event and well worth the long flight to Australia!

Balancing Your Training for Best Performance

When it comes to swim training, many swimmers and triathletes fall into one of two camps: those that train hard every session with little regard for their stroke efficiency and those who have been led to believe that swimming is entirely about technique work and that hard workouts should be avoided as they will ingrain bad stroke habits. However, too much focus on either pure technique work or hard fitness sessions without consideration for the other side of the equation is a recipe for underperforming.

Focusing on one area to the detriment of the other is the single biggest reason why swimmers and triathletes hit plateaus in their performance.

If you know how to balance out training and technique work within a weekly or monthly structure you will make the greatest improvements possible over time. Even then, you still need to take additional steps to adapt your pool stroke to the open water environment if this is where you will be racing, we will discuss this in detail later in Key 3. A plateau in your performance will occur when you have exhausted all avenues for improvement within that given area. If you only ever focus on one aspect of your swimming development, then chances are you are going to reach that plateau very quickly.

Paul all greased up and ready to tackle the English Channel, September 2011

As you will have noticed by now, the combination of these three elements of training, technique and open water adaptation form the 'Three Keys' to successful swimming covered in this book.

Swim Specific Fitness

If you are a triathlete, or are swimming alongside training in another sport, it is very important to appreciate that fitness is specific to the sport you are training in. In sports science this is a well proven fact [1, 2] and is known as the 'specificity principle'. Training in other sports – particularly those that involve different muscle groups such as cycling and running – will have very little benefit for your swimming. This is because an important part of your aerobic system is in the vein and capillary networks to specific muscles and in the cellular development within the muscles themselves. In other words, you need to train your swimming muscle groups in a way specific to the swimming. Far and away the best way to do this is by swim fitness training!

Emmy prepares to tackle a tough threshold session in the pool but it's all smiles here!

If you are new to swimming and have a high level of fitness in another sport then we are sure that you would have quickly and independently proven the specificity principle to be true! No matter how fit you are elsewhere, if you are new to the sport you will find it very hard at first. The good news is that after just a few weeks of introducing some training sets to your swimming you will take some good steps forward in swim specific fitness, which will make all of your swimming feel easier and so your time in the water much more enjoyable.

References

1. Millet, G.P., Candau, R.B., Barbier, B., Busso, T., Rouillon, J.D., Chatard, J.C. 2002. Modelling the transfers of training effects on performance in elite triathletes. *Int J Sports Med.* 23(1):55–63.

2. Gergley, T.J., McArdle, W.D., DeJesus, P., Toner, M.M., Jacobowitz, S., Spina, R.J. 1984. Specificity of arm training on aerobic power during swimming and running. *Med Sci Sports Exerc.* 16(4):349–54.

CHAPTER 25 Balancing the Different Types of Fitness Training

Structuring a Single Training Session

At Swim Smooth we like to use a very simple formula for constructing any training session. Following this structure helps you to break down a session and attain the right split between the warm-up, drills, heart rate build sets, main sets and cool-downs.

In this example we will use a total distance of 3.0 km for the session as an indicator for how much of each component you should look to include. You might normally only cover half this distance in your own training sessions, or you might cover more, in any case use this as a starting guide of what to include and when:

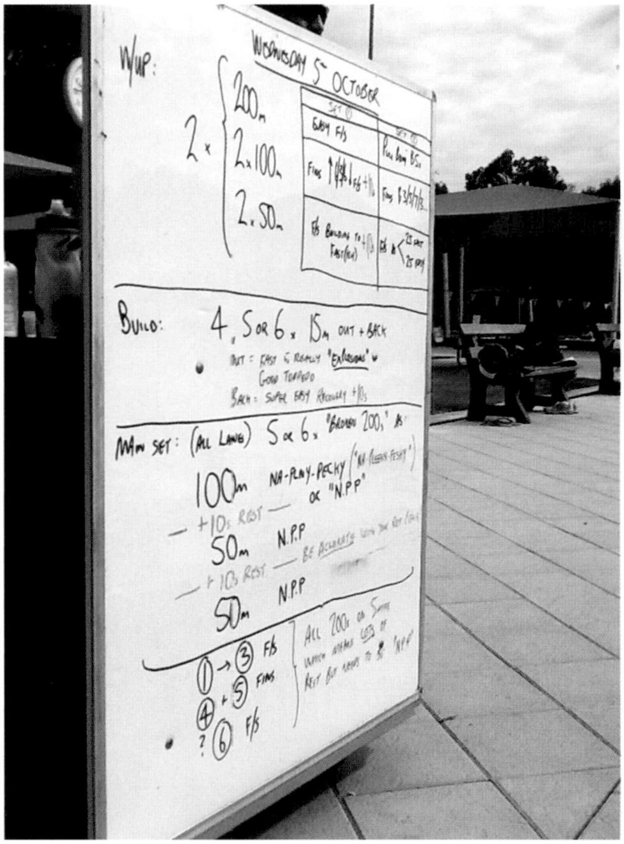

The session board for a Swim Smooth squad session at Claremont pool. Note the session is split here into warm-up, build and main set. The cool-down comes later.

1. **Warm-up totalling 400 m to 1000 m** – this should include the majority of your focused drills and stroke correction and be progressive in terms of intensity, building from an easy effort up to some mid-paced swimming.
2. **Build set totalling 200 m to 500 m** – these shorter sets are designed to elevate the heart rate and prepare you for a more active main set.
3. **Main set totalling 1200 m to 2000 m** – this set can focus on different areas, including technique and drills, shorter endurance

work, speed sets, threshold development or open water skills. We will look at these more closely in this chapter.

4. **Cool-down totalling 100 m to 400 m** – this is an important component of any session and should be included as a way of reducing the heart rate, flushing the body of lactate build up and to generally loosen off and feel good in your stroke.

Using this simple structure is an easy way to create some wonderfully engaging training sessions. To help get you started with this, in Appendix C we have listed six variations of each component which are loosely aimed at each of the six Swim Types. Use them to construct your own training sessions and so perfectly balance your technique, fitness and open water skills work. You can follow any of the sets for any other Swim Type, they will all be useful for your swimming.

PAUL: *Given the variety of the five types of main sets listed (including six open water skills sessions and six pure technique sets), our Swim Smooth boffins have calculated that by mixing and matching the sets you can create up to 5,100 unique training sessions to follow. Wow – that'll keep you going for a while!*

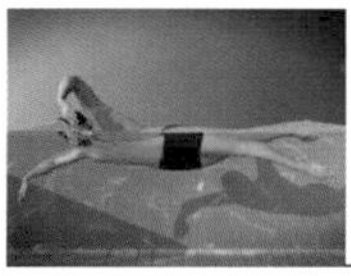

How Will the Different Types of Set Improve My Swimming?

We can break down the different types of main set as follows:

1. Speed or sprint work.
2. Endurance training or continuous swimming.
3. Threshold or 'Sustainable Speed' sessions.

Let's take a look at each of these training methods in that order. It's actually the order in which many Masters swimmers and triathletes prioritise their sessions, focusing a lot of training time on speed sessions, some time on endurance sets and relatively little time on sustained speed sessions. In Chapter 26 we will look at a different way to combine these sessions for best training effect as a distance swimmer has a very different set of priorities. By combining sessions in a different way you will soon be making some big strides forward in your swimming fitness.

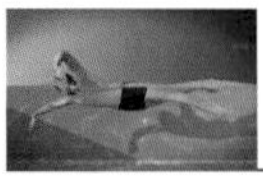

Session Type 1: Pure Speed or Sprint Work

For those of you who train with one of the many Masters swimming groups around the world, a large component of the training mix will be sprint work. This involves efforts at near maximum pace over short distances of 10 m to 200 m with large amounts of recovery between each interval. For many swimmers, this type of training is believed to be the best way of getting faster because they are swimming at very high speed. Certainly if you will be racing over sprint distances (25 m to 200 m) such sets should form a good portion of your training time as they are specific to your event. However, if your focus is on distances over 400 m in the pool, or on triathlon and open water swimming, too much training at this intensity can actually limit your endurance ability as we will see later on in this chapter.

Sprint training is essential if you plan to race in events of less than 200 m. If not then your valuable training time might be best spent with sub-maximal threshold sessions and aerobic endurance work.

Sprint sessions offer the swimmer significant rest periods between each interval to allow higher intensities to be held when swimming. The ratio of work to rest might be anywhere from 3:1 to 1:1 (or more). An example sprint set is:

8 × 50 m aiming for 40 seconds per interval with 20 to 30 seconds rest between each 50 m

In Appendix C you will find six specific sprint sessions that you can incorporate into your programme if you are seeking to improve your outright speed for shorter events below 400 m. If you are competing over longer distances and swimming five or more times per week, then you also probably have some scope to add this type of training to your weekly programme so long as it does not replace more essential threshold-based training.

Session Type 2: Endurance Sessions

In its simplest form an endurance session might be a long continuous swim at a steady pace, designed to build up your ability to swim for a prolonged period of time without stopping. It is very common to see swimmers who have only a very limited time in which to train (e.g. lunch breaks) jump into the water and simply swim continuously for the entire time they have available. This type of training has its merits, however if every session that you complete is swum continuously like this you could be missing out on developing your stroke technique and also run the risk of stagnating from swimming everything at the same steady pace.

The mental challenge of longer swims can be significant as you are stuck in your personal 'bubble' with very little outside interaction. Here James has used the acronym JKS (Just Keep Swimming!) to keep him motivated during the 20 km Rottnest Channel Swim. This phrase went on to become a mantra of our marathon swimming squad!

For those swimmers and triathletes attempting longer distance events (e.g. open water events longer than 2.5 km and triathletes training for a full Ironman), long continuous swims are a nice way of building your confidence that you can cover your target race distance. Later in Chapter 27 we will show you how to calculate the pace to hold for these swims so that you develop your base endurance whilst maintaining good form and technique. A classic mistake swimmers make with long continuous swims is to start too fast and then fade towards the end.

Breaking down these endurance swims into a series of longer intervals with a short rest in-between will help you maintain focus and motivation and also give you a chance to take on board fluid and nutrition for swims over 45 minutes in length. Fuelling correctly in longer sessions is critical to your successful completion of these sessions and how quickly you recover afterwards. We will cover some specific fuelling strategies for longer swims in Chapter 32.

An example of a simple endurance set might be 6 × 400 m at 75% effort with 30 seconds rest between each interval. Instead of thinking of this as 75% effort, you could swim this as 'threshold pace plus eight seconds per 100 m'. We will look at this form of pace calculation later in Chapter 27.

In Appendix C you will find six specific endurance sessions ranging in distance from 2.5 km to 6 km. These are designed to be completed without using one of the additional warm-up and build set suggestions as the warm-up is included within the main body of these sessions and encourages you to start off at a conservative pace as though you were starting a longer distance race. We would advise 10–15 minutes of light mobilisation and stretching work as per Chapter 29 before you start these sessions.

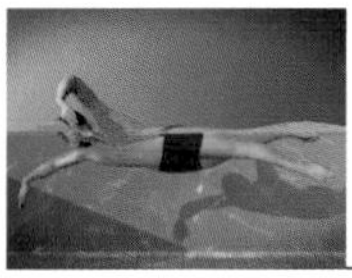

Session Type 3: Threshold or Sustainable Speed Sessions

At the heart of any good swim training programme is some dedicated work at threshold speed, often termed 'race pace' if your race distance is around 1500 m. Threshold speed is a pace that is tough enough to develop your aerobic capacity but not so strong that significant recovery is required between intervals. Generally speaking, recovery is faster from these sessions than from sets performed at a higher intensity. Developing your ability to swim well at this intensity is a key determinant of how well you will perform in races of 400 m and longer. As we shall see shortly in Chapter 27, we refer to this form of training as 'CSS' – short for Critical Swim Speed.

PAUL: *The ironic thing about this type of training is that as soon as the phrase 'race pace' is mentioned by a coach, swimmers act like a red rag to a bull, setting off way faster than they can sustain for the set. Don't make this mistake yourself, if you do you will soon blow-up and slow down – swimming most of the set at a slower pace than you otherwise could maintain if you had set off at the right pace. If this happens you have greatly harmed the training effect of the session and you will not develop your aerobic system to anywhere like the same extent as with a well-paced set. Arnies (from our Swim Type system, see Chapter 18) are particularly prone to doing this. I know from my own experience during my early days as a junior triathlete that the mention of the words 'race pace' or 'time trial' induces a sense of wild panic. If you try to remain calm in these situations and pace out such a swim perfectly, you might swim a PB straight away.*

Swimmers with very poor pacing always report that their swimming feels easy and smooth in the first couple of hundred meters but then their stroke quickly 'falls apart'. They might blame a lack of fitness, endurance or the inability to hold good form, and whilst this might partly be the case, nine times out of ten it is simply a pacing issue. Repetitively training like this is not effective at all and will certainly impede your long-term development. In fact inaccurate pace judgement is one of the main reasons swimmers and triathletes fail to reach their potential in the water.

Accurate identification of your own threshold (CSS) pace is very important and tuning into the feeling of this pace at the start, middle and end of a training session will allow you to better gauge your efforts. This important skill is what we call 'innate pace judgement' and developing yours will pay dividends during races when everyone around you starts too fast and then fades badly.

When performing a threshold set, the focus should be on swimming longer intervals at a challenging but sustainable pace with much shorter recovery periods between each interval rather than pure speed work. Many swimmers end up in a grey area between these two types of sessions, not swimming quite fast enough for it to be a speed set but taking too much rest between each interval for it to be a true threshold set.

ADAM: *A coach we work closely with in Montréal, Canada (Charles Gaston-Couturier) describes the challenge of a good training set using something he calls the 'Sweet Uncertainty Principle' based on work done by Brunelle in 1988 [1]. A good training set challenges you just enough so that you are a little unsure of whether you can complete the set hitting your goal times. If the set is clearly too easy you would lack stimulation and if the set is clearly too hard to complete this would be very negative and off-putting. Somewhere in between is the sweet spot of the perfect training set: you are uncertain of whether you can meet the goal times and motivated by the challenge of doing so.*

Swimmers in Perth prepare for their favourite 'Fresh and Fruity' threshold session with Coach Fiona Ford leading the way.

The ratio of work to rest should be 4:1 to 15:1 or shorter, e.g. 8 × 200 m aiming for 3'15" with 15 to 20 seconds rest between each 200 m. With such short recoveries it is essential to pace yourself through the set to be assured of completing the session whilst hitting the target times.

When you conduct training around this intensity you will be able to maintain much better form and technique than if you go off too fast and end up fighting the water. Many swimmers avoid training at higher intensities for fear of ingraining bad stroke habits but your stroke will only deteriorate if you pace things poorly and blow-up. At threshold pace it is perfectly possible to sustain great technique and you should not be avoiding this 'sustained speed' training, it is absolutely essential for your improvement.

In Appendix C you will find six specific threshold sessions that you can target for the main set of your harder training sessions. To perform these properly you will need to know your threshold or CSS pace; we will show you how to test for this in Chapter 27.

Reference

1. Brunelle, J., Drouin, D., Godbout, P., and Tousignant, M. 1988. La supervision de l'intervention en activité physique. Montreal: Gäétan Morin Editeur.

CHAPTER 26

A Simple Skeleton Structure for Your Swimming Month

Most triathletes are swimming between two and four sessions per week. As a Masters swimmer or as a pure recreational swimmer, you might have time in your weekly routine to swim more frequently. In any case, developing a good skeleton structure that you can adhere to on a weekly and monthly basis will ensure that you are maximising your time in the pool for your available training time.

Ideally, to see true improvements in your swimming you should aim to swim three or more times per week. We often see in our Swim Smooth Perth squads that those who go from swimming two times per week to three times per week really make some good gains in their swimming, often within just six to eight weeks of making this change to their programme.

Frequency will always trump volume, for example three 30-minute sessions per week will be more beneficial than one 90-minute session. Of course, you can only train in the time you have available and as long as you are realistic about what can be achieved if you only swim once or twice per week, then you will take away some of the frustration of expecting large gains for relatively little input.

Equally though, increasing your frequency from swimming six times per week to seven times per week might not result in any significant increase in performance at all and may risk lethargy, over-training and demotivation. There is nothing more important than turning up at training motivated about the session ahead and if you swim too often you risk losing this 'mojo'. If you're swimming five times per week or more and find that you are constantly dreading your swimming sessions and have no motivation for them, try dropping back by one session per week and see if you can regain your spark. Elite swimmers and triathletes are particularly susceptible to over-training, and making a marginal cut in training volume has been the key for many of them in making some big steps forward in their performance.

Paul and Martin plan the next phase of training for the Perth Swim Smooth squad.

More is not always better – effective training is about striking the right balance given everything you are trying to juggle in your training, work, family and social lives.

PAUL: *As a triathlete, coach and graduate of sports science, over the years I have invested a significant amount of my research and personal training time into devising the ideal training programme that has exactly the right training hours and precise training intensities. Ultimately this was a fruitless exercise as I found time and time again that what works for one athlete is simply not effective for another and that life events quickly ruin the prescribed training progression, often within just a few weeks of starting the programme.*

Instead, a much more pragmatic approach works best where you outline a basic skeleton structure which you work from loosely day to day, week to week and month to month. The structure gives you the right mix of sessions between technique development, steady endurance training, threshold sets and pure speed work which you can repeat over and over to give you the consistency you need. The pace of the sessions themselves is adjusted based on your performances as you go along, adapting to your current fitness levels to keep pushing you forwards.

Using such a skeleton structure when training is a very elegant and pragmatic approach and I highly recommend you use one yourself. In a moment we will look at some suggested structures for you to follow, depending on your ability level and the training time available.

In terms of scheduling additional recovery time into your plan I recommend you very much listen to your body here, especially if you are only training two or three times per week. In this situation it is unlikely that you are training enough to warrant additional recovery and so if you feel good, carry on training as normal. If you feel a little flat after a hard block of training then take an easy session or some additional rest.

My best results have always come from programmes that were simple, fun and motivating and that were laid out in such a way that I could consistently follow them week to week rather than the super whizz-bang scientifically prepared periodised programmes I've also tried to follow. Of course you have to have purpose and meaning behind what you do but if you are unable to adhere to a really sophisticated programme then you're not going to get the most out of it. At the end of the day life throws curve-balls at all of us when we least expect it and if you can't be flexible in your programme for risk of throwing that period of training out of the window entirely, then you're going to find yourself getting very frustrated very quickly.

Interestingly enough, this skeleton-structure approach was inspired by my own long-term coach and former British Triathlon Head Coach, Chris Jones. With all the great triathletes on the British World Class Triathlon Programme, we would all aim to keep things as simple and consistent as possible in our training routine. The training structure of elite athletes is nowhere near as technical as you might believe.

Recommended Skeleton Structures

Table 26.3 shows our recommended training structures, which are to be followed based upon how many times per week you are swimming. As you can see, we include a mix of all three of the training keys – technique, training and open water skills. You can follow these structures year round, performing your open water skills work in the pool when open water is too cold in the winter. As we will discuss in Key 3: Open Water Adaptation, developing and maintaining your open water skills is absolutely critical to swimming at your best in open water.

TABLE 26.3 Keep your training plan simple using one of these weekly skeleton structures. For specific sessions to follow, see Appendix C.

Swim Smooth's Suggested Weekly Training Structure Based on Frequency of Swimming								
Weekly Frequency	Week Number	Monday	Tuesday	Wednesday	Thursday	Friday	Saturday	Sunday
2 times / week	1		Technique			Threshold / CSS		
	2		OW Skills			Endurance		
	3		Technique			Threshold / CSS		
	4		OW Skills			Threshold / CSS		
3 times / week	1		Technique		Threshold / CSS		OW Skills	
	2		Technique		Threshold / CSS		Endurance	
	3		Technique		Threshold / CSS		OW Skills	
	4		Endurance		Speed		Technique	
4 times / week	1	Technique		Endurance		Threshold / CSS	OW Skills	
	2	Technique		Endurance		Threshold / CSS	OW Skills	
	3	Technique		Endurance		Threshold / CSS	OW Skills	
	4	Technique		Endurance		Speed	Technique	
5 times / week	1	Technique	Endurance		Threshold / CSS	Speed	OW Skills	
	2	Technique	Threshold / CSS		Threshold / CSS	Endurance	OW Skills	
	3	Technique	Endurance		Threshold / CSS	Technique	OW Skills	
	4	Threshold / CSS	Technique		Speed or REST	Technique	OW Skills	
6 times / week	1	Technique	Threshold / CSS	Endurance	Technique	Threshold / CSS	OW Skills	
	2	Speed	Endurance	Threshold / CSS	Technique	Endurance or LCS	OW Skills	
	3	Technique	Threshold / CSS	Endurance	Technique	Threshold / CSS	OW Skills or LCS	
	4	Speed or REST	Endurance	Technique	Threshold / CSS	Technique	OW Skills	
7 times / week	1	Technique	Threshold / CSS	Endurance	Technique	Threshold / CSS	OW Skills	Endurance or LCS
	2	Speed	Endurance	Threshold / CSS	Technique	Endurance or LCS	OW Skills	Threshold / CSS
	3	Technique	Threshold / CSS	Endurance	Technique	Threshold / CSS	OW Skills	Endurance or LCS
	4	Speed	Endurance	Technique	Threshold / CSS	Technique or REST	OW Skills	Technique

LCS = Long Continuous Swim. CSS = Critical Swim Speed OW Skills = Open water skills (pool or open water based on season)

Recommendation is to swim at least 3 times per week to see improvements. Only ramp up distances by <10% per week, having an easier recovery/adaptation week every 4th week. This easier week is less important if you're swimming <4 times per week.

Choose a skeleton structure and then construct your own training sessions from the session components listed in Appendix C to add variety and new ideas to your programme. You may of course be restricted by your local pool's lane swimming availability as to which days you can actually swim but if you aim to follow a structure similar to that outlined in Table 26.3 you will be on the right track.

ADAM: *In Table 26.4 you can see Paul's skeleton structure for his English Channel training in the six months building up to his crossing in 2011. Needless to say there's a lot of km's to be swum when preparing for a 7 to 17+ hour marathon swim such as this. Don't be intimidated by the distances he swam, or the paces he sustained, instead notice the components of training, technique and open water skills in the week and how he simply looked to repeat this week time and time again to prepare perfectly for the swim.*

TABLE 26.4 Paul Newsome's English Channel skeleton training structure. A balanced programme appropriate to your race distance and the training time available will make all the difference to your success in the water.

Day	Session Detail
Monday	Very easy 2–3 km swim including a range of drills to ensure good injury management **OR** Rest Day
Tuesday	Moderate 6–7 km pool swim including drills and a solid 4–6 km main set of 10 to 15 × 400 m at 1'24" per 100 m pace with 21 seconds rest between each 400 m (guided by my Wetronome).
Wednesday	Tough 9 km pool set swam on a 43 to 45 second per 50 m cycle, e.g. 20 × 50 m, 10 × 100 m, 5 × 200 m, 2 × 500 m, 1 × 1000 m, 2 × 500 m, 5 × 200 m, 10 × 100 m, 20 × 50 m. The cycle time includes any rest, so the faster you swim the more rest you get. I would typically average 1'18" per 100 m for these sets.
Thursday	Moderate 10 km cold (15°C/59°F) open water swim at an average pace of ~1'24" per 100 m including drink stops every 2 km for 15–20 seconds.
Friday	Steady 4–5 km pool swim focusing on drills and technique work.
Saturday	Hard 8 to 12 km cold (15°C/59°F) open water swim in rough water, aiming to hold close to 1'20" per 100 m.
Sunday	Goal session: 14 to 25 km cold (15°C/59°F) open water swim with paddler to practise, food and drink stops every 2 km. Aim to hold 1'24" per 100 m.

CHAPTER 27

Finding Your Critical Swim Speed

Becoming a Diesel Engine!

If you have a sprint background in the pool, or alternatively if you come from a team sport background such as rugby or football, you will probably have a natural disposition towards sprinting. Instead of sprinting powerfully over a short distance, a good distance swimmer has a very different physiology as they need to maintain a slower pace for a long time. However, the different energy systems are highly trainable and with the right training you will gradually transition towards the distance swimmer you need to be for open water races and triathlon.

Rory proudly wears his Swim Smooth Rottnest Channel Swim shirt. The shirt shows the breakdown of a swimming diesel engine!

At Swim Smooth we often use the analogy that sprinters are petrol (gasoline) engines and distance swimmers are diesel engines. The further your target event is the less fast-twitch speed matters and the sustained output of a diesel engine becomes more important. We are not talking about swimming at an easy pace here but a strong and sustained pace as you might in a bike time trial or distance running event.

For the rest of this section of the book we are going to look at something called CSS swimming. This is a form of training that focuses on developing you as a distance swimmer, turning you from that petrol engine into a swimmer who can sustain their speed over long durations. By following this form of training you may lose some of your ability to sprint but your sustained speed will be much higher. Figure 27.17 shows a hypothetical example of this transition from petrol to diesel engine.

To put some real numbers on this, take a look at Table 27.5 showing Paul's race speed at different distances before and during his English Channel preparation. Before training for the Channel Paul's training contained a mix of sprint work and CSS sets, during the training he switched almost exclusively to CSS training and endurance training. We can see that although he became slower over 50m, 100m, and 200m, by 400m he is swimming at the same pace and at longer distances significantly quicker. When you have to swim the equivalent of 100 × 400m to get across from Dover to France, sprint ability is not something you need too much of!

If you are a triathlete, you probably have a good idea already of what your running pace should be for a 10km event or how hard you could push on the bike for a 40km time trial. These paces correspond closely to something called your Lactate Threshold (or just threshold for short). This is the point at which lactate starts to gather in your blood stream, which happens when you start to become anaerobic. If you go faster than this pace you are on borrowed time and soon feel 'the burn' in your muscles which will force you to slow back down again. CSS is this point in your swimming, go faster than it and

PAUL: *I studied Sports and Exercise Science at the University of Bath and was also fortunate enough to be selected as an athlete for the British Triathlon World Class Performance Programme. On this elite programme we were regularly tested in the laboratory to examine our exact level of fitness and to give us precise training levels at which to train. This approach was highly scientific and I loved being part of it. Knowing how you should train and seeing the improvements as a result of this testing was very motivating indeed.*

However, whilst very useful, such testing simply isn't available to most age-group athletes around the world. The test procedures are lengthy, involve using a lot of expensive laboratory equipment and by taking lots of blood samples to monitor blood lactate they are quite invasive too. Fortunately there is an alternative way of assessing your swimming fitness that has all of the advantages of laboratory testing but with none of those downsides. The system is called Critical Swim Speed or CSS for short – here at Swim Smooth we are big fans of CSS training!

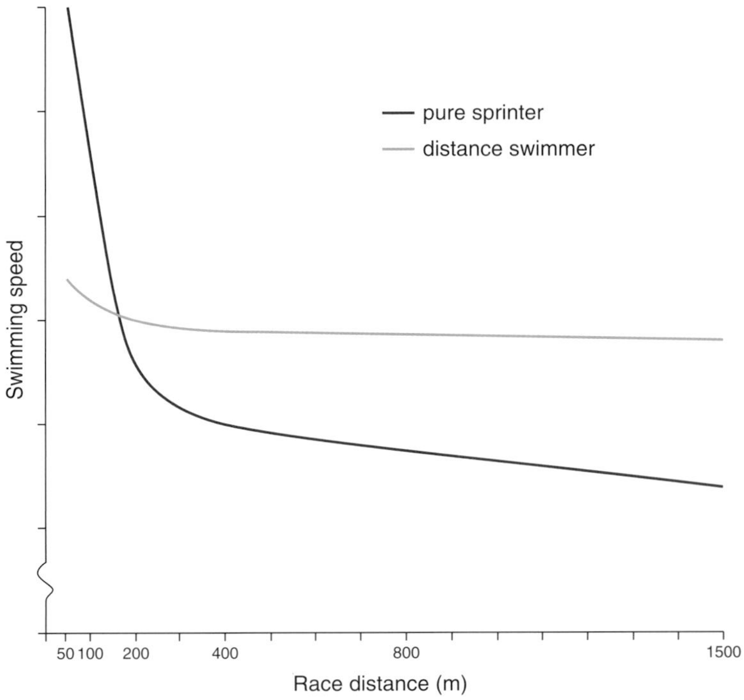

FIGURE 27.17 The speed profiles of two very different swimmers. The sprinter wins over very short distances, the distance swimmer over longer distances.

TABLE 27.5 Paul Newsome's race pace over different distances before and during his English Channel preparation.

Distance	Before English Channel Training	During English Channel Training
50 m	27.2"	29.5"
100 m	58.9"	62.1"
200 m	2'08"	2'10"
400 m	4'30"	4'30"
1000 m	12'00"	11'55"
1500 m	18'30"	18'08"
5 km	68 minutes	65 minutes
10 km	2 h36 m	2 h16 m
20 km	5 h24 m	4 h41 m

you will have to slow down, but swim at CSS and you will be able to swim for 800 m, 1500 m or even 3000 m if you are very well trained.

Threshold is an extremely important point in all endurance sports because it is fundamental to your physiology – if you can improve your fitness so that your threshold (and so CSS) is at a faster speed then you will race quicker in any distance event – even in ultra-distance events such as Ironman and marathon swimming. Other fitness factors such as your outright strength or your ability to sprint play an extremely minor part in distance races in comparison.

ADAM: *If you remember back to the 11-year-old girl story in the introduction to this book, you will recall how quickly she could swim despite having very low levels of outright strength. Here we have one of the main reasons to explain that – she has excellent aerobic fitness from training very consistently in her swim club. i.e. her CSS pace is high. Always remember that distance swimming performances are not about strength but aerobic fitness – it's about sustaining a good pace for a long time, not sprinting very quickly over a short distance. You need to develop this aerobic fitness in your swimming muscle groups to become a great distance swimmer and CSS training should play a major role in doing that.*

Improving your CSS is the key to improving your performance in any distance freestyle event. Training at this pace doesn't have to be a chore – it's actually quite good fun!

PAUL: *If you have used a power meter on a bike and read Coggan and Allen's excellent book 'Training with Power' (2006) you will be familiar with using the concept of Functional Threshold Power (FTP) to measure your threshold on the bike in Watts. CSS is the exact same concept but for swimming. In the controlled environment of a swimming pool we don't need something as fancy as a power meter to measure threshold, it can be defined as a pace per 100 m. As we shall see, rather than performing a 20-minute or 60-minute time trial to find FTP we perform two shorter swims in the pool and perform a calculation to find CSS pace.*

We recommend performing the CSS test approximately every four weeks to monitor fitness improvements. Once you know your CSS speed (say it is 1:40/100 m) you can then calculate your ideal training pace for endurance work (1:48/100 m) and for sprint training (1:35/100 m). Therefore as your fitness and CSS improves, your whole training plan adapts to keep pushing your fitness forwards. Combining CSS training with an outline skeleton structure (see Chapter 26) provides you with the perfect training routine that has the right mix of training levels, is flexible enough to handle life events and adapts to your fitness levels to keep pushing you forwards. In other words perfect training!

Next we will take a look at the test you can use to find your current CSS pace and go on to show you some training sets you can use to improve that pace over time and so become a faster distance swimmer.

The CSS Test

Follow this procedure to conduct a CSS test:

1. Swim an easy warm-up of between 600 m and 1000 m, including a variety of technique drills and a few short efforts to lift your heart rate.
2. Perform a 400 m time trial from a push (not a dive), count your laps right and accurately time it!
3. Recover for 10–15 minutes, including some easy laps of swimming to clear waste products from your muscles.
4. Perform a 200 m time trial from a push, again with accurate timing.
5. Easy cool-down.

ADAM: *Remember the anxiety you may feel at the mere mention of the words 'time trial'! Try to relax during the two swims and see what happens without any preconceptions or pressure. Whatever your times just see them as a stake in the ground at that point in time, the whole idea is that you improve them from here.*

Some important notes:

- Remember the test is about your <u>current fitness levels</u> so do not feel tempted to skip the test and put your all-time 200 m and 400 m personal bests into the calculation, unless you have just swum them!

- Your efforts need to be a true and accurate reflection of what you can currently do for that distance in order to produce a valid CSS figure. Ideally have someone take your splits every 50 m to check your pacing and try to swim each 50 m within a second of the others. Remember that a well-paced effort will feel quite steady at first but build in perceived intensity as it goes on: steady – tempo – hard – very hard.
- Carefully check that your results make sense, for instance you should have held a faster pace over 200 m than you did over 400 m, is that the case?

To determine what your CSS pace is in time per 100 m from your results the easiest way is to use the simple calculator at: www.swimsmooth.com/css. Or, if you would like to run the calculation yourself you can calculate your CSS pace as:

$$\text{CSS (m/sec)} = (400 - 200) / (T400 - T200)$$

Where T400 and T200 are your 400 m and 200 m times in seconds. Then convert your speed from m/sec into time per 100 m:

$$\text{CSS (sec/100m)} = 100 / \text{CSS (m/sec)}$$

SPORTS SCIENCE REFERENCES: *The method for determining CSS by using a simple non-invasive test, without expensive equipment, was put forward by Wakayoshi [1,2]. This test was simplified in 1993 by Ginn [3] to using just two test swims of 400 m and 50 m at maximum pace to evaluate a swimmer's aerobic capacity and identify the anaerobic and aerobic components of their fitness. It has been further refined by MacLaren and Coulson [4] who demonstrated that the best distances to choose for a CSS test set are 400 m and 200 m. These are the time trial distances that we now use within Swim Smooth.*

Your resultant CSS pace might at first glance appear a little easy for those of you with experience of interval training but remember that CSS is about a hard 1500 m pace. Certainly you could swim quicker than CSS in an intervals session with lots of recovery but CSS sets should be performed with short recoveries so that the training effects are focused on the energy systems used in distance swimming, not sprinting.

Re-test your CSS pace approximately every four weeks to make sure that you are setting your training intensities properly and thus getting the best out of your training time. The ultimate goal is for your CSS pace to increase, if it does you are pretty much guaranteed to be swimming quicker in your races. This is even the case if you are racing in ultra-distance events that take place well below lactate threshold pace, this is because the same energy systems are used at these slower paces too and from their enlarged capacity for work you will be able to sustain a faster pace for longer.

Improving Your CSS

The key to improving CSS is to perform sets with short recoveries with a strong focus on pacing them correctly. When you swim at your CSS pace the feeling is one of being 'uncomfortably comfortable' – it is hard work but you can sustain your technique and speed throughout a training set. It is very important that you do not start these sets too fast and then blow-up!

Here are four example CSS sets:

1. 20 × 100 m with 15 s recovery between each.
2. 10 × 200 m with 20 s recovery between each.
3. 5 × 400 m with 30 s recovery between each.
4. 3 × 600 m with 45 s recovery between each.

PAUL: *During a CSS set, I often ask our swimmers what the pace feels like to them on a scale of 1 to 10 (where 10 is impossibly hard) – we are looking for scores of 6 to 6½ in the first few hundred meters before rapidly building up to 7½ to 8 out of 10 for the majority of the set before peaking at 9+ by the end. Obviously the numbers themselves are quite subjective but the important point here is that you will begin to correlate how CSS pace feels as the set goes on. This will help you develop your innate pace judgement which is a critical skill for distance swimmers. Pacing out your races correctly through the start, middle and end phases will give you a huge advantage over your competition on race day.*

These total around 2000 m which is about right for fast swimmers with a CSS of around 1:10 to 1:25/100 m. As you will see in the training sessions in Appendix C, the length of the sessions become shorter for slower swimmers so do not be put off if these distances appear more than you would normally do in an entire session!

Or you can get a little more creative and really test your pacing abilities with something like our 'Goldilocks Set' swum straight through:

- 4 × 100 m with 15 s recovery.
- 1 × 200 m with 30 s recovery (Baby Bear!).
- 4 × 100 m with 15 s recovery.
- 1 × 300 m with 30 s recovery (Mama Bear!).
- 4 × 100 m with 15 s recovery.
- 1 × 400 m and finish (Papa Bear!).

In practice, CSS pace feels significantly steadier than a truly hard interval session but is maintainable for a much longer period of time if paced correctly. In the example of the Goldilocks set above it is easy to get carried away on the 100 m intervals thinking the pace is too easy but then find it impossible to hold the same times as you progress through the 200 m, 300 m and 400 m intervals. Aim to keep everything the same pace even if it feels too easy at first – this will really help you develop your pacing skills.

CSS VS. RACE PACE

As a rough gauge, you can calculate your race pace over various distances relative to your CSS pace :

- 400 m: CSS pace - 2–4 sec per 100 m.
- 1500 m/1900 m: CSS pace.
- 3.8 km/5 km: CSS pace + 2–4 sec per 100 m.
- 10 km: CSS pace + 6–10 sec per 100 m.
- 20 km: CSS pace + 10–20 sec per 100 m (factoring in feed stops of 20–30 sec every 25 minutes or so).
- English Channel (38 km): CSS pace + 20–30 sec per 100 m (factoring in feed stops of 20–30 sec every 25 minutes or so).

Of course you also need to train your endurance sufficiently to maintain these paces over the longer swims!

Don't I Need to Swim Faster than My CSS Pace to Improve it?

You will have noticed that CSS training sets are swum at current CSS pace in order to become faster. For many swimmers this seems counter-intuitive, going against the commonly held belief that the key to becoming faster is to *'train at a much faster pace and my body will get used to it'*. Unfortunately this logic is flawed because the body does not work like that. When you train significantly faster than threshold you end up splitting the training effect into your anaerobic system too – which you don't need to develop as a distance swimmer. You also give your body a much greater recovery task after the session, which means it has less energy left over to make the fitness adaptations you are looking for. The end result is that training significantly above CSS pace gives you less development of your threshold speed.

Coaches Martin and Gabby explain the importance of correct pacing prior to a CSS set.

The research by MacLaren and Coulson [4] backs this up, demonstrating that threshold-paced training significantly develops CSS but much harder paced anaerobic sprint training often results in a slowing of CSS pace. Still not convinced? Compare this form of training to weight training. Say you wanted to increase your maximum bench press. You can currently lift 50 kg and want to get to 60 kg. You can't go and lift 60 kg – you're not strong enough. But by doing sets at 45–50 kg your body adapts and improves. To stress a body system and prompt an adaptation you just need to approach your current limit or threshold.

Many Masters swim sessions do focus on short, sharp speed sets as their swimmers will be competing in pool-based sprint events. If you are a triathlete or longer distance pool or open water swimmer, you need to be wary of doing too many high intensity intervals at the expense of more steady-state CSS work. Unfortunately, many view these longer, harder sets as dull or even antisocial but when faced with limited training time you need to be assured that the work that you are doing is paying the biggest dividends. Once you get into the swing of CSS work you will find it challenging and be motivated as a result, especially when you see your performances improve. Gathering a few friends together to swim these sets always makes things more enjoyable and is highly recommended.

So, No More Sprint Training?

You can certainly still include some anaerobic work and short sprints in your training – they're good for your swimming technique in themselves: they give you a 'feel for the water' at higher speeds and they train your nervous system to recognise the higher forces associated with producing greater power output. Sprint races can also be a lot of fun between friends and should not be discounted because they are not specific to distance swimming.

What we are suggesting is that you shift your key training sets away from anaerobic sprint sessions to CSS work if you are focusing on events over 400 m. In practice this means slowing the pace a touch and shortening the recoveries – making the speed more sustained.

Pacing Your CSS Sets Correctly

Think of your CSS pace as a single reference point from which all your other training paces are calculated. In the training sets in Appendix C we use this principle, giving you a target pace for different sets in reference to your CSS pace. For example a simple endurance set for a swimmer with a CSS of 1:40/100 m is:

1000 m at CSS pace + 10s per 100 m, i.e. 1:50/100 m
800 m at CSS pace + 8s per 100 m, i.e. 1:48/100 m
600 m at CSS pace + 6s per 100 m, i.e. 1:46/100 m
400 m at CSS pace + 4s per 100 m, i.e. 1:44/100 m
200 m at CSS pace + 2s per 100 m, i.e. 1:42/100 m

PAUL: *Using one of these devices in this manner is quite an experience, it is like swimming against the red World Record line that follows swimmers up and down the pool at the Olympics. It has a nagging habit of catching you up if you set off too fast!*

You will have noticed by now that these paces are very specific and would make pacing them using a watch or pool clock quite difficult. The solution to that problem is to use a Wetronome or Tempo Trainer Pro, which are beepers that you place under your swimming cap. In lap-interval mode they can be set to beep at the exact pace that you want to be holding, for instance 1:40/100 m pace is 25 seconds per 25 m. So by setting the device to beep to you every 25 seconds you can pace your swim to be at the end of the 25 m lap (or half lap in a 50 m pool) when it beeps. This gives you an amazing control over your swim pacing and greatly simplifies the process, allowing you to switch off and concentrate on your swimming and holding good form – these beepers make the perfect virtual training partner for your CSS sessions.

Confusing CSS Test Results

From time to time you might get some unexpected results from the CSS calculation, especially if you are comparing results from different swimmers. The most common of these is where one swimmer has faster 200 m and 400 m time trial results than another but ends up with a slower CSS – which at first sight seems very strange. To understand this result we must remember that CSS pace is slower than both 200 m and 400 m pace and is much closer to 1500 m pace, take a look at Figure 27.18 to see the speed relationship for two such swimmers. Our faster swimmer is much quicker at 200 m but only slightly faster at 400 m, this drop off in pace between the two indicates the swimmer is faster at these speeds by virtue of a very strong anaerobic capacity, not because they have a higher CSS. In fact when we extrapolate the results out we see that this swimmer actually has a slower CSS and would be slower at 1500 m and beyond.

The Wetronome and Finis Tempo Trainer Pro - one of these beepers will make the perfect virtual training partner for you!

One problem to be aware of is if you have erroneously timed the two time trials and included a 400 m time that is a faster pace than the 200 m time – a clearly impossible result. The calculation will produce some very fast CSS figures in this situation!

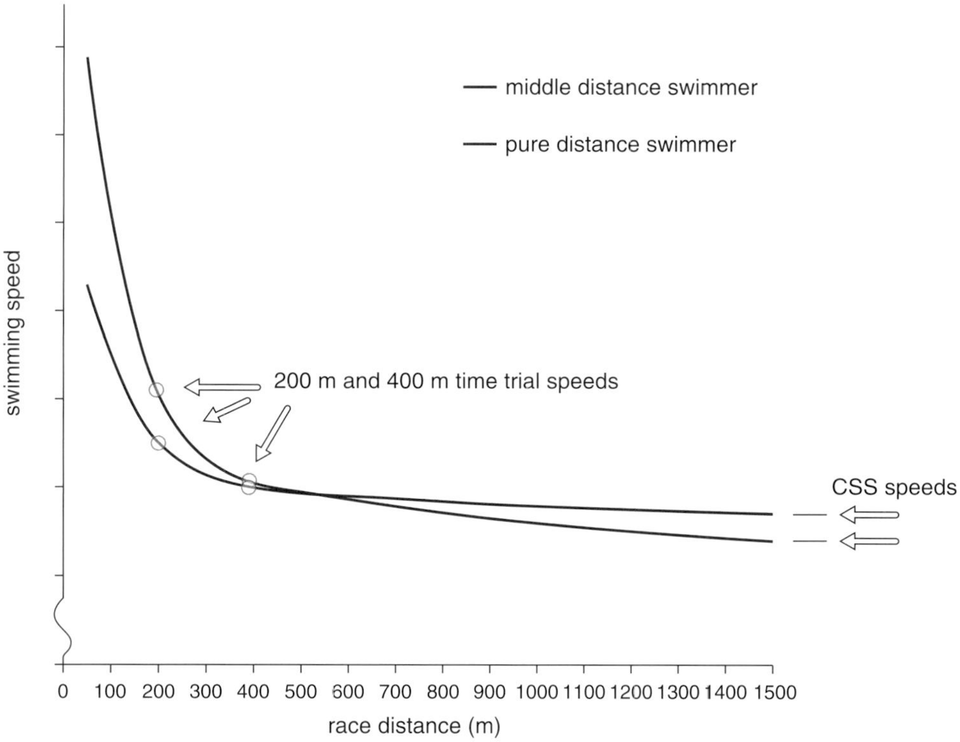

FIGURE 27.18 Middle distance and distance swimmers compared. The middle distance swimmer's 200 m and 400 m speeds are quicker but they have a slower CSS pace as the drop off between the 200 m and 400 m speeds is much steeper so this trend will continue. See our CSS calculator at www.swimsmooth.com/css.

References

1. Wakayoshi, K., Ikuta, K., Yoshida, T., Udo, M., Moritani, T., Mutoh, Y. and Miyashita, M. 1992a. Determination and validity of critical velocity as an index of swimming performance in the competitive swimmer. *Eur. J. Appl. Physiol.*, 64, 153–157.

2. Wakayoshi, K., Yoshida, T., Udo, M., Kasai, T., Moritani, T., Mutoh, Y. and Miyashita, M. 1992b. A simple method for determining critical speed as swimming fatigue threshold competitive swimming. *International Journal of Sports Medicine*, 13, 367–371.

3. Ginn, E. 1993. 'The application of the critical power test to swimming and swim training programmes', National Sports Research Centre.

4. MacLaren, D.P.M., Coulson, M. 1999. Critical swim speed can be used to determine changes in training status. In: *Biomechanics and Medicine and Swimming* VIII, edited by Keskinen, K.L., Komi, P.V., Hollander, A.P., Jyväskylä: Grummerus Printing, p. 227–32.

CHAPTER 28

Pace Awareness in the Pool and Open Water

PAUL: *Getting used to accurately pacing yourself over progressively longer intervals is absolutely essential. Besides the necessity to train at a pace appropriate to your race distance, the biggest skill you will develop is the ability to control and manage your effort over time. In the heat of a squad session, pacing can go straight out of the window as swimmers try frantically to keep up with the person in front of them. In our Perth Swim Smooth squad sessions, the leader of each lane is instructed to use a beeper under their swim cap set at the right target pace for the lane, all the other swimmers in the lane have to do is set off five seconds behind the swimmer in front and maintain that gap. This takes the pressure out of these types of sessions and encourages the lane to work together as a team, each happy to take their turn at the front with the beeper.*

Whilst it sounds simple to maintain a given swimming pace, in practice all sorts of things can affect how well you develop this skill, not least your competitive urge and the notion that a training session should feel hard from the very first lap for you to maximise the benefit from it. Instead of this, think of a CSS session as part training, part technique — the technique being your ability to pace things out well. The two go hand in hand: by sticking to your goal pace accurately you will maximise the training effect of your session.

ADAM: *Did you know that over 90% of all endurance world records for running (track) and swimming (pool) have been achieved through perfectly even pacing or with a 'negative split' – i.e. finishing faster than you started? Pace judgement is an absolutely essential skill for great distance swimming and with CSS training you will really start to develop yours.*

Watches such as the Finis SwimSense, the Garmin 310XT (and the newer 910XT) and the Swimovate Pro can help you monitor your pacing consistency. You will need a GPS device such as the Garmin to monitor pace in open water. In the future we expect this technology to keep evolving becoming ever more accurate and cheaper too.

Developing Pace Awareness in the Open Water

In the pool you can easily monitor your swimming pace and your strokes per length to assess your consistency but in open water neither of these variables is easily measured. Elite open water swimmers do monitor one metric though to ensure some consistency and that is stroke rate – how many strokes they take per minute. Normally this information is fed to the swimmer from a coach on a support boat and in general the target is to avoid stroke rate dropping by more than 10% over the course of a race.

Every swimmer has their own unique stroke rate that they can sustain. As an extreme example of how consistent an elite swimmer can be, Shelley Taylor-Smith (seven-time World Marathon Swimming Champion) held 88 SPM (strokes per minute) for a distance of 70 km from Sydney to Wollongong (Australia) only varying by ±5% over this epic 12-hour challenge. Amazing!

Probably the biggest single difference between an amateur and a professional endurance athlete is their ability to feel exactly what level of perceived exertion they are holding for a set distance. Every single session they do, elite swimmers are tuning themselves into what it feels like to hold a certain pace over a specific distance.

ADAM: *Grant Hackett is reputed to have been able to hold multiple 100 m intervals in the pool all within 0.4 seconds of each other without using a pace clock – an amazing feat when you consider that most amateur swimmers will vary by 2 to 12 seconds over a similar set with the assistance of a pace clock! With good training preparation you too can tap into this deeper understanding of what perceived exertion and pace you can truly maintain over a given distance. You won't always get this right but when you do get it wrong you should try to learn as much as possible so that you can improve your pacing ability in the future.*

It is very difficult to accurately judge what pace you can hold for an open water event given all the external factors that are out of your control such as waves, chop and currents. Sometimes giving yourself a very strict target pace can be psychologically detrimental, especially if you are dropping off this pace for reasons out of your control. By getting to know your body better and knowing exactly what level of fitness you have in the pool at any point in time, you can improve your ability to judge the right pace whatever the external influences. The key to good pacing is the pace you set in the first 20% of your race when you are fresh, this will ultimately determine how successful you are in that event. The more refined and developed your innate pace judgement, the more accurate you will be at pacing this first section of the race.

PAUL: *In my training for my English Channel swim in September 2011 I used a Garmin 310XT GPS device under my swim cap in all my open water sessions so that I could assess my ability to hold a straight line in the open water and to see how far and fast I'd actually swum. Whilst I couldn't see this data as I was swimming, I did use the Garmin to beep at me every 500 m which kept me focused on just the next seven minutes of swimming rather than thinking about the very long training session as a whole. When the Garmin was downloaded, I could clearly see how well I'd been pacing myself and whether or not I needed to make any changes to my pacing for future sessions. It was a brilliant tool to use and one which I can highly recommend!*

Summary

Overall

Time:	02:20:37
Distance:	10.01 km
Elevation Gain:	220 m
Calories:	558 C

Timing Pace Speed

Time:	02:20:37
Moving Time:	02:11:24
Elapsed Time:	02:20:37
Avg Pace:	14:03 min/km
Avg Moving Pace:	13:07 min/km
Best Pace:	04:40 min/km

Elevation

Elevation Gain:	220 m
Elevation Loss:	228 m
Min Elevation:	-13 m
Max Elevation:	11 m

Laps 21 View Splits

Split	Time	Distance	Avg Pace
1	00:06:52	0.50	13:45
2	00:07:00	0.50	14:01
3	00:06:49	0.50	13:38
4	00:06:55	0.50	13:51
5	00:07:12	0.50	14:24
6	00:07:20	0.50	14:41
7	00:06:46	0.50	13:32
8	00:06:46	0.50	13:32
9	00:07:52	0.50	15:44
10	00:06:58	0.50	13:56
11	00:06:48	0.50	13:38
12	00:06:26	0.50	12:53
13	00:07:10	0.50	14:20
14	00:07:03	0.50	14:06
15	00:06:55	0.50	13:51
16	00:06:45	0.50	13:31
17	00:07:23	0.50	14:47
18	00:07:01	0.50	14:03
19	00:07:06	0.50	14:13
20	00:07:07	0.50	14:15
21	00:00:15	0.01	20:00
Summary	**02:20:37**	**10.01**	**14:03**

Tracking data recorded by the Garmin 310XT and 910XT software is extremely useful for assessing your performances in open water.

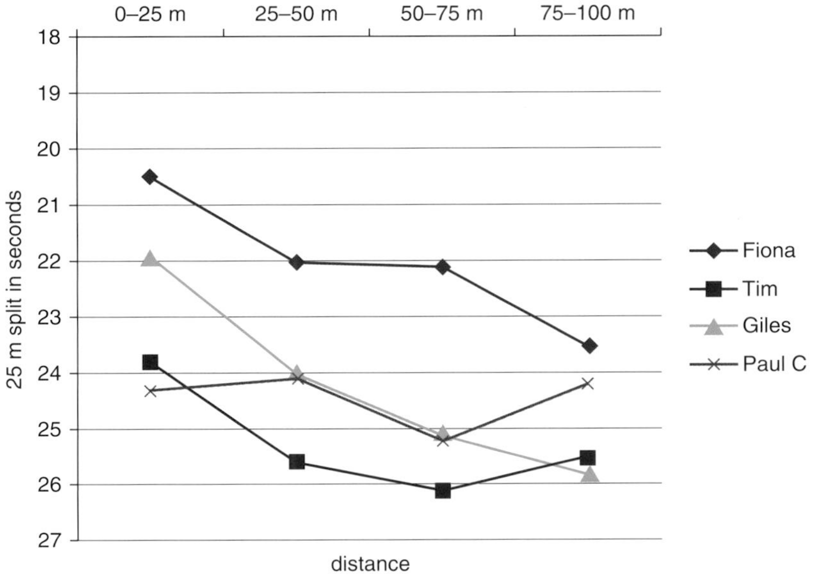

Pacing yourself is not easy – in fact even coaches find it hard! Here is some data from our first three-day coaches' course in 2010. We filmed the coaches for stroke analysis over 100 m but then checked their pacing each 25 m. Notice how Fiona, Giles and Tim slowed down lap by lap but Paul C did a good job!

Summary

Developing your swim specific fitness doesn't need to be a chore or a risk to your stroke efficiency. If you seek to be the most proficient swimmer that you can, developing a good balance between your swim fitness and your stroke technique is imperative. Don't be afraid to push your limits a little bit – you might be surprised at just how quick you can go with a solid block of training behind you!

Further Resources

If you are out of town on business or holiday and searching for a pool to train in, check out swimmers-guide.com which aims to list every pool in every town in every state in every country around the world and features handy pricing information and details of the pool timetables.

Well worth checking out!

CHAPTER 29

Dry-Land Conditioning

To Gym or Not to Gym, That is the Question!

One of the most frequently asked questions at the end of our full-day Swim Smooth Clinics is 'do you recommend gym training for swimmers and triathletes?' Our answer is that it depends, mostly on whether you have enough time available in your week.

In an ideal world we would all be full-time athletes with access to well-equipped gyms and physiotherapy, pilates and even yoga classes. In this situation you would definitely benefit from such conditioning work to help you become a more balanced athlete but in reality most of us are time-strapped and the danger of introducing significant conditioning work to your programme is that you would have to cut back on the swimming itself to fit it in.

With this in mind we have designed a flexibility and conditioning routine that you can complete quickly and efficiently both before and after swim training or even in front of the TV!

What is Dry-Land Training?

Dry-land training can be loosely categorised into three main areas:

1. Flexibility and mobility.
2. Core stability and rehabilitation.
3. Strength training.

PAUL: *Dry-land training derived its name from the fact that many of the world's elite swim programmes would engage their swimmers in conditioning exercises on the pool deck immediately before and after training in the water. Australian swimming legend Ian Thorpe was famous for arriving at training 30 minutes prior to every session to work on his mobility and flexibility. This extra conditioning work has often been cited as one of the reasons why he was so successful in winning multiple Olympic Gold Medals. Whilst we will probably never reach the same levels of flexibility and conditioning that elite swimmers have, making improvements in important areas can help you make large improvements to your stroke technique.*

1. Flexibility and Mobility

When it comes to swimming, a big limiting factor for many triathletes is a lack of flexibility. Poor flexibility can give rise to many stroke technique flaws including crossovers, dropped elbows and sinking legs, all of which will severely limit your potential in the water. Swim, bike and run training keeps us very busy but improving your flexibility doesn't have to eat into your training time, you can make some big improvements by performing a stretching routine in front of the TV in the evening.

In particular, triathletes and swimmers needs to focus on the following areas when stretching:

- Upper back / shoulders.
- Hips.
- Ankles.

Studies show that to avoid injury athletes should either stretch regularly or not at all [1] – it tends to be those athletes who stretch every now and again that experience issues with muscle injury and strains. For this reason you should keep stretching regularly to avoid injury and always warm up properly beforehand. Think of your muscles and tendons as a little like toffee – when cold they are brittle and subject to micro-tears if over-stretched, with some gentle mobilisation and warming up they become a lot more pliable.

Stretching prior to a training session should only be used to gently loosen off and not to develop muscle length or range of motion. Such work is best left until after training or in a specific stretching session where you warm up beforehand. Stretches should never be painful and should never use a bouncing action.

Aim to hold each stretch for approximately 20 seconds and repeat each two to three times. Practise deep controlled breathing while stretching.

Stretching: Upper Back and Shoulders

Doorway Chest Stretch. Standing in a doorway or beside a post, place your arm in the position shown with your elbow at a right angle. Gently press forwards with your chest and feel the stretch across the front of your shoulder and through the pectoral (chest) muscle. Avoid pushing the shoulder itself too far forward – instead think of drawing your shoulder blades together and back.

Telescope Arms and Rotation Stretch. This looks complicated but is easy when you get the hang of it! Start by lying on your side with knees bent to approximately 90° and one hand on top of the other. Take a deep breath in and as you exhale rotate the top arm all the way over to open yourself out into a crucifix position whilst following the arm with your gaze. Take a few deep breaths in this position and feel your back and shoulders sinking into the ground with every exhale.

This fantastic stretch develops your chest, shoulder and back mobility all in one. Take care to perform it in a slow controlled manner and do not attempt it if you have had any major back problems in the past.

Triceps and Lats Stretch. Place your hand behind your head and lean to the side into a wall or against a post. Relax into the position and feel the stretch through your triceps and lat muscles.

Forward Lean Shoulder Stretch. Whilst kneeling, lean forwards with your hands extended out in front of each shoulder. Feel the stretch through the shoulders and chest and underneath the armpits.

Hip Flexor Stretch. A lot of time spent sitting at a desk and training on the bike can result in the hip flexor muscles at the front of the hip becoming short. When trying to maintain a horizontal position in the water to reduce drag, this tightness in the hips can pull your legs forward and lower in the water. Regular stretching of the hip flexors will help improve your body position in the water.

Settle into the position shown with your lead leg angled 90 degrees at the knee and your rear leg stretched out behind you. Keeping your body vertical and strong, gently push your hips forward and gently squeeze your glutes (your buttock muscles). You will feel the stretch through the front of the hip and possibly into the quadriceps. As a triathlete, think of this as one of your key stretches.

Seated Ankle Stretch. In the Swim Smooth squads in Perth, we perform very few kick sets with our triathletes, preferring instead to perform drills using a pair of longer flexible flippers, which help to stretch off your ankles. This is a very good use of your time as you develop your stroke using a specific drill and stretch your ankles simultaneously. Outside of the pool you can also use the two stretches shown to assist in stretching off your ankles.

Left: Sit on the floor with one leg extended in front and the other bent across the top. Hold the top leg as shown with the hand gently pulling the foot towards you. The stretch is felt through the top of the foot and into the shin.

Right: In a kneeling position, place your feet out straight behind you. If you are quite inflexible through the ankles you will feel the stretch through the top of the feet and into the shin. You can lift one knee at a time to develop this stretch further. Avoid this stretch if you have ever had any knee issues.

Calf and Plantar Fascia Stretch. If you find that you are prone to cramping when wearing flippers then there is a strong likelihood that you are very tight in your calf muscles and in the plantar fascia in the arch of the foot. Include these stretches regularly in your routine to loosen off these areas and reduce your incidence of cramp in the future.

Toes curled under stretch (left). Stay in a kneeling position but tuck the toes under the foot and onto the floor. You will feel the stretch through the sole of the feet. Proceed gently with this stretch if you are tight in this region, little and often is best.

Calf stretch (right). Crouch down with foot kept flat on the floor and the other pointing back underneath you. Keep your body weight over the foot which is flat on the ground and feel the stretch through the lower calf muscle (soleus).

2. Core Stability and Rehabilitation

In Chapter 10 we looked at how you could improve your use of your upper core (shoulders / upper back) and lower core (lower back / abdominal) muscle groups to improve your posture whilst swimming. Here are a few key exercises that you can use at home or in the gym to improve your general conditioning in these areas. Given that core stabilisation training initially requires some skill in order for you to feel the correct muscles activating, we would highly recommend seeking the assistance of a personal trainer or physiotherapist to take you through these exercises.

Core stability became very popular in the mid to late 1990s together with an increasing interest in pilates, yoga and the combined 'yogilates'. Core stability is the interaction of coordination and strength of the abdominal, back and glute muscles during activity to ensure that the spine is stabilised and provides a firm base to support both basic and powerful everyday movements of the arms and legs.

Core stability training is an essential component of sport performance and plays a key role in injury prevention. The core muscles are the deepest layer of muscles within the torso and include the abdominals, lower back, buttock and hip muscles, which surround the pelvis. Developing a solid foundation within your torso will then allow you to generate powerful movements from your trunk outwards.

In a nutshell, core stability:

- Improves posture.
- Maintains healthy and balanced muscles.
- Enhances physical functioning in everyday activities ('Functional Fitness').
- Facilitates powerful movements such as those executed during sport.
- Helps to protect joints and muscles from injury.

Neutral Spine

The idea of a neutral spine relates to setting your trunk before you begin a core stability programme. By finding your neutral spine position you are activating the key core muscles within your torso, which need to be 'turned on' prior to executing coordinated movements. Here's how:

1. Start by lying flat on your back on a mat or comfortable carpeted floor with your knees bent.
2. Place your arms by your sides so that your elbows are straight and your shoulders relaxed.
3. Slowly take three deep breaths in and out to try and release any stress and relax your body.
4. Gently and slowly tilt your pelvis so that you are flattening your back into the floor. Avoid lifting your buttocks. Try to isolate the movement so that only your pelvis is moving.
5. Now tilt your pelvis in the opposite direction so that you are arching your lower back. Again try to keep the movement isolated to your pelvis.
6. Repeat steps 4 and 5 a few more times. By tilting your pelvis you are performing what is called an anterior pelvic tilt (arch back) and a posterior pelvic tilt (flatten back).
7. Now to locate your neutral spine, find the middle position between flattening and arching your back.

Here are four simple exercises that you can use to improve your core conditioning:

Controlled Roll Ups
Lie flat on your back on the floor, legs straight out in front of you placing your arms and hands by your sides. Gently and slowly lift your head off the floor and draw your lower stomach to spine as you slowly start to sit up. Slowly breathe in as you continue sitting up until you are straight, then pause. Begin rolling back down whilst breathing out. Start at your pelvis and slowly unfold your spine as you return to the starting position. Repeat 10–15 times.

Bridging
Lie flat on your back, find your neutral spine and draw your lower stomach in. Slowly push down through your feet and lift your bottom right up so that your trunk is straight with your shoulders, hips and knees in a line. Breathe in as you lift and out as you lower, and hold the lift for 5–10 seconds thinking of squeezing your buttocks as you lift. Repeat 10–15 times.

Wall Squats
Standing with your back to the wall take one step away with both feet whilst keeping your back to the wall. Your toes should be in line and slightly turned out. Find your neutral spine position and draw your lower stomach in. Holding this position, slowly perform a half squat keeping your bottom against the wall. Hold the squat for five seconds and then lift to return to the start. Complete three sets of twelve squats.

Front Plank
Place your elbows on the floor shoulder width apart and directly under your shoulders. Supporting yourself on your elbows and toes, be sure your body is in a flat line with no dip or arch in your spine and with your bottom tucked in. Keep your spine neutral and draw in your lower stomach. Hold this position for 20–30 seconds and then rest for 30 seconds, repeating three times. As you get stronger challenge yourself by trying to hold the position for longer each time.

The Y-T-W-L

Here's a dry-land exercise we have borrowed from physiotherapists to help you tune into drawing your shoulders together and back (technical term 'scapular retraction'). We are sure you are familiar with the Village People's hit song from the 1970s: 'YMCA'. We are going to do the Y-T-W-L instead!

Standing in some space, draw your arms up into a Y position beside you. How do they naturally sit? Do they tend to lean forwards like Paul's position on the left? Maintaining this position, focus on drawing your shoulder blades together and back and notice how your arms come back in line with the body. That's good posture in action! Avoid arching your lower back as you do this.

Run through each of the Y-T-W-L positions, holding each position for around ten seconds; the exercise gets progressively harder to stabilise through the four positions!

The YTWL is a great exercise to add into any stretching and conditioning routine that you have in place. You can practise it immediately before a swim or even between sets in the shallow end of the pool. Over time the YTWL will give you a greater awareness of your posture and help you improve it.

In Chapter 30 we will look at some more functional rehab-style exercises for the upper back and shoulders that will help to ward off shoulder injury.

3. Strength Training in the Gym

When considering introducing traditional gym strengthening exercises into your swimming programme we would encourage you to always ask the question 'how specific is this exercise to my swimming?'. Swimming is not ordinarily limited by strength in the true sense of the word, which is probably best demonstrated by the example of the 11-year-old girl who so easily cruises past you in the pool and yet would never come close to matching your strength in the gym as an adult. Despite swimming not being limited by strength, some swimmers and triathletes like to add a gym strengthening programme to their routine during the winter months and we would not discourage you from doing so if you are seeking a little general conditioning and toning.

We would, however, encourage you to avoid too much emphasis on lifting heavy weights, especially those focused on the muscles at the front of the shoulder and chest (e.g. shoulder and bench press). If performed excessively these exercises can limit mobility in the shoulders and also bring you into a rounded-shoulder posture that could harm your alignment in the pool. In fact, most swimmers and triathletes that we see who have a background in weight training are limited by those two factors: posture and mobility.

If you are going to use the gym we suggest you focus your attention on the following exercises that will help maintain and improve your swimming posture:

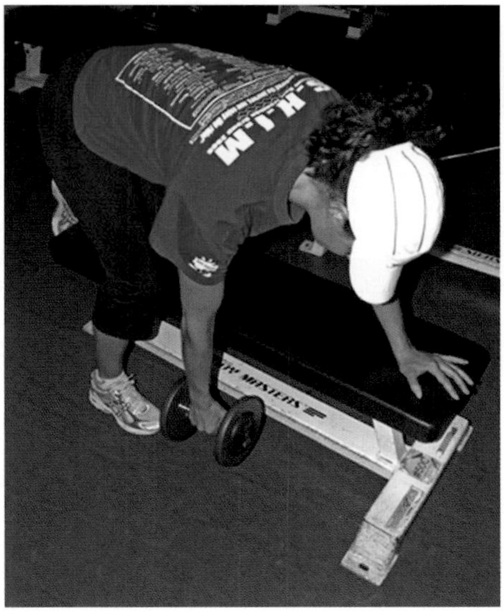

Barbell Row. This exercise focuses on the shoulder and scapular region muscle groups. Use a light weight for this exercise and keep the shoulder horizontal, aiming for 2–3 sets of 12–15 reps with each arm.

Lat Pull Down. A great exercise for assisting with good posture and alignment of the upper back. Keep your spine straight when performing this exercise and keep the weight light. Aim for 2-3 sets of 15–20 reps.

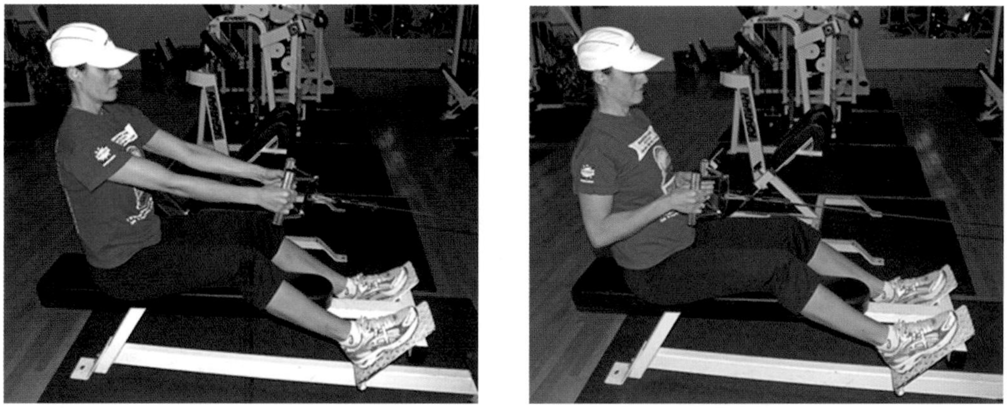

Seated Upright Row. Another excellent exercise for helping you to focus on drawing your shoulder blades together and down when you swim. Keep the spine straight and again use a light weight. Aim for 2–3 sets of 15–20 reps.

Travelling Away from Home?

At Swim Smooth we are fans of the GymStick system for when you are away travelling and are without access to a pool. A GymStick is very portable and features two therabands which you can use for stretch cord work as well as the basic functions of the stick. Find out more at www.gymstick.net.

Use The GymStick and included Therabands to perform a wide variety of conditioning exercises. Use the Therabands (bottom) to practise the catch phase of the freestyle stroke against mild resistance, emulating good posture and that high elbow position.

Reference

1. Fradkin, A.J., Gabbe, B.J., Cameron, P.A. 2006. Does warming up prevent injury in sport? The evidence from randomised controlled trials? *J Sci Med Sport*. 9(3):214–20. Epub 2006 May 6.

CHAPTER 30

Prevention and Management of Shoulder Injuries

Shoulder pain and injury is very common amongst freestyle swimmers and is caused by repetitive stress placed on the shoulders during each arm stroke. At least 80% of adult swimmers will experience some form of shoulder pain in their swimming lives and such pain should be taken very seriously so that it does not lead to a full-blown injury and time out from swimming. Most elite swimmers train for around 40-70 km per week, which adds up to well over two million strokes per year – that is an awful lot of potential stress on their shoulders. In fact, in elite swimming circles shoulder injury was so common that it used to be considered a fact of swimming life, just something they had to live with. Fortunately these days we understand that the stress on the shoulders is dramatically affected by stroke technique and that by correcting your technique we can greatly reduce stress on the joint, quickly reduce symptoms and go on to cure the condition.

Avoid shoulder injury at all costs, it will ruin the consistency of your training, which is absolutely key to your success as a swimmer.

An absolutely vital aspect of your preparation as a swimmer is consistency in your training; if you need time out of the water to recover from an injury you will lose the fitness gains that you would otherwise have achieved. For this reason if you suffer from any form of pain in your shoulders you need to take immediate corrective action using the advice in this chapter.

Shoulder Injury Signs and Symptoms

Shoulder injury may begin as mild pain in the shoulder, which is only felt when swimming but can quickly progress to moderate or severe pain felt while performing caily activities and while sleeping. Early on, symptoms will subside shortly after swimming; however, if there has been no period of rest or treatment, pain may come on sooner and persist with other activities involving shoulder movements. Common symptoms of swimming shoulder injury include pain, limited movement, a painful arc, muscle weakness, tenderness to touch, clicking noises or catching sensations.

PAUL: *I vividly recall a conversation I had with my long-term coach Chris Jones (former British Triathlon Head Coach) about one of the other junior athletes on the British Triathlon team with me at the time, Tim Don. Tim had just won the World Junior Triathlon Championships in 1998 and Chris had asked Tim about the factors involved in his success and his rise to prominence. Perhaps the key point that Tim highlighted was his consistency of training – he hadn't picked up a single injury in the past three seasons. This, combined with an excellent and balanced training programme, had allowed him to lift his game and dominate the world junior triathlon scene – something I could only ever dream of!*

Thinking back to my own training in that period, my incidence of injury was quite high and my progress was constantly being stalled by time out from training. If there's one thing guaranteed to help you improve, it's consistent practice of correct training methods. Likewise, if there's one thing guaranteed to throw a spanner in the works, it's an injury! Please be super-proactive with your stroke technique to avoid injury, use pre-swimming exercises to loosen off before swimming and take a sensible approach to your overall training load. Don't panic if you already have a shoulder injury, use the advice in this chapter to get it quickly under control.

Pain can be felt in the top, front, side or back of the shoulder and may even radiate down the arm to the elbow. Swelling and torn tissue may also be present, however it is most likely this will only be seen by ultrasound examination.

Take Immediate Action

As soon as you experience any shoulder pain or injury always seek medical advice from a physiotherapist, athletic therapist or sports doctor as soon as possible in order to determine the severity of the injury and to begin rehabilitation. Also immediately reduce or stop training to prevent the pain and swelling from continuing. Resting from activities or movements which aggravate pain is critical and applying ice to reduce inflammation is also key to a successful and fast recovery.

Secondly, make sure that you address areas of your stroke technique that can be causing or aggravating the injury using the advice that follows in this chapter. Whilst rehabilitation is important, without addressing your stroke technique an injury could quickly return.

Finally, as part of your rehabilitation, introduce the strengthening and stability exercises into your training programme so as to maintain muscle balance around your shoulder joint, which will help to maintain healthy strong shoulders and upper back. Before training always warm-up and stretch lightly but do not over-stretch your shoulders as too much flexibility can also be detrimental.

What is the Cause of Shoulder Pain?

Shoulder pain is commonly classified into three categories:

1. Shoulder Joint Impingement

Shoulder Impingement is a compression or squashing of the structures within the top of the shoulder joint (subacromial space). Within this space lie muscular tendons (e.g. the rotator cuff), and the fluid filled sac that prevents muscle on bone traction (the subacromial bursa). Impingement arises due to the thickening or swelling of the structures within the space or upward migration of the ball in the shoulder joint, caused by having poor posture or poor biomechanics while swimming.

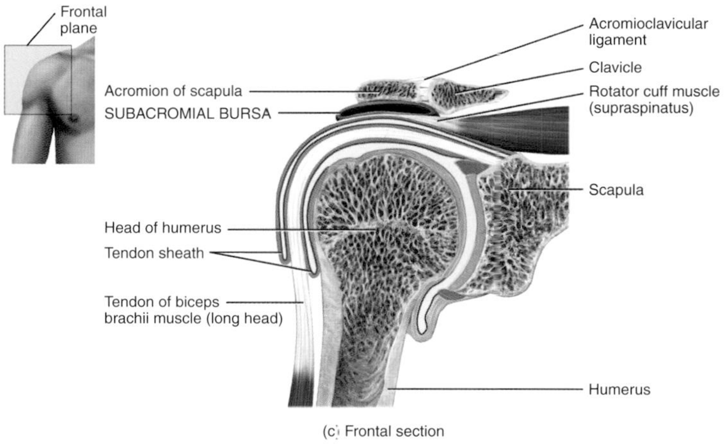

FIGURE 30.19 The shoulder joint showing all the structures of the rotator cuff which may become thickened or swollen from poor posture and biomechanics when swimming which can lead to impingement. (Source: *Principles of Anatomy and Physiology 13th edition*, Gerard J. Tortora, p. 311).

2. Overuse Injury

Overuse injuries are generally defined as tendonopathies, which is where there is injury to or degeneration of the tendon of a muscle, which may or may not be accompanied by inflammation. Damage to a tendon tissue occurs when the load applied exceeds the strength of the tendon either over time or in a single incident. Tendon injuries can be very difficult to treat because tendons have a poor blood supply and totally resting a tendon to allow it to heal is hard to achieve in daily life.

3. Joint Laxity/Instability

Joint laxity or instability normally develops over an extended period of time if there is no traumatic injury to the shoulder joint. Gradual deterioration in the ligaments and inhibition of the rotator cuff muscles leads to laxity or loosening of the shoulder joint. If this is not addressed instability of the shoulder can occur which may lead to a tear in the lining of the socket of the shoulder joint (a capsular lesion).

Elements of each of these three patterns can coexist and are often interrelated. For example, a swimmer who has been diagnosed with a rotator cuff injury will experience pain, which prevents the muscles from working properly thereby allowing the ball (head of the humerus) to move more in the socket. Overall, the shoulder joint moves more than normal which can lead to laxity or instability of the shoulder. This laxity allows the ball to migrate upwards in the socket (glenoid fossa), which causes impingement or compression of the structures in the top of the shoulder.

Many factors can cause shoulder injury. Broadly speaking these can be split into two key areas, both of which you should address to help prevent and rehabilitate sore shoulders:

1. Poor stroke technique and sudden increases in volume and/or intensity within your programme.
2. Poor posture and mobility in your neck and upper back as well as muscle imbalance around your shoulders.

In the rest of this chapter we will look at each of these areas and how to address them to fix a shoulder problem.

Shoulder Injury: Stroke Technique and Training

The classic stroke technique flaws that cause shoulder injury are as follows, refer to Figure 30.20 to view pictures of them and how to correct them:

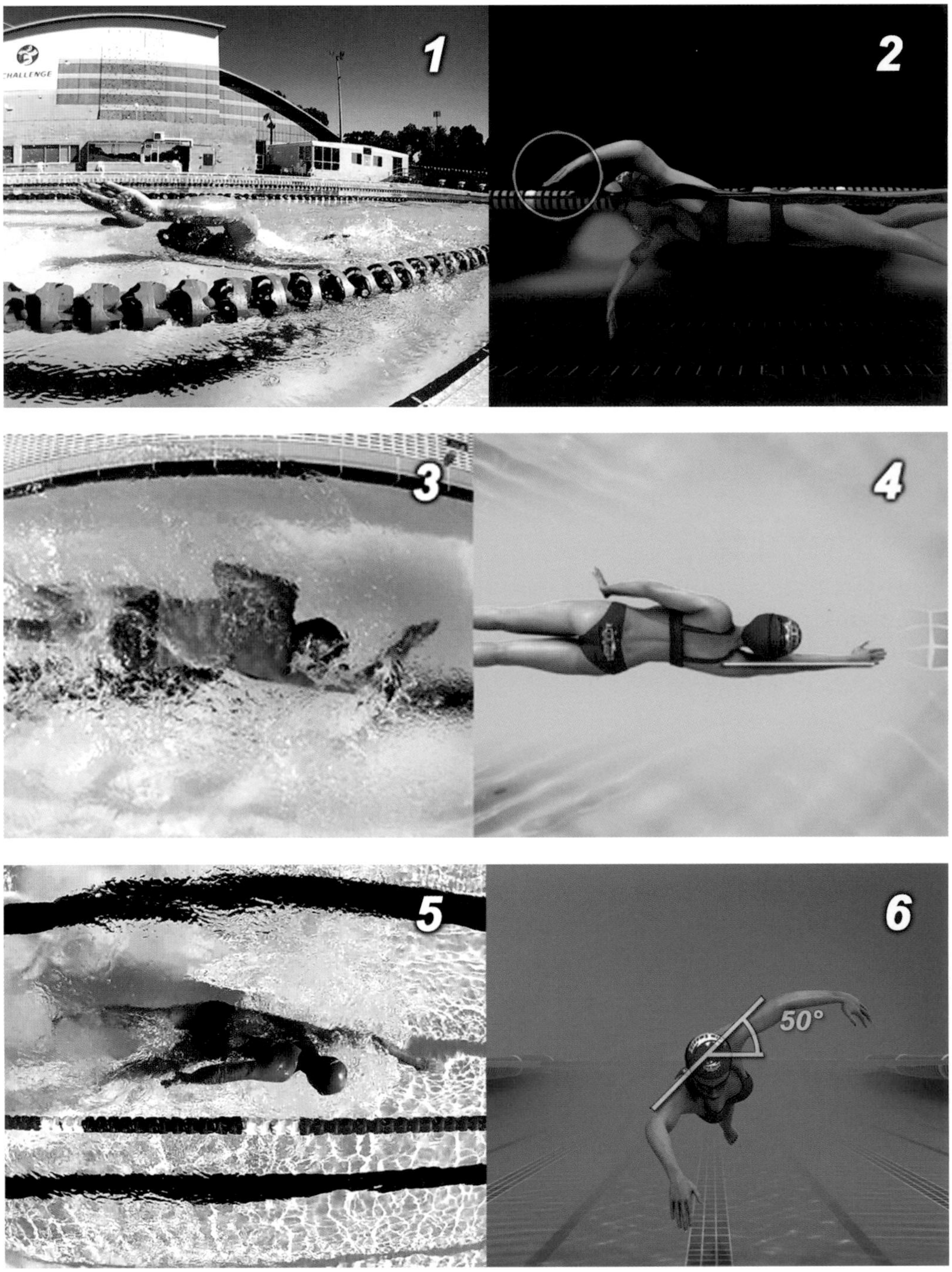

Continued

FIGURE 30.20 Common stroke technique flaws causing injury.

A Thumb-First Entry into the Water

To enter into the water thumb first (1) the swimmer must internally rotate the shoulder, which reduces the subacromial space and places the rotator cuff muscles in a high-risk position. Ironically enough this hand entry had been taught for many years as a way of improving how smoothly the hand entered into the water. Whilst you might get away with this if you are 11 years old with good flexibility and rotation in your stroke, as adults we need to be much more careful and modify our strokes to use a fingertips-first entry as demonstrated by Miss Smooth (2). This will keep your shoulder in a much more neutral position.

A Crossover Upon Hand Entry

Evident in over 70% of the swimmers we work with, a midline crossover (3) has a similar effect to that of a thumb-first entry (squashing the front of the shoulder). If a crossover is combined with a thumb-first entry this will almost certainly lead to a shoulder injury. To straighten your hand entry, visualise the middle finger of each hand extending straight forward in front of the same shoulder, not across, as demonstrated by Miss Smooth (4).

Poor Body Rotation

Many swimmers who were taught to swim by the Red Cross in the 1950s, 1960s and 1970s were taught that body rotation along the long axis of the spine was a bad thing and a waste of effort (5). Conversely in the 1990s there was a strong and concerted effort to encourage swimmers to rotate to a full 90° by 'stacking their shoulders'. Neither method is correct but both still persist in some swimming programmes today.

To avoid shoulder injury, good body rotation between 45° and 60° is essential on every stroke (not just when you are breathing) and aids the recovery phase of the freestyle stroke by allowing the arm to clear the surface of the water without excessive internal rotation of the shoulder. This is best demonstrated by the land-based exercises as listed in Chapter 11. To avoid shoulder injury and improve your stroke efficiency, aim for rotation along the central axis of the spine demonstrated by Miss Smooth (6).

A Straight Arm Catch and Pull-Through

A straight arm pull-through is another very common stroke flaw and is a precursor to shoulder injury in many cases. When the arm pulls through with a straight elbow (7) it creates a large amount of force on the unstable and relatively weak shoulder and rotator cuff muscles. This is exacerbated if the swimmer trains with large hand paddles as they put further force through the shoulder when in a very compromised position.

Large hand paddles have a bad reputation for causing injury for this reason, but it is not directly the fault of the paddle, it is poor technique combined with a large paddle that creates shoulder injury. In fact when used in moderation with a bent elbow pull (8), hand paddles carry a very low injury risk.

An Excessive Flick at the Exit (Push) Phase

Some coaches and swim programmes encourage their swimmers to 'finish strong' at the back of the stroke by emphasising the push immediately prior to the hand exiting the water at the rear of the stroke. This causes the swimmer to hyper-extend the elbow (9) and excessively internally rotate the shoulder. As well as stressing the shoulder joint, the hyper-extension at the elbow can cause a condition called medial epicondylitis ('Golfer's Elbow'). Swimmers who overly lengthen their freestyle strokes are particularly susceptible to this condition.

Instead of locking out straight, the arm should exit the water with a slight bend of around 150° at the elbow. The palm of the hand should be turned in slightly towards the thigh to complete the stroke smoothly (10).

A Sudden Increase in Training Volume or Intensity

It is very important that you do not suddenly increase the volume of your training by more than 5% to 10% per week. Sudden jumps in volume or training intensity can trigger shoulder injury, especially if any of the above stroke flaws are in place in your stroke. This should not put you off fitness training as part of a balanced programme but take care to build things up progressively, especially if you are suddenly inspired (as we hope you will be!) with the large variety of training sets in Appendix C.

Other aspects to watch out for are adding too much pull buoy, paddles and bands work to your swimming sessions, especially if you have poor catch mechanics and limited body rotation in your stroke.

Shoulder Injury: Posture, Mobility and Muscular Imbalance

In freestyle swimmers, there are particular muscle groups which tend to be strong and tight (internal rotators – pectorals and latissimus dorsi) and ones which are weak and lengthened (external rotators and middle and lower trapezius muscles). These imbalances lead to altered biomechanics and so a predisposition to injury. An essential path to reducing the abnormal imbalances in your shoulders is to include a cross training programme in your exercise regime. Strengthening the less dominant muscles used in swimming and maintaining good flexibility in your shoulder and thoracic spine will greatly reduce the likelihood of shoulder pain and injury.

Follow the six specific exercises below to reduce the stress on your shoulders.

Maintaining Thoracic Spine Flexibility

A slumped posture is becoming more and more prevalent in the average population as so many of us now have desk jobs and spend large parts of our day sitting at computers. With our shoulders slumped forward and our chins poking out, our upper back and thoracic spine begin to morph into a hump back, which in physio terms is referred to as a kyphosis. In swimmers, a mild kyphosis is common due to the nature of the freestyle stroke and the overuse of the muscles at the front of our shoulders pulling us into a rounded shoulder position. This kyphosis can lead to a loss of flexibility in the thoracic spine which in turn can result in excessive flexibility in our shoulder joints. Thoracic extension and rotation are two exercises which will maintain a flexible thoracic spine and so keep the shoulders free from excessive load.

Poor posture at your desk can be problematic for your swimming and the health of your shoulders. Left: Posture is poor due to a slouched position with the chin poked forwards. Middle: Posture is good with a straight, tall back, feet flat on the floor and shoulders back. Right: Good posture is being over-exaggerated which places too much load on the lower back.

I. Thoracic Extension Using a Towel Roll

Referring to Figure 30.21 place a rolled hand towel on a carpeted floor (1) and lie on your back with the towel under you so that it sits along your spine between your shoulder blades (2). Let your head fall back onto the floor above the towel (if this is uncomfortable for your neck you may use a low pillow to support your head). Straighten your legs and let your arms rest by your sides with your palms facing up (3).

Hold this position for two to three minutes and as a progression move your arms over your head in a snow angel fashion to increase the stretch and lengthen out the muscles at the front of the shoulders (4).

FIGURE 30.21 Thoracic Extension Using A Towel Roll.

FIGURE 30.22 Telescope Arms Exercise

2. Telescope Arms

Referring to Figure 30.22 lie on your side with your knees and hips bent to 90° and your arms stretched out, one on top of the other at shoulder height. Begin the stretch by reaching your top hand past your bottom hand as though you are reaching toward the wall in front of you. Keeping your elbow straight and rotating from your trunk upwards (avoiding rolling your hips), reach your arm toward the ceiling and back toward the opposite wall as though you are carving an arc in the air. Your goal is to finish the stretch with your upper shoulder on the floor. Repeat four to six times on each side.

3. Scapular Setting

Scapular setting is important to re-establish a more balanced position of the humeral head (ball) in the glenoid fossa (socket) thus improving your overall shoulder posture.

Sitting upright in a comfortable chair, gently pull your chin in and open your chest. As you do so, imagine pulling the lower part of your shoulder blades together without arching your back or

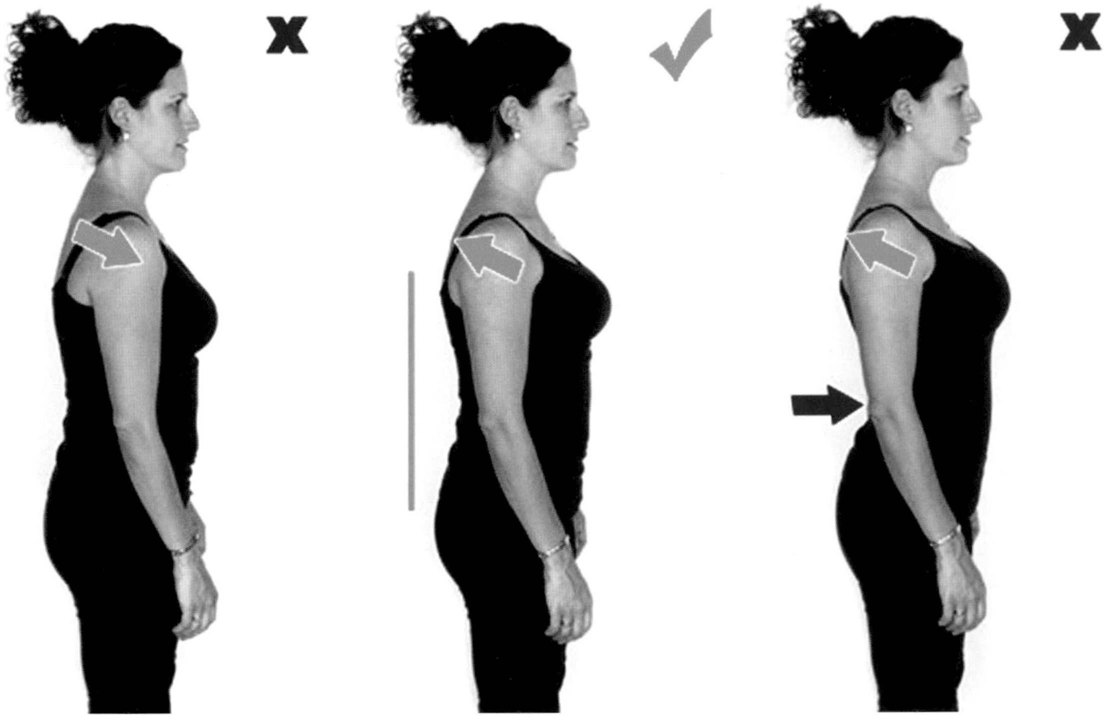

FIGURE 30.23 Develop an improved posture using Scapular Setting. Do not overexaggerate the position and arch the lower back (right).

throwing your rib cage forwards. Only a 30%-40% effort should be used to perform this exercise and you should not feel any tension in your shoulder blades or neck. Keep breathing normally and aim to hold the position for 1-2 minutes until it becomes comfortable, then aim to hold it for longer periods during the day.

Repeat this exercise frequently throughout the day in sitting and standing positions. As a progression try the same position lying on your front with your arms at your side, this will allow you to train these muscles in a prone posture similar to swimming.

4. Shoulder Shrugs

Shoulder shrugs address weakness in the upper trapezius muscle, which is often seen when the shoulder on one side is depressed or sits lower, this is normally the shoulder experiencing shoulder pain.

Start by standing with your arm slightly away from your body, elbow straight and your palm facing forward (1). Set your shoulder as in the previous Scapular Setting exercise and hold this position. Gently shrug your shoulder toward your ear, hold for 1-2 seconds (2) before lowering.

Repeat three sets of the exercise, each with 10-12 repetitions. As a progression you can add a light hand weight if control allows (3 and 4). Start with 1 kg and progress to 3 kg.

FIGURE 30.24 Shoulder Shrugs with and without weights.

5. Seated Row Using Theraband

A seated row aims to strengthen the muscles at the back of the shoulder between the shoulder blades, which help to stabilise the scapula and improve overall shoulder position and biomechanics.

Use a piece of theraband anchored to a door knob or railing at belly button height, stand or sit holding one end of the band in each hand with it taut and slightly stretched in front of you. Start with your elbows straight and shoulders slightly rounded (1 and 3). Leading with your elbows pull your hands toward you bringing them toward the outside of your chest (2). As you pull the band to your chest gently pull your shoulder blades together (4).

Repeat three sets of 10-12 repetitions each. As a progression increase repetitions to 15-20 and then increase the resistance by using a stronger theraband.

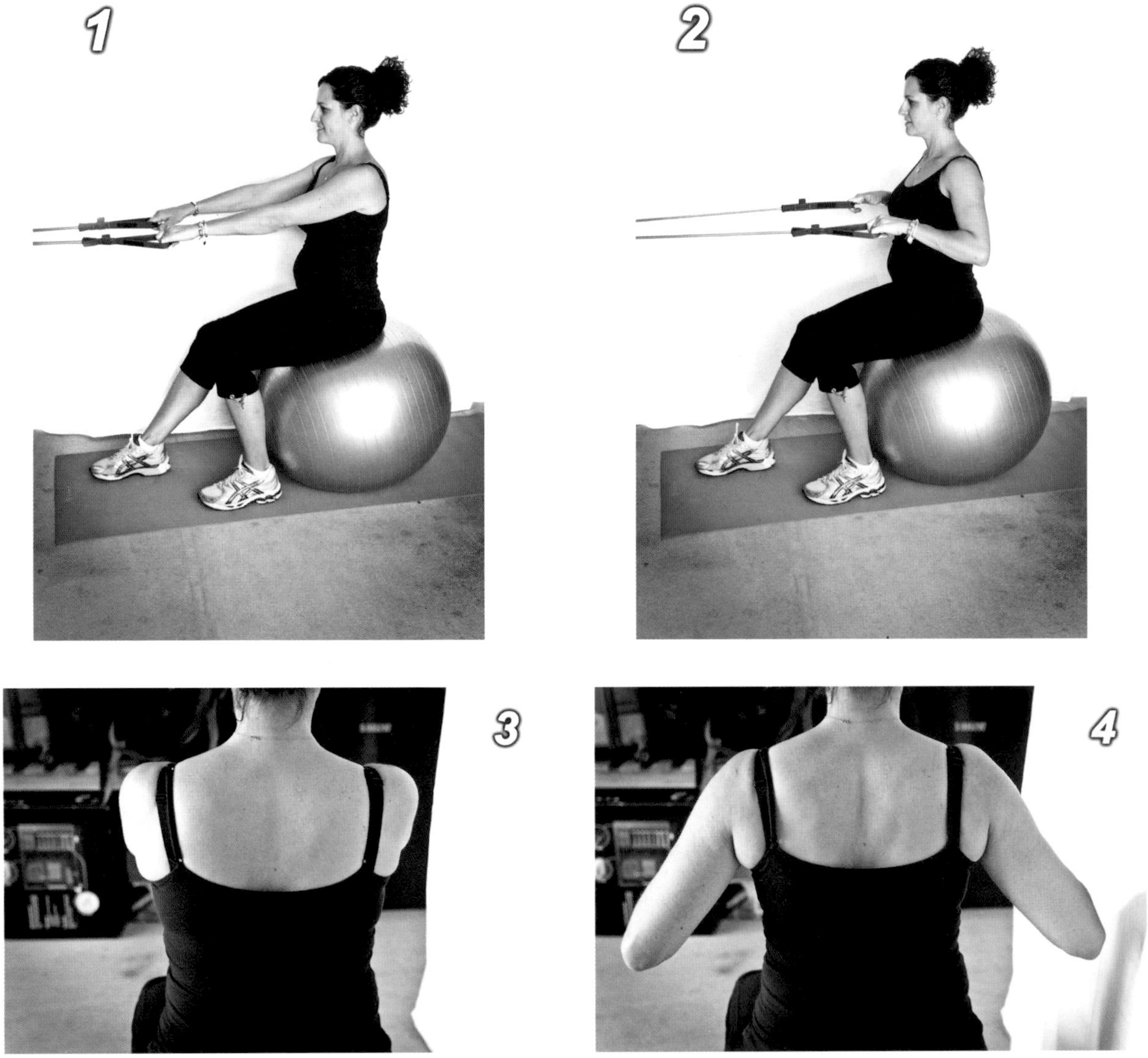

FIGURE 30.25 Seated Row Using Theraband.

6. External Shoulder Rotation with Theraband

This external shoulder rotation exercise focuses on improving strength in the back of the shoulder primarily in the rotator cuff muscles. This exercise helps to re-balance the rotator cuff muscles and improve the position of the humeral head (ball) in the glenoid fossa (socket).

Anchor one end of a piece of theraband to a door knob and stand with your unaffected shoulder beside the door. Hold the end of the theraband on your affected side and stand so that the band is taut with your elbow bent to 90° and your upper arm along your side. Your wrist should be level with the door knob. Set your shoulder as in Exercises 2 and 3 and then gently pull the band away from your mid-line pivoting at your elbow.

Repeat three sets of 10-12 repetitions of this exercise. As a progression increase to 15-20 repetitions then increase the resistance by using a stronger theraband.

FIGURE 30.26 External Shoulder Rotation Using Theraband.

CHAPTER 31 Pool Skills

If you are considering joining a triathlon club or Masters swim squad to improve your swimming, the simple tips in this chapter will help you fit in more quickly. Joining a squad does not need to be a confronting experience and you will certainly find many other swimmers at a similar level to yourself all keen to improve their swimming. This can be very motivating and we would always recommend that swimmers and triathletes aim to do at least one squad session per week under the guidance of a coach.

Squad Training and Lane Etiquette

Here are our top 10 tips on surviving your first few squad sessions with correct lane etiquette:

1. Unless otherwise advised, use the pool clock to set off exactly five seconds behind the person in front of you. You should not try to catch them up, as whilst this gives you a draft and makes it feel easier, you are not then getting the best possible workout that you could and it can also annoy the person in front. The coach will announce when drafting is actively encouraged but normally keep your distance to allow everyone to perform at their best, especially on technique sets.
2. Always keep close to the lane rope and swim in the circular direction advised on the plaque at the end of the lane, either clockwise or anticlockwise. If there is no sign, observe what others are already doing in the lane and aim to replicate that – here in Australia the convention is to always swim clockwise but in the UK lanes alternate clockwise and anticlockwise. Stay close to the lane rope and avoid swimming in the middle of the lane as this is when head-on collisions occur or accidental clashing of arms.
3. If someone is catching you up and you are aware that they wish to get past you, either pull tight in towards the lane rope so that they can overtake (but still keep swimming and reduce your speed a fraction) or better still, when you reach the end of the pool pull off to the side, stop and let them past.
4. Be vigilant when you are pushing off in the middle of a set – is someone coming up to the wall where you are to turn? If so, don't push off immediately in front of them as this is somewhat rude. Let them past and then when it is clear jump into a spot behind them.
5. Aim to start each and every lap with a good torpedo push off, they really pay dividends for your posture and make you look quite the 'pro'!

6. When using fins or pull buoys, chances are that the speed or 'pecking' order of the lane may change. If you know that you are particularly quick with fins on, don't be afraid to ask to go in front of the person in front of you or even lead the whole lane.
7. Aim to pace yourself well, this is ultimately what keeps the lane flowing effectively and what makes the most out of your own practice time.
8. Aim to do your drill and technique work to the best of your ability, do not feel pressured to rush through this aspect of the session. A drill worth doing is a drill worth doing well – always remember that.
9. Try to keep all of your kit neatly organised on the pool deck – a mesh kit bag is highly advisable and prevents other swimmers mistakenly walking off or using your kit. Also, naming your kit in bold black marker is always worth doing!
10. Lastly, be nice to your fellow lane swimmers. It might be early in the morning or late at night and we can all be a little grumpy at these times but there's never an excuse to get irritable with anyone in your lane. If there's a problem, let the coach know or just diplomatically address it with your swimming buddy.

Tumble Turns

Tumble turns can take a bit of practice to master but with a few simple tips, you too can be flipping at the end of each length very effectively. Tumble turns save you time and also maintain the flow and rhythm of your stroke better than a touch turn but they are by no means compulsory in any squad session. Many swimmers worry about the disorientation of being upside down whilst trying to coordinate a roll over in the water or fear bashing their legs on the side of the pool from being too close. Instead aim to swim in positively, achieve a tight tuck and firm foot plant on the wall – confidence is the key to a successful tumble.

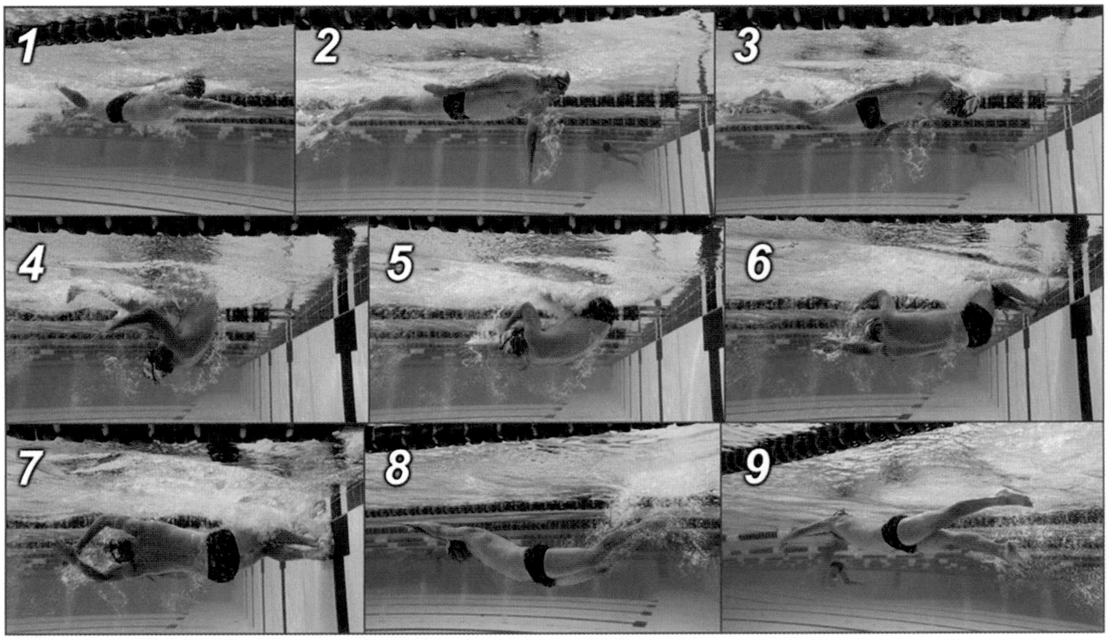

FIGURE 31.27 A great tumble turn has the above steps.

1. Approach the turn with confidence but avoid lifting the head too high or out of the water completely to 'spot' the wall (a very common mistake for beginners).

2-3. You should commence your turn between the black 'T' on the floor of the pool and the wall, i.e. about 1m (3 ft) away – if you really stretched out with one hand you should just about be able to touch the wall.

3. Tuck your chin into the chest and bring your arms down by your sides.

4-5. Think about getting into the tightest, smallest ball that you can – this will help you flip over faster than if you stay outstretched. Bring your knees into your chest. At this point if you were to open out you'd be perfectly on your back. Start bringing your hands back above your head.

6. Keep the knees, ankles and feet together and aim to plant them firmly on the wall with your toes pointing to either 10 o'clock or 2 o'clock on the wall. Note: you do not have to attempt to add in a full twist at this point so that your feet would be pointing to 6 o'clock.

7. Aim to make contact with the wall with your knees bent at about 90° – much more or less than this and you will struggle to get a good drive off the wall.

8. As you drive off the wall, strive to stretch out in a full torpedo (streamlined) position. Add in a few freestyle flutter kicks or dolphin (butterfly) kicks to emphasise your speed off the wall and rotate fully back onto your front.

9. Maintain the streamlined torpedo and aim to break out into your full stroke at about 5 m (15 feet) from the wall.

Dives

Some swim squads like to finish a session with some sprints from the deep end of the pool from a dive start – these are great fun and they sharpen up your pool skills. Whilst not compulsory, learning to dive properly can be a lot of fun and if you are planning on racing in the pool it will really give you a good advantage especially in the shorter sprint events.

IMPORTANT: Always ensure that you check the depth of water that you are diving into and that there are no foreign obstacles or other swimmers that might get in your way and cause you harm. There is a risk of neck and spinal injury from diving into any body of water but if the depth is greater than 1.8 m (6 ft) and you execute a shallow racing dive into clear water the biggest risk that you face is a painful and embarrassing 'belly flop'. If learning to dive, always seek the assistance of a qualified instructor and if you feel at all uncomfortable it is advisable to give it a miss and try again another day.

Referring to Figure 31.28 here are our key tips to performing a successful racing dive:

1. In a race the starter will call you onto the blocks with a series of short, sharp whistles to quieten the crowd followed by a longer whistle to invite you to step up.
2. You can choose to go from the side of the pool or off the special dive blocks which feature at many competition pools. Being higher and angled slightly down at the front, blocks allow the swimmer to gain a little more height (and with it, distance) when they dive, which can make for a cleaner entry into the water. You have three basic stances which you can try in order to ready yourself for a good dive: 1) the classic start – feet together and hands reaching either side of the feet as you fold yourself over at the waist; 2) the competition start – feet about shoulder width apart and hands reaching between the feet, using the lip of the block to pull up against and gain traction on the block and coil

Figure 31.28 The dive start.

the body like a tight spring; 3) the track start (shown) – a similar hand position as the classic start, but one foot is placed back in a similar stance to how a track runner might start – this will typically be your strongest leg. Experiment and see which gives you the fastest reaction time and power off the blocks.

3. The starter will start you off with the instruction 'take your marks...' and then follow with either a whistle, gun blast or a simple 'go!'
4. Keep your chin tucked into your chest and spring your arms out in front of you to form a streamlined torpedo whilst driving off the block with the legs aiming for both a little height and a good bit of distance. If you lift your head and look forward too much you will cause your legs to drop too low and you will hit the water stomach and chest first (the 'belly flop'). Tucking your chin in too tightly and spearing the water at too great an angle will force you into a nose dive and send you too deep into the water.
5. Once in the water, keep your hands together and commence a powerful kick to maintain your speed before breaking out into your full stroke just as per any normal push-off.

In our Swim Smooth Perth squad sessions we perform very little of the other three competitive strokes: butterfly, backstroke and breaststroke. Whilst these strokes can benefit your freestyle by developing better muscular balance across the body, if you are only swimming two or three times per week and training for a triathlon or open water swimming event, we would advise you to keep your training as specific as possible and focus on mastering the freestyle stroke. However, it is still useful to know some tips on performing the other three strokes and using them in your warm-ups, and particularly cool-downs, as a good way to vary your programme.

Butterfly – often seen as the hardest competitive stroke, butterfly can be challenging because it requires excellent rhythm and timing, good flexibility and a strong leg kick. The stroke undulates around the short axis of the spine and in this respect is more similar to breaststroke than freestyle and backstroke. The best way of visualising a good butterfly stroke is to think of yourself moving through the water like a dolphin. Both arms work together above and below the water with a more rounded recovery than in freestyle – probably one of the reasons why many Swingers are good at butterfly! You do need to be cautious, however, as the lack of long axis rotation in butterfly can increase the load on your shoulders so you should limit the volume of butterfly in your programme.

The key to butterfly is to breathe and then quickly drop your chin back down onto your chest.

Performing butterfly with fins is a great way to develop a feel for the undulated action of the stroke, it can also tone up your mid-section and when done gently can help to loosen off a tight lower back. The key to a good butterfly stroke is to ensure that as your head comes up out of the water to take a breath, you do this quickly and focus on getting your chin down onto your chest as quickly as you can. This will help the torso dive back down into the water and assist the arms with their recovery over the top of the surface.

Backstroke – very similar to freestyle with respect to long axis rotation, backstroke is effectively the reverse of freestyle and is often used as a way of stretching out during a cool-down and working the muscles in the opposite direction. To be good at backstroke having a strong leg kick is essential. If you don't have a strong kick and want to try some of the beneficial aspects of the stroke then try wearing a pair of fins.

One of the keys to a great backstroke is to make sure your head is pushed back into the water.

Another important feature of backstroke is to keep your head back. We often tell the children who we work with to imagine that they have to keep their noses in the air like a 'posh' person would walk around. This stops the common mistake of bringing the chin towards the chest, which causes the swimmer to sit up in the water and drop the legs and buttocks down low.

Breaststroke – whilst used by many swimmers who cannot swim freestyle, breaststroke is actually the least economic and slowest stroke due to the width of the body cutting through the water during the wide 'frog' kick. The reason breaststroke is favoured by many swimmers is because of the ease of lifting the head out of the water to breathe. Coordinating breathing in the freestyle stroke can initially be quite daunting whereas breaststroke is significantly easier and for this reason is a very valid way of becoming accustomed to the water when starting out in swimming.

A fast breaststroke uses a snappy arm movement, returning to the front of the stroke as soon as possible.

Good breaststrokers often have very good hip flexibility, which helps with the angles required to gain a propulsive kick. The key to a good breaststroke is good coordination between the arms and legs and to aim to reduce the frontal profile by not pulling or kicking too wide. A simple focal point for developing a better breaststroke is to focus on snapping your elbows into your sides as you pull through and then driving your arms forwards in as sleek a motion as you possibly can. Try visualising scooping out a bowl of cake mix with your hands as they pull through to develop this motion!

Individual Medley – Swimmers can bring all four competitive strokes together and perform an Individual Medley ('IM') which consists of 25 m, 50 m or 100 m of each stroke in succession without stopping in the following order: butterfly, backstroke, breaststroke, freestyle. If performed as part of a medley relay team with three other swimmers, the order of the strokes is slightly different: backstroke, breaststroke, butterfly, freestyle.

For more experienced swimmers, completing a 400 m IM always proves to be a good challenge and is worth swimming every now and then to spice up your training regime.

The Most Important Walk in Swimming

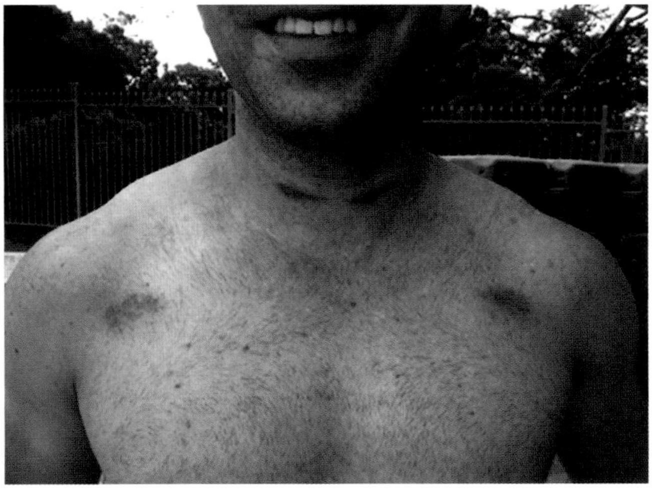

A final tip: guys, don't forget to shave that 5 o'clock shadow before you swim!

It might be as little as 10 metres but the walk from the changing rooms to the pool can really define your swimming. If you've been learning freestyle or working on improving your stroke then you should feel proud of yourself. Most people in the world cannot swim and many in the Western world do absolutely no exercise at all. You may not be the fastest swimmer in the world but that is absolutely fine thank you – so start walking out onto the pool deck tall and proud. Like your mum used to say: 'head up, shoulders back, chest forwards!'

Adopting some positive body language and being confident in what you are doing will make a real difference when you start swimming. For one thing it will improve the positivity and rhythm in your stroke, which can only be good for your technique. And, if you can carry forward that shoulders-back posture into your stroke you will start to 'Swim Proud', which is great for your alignment in the water.

CHAPTER 32

Nutrition for Longer Sessions and Races

At Swim Smooth we are often asked questions about what food and drink swimmers and triathletes should be using when they train and race to keep themselves fuelled and hydrated. Getting this aspect of your training preparation right is very important and will also determine how well you perform in training sessions and how quickly you recover afterwards. Studies have shown the negative effects of dehydration on performance as being anything upwards of 20% and if you have ever depleted your energy strokes and 'hit the wall' whilst you have been training you will know the profound effect that this also has.

Whilst we believe in a balanced wholefood diet outside of your training and racing, here are a few tips on what you can do immediately before, during and after training to supplement your fuel stores and maintain your hydration levels. We have written our advice on this as a direct response to an email we received recently from one of our swimmers who is contemplating the challenge of the 20 km Rottnest Channel Swim in February 2012:

> *Hi Paul,*
>
> *I have been doing the Saturday morning set the last three weeks with Stu and Clare and feel like I am pretty close to running on empty after about 4 k.*
>
> *You mentioned using carbohydrate gels in one of the sessions last week – would it just be one of those after 3 or 4 km? In terms of fluids – just water or a Gatorade or similar?*
>
> *Would you recommend anything before a 5–7 k swim – bananas, muesli bar??*
>
> *Where do you get the carbohydrate gels?*
>
> *Cheers,*
>
> *Chris*

There are a couple of things worth pointing out with respect to training and racing nutrition to fully answer this question Chris:

1. When training early in the morning your body has slept for 6–8 hrs and whilst this requires less energy than when you are awake, you still do burn calories whilst asleep. Although some swimmers

Food, food, glorious food! A collection of possible food and carbohydrate drink mixes for your training and racing.

prefer training on a totally empty stomach, we highly recommend having something before training to top up your muscle and liver glycogen stores. I personally have 'Weet-bix' cereal with hot milk and a sprinkle of sugar washed down with a vitamin drink, which I find works really well. Other people might have a banana, muesli bar or some toast and honey or jam. I will often sip on a bottle of water on my way to the pool to top up my hydration levels.

2. Your body typically stores enough fuel in the form of carbohydrate (glycogen) to last you through 1½–2 hrs of moderate to hard intensity training. In general you want to avoid becoming depleted so it's important that you top-up your energy during any session lasting over an hour. When you exercise very lightly you use a larger portion of stored fat as your fuel source but as soon as intensity starts to lift above 70–75%, an ever greater share of your fuel source starts to come from carbohydrates. Given that this session is long (5+ km) and it becomes progressively faster, it has the potential to be a real drain on your glycogen stores. As you get fitter, the body becomes better equipped for utilising stored fat as a fuel source but your pacing in the first 1–2 km of a hard set like this is important as well – go off too fast and you will immediately start draining your carbohydrate stores which will leave you wanting later in the session or race.
3. Personally I alternate between drinking 250 ml of Gatorade (mixed into the recommended 6–8% solution) every 25 minutes with 250 ml of Gatorade or water together with a carbohydrate gel like a GU. Some say you should never ingest a gel and Gatorade together (or similar carbohydrate rich drink) as the sugar solution might be too strong in your stomach and can cause gastro-intestinal problems. Whilst this is true for some, it's not true for everyone – which is why you should use your training sessions as a way of experimenting with what works best for you. My little formula gives me 500 ml of fluid per hour plus 30 g carbohydrate from the Gatorade and 25 g from the gel (55 g total). This is somewhat lower than the standard recommendation often made to triathletes of 1g/kg/hr (75 g per hour for someone of my size) plus 600-1000ml of fluid per hour. I've always found the greater total fluid and fuel volume more of a source of stomach upset than combining a gel together with Gatorade, but as I say this is highly individual and something to test out thoroughly yourself.
4. These days carbohydrate sports gels can be bought at many sports stores or online. Whilst I use Gatorade most often as my drink source (because of its wide availability in supermarkets) other brands offer more sophisticated carbohydrate drinks too. 'Pure Sport' is a drink that we're

currently trialling (as used by Mr Michael Phelps himself). This contains a little protein as well as carbohydrates and electrolytes – the carbohydrates are for fuel, the electrolytes are to replace lost minerals through sweat, and the protein is to enhance recovery and reduce muscle damage. Other good brands include Powerade, Science In Sport and Powerbar.

5. Not everyone likes to consume a gel due to the texture, so experimenting with things like Powerbars, cereal bars, honey sandwiches and bananas are also a worthwhile thing to do to find out what works best for you, albeit they are generally harder to eat and digest than gels. On my Rottnest crossings (and for the English Channel) I took a large variety of things with me (some of which are comfort foods and make me feel good if I'm getting low, e.g. Fry's Turkish Delight – yum!) just in case I fancied something different. When I swam the English Channel, despite being in the water for a little over 12 hours, I hardly strayed from my original Gatorade and GU gel plan but it was good to know that I had something different readily available if I wanted it.
6. Whilst it's fair to say that sweat and evaporation rates are a lot different on land than in the water, you do still lose fluid in the water, so rehydrating is essential. If you are not needing to urinate every 60–90 minutes whilst training, you could be starting to become dehydrated. Equally, over-hydrating (more than 1.2 litres per hour, especially as plain water) can be extremely dangerous due to an effect known as hyponatremia, which is where you flush the body's cells of their sodium stores. So whilst my 25-minute fuelling and hydrating strategy works for me, you should experiment between 15 and 35 minutes to see what works best. In a pool session when you are not swimming continuously it is advisable to have a water bottle for little sips in between your major fuel stops.
7. If you finish a session completely drained of fuel then it's going to take you a much longer time to recover. We get fitter (and faster) through a good balance of hard work and recovery. Take too long recovering between sessions and you will feel much less energetic at your next session. Consequently you always end up performing below par and never see the big improvements. This is why fuelling is so essential for effective training.
8. Aiming to get in 20–30 g of carbohydrates immediately after a long session like this will really pay dividends – a Nutella sandwich is always a favourite for me within 20 minutes of finishing a tough session. Things like Sustagen drinks are also a good way of recovering post session too.

This is certainly not an exhaustive section on sports nutrition but the take home points are: don't skip on nutrition, experiment with what works best for you and don't forget to consume some carbohydrate rich foods immediately after training to aid rapid recovery and reduce the urge to snack on fatty foods later in the day.

KEY

3

Open Water

Skills, tactics and stroke adaptations for swimming in open water

The Importance of Open Water Skills

When discussing open water events with swimmers, one of the most frequently asked questions we are asked is:

'What time do you predict I can do for open water swim X?'

As we saw in Chapter 27, knowing your current level of swim specific fitness (your CSS pace) is a key predictor of your performance for distance swimming in the pool. However, knowing this threshold pace will only give you a guesstimate of what you might be capable of in the open water.

Swimming well in the open water requires you to be proficient in a wide variety of areas within swimming including:

- **Managing anxiety** and the feelings of claustrophobia that can come from the 'washing machine' effect at the start of a race.
- **Sighting** and the ability to swim straight between marker buoys.
- **Drafting** faster swimmers for improved times or with swimmers of similar ability for less energy expenditure.
- **Turning** and improving your speed around buoys with maintenance of good rhythm and momentum.
- **Effective wetsuit swimming** by adapting your stroke to work with, not against, the rubber of the suit.
- **Strategies** to adapt to a variety of open water conditions, both technically and psychologically.

In an effort to constantly refine your technical capabilities in the pool it is very easy to forget about honing your open water skills until the start of the summer race season. However, to swim effectively in open water these skills need to be developed and refined all year round with just as much priority as traditional stroke technique work. This can be done very effectively – whilst having a lot of fun – in the pool during the winter months. As we shall see, developing these skills in the controlled environment of a pool is easier in many regards than in an open water environment.

Working on improvements in your stroke mechanics is very important and you can certainly make significant gains in this area in the pool. However, studies have shown that an effective drafting technique can save you up to 38% of your energy expenditure [1]. This is a staggering saving and to be honest one that you would struggle to match by improving your stroke mechanics alone, at least in the short term.

If you add into that equation further improvements in handling anxiety, sighting, navigation skills and the ability to swim straight without a black line, then you can understand why Swim Smooth is so passionate about giving your open water skills the attention they deserve all year round. What's more, developing these skills can be a lot of fun and help to break the monotony of following the black line endlessly up and down the pool.

PAUL: *Here in Perth we run an open water skills session once a week all year round. This takes places on a Saturday lunch time and is a favourite session of local triathletes and open water swimmers – even in the middle of winter. We have a lot of fun and it's personally my favourite session of the week to coach!*

Age-group triathletes are particularly time poor as they must split their training time between three sports, around a full time job and having a healthy family life too. This shortage of time in the water makes it even more critical to focus on the right things when you are training. If you are a time strapped triathlete looking to improve your swim performances, make sure that you practise your open water skills regularly, ideally at least once a week.

ADAM: *During every Swim Smooth Clinic we run we ask swimmers if they regularly practise their stroke technique by working on appropriate drills in the pool. Nearly every hand is raised – great! But when asked who practises their open water skills regularly, very few hands go up. This highlights a real imbalance in most swimmers' approach to the sport – don't make this mistake yourself!*

Open Water vs. Pool Swimming

Just like swimming in the pool? The Indian Ocean was pancake flat before this Ironman swim start.

A small plea from us: never be sold on the illusion that swimming in the pool is exactly the same as swimming in the open water. The fact is that the two can be incredibly different. The contrast is akin to road cycling on smooth flat asphalt, versus a technically challenging and hilly mountain bike trail. Make a commitment to get better at all of these skills at any time in the season and you'll be translating and adapting your smooth freestyle pool stroke more efficiently to a variety of conditions in the open water. In the next six chapters we show you how.

Reference

1. Chatard, J.-C., and B. Wilson. 2003. Drafting Distance in Swimming. *Med. Sci. Sports Exerc.*, Vol. 35, No. 7, pp. 1176–1181.

CHAPTER 34 Managing Anxiety

PAUL: *Back in 2001 I was asked to do some wetsuit testing for a popular UK triathlon magazine whilst on location at the inaugural UK Half Ironman championships in Llanberis, North Wales. A large marquee was erected at the event and athletes were able to mingle and look at all the latest training gear whilst asking questions of the professional triathletes and seeking useful tips.*

I remember being questioned by one of the local athletes who would be doing his very first triathlon at the event the following day. Like many novices he was very apprehensive about the thought of swimming in the dark and cold Llyn Padarn lake having had very little experience up to this point. As I was about to start offering a few tips of advice to the athlete, his father came over and interrupted us. He was a rather burly and forthright Welshman who had his own thoughts about how his son should approach the event. Knowing the area well, he proceeded to tell us a tale about how several plane and helicopter crashes had occurred at the site with the most recent being an RAF Wessex helicopter crash in 1993.

His Dad then thought it humorous to tell us that the bodies were never recovered and to just imagine one floating up to the surface whilst we were swimming! Obviously this threw the poor young guy completely but that very afternoon I went for a swim in the lake to test several wetsuits and all I could think about was this story to the point of it bringing on quite a severe panic attack. I've never swum so fast back to shore in my life!

Anxiety attacks in the open water are very common and can affect swimmers of any ability level, the only common denominator sometimes being those who have more vivid imaginations. The possibility of anxiety attacks should be taken seriously as they cannot only ruin your race but your overall confidence in your swimming ability too.

If you ever feel anxious in open water – or in the pool – here are some important coping strategies that you can use to help you overcome those feelings:

1. **Remember You Are Not Alone**. Many of us are embarrassed to even admit that we feel uncomfortable swimming in open water but most swimmers suffer some level of anxiety to a greater or lesser extent. Try talking openly with others about how you feel and this will help you identify what in particular triggers the feelings of panic. Half the battle when tackling anxieties is working out what it is that specifically brings on an attack – for example it could be swallowing

During the anxiety of an open water swim start it is essential that you block out everything around you and focus just on yourself.

some water and fearing you're going to choke or perhaps losing your orientation and sense of direction. Other common triggers can be the cold itself, fear of the deep, fear of marine life or swimming into reeds. The reasons will be very personal to you and your circumstances.

2. **Become Selfish**. When you're training in the pool and thinking about your technique, you're only ever concerned about yourself and how well you're performing the exercise. The environment is calm and controlled and you can go about your task easily. As soon as you enter open water that calm internal focus can be rapidly replaced with thinking about external factors which are out of your control such as other swimmers, waves, fish, the thought of touching something, etc. A key skill for swimming well in open water is to block out those thoughts and return your focus on to you, your stroke and your breathing. We call this 'becoming a selfish swimmer'!
3. **Use Cue Words**. Often referred to as mantras, repeating cue words such as *'relax'*, *'breathe'*, *'control'*, *'smooth'* can help keep you focused on the here and now of each stroke rather than letting your mind wander to things out of your control. One of our best teaching mantras that also works well in the open water is *'breathe-bubble-bubble-breathe'* as outlined in Chapter 7. Give it a try – simplicity of focus is key in the open water.
4. **Practise With Friends**. Any time you go for a swim in the open water you should set up some practice sets with a group of friends. Swimming in a group supports everyone's safety in the water and with the support of non-threatening, non-competitive training partners you will really start to tune up your skills and grow your confidence. Practise some of the more advanced concepts like drafting and open water turns in the pool first so that you get a good head-start before using them in open water.

PAUL: *If you only remember one open water tip from this book, let it be to remember to exhale into the water at the start of a race. When the gun goes off far too many swimmers set off at break-neck speed, hold their breath and so become very tense. Holding your breath is a sure-fire way to trigger a panic attack and potentially ruin your whole race. By all means set off at a good pace but remember to breathe out under the water as though you are sighing and you'll have a fantastic swim!*

CHAPTER 35 Swimming Straighter

PAUL: *We started this section with a very common question: 'How fast do you think I can swim this event in the open water?' I was asked this exact question by an athlete that had just started swimming with us in early 2010, prior to the Busselton Half Ironman.*

Dan is a very dedicated athlete who seeks to improve his times in all three disciplines and often uses the latest technology to help him in this quest. Given that he'd been training consistently for the event in the pool and knowing that his CSS (threshold pace) was exactly 1:48/100m, I thought that this pace would be a reasonable goal to aim for during the 1900m swim leg. Although a Half Ironman swim is normally just below CSS pace I took into account that Dan is a leg-sinker (and still at that point very much an 'Arnie' Swim Type, see Chapter 18) and so would gain considerable assistance from the buoyancy of his wetsuit. I quoted a target of between 34 and 35 minutes for the swim having the exact figure of 34 minutes and 12 seconds in my head. Given that I'm often very close in my predictions, I was confident that this would be a good goal to aim for.

Part of Dan's GPS plot indicating inaccuracies in the ability to swim straight in the open water.

On race day I waited at the swim exit to see all my athletes complete the swim discipline. After 35 minutes Dan hadn't exited the water; 37 minutes – still no sign; 40 minutes – nothing. By 42 minutes I started to get very concerned that he had suffered a bad cramp or had succumbed to some kind of marine life attack, God forbid. Ten minutes after his allocated goal time Dan came running out of the water, seemingly very happy with his swim, stating that he felt great. All I could think was how disappointed Dan would be when he saw his time – he had averaged 2:13/100m or 25 seconds per 100m slower than what I thought he would.

After the race I discovered that Dan had swum with a waterproof Garmin 310XT GPS device under his swim cap, which had recorded his entire swim path. On analysing the data we found that instead of covering 1.9km, Dan had actually covered 2.33km. More than 22% too far! This was an incredibly insightful piece of data only made possible with the advent of waterproof GPS devices like the Garmin. What was also interesting to see was that Dan had indeed averaged 1:48/100m for the 2.33km that he had covered, exactly as I thought he would.

Dan would go on to use his Garmin to improve his ability to swim much straighter in future events and knock off massive chunks of time by addressing this aspect of his swim preparation. Prior to GPS tracking we could only ever guesstimate how much extra distance someone might be swimming off course but now we have the technology to find out. Whilst Dan's example might sound quite extreme, as we see more and more GPS data at Swim Smooth we find that swimming 10% or more too far in a race is really very common. If you don't swim as well as you expect in open water then investing in a GPS watch and wearing it under your swim cap could be exactly what you need to find out what's going wrong. For Dan discovering this and gaining the motivation to improve this aspect of his swimming was worth a massive 10 minutes over 1.9km!

Let's take a look at some of the tactics Dan used to prepare more specifically for open water swimming:

1. Avoiding Crossovers

As discussed in Chapter 10 of this book, crossing over in front of your head as your hand enters into the water is an extremely common stroke flaw; in open water that crossover pulls you constantly off course. Crossovers are normally at their worst when breathing as your thoughts are simply about getting in air and you forget your stroke alignment, so it is no coincidence that most swimmers go off course when breathing.

Without the constraints of the pool lanes and a black line to follow you can be pulled a long way off line and add considerable distance to your swim. Use the side kicking drills and visualisation in Appendix A to improve your swimming posture and alignment in the water. Also shift your focus when breathing back to the alignment of your lead hand; to do this you might count each stroke by repeating to yourself '*1-2-straight-1-2-straight*' where the word '*straight*' coincides with your breathing stroke.

2. Bilateral Breathing and Frequency of Sighting

We are big fans of bilateral breathing at Swim Smooth for the simple reason that it naturally helps maintain the symmetry of your stroke and so helps you swim straighter in open water. Even if you only treat bilateral breathing as a training practice you then have the choice of either side to breathe to unilaterally whilst racing. We have heard some swimming coaches state that you should only ever breathe to one side in open water as this gives you a greater oxygen uptake. This makes sense, however, usually the reason swimmers start to feel starved of oxygen is due to the fact that they are not exhaling properly into the water between breaths. By improving their exhalation such swimmers find it much easier to breathe bilaterally even at racing levels of effort. Also, as we mentioned earlier, holding onto your breath is never a good idea as it can bring on anxiety attacks followed by hyperventilation.

Many unilateral breathers accept the fact that they might lose stroke symmetry and swim off course as a result; to counter this they sight forwards more frequently to correct their course. The problem with this solution is that sighting carries an energy cost of its own as you have to lift your head to breathe which sinks your legs downward even in a wetsuit. In an ideal world every swimmer would be able to swim so straight that they would never have to sight but everyone is eventually moved off course slightly by waves, current and even other swimmers. The key point here is that the less often you need to sight the faster you will swim and the best pathway to swimming straighter is bilateral breathing.

ADAM: *You can experiment with keeping your eyes closed in a safe open water environment or an empty pool without lane ropes to see how straight you can swim. The furthest you can travel without moving off course is the answer to how often you should be sighting, give or take a few strokes – at least in calm conditions! Take caution when attempting this though, as hitting an object in the water when swimming can be potentially injurious! Another way of performing a similar exercise is to have your eyes closed when your head is down but then open your eyes whenever you go to sight forwards. This can help to simulate the sensation of swimming in murky water conditions.*

3. Minimal Head Lift When Sighting

Every swimmer needs to sight forwards in order to stay straight but developing the movement and timing of their sighting technique is something very few people practise regularly. The most common mistake to make when sighting forwards is to lift your whole face out of the water and try to sight and breathe at the same time. In order to lift your head out sufficiently to breathe, the legs have to sink dramatically adding to your drag profile in the water, even when wearing a wetsuit.

A good sighting technique involves lifting just your eyes out of the water and then rolling your head to the side to breathe, this should happen in one smooth fluid

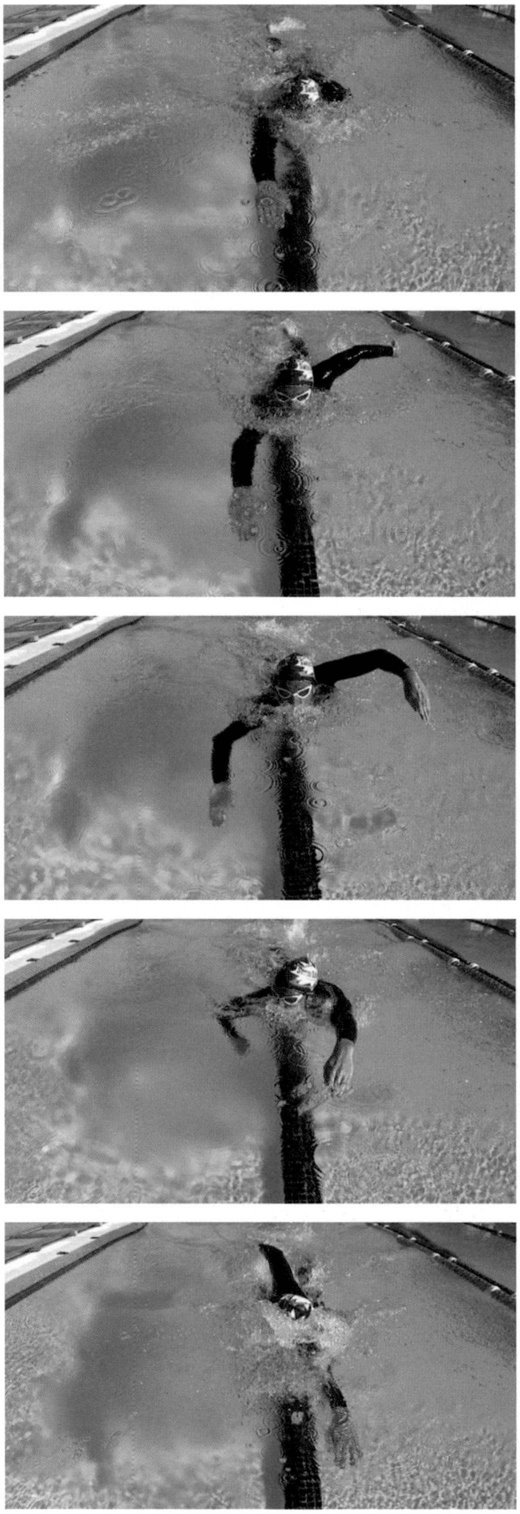

Sighting technique sequence: lift your head just enough to sight forwards and then breathe to the side.

movement. If you were about to breathe to your right, you would press down slightly with the right arm as you pull through so as to raise just your eyes above the water line before continuing to roll the head with your body's natural rotation to the right and take a breath as normal.

Do not try and hold your head up high for several strokes until you can see exactly where you are going with a waterpolo style of stroke, that is extremely fatiguing. If you do not see where you are going on your first sighting stroke then do not panic, just try again in a couple of strokes time. You will not always get a clear view every time you sight forwards but by sighting two or three times in a row you will gradually change what is initially a fuzzy picture into a clearer view of where you are going. Once you have that image in your head of where you are heading, lock onto it and focus entirely on cutting as straight a line as possible to that point.

4. Sighting on Large Immovable Objects

This is a classic tip. Before the start of your open water event, walk around as much of the swim course as you can and get down as close to water level as possible to line up the marker buoys with fixed points on the horizon. A large object on the horizon could be significantly easier to see than a turn buoy whilst swimming in a group of swimmers during the race. Suitable objects might include the peak of a hill or mountain, a large building or trees.

By correctly lining these points up before the start and then aiming towards them when the gun goes off, you stand a much better chance of swimming in a straight line between the turn buoys. At many locations it might only be possible to line up the first marker buoy from the start line. If that is the case, then work out as many sighting points as you can for other sections of the course. If your swim will be in a river or following the line of a shore, make sure that you gauge the distance well in order to swim parallel and straight. Keep a check on this every time you breathe to your side.

5. Don't be a Sheep

When drafting behind another swimmer it is very easy to fall into a false sense of security and think that the lead swimmer will track accurately towards the next buoy. Even the best swimmers in the world can drift off course sometimes, so maintain your own responsibility for swimming straight by regularly sighting and adjusting your position if necessary. If your lead swimmer does drift off course you will have to weigh up the benefit of the draft versus swimming in a straight line. This is not always an easy decision and you may have to risk the success of your swim on this choice.

ADAM: *It's well worth investing in a couple of pairs of goggles (preferably of the same design that you know fit you well) with different lens tints for the different lighting conditions that you may experience. Cool mirrored lenses will be too dark in low-light conditions no matter how good you look wearing them! Equally, a clear lens in low early morning sunlight can be dazzling.*

Choose goggles which do not leak, have good anti-fog properties and won't dislodge easily if you happen to get a knock from another swimmer. Avoid touching the inside of the lens with your greasy fingers (especially if you've used them to apply sunscreen or wetsuit lubricant) as this will ruin the anti-fog properties very quickly. You won't notice your goggles if they are working well but a goggle malfunction could cost you your race.

Drafting Effectively

Swimming behind or to the side of another swimmer to gain an advantage from being in their wake is called 'drafting'. As we will see later, studies have shown up to a 38% saving in your energy expenditure from drafting another swimmer – that's a huge saving and equivalent to what you would gain from being tucked up behind a couple of cyclists in a pack if you ride a bike. The benefits of drafting in open water are so great that it is essential for you to become comfortable drafting other swimmers and fine tune your skills in a variety of different positions and situations.

ADAM: *If you are new to open water swimming or triathlon then you may be wondering if drafting behind another swimmer is legal. Don't worry, it most certainly is! Unlike in a cycling time trial or non-drafting triathlon bike leg, drafting behind other competitors is very much seen as part of the sport of open water swimming and something that you should be looking to become accustomed to and maximise to your advantage.*

PAUL: *In our squad training sessions over in Perth, I am very keen to know and monitor the performance of our swimmers. The best way of doing this is to use a regular time trial over a distance such as 400 m or 1000 m in the pool. I don't think anyone looks forward to time trials as there is certainly no hiding from the results but it's only through measuring your performance that you'll really know whether or not the hard work you are putting in is paying off. Time trials are also an excellent way to assess your key open water skills like drafting.*

In October 2010 I decided to run a 1000 m time trial for our squads but with a slight twist. In our 5:30 am Tuesday session we have four lanes of differing abilities:

Lane 1 (the 'fast lane') has swimmers capable of around 20 minutes for 1000 m.
Lane 2 (the 'faster lane') is capable of approximately 17-19 minutes for 1000 m.
Lane 3 (the 'even faster lane') around 15-16 minutes for 1000 m.
Lane 4 (the 'fastest lane') is capable of sub-15 minutes for 1000 m (most swimming around 13 minutes).

Drafting in open water is perfectly legal and when performed correctly is a huge strategic advantage.

We performed a 1000 m time trial and the eight swimmers in lane 1 averaged 19 minutes and 12 seconds. This was a very pleasing result and a good sign that their hard work was paying off. Unbeknownst to them though, we would be repeating the same exercise again in just two weeks time but this time drafting one behind the other would be actively encouraged!

For this second time trial we invited two of the swimmers from lane 2 to swim at the front of lane 1 with the instruction for them to set the pace at their personal best time from two weeks previous. This equated to 17 minutes and 41 seconds for the 1000 m, a pace which they successfully repeated. The other swimmers in lane 1 started immediately behind and had the sole goal of trying to stay on the toes of the swimmer in front for the entire 1000 m. Knowing that these lane 2 swimmers were significantly faster, many shuddered at the thought of how hard this task would be but, lo and behold, every single swimmer in lane 1 went on to swim 17 minutes and 41 seconds! An improvement of 91 seconds (or nearly 100 m in distance) from just two weeks previous.

Even 'a healthy sprinkling of Swim Smooth magic' in the areas of training and technique could not give these swimmers that increase in speed in two weeks – it was down to the benefits of drafting faster swimmers.

Despite their excellent performances some of the swimmers said that they didn't enjoy the experience of swimming so close to others and that it felt claustrophobic. This is a fair observation, especially for those newer to open water swimming. However, in the Swim Smooth offices we receive many emails from swimmers around the world who are frustrated that they are under-performing in open water and want to know how to improve. A typical comment we hear is 'once I get through the start I try to find some clear water and then lengthen out' but there-in lies the problem: clear water is the last thing you should be seeking in open water if you want to achieve your best performances, you should be looking to draft all the time and prepare in training to be comfortable doing so. Could this be the source of your own open-water plateau?

The potential speed improvements gained by drafting effectively make an interesting comparison to those made by improving your conventional stroke technique or fitness. By drafting effectively you stand to gain between 30 seconds and two minutes per kilometre swum, a very large chunk of time which you cannot stand to ignore. Improvements to your speed from stroke technique gains or swim specific fitness may be less than this amount individually but each should be looked at as an important component of your entire preparation. We'll show you later in Appendix C how you can combine these elements in your training sessions to give you the maximum performance gains for your swimming. The ability to draft effectively takes skill and a certain tenacity, it doesn't just happen without practice. If you are planning on competing in triathlon or open water swimming events then you should be practising these skills in a structured manner all year round, just as you would your conventional stroke technique. Very few swimmers and triathletes do this, offering you the potential for a distinct competitive advantage!

Technical Aside

If you are interested in the research behind drafting here's an overview of the key studies:

ADAM: *The technical term 'metabolic cost' refers to the energy used by the swimmers. You can equate it to your physical effort: a reduction of 20% metabolic cost is a 20% reduction in your workload.*

A collaborative study in 2003 between Jean-Claude Chatard of the University of Saint-Etienne in France and Barry Wilson at the University of Otago in Dunedin, New Zealand [1], aimed to show just how much benefit there is to be gained from swimming behind, or to the side of, another swimmer in a fixed flume tank environment. The study examined which were the most effective positions (to the side or behind) and also the optimal distance to be from the lead swimmer. The study concluded that sitting approximately 50cm behind the lead swimmer reduced the draftee's metabolic response between 11% and 38%. The large range in the result possibly indicates just how skilful this practice is, with those more technically proficient at drafting being able to reap the biggest rewards.

Several other studies have also shown similar savings. Delextrat et al. in 2003 [2] found a 10-24% reduction in the metabolic cost of swimming when drafting was compared with swimming solo. In a 1998 study of elite triathletes, Chatard, Chollet and Millet [3] found up to a 3.2% improvement in direct speed (around 40 seconds per 1500 m). Interestingly, this latter study indicated that those of very lean muscle mass saw the biggest gains from drafting, potentially because the elevated speed assisted in their horizontal body position in the water – Arnies take note!

How to Draft

There are two distinct positions in which you can draft:

1. Directly Behind a Faster Swimmer

If you have swum in a busy squad session then this position will be well known to you! The effect of swimming directly behind another swimmer is the reason why many swimmers prefer to swim in

The simplest way to draft – directly behind another swimmer.

second or third place rather than lead the lane. It is significantly easier to swim behind another swimmer and the closer you can get to them the easier it will be. Conversely though, spend too much of your time swimming like this in a squad session and you might not be developing your aerobic capacity to its fullest!

Of the two ways to draft, this is by far the most common to see. Try to get as close as possible to the person in front of you but do not actually touch their feet. This is all too easy to do but will probably annoy them and risk you receiving a sharp retaliatory kick! If you end up pushing down on their feet this will increase their drag and slow them, and ultimately you, down.

PAUL: *When you see elite triathletes and open water swimmers drafting one behind the other they are very skillful at maintaining just the right distance behind the swimmer in front to gain the maximum draft and be the least annoying that they can be to the person in front. It's not advantageous to be a nuisance by constantly tapping on the toes of the person in front of you and these elite swimmers know that first-hand, waiting patiently for when they might strike and come around their leader to win the race. One way they do this is by stroking quite wide around the feet of the swimmer in front, thus bringing their head and chest even closer to the leader. This takes quite a bit of courage as a misplaced kick can easily end up knocking them in the jaw!*

Cyclists in a peloton often use tactics to subtly slow their pace and control their distance to maintain the optimal position by becoming less aerodynamically efficient, i.e. sitting up or moving out into the wind momentarily. Elite swimmers might adopt similar tactics by applying the brakes with the lead hand in the same manner that an Overglider might unwittingly do when trying to really lengthen out. The elite swimmer uses this to slow their pace though, whereas the Overglider will feel that they are gliding more and incorrectly assume that they are becoming more efficient as a result. This is just another example of how perception and feel can be quite different to what is happening in reality.

ADAM: *The other Swim Smooth coaches and I refer to something called the 'Lane 1 Magneto Effect'. This is where the lane one swimmers in our squads gravitate towards each other despite us setting them off at 5 or 10 second intervals. Normally within 100 m-200 m of any set they are all circulating round as one big group in the lane! They have intuitively learned that there's a distinct advantage to swimming close behind another swimmer and at the start of any swim put in a big effort to catch the person in front.*

2. To the Side and Within the Wake of a Faster Swimmer

Each swimmer creates a V-shaped wake when they move forwards in the water, the size of this wake will be determined by the size of the athlete and also their speed. By sitting to one side of the swimmer, positioned so that your head is somewhere between their hips and chest, you will be within this wake and can experience a very powerful drafting effect. The key to this skill is to be able to adjust your stroke rhythm so as to synchronise your stroke timing with theirs. This is important otherwise your arms will clash and both of you will become frustrated.

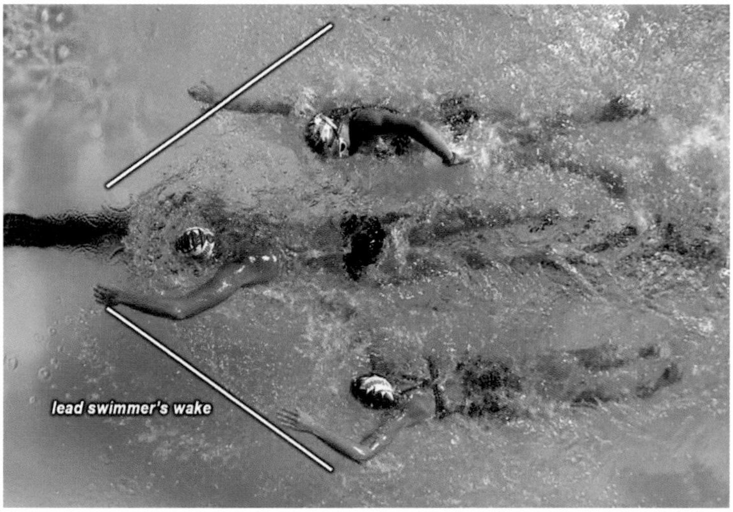

A more technical way to draft is close to the side of the lead swimmer, within their wake.

From the perspective of breathing easily it would make sense to breathe away from the person you are drafting so that you're breathing into undisturbed water. Unfortunately, doing this tends to pull you wide of the other swimmer, which can easily drop you out of the draft zone and lose you all the benefit of it. For this reason the golden rule is to always breathe in towards the stronger swimmer even if this makes breathing itself slightly harder. This is one occasion where unilateral breathing (breathing to

The perfect way to train in open water is by taking a coached skills session like this Swim Smooth one in Perth.

one side only) is advantageous to you. Of course you still need the ability to breathe to either side so that you can draft on either side of a swimmer as opportunities present themselves during a race.

A further advantage of drafting alongside another swimmer in this manner is that should you start to get dropped you can move directly behind to jump onto their feet, providing you with a very useful lifeline.

PAUL: *You will encounter situations in races where you are drafting another swimmer and feel that the pace is too easy for you. Before trying to break free by yourself, contemplate how much benefit you might be gaining from the draft and if this could explain why it feels quite slow. Often moving out of the draft and going solo becomes a shock as the extra effort of swimming by yourself suddenly catches up with you. You might also finish the swim and find the swimmer you overtook happily swimming on your toes!*

If you are really in a group of swimmers that are too slow for you then you will need to break free and swim solo but a better strategy might have been to start slightly quicker to find a better group to swim with. Your innate pace judgement is important here as it will help you judge your own pace and those of others around you at the start of a race, allowing you to look for swimmers slightly faster than yourself to latch onto in the first 50 m or 100 m. Of course if you know your competition well then you can simply line up directly behind a swimmer slightly faster than yourself before the race starts and stick to them like a limpet when the gun goes off! This tactic has personally served me well in many races and seen me significantly outperform where I would otherwise finish in a race.*

*Pace judgement is a very important skill in swimming and one that you can fine tune by using your training sessions in the pool. We looked at this in Chapter 28.

References

1. Chatard, J.-C., and B. Wilson. 2003. Drafting Distance in Swimming. *Med. Sci. Sports Exerc.*, Vol. 35, No. 7, pp. 1176–1181.
2. Delextrat, A., V. Tricot, T. Bernard, F. Vercruyssen, C. Hausswirth, and J. Brisswalter. 2003. Drafting during Swimming Improves Efficiency during Subsequent Cycling. *Med. Sci. Sports Exerc.*, Vol. 35, No. 9, pp. 1612–1619.
3. Chatard, J.C., Chollet, D., Millet, G. 1998. Performance and Drag during Drafting Swimming in Highly Trained Triathletes. *Med Sci Sports Exerc.* 30:1276–1278.

Turning Around Buoys

PAUL: *The annual 'Swim Thru Perth' race is a 4 km swim in the Swan River from Barrack Street Jetty to Matilda Bay and is Australia's longest-running open water swimming event, having been inaugurated in 1919. The musician and artist Rolf Harris famously raced the 4 km in the early 1950s swimming backstroke. At the time Rolf was the Australian junior backstroke champion and a very handy swimmer by all accounts.*

I have competed in this event most years since I moved to Perth in 2002 and one incident springs to mind when discussing turning around buoys and the general mêlée of swimming in close quarters to other swimmers. The gun had gone off and we were into the first few hundred meters of the swim when I first became aware of a swimmer alongside me who I just couldn't seem to shake off. We were constantly bumping into each other in a bid to pick the straightest line, neither wishing to concede an inch or wisely choosing to sit back and jump on the other's toes for a nice draft.

The swim course is one long straight-line with a final very sharp right-hand turn with 80 m or so to the finish. By this point we had been duelling it out for just over 48 minutes and clearly whoever made it first around that buoy would beat the other. I felt a hand reach out and grab my shoulder, ducking me several feet under the water. Coming up and gasping for air, another hand perfectly connected with the same shoulder and forced me down once again. Fearing more that I would drown at this point, and less that I would win our mini-race, I had no other choice but to jab the assailant in the ribs with my elbow whilst under the water to ensure that I did actually resurface. Sadly the damage was already done and I came off second best across the finish line.

Being deliberately dunked in this way is incredibly rare but it highlights that there will be times in open water where your reserve will be tested. Rather than shying away from swimming close to other swimmers, practise getting close to your training buddies and become accustomed to the odd small knock without it putting you off your stroke. Inevitably you will experience a few knocks and bangs whilst swimming in open water – most of which are entirely accidental. They're never pleasant but become experienced swimming in close proximity to other swimmers and those knocks won't put you off enjoying this great sport.

To turn past a buoy, slide your inner arm past the buoy, flip onto your back and then back onto your front.

The thought of the washing machine effect as swimmers converge on a turn buoy in a triathlon or open water swim can be very intimidating to those new to open water swimming. Many worry about getting caught up on the fixing rope or being pushed under water by their competitors (a very rare occurrence). These fears are mostly groundless but there is little wonder many swimmers give turn buoys a very wide birth adding considerable distance to their swims. You might also feel the need to switch to head-up breaststroke round the buoy in an effort not to get swamped. This will ruin the rhythm and flow of your swim though and can result in other competitors swimming into the back of you.

By working on improving your turning technique you can swim through these areas of the course in a much more effective (and impressive!) manner:

1. **Get Ahead.** If you have been swimming side by side with a couple of other swimmers, it will serve you well to make sure that you are the first around the buoy. Put in a short burst of speed about 25 m before the turn to get there first.
2. **Corkscrew Roll.** As you approach the buoy, keep in close and aim to slide the hand closest past the buoy and roll over onto your back and then continuing the roll immediately back onto your front. Add in a little twist as you do so and this should give you a neat 90° turn without breaking your stroke rhythm.

   If you wish to turn left, it's your left hand that should slide past the buoy to start the process and for a right turn, your right hand should slide past. For very tight turns try combining two consecutive rolls to bring you around the buoy quickly and efficiently. This skill does take some time to master but it is a lot of fun and practice makes perfect!
3. **Know Your Bearings.** Once you are around the buoy focus immediately on locating the next marker buoy, do not dilly-dally here! Quickly seek out the mark and get a clear bearing on it, making use of any landmarks in the background to assist you. Keep the surge going at this point and you might just drop the guys who went into the turn with you.

PAUL: *Larger marker buoys at the bigger events will float very high on the water such that they create a body width's gap under the buoy as the design tapers underneath. Avoid getting so close that you find yourself in this gap as it can be very difficult to escape without the room to bring your arm over the surface of the water!*

CHAPTER 38

Better Wetsuit Swimming

Most swimmers have a good appreciation of the potential performance gains of swimming in a wetsuit, mostly from the increase in buoyancy offered by the suit. A low-lying body position in the water is the biggest factor holding back many lean male triathletes so it is little wonder they experience the biggest improvements of all swimmers from wearing a buoyant wetsuit.

ADAM: *We conduct a lot of wetsuit testing with different styles of suits and different types of swimmers in Perth. In a well fitting suit, we often see time savings of up to five minutes over 1500 m in swimmers who have very 'sinky' legs. Amazing! As we shall see though, some other swimmers don't enjoy swimming in their wetsuits at all.*

PAUL: *I have been working with double Ironman winner Kate Bevilaqua for the last 12 months over in Perth. Kate is a fantastic athlete but is someone who finds swimming in a wetsuit very awkward indeed. It is true to say that most swimmers are substantially faster in a wetsuit than without, however Kate finds the exact opposite: she feels it is slowing her down. Many triathletes are held back by a very poor body position but conversely some have very good natural buoyancy and find that the addition of a neoprene suit actually lifts them too high out of the water. This is the problem that Kate was experiencing.*

Kate was giving away the best part of ten minutes to the other professional women in the Ironman swim when using a wetsuit. At this level of competition this is a massive amount of time and a real Achilles heel in her racing. Between Ironman Western Australia (December 2010) and Ironman Lanzarote (May 2011) we lowered Kate's swim time from 61 minutes to 53 minutes. How did we do this? Technically Kate swims very well in the open water without a wetsuit

Working with Kate in the pool in Perth.

Kate has a super high body position in the water, especially in her wetsuit. She can easily afford to use a forward-looking head position with her stroke.

but as soon as she put on her suit she felt like she was going backwards. We took a close look at why this was happening.

With our Swim Types system we identify the 'Kicktastic' swimmer who typically suffers in a wetsuit from this loss of balance; as the name suggests these swimmers like to use a strong 6-beat leg kick but wetsuits tend to bring them so high at the rear they start to kick into thin air. We identified Kate as a bit of a Kicktastic through listening to the issues that she found she was experiencing during racing. Some Overgliders who have adopted a very low head position report this same unbalanced sensation in a wetsuit.

If like Kate you feel unbalanced or too high at the rear in your wetsuit it is doubtful that you are actually slower in it; much more likely is that you gain less from a suit than other swimmers you train with and so end up looking slower relative to them. The only way to be sure is to perform a time trial with and without the wetsuit in the pool. Either way, it is a very frustrating situation to be in, especially if you have invested quite a bit of money in your wetsuit.

Many Kicktastics and Overgliders have developed their swimming with the idea that they should always keep their eyes looking straight down with a very low head position. The belief here is that doing so helps lift the hips and legs higher in the water and so reduces drag. However, for those who already have good natural buoyancy in the water wearing a wetsuit can substantially change their balance. In maintaining the same head position with the wetsuit on, the feet of these swimmers will often pop up out of the water leaving them feeling very unbalanced.

Kate also felt like she was not strong enough to use her wetsuit, that her shoulders would fatigue very quickly when using one. She experimented with a short-sleeve suit but whilst her shoulders felt a little looser, she still wasn't performing as well as she would like in it.

Kate benefited from using a straighter arm recovery.

To dramatically improve Kate's swimming performance:

1. We asked her to forget the notion of looking down but aim to look forward in the water by about 1.5 m (5 feet). This brought her legs back down into a usable and more stable position without reintroducing drag. This change also helped her substantially improve her drafting ability by being more aware of other swimmers around her from whom she could gain a tow.
2. We asked her to forget the notion of swimming with a classic high-elbow recovery over the water, which causes premature fatigue in the shoulders when working against the restriction of the wetsuit. A straighter arm recovery increased the range of movement and relaxation in her shoulders.
3. We encouraged Kate to swim more regularly in the wetsuit (both in the pool and open water) and objectively test against the stopwatch which changes were having the greatest impact.
4. We refined her drafting skills and then ensured that she practised these skills as regularly as possible with faster swimmers.

Kate's story not only shows how important it is to swim with the right stroke technique in your wetsuit but also the wider potential for making improvements in your performance by adopting the right changes to your stroke for the conditions and environment you are racing in.

Whether you are already swimming well in a wetsuit or not, there is plenty of opportunity to improve your performances further using the following tips:

1. Get the Right Fit

These days many triathletes buy much of their equipment from on-line stores but a wetsuit should always be tried on before purchasing. Ideally visit a retailer who stocks a range of different suits and be fitted out by an expert. Many stores now have Endless Pools to allow you to test suits before purchasing them, an extremely worthwhile exercise.

Like running shoes, you are not looking for the best looking or most expensive suit, you are seeking one that both fits you well and is matched to your stroke type. Take a read through the Swim Types section of this book to discover your Swim Type:

- If you are an Arnie, Bambino or Overglider* you are normally suited to a thicker suit with more buoyancy, especially in the hips and legs.
- If you are a Kicktastic, Swinger or Smooth then a thinner suit with greater flexibility is better matched to your needs.

*Overgliders fall into two camps with respect to body position: those with very slow stroke rates (under 48 SPM) and with very obvious pauses at the front of the stroke will normally have low sinking legs due to the deceleration in the stroke causing them to sink downwards and would thus benefit from a more buoyant suit. Those with less obvious dead spots and reasonable stroke rates (over 54 SPM) will normally sit very horizontally in the water and as such will benefit from a thinner, more flexible suit. Of course, those in the first scenario (Classic Overgliders) would do well to improve the inefficiencies in their stroke initially, which would then result in the win-win situation of being faster, smoother and more horizontal even without a wetsuit!

2. Spend Time Putting it on Properly

Allow yourself some time to put on your wetsuit before the race rather than leaving it to the last moment and trying to put it on frantically. Here are some tips on how to do this properly:

- Place a plastic bag over your foot like a sock and then slide the wetsuit on like a pair of trousers (Figure 38.29-1), removing the bag once the foot is through the leg of the suit.
- Slowly creep the wetsuit material up bit by bit starting at the ankles and working it up into the crotch area (Figure 38.29-3 and 38.29-4). Use a pair of gardening gloves with rubber grips to help with this and to avoid putting a hole in the wetsuit with sharp finger nails.
- Work the material up high enough that it leaves about 10 cm (3–4") of ankle and lower leg showing. This will let you move the maximum amount of material up so that the crotch is quite tight. If the suit

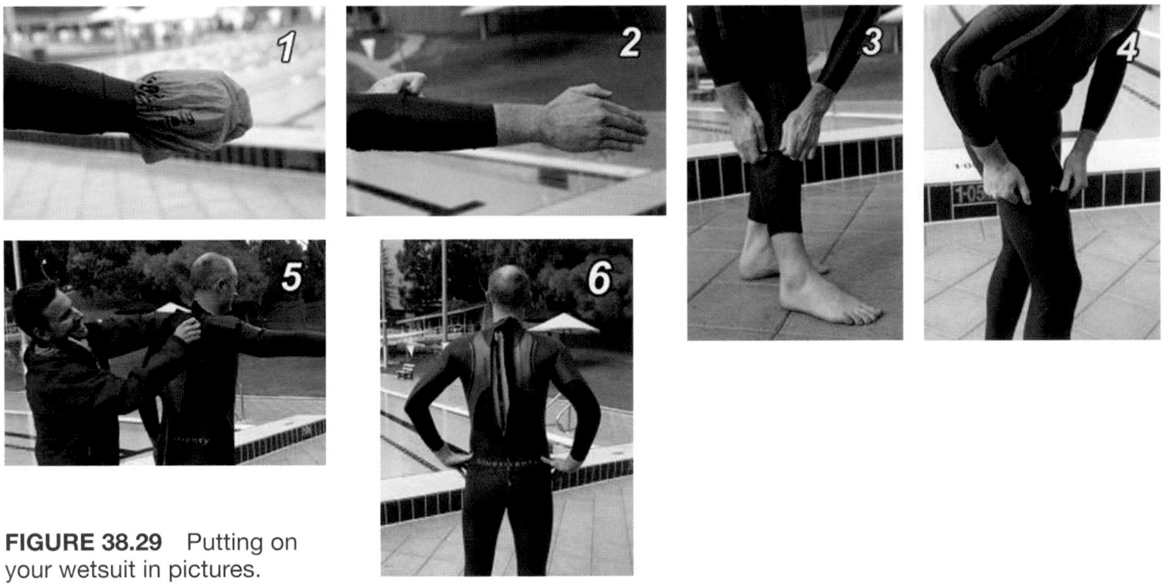

FIGURE 38.29 Putting on your wetsuit in pictures.

is loose around the crotch area then the suit will be hard to run with into transition and will make your hip flexors work overly hard whilst swimming.

- Repeat the plastic bag trick for the arms, allowing 5 cm (2") of wrist to show once the suit is over the shoulders (Figure 38.29-2).
- Before zipping up, ask a friend to help shoe-horn you into the suit from the back (Figure 29-5) by sliding one hand down the back of your arm and carefully working the wetsuit with the other hand over your shoulders. This will take a couple of extra minutes but it is time well spent as this will give you a much freer feeling around your shoulders during the swim.
- Squeeze your shoulder blades together and down as your friend zips you up (Figure 38.29-6).
- Finally, be brave and let a little water in at the neck when you first get into the open water. This will provide a bit of natural lubrication between your skin and the rubber suit that will make for freer movement in the upper torso.

3. Use a Lubricant in Areas that Chaff

The neck and armpits are common areas of wetsuit chaffing, particularly in the sea or ocean where the salt can add to the level of abrasion. Apply wetsuit lubricant to these areas to help the neoprene and your skin slide past each other.

Also try smearing some lubricant on the suit around the ankles and wrist which will help the suit slide off easier as the material rolls over itself. Some swimmers who really struggle to remove their wetsuit have resorted to cutting a few inches off the legs at an angle. If you do this be aware that you will lose some buoyancy in the legs and there's no going back when it's done!

PAUL: *Personally, despite the warnings from manufacturers, I still use Vaseline as a lubricant on my wetsuit. Either that or my new favourite Bepanthen (Australian baby rash cream) – can you tell that I'm a new father? If you're going to use an oil based lubricant, make sure that you take the time to clean it off properly after your race as it can degrade the material and shorten the life of the suit.*

ADAM: *Don't fight against the suit, work with it. Try altering your arm recovery over the top of the water to a straighter arm style as we did with Kate, this will avoid tension and premature fatigue in the deltoids. If your arms and shoulders become tired when swimming in a suit are you trying to swim with a classic high-elbow recovery? The solution to this problem isn't to get in the gym and build up your strength as the extra muscle bulk may actually make the problem worse. Instead, work on a relaxed but straighter arm recovery style. As a bonus this will help give you greater arm clearance over the surface in rougher conditions.*

Open your elbow angle out in a wetsuit to create a straighter arm recovery, thereby avoiding wetsuit fatigue.

PAUL: *In some open water swimming and warm water triathlon events around the world 'swim skins' like the Blue Seventy Point Zero Three (TX) are still allowed. These suits are like a very thin wetsuit which provide marginal buoyancy benefits, warmth, sun protection and also enhance proprioceptive control through the core abdominal region. The surface of the suit is also aqua-phobic meaning that you slide through the water very easily. We have tested them extensively in the warm waters here in Perth and have found them to be amazingly quick. If your budget will stretch to one we'd highly recommend them for warm water swims.*

Adapting Your Stroke to a Variety of Conditions

PAUL: *In February 2011 I took a group of our Swim Smooth Perth squad swimmers down to the 4 km Busselton Jetty Swim, a three hour drive south of Perth. This is one of the most popular open water swims on the calendar and conditions are usually relatively flat. The Busselton Jetty is the longest jetty in the southern hemisphere and extends just under 2 km out to sea with a slight kink in the middle. Navigation in this event is relatively simple – keep the jetty on your left side all the way out to the end, swim round the very end of the jetty before returning on the other side, still keeping the jetty on your left. Simple.*

On this particular year though a strong wind had stirred the Indian Ocean up considerably with a significant swell running from right to left across the course as you looked out to sea. It made for extremely challenging conditions such that it was nearly impossible to breathe to the right on the outward leg and equally impossible to breathe to the left on the return leg. Attempting to breathe towards the direction of the oncoming swell resulted in a nasty mouthful of salty water! Those swimmers unable to adapt their breathing patterns were at a severe disadvantage, which saw over 60% of the field withdraw from the race.

Just three days before the event I had set a training session for my swimmers of 15 × 100 m with 20 seconds rest between each. The goal was to hold their best maintainable pace for the whole set. This set is nothing new or unique and all the swimmers had performed this sort of set before. What we did do though was instruct all the swimmers that they must only breathe to their left for the first five repetitions, only to their right for the next five repetitions and finally bilaterally (every three strokes to both sides) for the last five repetitions.

Looking at the weather forecast it was my belief that the conditions down in Busselton could prove challenging and I didn't want to risk the old adage of 'failing to plan is planning to fail'. During the set the swimmers monitored their times per 100 m for each of the three breathing patterns to identify how much faster and more comfortable they were on one side versus the other. What was very interesting was that whilst for some breathing to their weaker side felt unusual, the time differential to their stronger side was much smaller than anticipated. This simply showed the swimmers that if they had to breathe to their non-dominant side because of conditions, they wouldn't lose much or any time in doing so. This was a great confidence booster to them when they got in the water on race day.

I'm very pleased to report that of the 34 squad members who raced from our team, not a single person pulled out of the event and of the 1000+ entrants we claimed three top-10 finishes overall and eight individual age-group gold medals. A very successful day for Swim Smooth!

IMPORTANT!

Remember, when practicing in open water always ensure that you are swimming with a buddy and that someone on the shore knows where you are. Also ensure that there is adequate safety support at your swimming venue in the event of a problem. In conditions where there are swells, tides, currents and cold water, if you are in any doubt about your ability to cope, DO NOT attempt to swim.

The following tips are designed to provide food for thought and to encourage you to experiment in a range of open water swimming environments with subtle (or sometimes substantial) adjustments to your stroke technique.

1. Flowing Rivers

Salt water in the sea or ocean is significantly more buoyant than fresh water in lakes and rivers, something you will notice immediately when swimming without a wetsuit in these environments. Most swimmers welcome any increase in buoyancy as it helps improve their body position in the water. When swimming in fresh water you may wish to adapt your stroke for the reduced buoyancy by tilting your head subtly down to lift your backside and legs higher.

When swimming in a flowing river and where access will permit, aim to swim close to the bank when you are swimming against the current and in the middle of the river when the flow is pushing you along. The greatest flow is normally in the middle of a river with a reduced flow nearer the banks; make the most of this effect by adjusting your position depending on your direction of swimming and you can save a lot of time on your swim.

2. Lakes

The threat from marine wildlife in lakes is very low but they can be quite eerie to swim in if they have dark and murky water. In most locations around the world lakes are quite cold too. Both of these factors can exacerbate feelings of anxiety or panic when swimming.

Getting into cold water is often more of a mental than a physical challenge.

When entering a lake do so slowly and pause when thigh deep to splash some cold water over your face two or three times. The receptors that set off the gasp-panic response to cold water are all centred around your eyes and cheek bones and splashing water here will allow your body to adjust before you start swimming. Also try splashing water on your chest and back if you are not wearing a wetsuit or pull out the neck of your wetsuit to allow some water to run down your chest. This might feel uncomfortable but you will be calmer and less likely to panic when you first start swimming. The hardest part about any cold open water swim is just getting started – after preparing properly, turn your brain off and get on with it. A quiet brain's a good brain in this respect!

WARNING: When swimming in water temperatures of less than 15½°C (60°F) with (and especially without) a wetsuit there is increased risk of becoming hypothermic. Significant care and attention should be exercised whenever considering a cold open water swim. The International Triathlon Union rules state that whilst wetsuits are forbidden in temperatures greater than 22°C (72°F), they are mandatory below 16°C (61°F) for all age-group competitors. All triathlon swim legs are now cancelled in temperatures less than 13°C (55°F) irrespective of distance. FINA also regulates the World Cup 10km open water swimming events to between 16°C (61°F) and 31°C (88°F). Some of the world's more notable ultra-marathon events (e.g. the 34km Lac Magog swim in Canada) have seen temperatures down at 11°C or 12°C (52°F to 54°F) in the past but swimming for this duration in these temperatures without a wetsuit takes significant training and adaptation, often including substantial fat gain for insulation. DO NOT underestimate how potentially dangerous swimming in very cold water can be.

3. Sea and Ocean

Whilst the wake and waves generated by other swimmers can turn any flat water into a turbulent mess, it is in the sea and ocean that you're likely to face the most challenging conditions and where you will need to adapt your stroke technique the most.

When entering rough water from the shore, it's essential to go under (not through or over) breaking waves. Ensure that you know what is underneath you and if it is safe to do so, dive under the waves with both arms extended to protect your head. If the water is shallow and the bottom sandy, grab onto some sand to prevent you being pushed back by the wave and once it has past, drive off the bottom towards the surface and start swimming. You may need to repeat this a few times until you are past all the breaking waves.

A straighter arm recovery and higher stroke rate will serve you very well as you make your way through the swell and chop. There are no prizes here for a pretty stroke and this is one of the reasons why many of the world's best open water swimmers and triathletes have seemingly scrappy strokes in the pool but excel in rougher water where momentum and rhythm is key. We call swimmers with this style of stroke 'Swingers', as explained in Chapter 22.

Dead spots, overgliding and slow stroke rates significantly inhibit open water swimming in challenging conditions. It's no wonder that many of the world's top open water swimmers have stroke rates in excess of 85 strokes per minute (SPM) and can hold this rate for hours on end. They might not have the longest strokes in the world but in open water, the rhythm, momentum and a certain degree of punch are perfectly suited to the environment. You might not be able to match their incredibly fast stroke rates but even aiming to lift your own by 5-6 SPM will make a difference. Revisit Chapter 14 for more information on increasing your stroke rate.

Always make sure you have adequate water support at your venue to ensure your safety.

Also remember that in rougher conditions you will sometimes be forced to breathe to one side over the other based on the direction of the swell – don't be caught out by an inability to

Swimming well in rough conditions requires constant application and a lot of determination.

breathe to both sides. At points in the course with the swell behind you, you will be able to lengthen out your stroke and adopt a stronger kick to ride the waves home. Watch elite surf-lifesavers in these conditions to pick up valuable tips.

All of this may feel a little intimidating if you are used to developing a nice smooth relaxed stroke in the pool but fear not, you can learn to adapt your stroke to cope with this environment and it is great fun when you have got the hang of it. If you know that everyone else is going to struggle in these conditions but that you can lift your stroke rate and punch through the waves and chop then you are going to really excel in your races. Most of all, learn to love the experience: it's akin to the challenges of a hilly cycle ride or technical MTB trail versus a 'boring' flat time trial!

PAUL: *A question we often get asked is 'Where should I position myself at the start of a race?' Many new swimmers have been told to hang back and stay out wide to avoid the hustle and bustle of the start. Whilst we would never encourage anyone with limited experience to head right to the centre of the mêlée, it's often a mistake to go too far back and wide as well. The last thing you want to do is add a large amount of extra distance by taking a long path to the first buoy or get caught behind many slower swimmers by starting right at the back.*

Even if it's your first ever open water event, you should have spent enough time practicing the skills outlined earlier in Open Water Adaptation (Key 3) to become familiar with swimming at close quarters with other swimmers. Far too often we hear from swimmers whose very first experience of swimming in open water was during a race. This is a recipe for disaster as you seriously risk a panic attack and being put off this great sport for life. If you have worked on your specific open water skills both in the pool and in open water training, there's no reason why you cannot start amongst other swimmers of your speed and take the shortest line to the first buoy. Who knows you might just surprise yourself by finding an excellent draft and having a great swim even if you do get a little jostled occasionally. Through proper preparation you'll know what to expect, how to tackle it and take advantage of the conditions.

Above all else, have fun out there!

Further Resources

For more information on open water swimming and suitable venues around the world in which to practise and race, check out: www.openwaterpedia.com. Openwaterpedia is a multilingual online reference and research tool for the open water swimming community. Athletes, coaches, administrators, race directors and fans of open water swimming can post, learn and modify information, photos and videos that are relevant to the sport. Openwaterpedia covers people, places, products, services and events where anyone and everyone can freely add to the global knowledge base of the sport.

Appendices

APPENDIX A

Swim Smooth Drills

This appendix covers the key Swim Smooth drills. Each drill is referred to and discussed in the main text of this book.

The purpose and focus of each drill is described clearly. Take the time to read the descriptions carefully and refer back to reflect on the tips once you have tried the drill. Whenever you perform a drill you should always be aware of the purpose of doing it and the key focus points of the drill; never swim drills for the sake of them without a clear purpose in mind.

Drills are a very powerful way to improve your freestyle swimming. They are so effective because:

- They break down the movement patterns of swimming to help you rectify bad stroke habits.
- They can slow things down to give you time to think about an area of your stroke.
- They can isolate a particular area of the stroke which must be peformed well in order for you to swim the drill successfully.

You can use all the drills in your training but focus particularly on those that are specific to your individual stroke style and needs. See Appendix C for example stroke technique sessions and Chapter 17 on Swim Types where we examine individual stroke styles in detail.

One important thing to bear in mind: if you initially find a drill challenging this is normally a sign that it is focusing on an area of your stroke technique that needs work. Don't shy away from drills that you find hard – instead work on performing them well and this will make a positive impact on your freestyle stroke technique.

Use of Fins

The Swim Smooth drills make extensive use of fins (flippers) as they are extremely valuable when developing your stroke technique. They offer you support and propulsion to help you perform the exercises in a relaxed manner. Fins are not cheating if you know why you are using them and have a specific purpose in mind, e.g. working on your swimming posture.

Some pools, particularly in the UK, have banned the use of fins during public swimming sessions. This is very unfortunate for swimmers trying to develop a good stroke technique, so much so that it is well worth approaching your pool's management to ask if a specific lane or specific time slot can be allocated where fins are allowed.

Using fins during your technique training is so important that it's well worth the journey to a pool slightly further away from you to use them. As a last resort perform the drills without fins but shorten the duration of them. For instance 6-1-6 could be shortened to 4-1-4 or even 2-1-2 and 50 m of a drill could be shortened to 25 m.

Swimming these drills without fins is a major disadvantage, seek out any opportunity you can to find a specific session or pool where you are allowed to use them.

A Modern Drill Pack

If you're an experienced swimmer you will notice that one or two 'classic drills' are missing from this pack. These are deliberate omissions either because they emphasise parts of the stroke which are now understood to cause injury or be inefficient, or because superior modern drills exist with the same purpose. You might notice the following drills are missing:

Catch-Up is one of the oldest drills and involves swimming with a full catch-up of the arms at the front of the stroke. The purpose of the drill was to emphasise a front quadrant style of swimming but at the same time it flattened body rotation and ran the risk of the swimmer over-emphasising the catch-up style. We recommend the 6-1-6 drill as a direct replacement, it emphasises body rotation to a much greater extent and helps the swimmer set up for a great catch and pull-through.

Traditional Single Arm was swum with one arm out in front of the swimmer, and the other arm stroking. The idea was to isolate an individual arm pull so that the swimmer could focus on it. The weak point of traditional single arm drills (which were sometimes performed with a kick-board held in the lead arm) is that they teach the swimmer to catch the water whilst they are flat on their front. This is bad practice and tends to reduce a swimmer's body rotation. 6-1-6 and Unco drills are superior modern drills used for these purposes.

Swimming With Fists is a way of reducing the effective area of the hand so that the swimmer is encouraged to use their forearm as a paddle. This is a good concept but modern paddles such as Finis PT Paddles are a superior way of achieving the same effect. Swimming with fists causes the swimmer to tense up while in contrast specialist paddles allow the hand to stay in a natural relaxed position. These paddles also leave the fingertips in the waterflow which helps maintain feel whilst still reducing the effective area.

Kicking With A Board is used by junior and Masters squads to develop a swimmer's kick power. Most adult swimmers do not have the ankle flexibility to kick well with a board as the lift at the front worsens the working angle of the foot against the water – in many cases reducing propulsion to zero. If you are keen on introducing some kick work into your training then we recommend kicking without a board in a torpedo position unless you have very flexible ankles.

In the Swim Smooth squads in Perth we perform very few dedicated kick sets. Instead, the kicking performed using fins during drills helps to stretch off the swimmer's ankles and bring their legs into a better kicking position. This, combined with specific use of the *Ballet Leg Kick* and *Torpedo Kick And Swim Back* drills, is our preferred approach to improving an adult swimmer's kick.

As discussed in Chapter 9, for adult swimmers tackling distance swimming events, we are not normally looking to create much kick propulsion. The objective is to improve their kick technique so that the legs are lifted high and together with minimum effort and produce the propulsion from the arm stroke combined with body rotation instead.

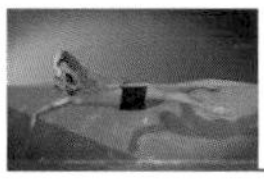

Sink Downs

Exhaling constantly through your mouth or nose as you swim is an essential skill for efficient freestyle. Exhaling constantly sounds easy but can be a challenge to get the feel of to begin with, especially if you have many years of holding your breath underwater behind you.

Tread water and take a breath in

Exhale smoothly through your mouth or nose

With a good exhalation you
should sink down easily

When you've exhaled fully,
lightly push up to the surface

To help develop your exhalation technique use this sink down exercise at the deep end of your pool. Sink downs are an excellent way to start your swimming session, even before your warm-up.

Tread water and take a breath before bringing your arms down by your side and start exhaling into the water. You're aiming to sink straight down to the bottom without any pauses or delays. Experiment between exhaling from your mouth and nose to see which is most natural to you.

Tipping Point

When you exhale you may find that you struggle to sink or that you might sink a little and then come back up to the surface. That's a sign that you're not exhaling quickly enough and that perhaps you are subconciously holding on to your breath.

If you initially sink a little but then immediately return to the surface don't give up, keep exhaling! You will find that you pass through a tipping point and then start to sink down again. As you continue to practise your sink downs aim to get to this point more quickly and sink straight down without the initial delay near the surface.

Relaxation

The key to getting rid of the air in your lungs is relaxation, if you're anxious in the water then this will

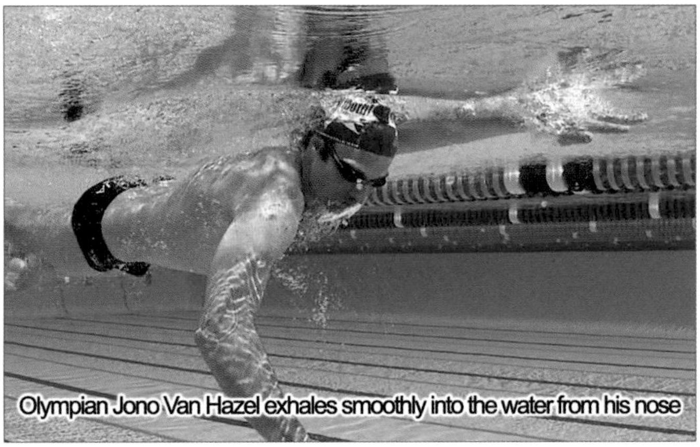
Olympian Jono Van Hazel exhales smoothly into the water from his nose

hold you back from exhaling properly. Imagine you've had a stressfull day at work and you get home and collapse onto the couch with a big sigh. That is exactly the feeling you're aiming for as you swim – the sensation of sighing into the water.

Also experiment with making sounds as you exhale. Try a 'brrrrrr' sound through your lips like a motorbike or humming through your nose. As overly simple as this sounds, these cues really can help you tune into exhaling into the water in a relaxed way.

Caution for Beginners

If you are new to freestyle swimming it is well worth getting a friend or coach into the water with you to make you feel more comfortable.

A bit of moral support can go a long way here as you become accustomed to having your face under the water.

Three in a Row

When you are able to sink down smoothly and quickly, move on to performing three sink downs in a row. This makes the timing much more like swimming:

- Take a breath and sink down ridding your lungs of air, when you are empty of air push off and return to the surface.
- As soon as you surface take an easy deep breath in and sink down straight away again.
- Repeat this three times through.

The key point to this exercise is that you are either inhaling or exhaling, you are never holding your breath. As soon as you have completed the three sink downs, push off from the end of the pool and start swimming using the *breathe - bubble - bubble - breathe* mantra.

breathe - bubble - bubble - breathe

As you swim repeat the phrase *breathe - bubble - bubble - breathe* to yourself. Literally say 'bubble' into the water to remind you to exhale; on a breathing stroke say breathe to yourself as you rotate and take a breath in.

This mantra helps you to coordinate bilateral breathing and exhalation together. We're confident that you'll find it useful to combine these two important areas of good freestyle stroke technique.

As you get good at sink downs, set yourself ever harder challenges
to push your relaxation skills!

Ballet Leg Kick

Ballet Leg Kick focuses on improving your kicking technique so as to reduce drag and improve your body position in the water. You'll need a deep end to your pool where you can't touch the bottom.

Support yourself on the side of the wall, with one hand lightly holding the pool edge for support. Rest the inside leg and kick back and forth with the outside leg. Place your outside hand on your hip.

As you kick back and forth point the toes and turn them slightly inwards; drive the kicking movement from the hips. The knee should be soft and relaxed but not driving the kick, it should flex only slightly with the kicking action.

Perform the following sequence:

- Increase the width of the kick to move further backwards and forwards. Squeeze your backside to drive the movement.
- Gradually shorten the kick, scissoring back and forth by about 60 cm and then kick as hard as you can for five seconds. Really go for it but maintain the good kicking action!
- Swap sides and repeat with the other leg.

The high-effort kicking action helps your nervous system learn an improved kicking technique. Immediately after the drill swim 100 m of easy paced freestyle, simply thinking about pointing your toes and brushing the big toes lightly as they pass. As you swim, how does your body position feel? Are your legs higher? Do you slip through the water more easily?

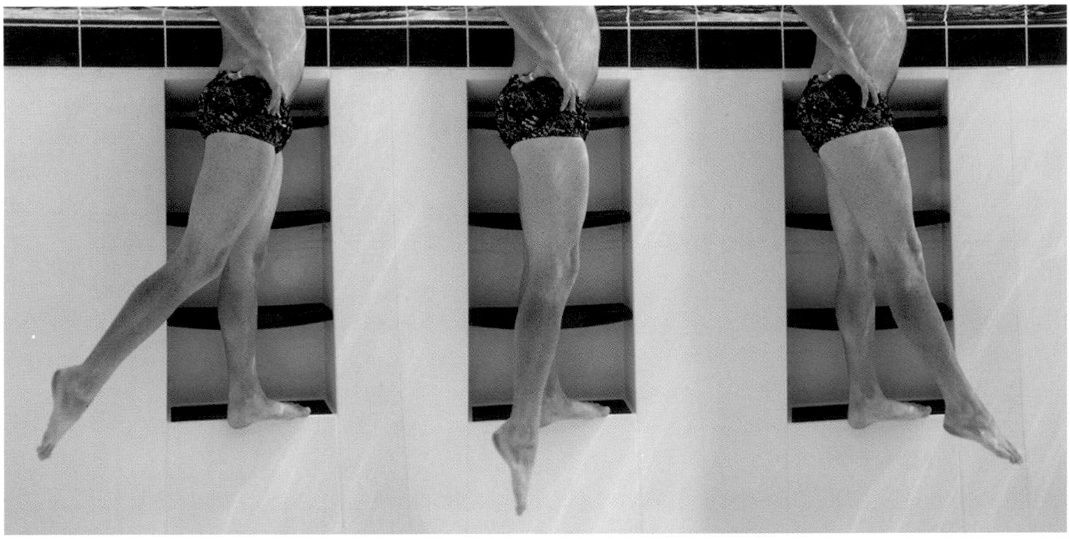

Move on to the *Torpedo Kick and Swim Back* exercise to further reinforce your kicking technique. If you are a 'leg sinker' with a low body position both of these exercises should be very beneficial to you.

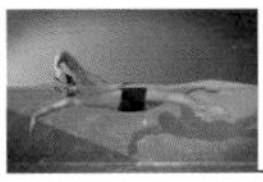

Torpedo Kick and Swim Back

To develop and refine your kicking technique use this exercise, which is based on kicking in a torpedo position. This streamlined position is the same one you should be using every time you push off from the wall, it's the lowest drag position that you can achieve whilst swimming.

Place one hand on top of the other and tuck the top thumb around the side of the lower hand. Then reach as high and tall as you can to produce the tuck. If you are flexible enough you should be able to tuck your arms behind your head.

Kick Development Sequence

From the end of the lane push off in your torpedo tuck and kick as hard as you can until you run out of air. Aim to be about 50 cm or 1½ ft under the water as you kick along.

When you run short of air stop and tread water for a few seconds to catch your breath. Then swim easy freestyle back to the wall that you came from: kick gently and simply focus on tapping your big toes as they pass.

How does your body position feel when swimming back? Higher? Do you feel like you're cutting through the water more easily? Be careful not to over-kick when swimming back, compared to the hard kick during the torpedo it will feel like nearly no kick at all!

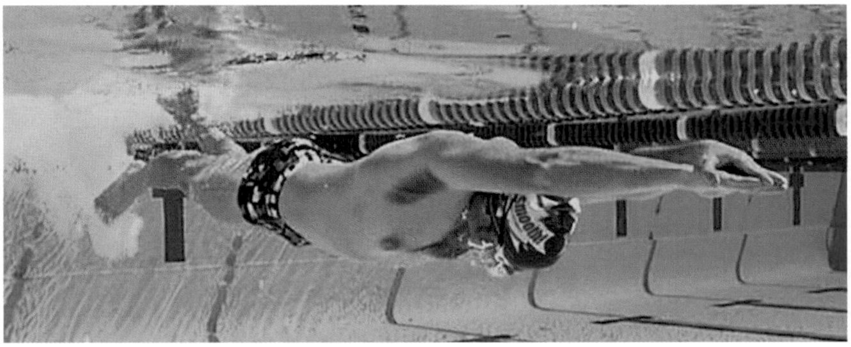

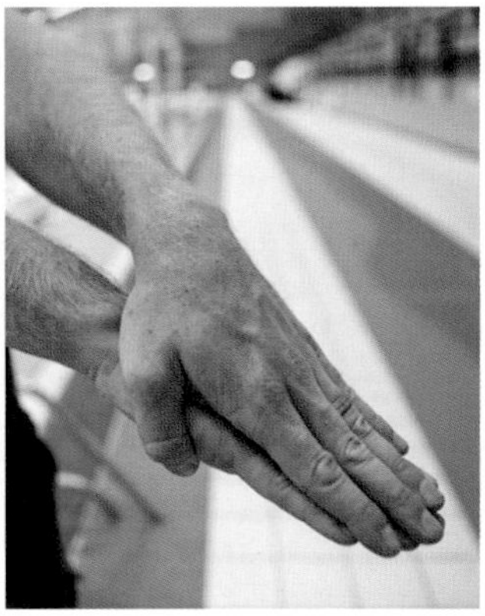

Kicking Focus

Repeat this exercise through, each time using one of the following focuses as you streamline and kick:

- Turn your toes inwards slightly and lightly brush them together as they pass.
- Squeeze your backside as if you have a coin between your bum cheeks!
- Stretch through the core, stretching your rib cage away from your hips.
- Think about tiliting your pelvis upwards slightly (as if lifting your backside towards your lower back).

Which felt best to you? Which created the most propulsion? Move on to swimming 200 m easy freestyle thinking solely about your chosen focus. You can return to your chosen visualisation any time you swim if you feel as though your stroke is becoming ragged.

Kick on Side

Kicking on your side seems like a simple idea but don't let that fool you, this is a very powerful drill. This exercise and its progressions, *6-1-6* and *6-3-6*, are at the core of the Swim Smooth drill pack.

Traditionally swim coaches used side-kicking exercises to help swimmer's become accustomed with swimming on their side to develop their body rotation. This is a worthy goal but Swim Smooth use these drills to develop two other critical parts of the freestyle stroke:

- The swimmer's posture and alignment in the water.
- An excellent catch set up position.

Use these drills to improve these two aspects of your swimming and you can dramatically increase your speed and efficiency in the water.

Side Kicking

Use fins and push off from the end of the pool, bringing yourself perfectly onto your side at 90°. Kick at a steady pace and take your lower arm out in front of you and rest your top arm lightly by your side. Face downward and exhale into the water whilst you are kicking. When you need to take a breath simply turn your head to breathe before returning it to the water:

Look straight down, you will feel like
you're looking past your armpit

Without any further thought, try this exercise and see how you perform. Do you track straight or weave about in the lane? Perform a single arm stroke to swap sides after 25 m, are you better or worse on the other side?

Now try the exercise again and become aware of the position of your lead hand. Is it pointing arrow straight down the pool or across the centre line? If it's crossing over it's very likely that you do the same thing when extending forwards in your full freestyle stroke.

Refer to Chapter 10 on posture and remove the crossover by improving your swimming posture, drawing your shoulder blades together and back. You will track a lot straighter and you should also find it easier to stay perfectly on your side as you perform the drill having much better support from the lead hand.

Your objective is to transfer this improved posture into your full stroke. The *6-1-6* and *6-3-6* drills will help you do that.

Draw your shoulder blades together and back to bring your lead hand straight
don't think about going wider, think about becoming straighter!

Hand Position

As you perform the drill, also check your elbow, wrist and fingertip positioning. Is your elbow higher than your wrist and your wrist higher than your fingertips? Is the palm of your hand facing downward? All of these elements should be in place when performing side kicking. If your hand is angled to the side (like a karate chop) or your elbow and wrist are dropped then it's very likely that these stroke flaws are present in your full stroke too.

Bring the palm of the lead hand to face the bottom of the pool and tip the wrist very slightly so the fingers are lower than the wrist. Don't do this too much or you will feel your hand being pulled down towards the bottom of the pool. If you have a tendency to bring your fingertips towards the surface of the water think about going a little deeper with the whole arm. This will leave you in a much better catch set up position.

With your hand angled correctly now check the position of your elbow, is it dropped down low in the water? Bringing it higher than the wrist will give you a lot more support. The shape you make between your elbow, wrist and fingers is slightly curved, like the shape of an aeroplane wing.

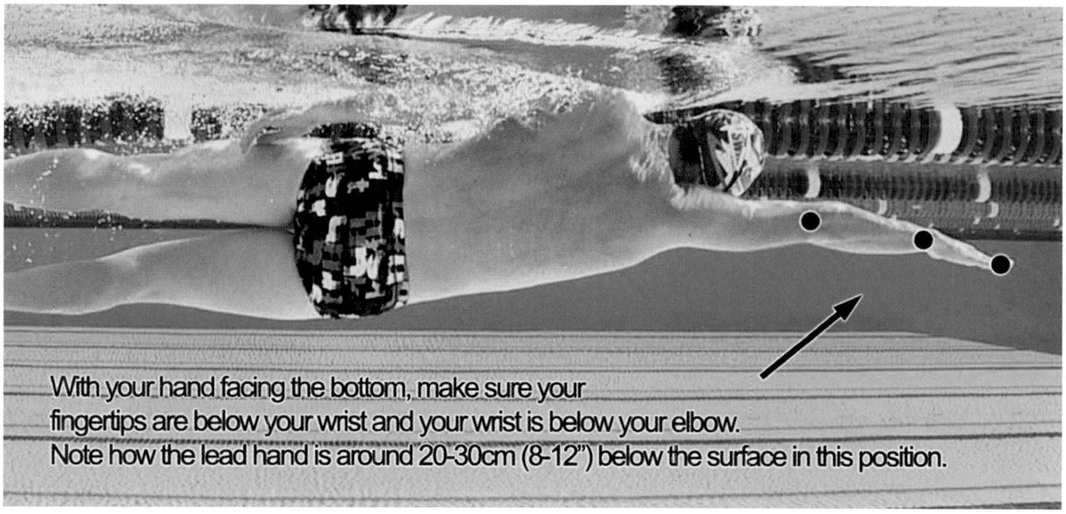

With your hand facing the bottom, make sure your
fingertips are below your wrist and your wrist is below your elbow.
Note how the lead hand is around 20-30cm (8-12") below the surface in this position.

6-1-6

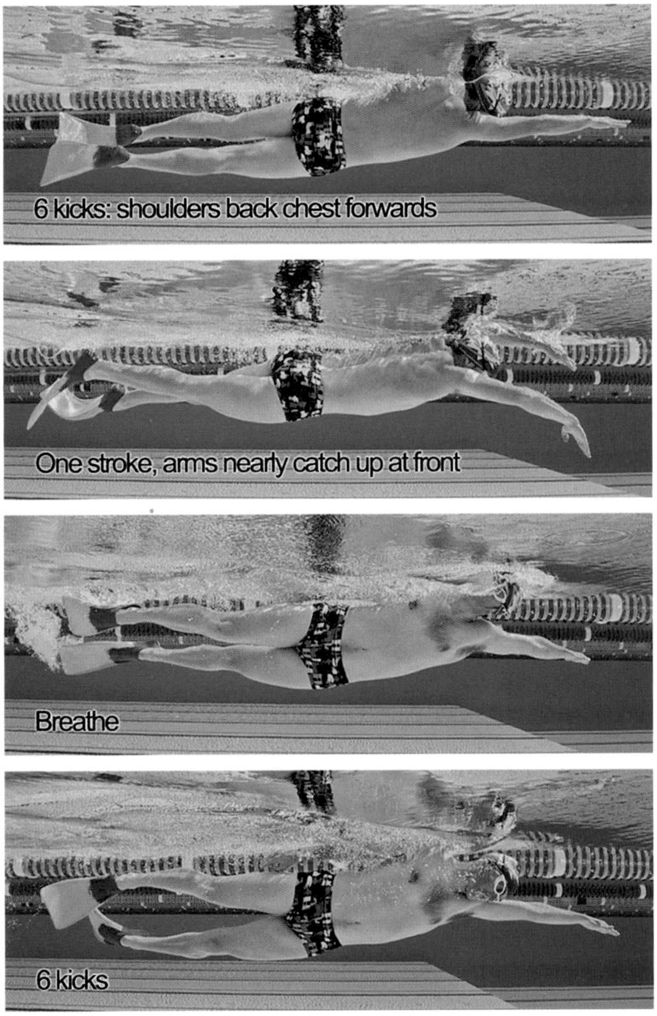

6 kicks: shoulders back chest forwards
One stroke, arms nearly catch up at front
Breathe
6 kicks

6-1-6 is a progession of the *Kick On Side* drill. Develop your alignment, posture and hand set up position before moving on to *6-1-6* and then *6-3-6*.

6-1-6 involves kicking on the side in the same manner as side kicking for around six kicks. Use this time to tune into your posture and alignment again and then perform one stroke to swap onto the other side. Continue on this side for six more kicks before swapping sides again.

As you perform the arm stroke recover the back hand over the top of the water first and keep the lead hand in position. Let your hands nearly catch-up in front of your head before starting the underwater stroke to rotate onto your other side. In your full stroke you would not fully catch-up in front of your head in this manner but this is good technique for *6-1-6*.

If you are a Bambino or an Arnie Swim Type you may find that you have a strong tendency for the lead hand to collapse down before the recovering arm reaches it. That's fine and perfectly normal.

If you struggle to keep it in front, try using something as a relay baton, in Perth we use Berrocca vitamin tubes. Keep this tube held between the thumb and first finger of your lead hand and when the top hand comes over, transfer it into your other hand. This will help you coordinate the catch up action.

The timing of the breathing is important in *6-1-6*: take the breath immediately after the stroke, not before! So the drill is really *6-1-breathe-6*.

This makes the breathing timing as close as possible to full stroke freestyle.

6-1-6 challenges you to maintain your hand positions and posture during the arm stroke. It's common to see swimmers crossover or drop their elbow as the new hand enters the water and then immediately correct themselves. Instead of doing this, aim to enter straight into the correct position by maintaining your posture during the stroke. A good indication that you are doing this right is in how straight you are able to track down the pool.

Over-Rotation

With side-kicking drills you may feel unstable on your side as if you are going to topple onto your back. If your lead hand is not crossing over in front of your head then the cause is likely to be that you are slightly over-rotated beyond 90°. To improve this, bring your resting hand towards the front of the thigh as if it is in a jeans pocket. That should help you regain your balance.

It's worth highlighting that whilst these drills bring you to 90° of rotation, in your normal stroke we are looking for 45–60°. The drills emphasise the rotataion with the view that you will transfer some of it into your full stroke.

6-3-6

As a further progression to *6-1-6*, kick on the side for six kicks before performing three strokes, each nearly catching up in front of your head. Perform each stroke with perfect alignment and a great catch set-up position - fingertips below wrist and wrist below elbow.

If you can, breathe immediately after the three strokes: *6-3-breathe-6*. If that's too little breathing, add in a breath during the arm strokes as well.

Middle Finger Visualisation

A useful visualisation whilst side kicking, and during the arm strokes in *6-1-6* and *6-3-6*, is to think solely about the middle finger on your lead hand and where it is pointing. Keep it pointing straight down the lane at all times. Use this visualisation during full-stroke freestyle too, to help you maintain your alignment as you swim and avoid crossovers.

Progressing to Full-Stroke Freestyle

The sequence of side kicking, *6-1-6* and *6-3-6* progressively builds up the freestyle stroke whilst focusing on your posture and alignment in the water and your catch set-up position with the elbow higher than the wrist and the wrist higher than the fingertips.

The next step is to perform some full-stroke freestyle. We recommend that you perform this immediately after performing the drills, whilst you still have your fins on. For instance:

3x 100 m as : 25 m kick on left side + 25 m kick on right side + 50 m freestyle

4x 100 m as : 2x : 50 m *6-1-6* + 50 m freestyle
2x : 50 m *6-3-6* + 50 m freestyle

As you enter into full-stroke freestyle following the drill think about maintaining your alignment and extending your hand in front of the same shoulder.

For examples of how we recommend integrating these drills into full training sessions see Appendix C.

Broken Arrow

The *Broken Arrow* drill is designed for swimmers with tight shoulders and upper backs to help them loosen off. It's a derivative of the *6-1-6* drill and should always be performed wearing fins.

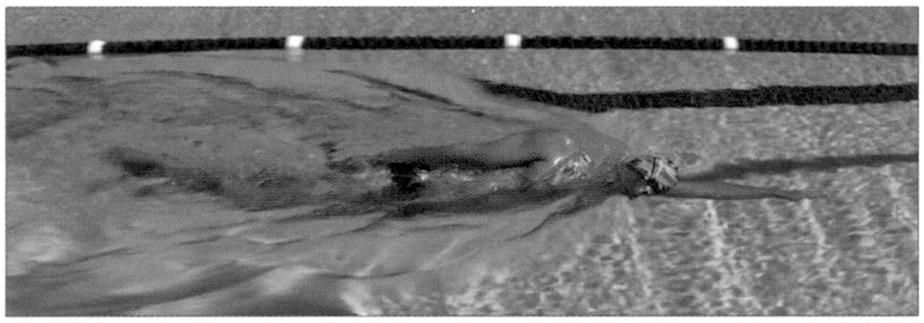

Whilst paused in this position, sink the arm down in to the shoulder socket

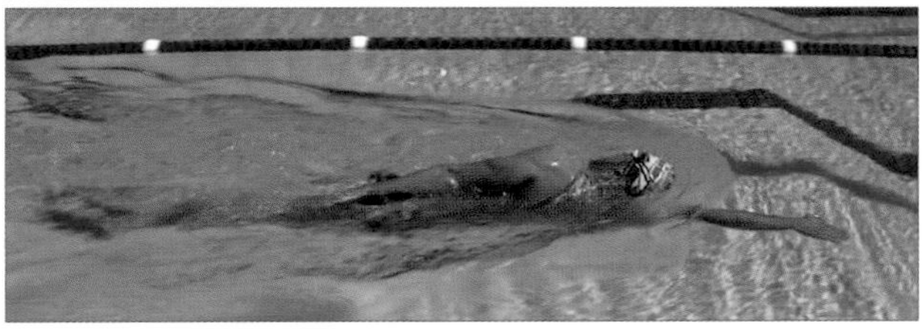

As in *6-1-6*, kick on the side but without delay take the top hand and raise it up vertically over your head and pause it there for two seconds. This is your 'arrow'. After pausing for a second, break the arrow by bending at the elbow and then spear into the water in front of the head.

Rotate on to the other side and breathe before returning your head to the water and lifting your arm on that side.

The mantra of the drill is:

up - break - spear in - breathe -
up - break - speak in - breathe.

Whilst your arm is vertical, think about sinking your arm down into the shoulder socket for two seconds before breaking the arrow. This helps you to improve your swimming posture by engaging your scapular.

When you have a feel for the rhythm of *Broken Arrow*, maintain a focus on your lead hand, keeping it straight and aligned by drawing your shoulders back and together.

Using Broken Arrow

You can swim *Broken Arrow* at any time but as with *Shoulder Tap*, it's a perfect drill to add to your warm-up to help you loosen off your shoulders.

A good warm-up is:

200 m easy freestyle
300 m with fins as 3x:
  { 50 m Broken Arrow + 50 m freestyle }
100 m easy freestyle with pull buoy

Popov

Kick on side facing down
Slide thumb up to armpit
Back down to hip
Up to armpit
Through and stroke onto other side
Breathe
Return face to water

The *Popov* drill is used to develop your body rotation and a classic high elbow arm recovery. The drill is named after legendary Russian sprinter Alexander Popov who won the 50m and 100 m freestyle at both the Barcelona and Atlanta Olympics. Alex used the *Popov* drill successfully in his own swimming preparation.

To perform *Popov*, wear fins and push off from the end of the pool. Move into a side lying position with the bottom hand in front as in all side kicking exercises.

Slide the thumb of the top arm up to the armpit. Then return it to the hip before sliding it to the armpit again, at which point bring the hand over and spear into the water to change sides.

The movements of the drill are relaxed and quite slow, don't force or hurry them. The "*up - down - up - and through*" should be continuous and without pause.

If you are very tight in the shoulders you may not be able to reach your armpit with your thumb. In which case perform the drill with the elbow opened out slightly, coming within a few inches of the armpit.

Popov helps you to develop a good sense of balance and core control in the water. The drill also emphasises a classic high elbow recovery over the top of the water.

High elbow recoveries are seen by many swimmers as an elegant and gracefull way to swim. Whilst this is certainly true, be aware that such a recovery may not suit your individual style. See Chapter 17 on Swim Types.

If you intend to swim in open water you will also need to open out the elbow angle so as to gain sufficient hand clearance over disturbed water.

Shoulder Tap

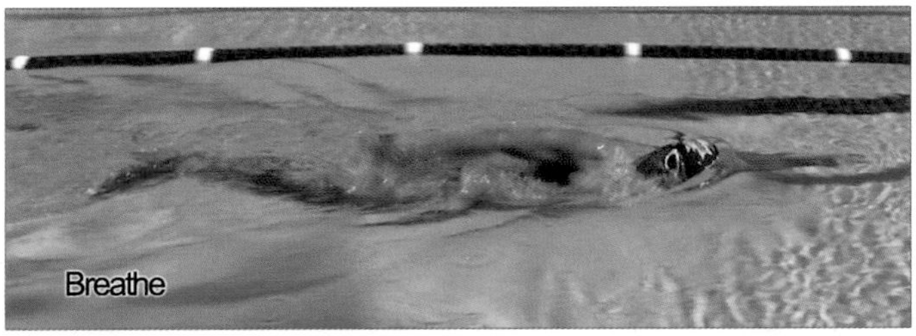
Breathe

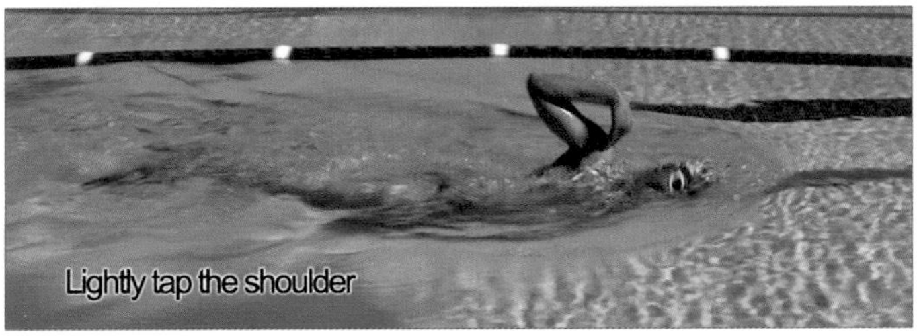
Lightly tap the shoulder

The drill emphasises a high recovery over the water

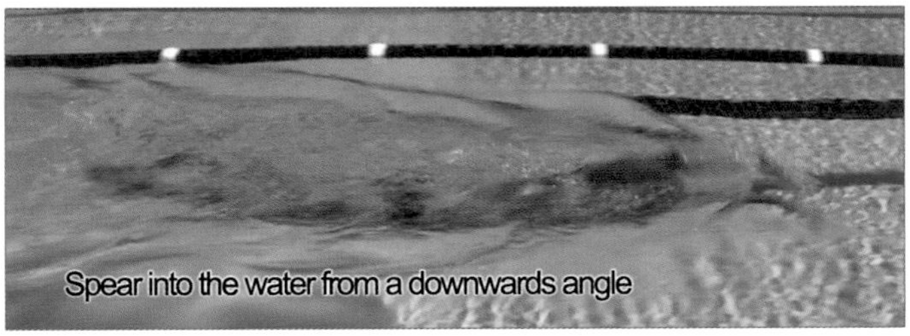
Spear into the water from a downwards angle

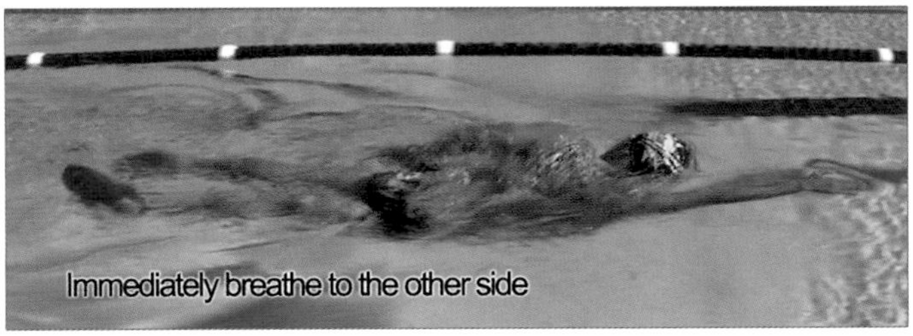
Immediately breathe to the other side

Shoulder Tap is an excellent drill to work on if you want to achieve a positive spearing hand entry into the water. If you tend to splash down with a flat hand or drop the elbow in first as you enter into the water, *Shoulder Tap* is for you. You can also use it to help undo a thumb-first entry with the palm facing outwards.

Use fins and perform a catch-up style of stroke where the hands nearly meet at the front. As the top arm recovers over the water, tap the shoulder lightly and then spear in fingertips first. Make sure the palm of the hand is facing downward as you do so.

To help drive good rotation in the drill, breathe on every single stroke to both sides! The mantra of the drills is:

breathe - tap - spear in . . .
breathe - tap - spear in . . .

After performing the drill keep the fins on and transition to full-stroke swimming focusing on good body rotation and a spearing hand entry into the water from a high angle :

e.g. 4 × 100 m as: 50 m *Shoulder Tap* + 50 m freestyle

When transitioning to freestyle, imagine a small fish is swimming just in front of you in the water. As you recover the arm and enter into the water you're aiming to spear the fish just in front of your head. This visualisation will help you to develop the positive spearing entry you need in your stroke.

Shoulder Tap can help loosen off your shoulders too, which makes it an excellent drill to include in your warm-up.

Doggy Paddle

Doggy Paddle is perhaps the oldest drill in the book but it's a great one none the less! This version is swum with more rotation than kid's doggy paddle and is known as 'long-dog' in some parts of the swimming world.

Doggy Paddle is a powerful drill for developing your catch and 'feel for the water' as it forces you to develop an early bent elbow catch. Performing the drill with a straight arm catch, which many swimmers use in their full stroke, is nearly impossible!

If you struggle to perform the drill it's likely that you are in the habit of catching the water with a straight arm, in which case this drill will be very useful for you indeed.

Performing Doggy Paddle

As with sculling drills, always use a pull buoy with *Doggy Paddle* to avoid any assistance from the legs. Push off from the wall and start performing strokes, returning the recovering arm forwards underwater.

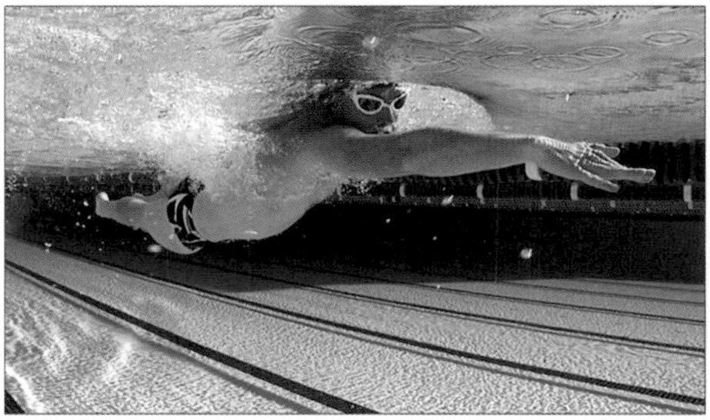

This underwater recovery might feel odd at first. Don't worry too much about your return path, simply slip the hand forwards fingertips first as easily as you can.

Emphasise 'reaching over the barrel', bending your elbow right at the front of the stroke and exaggerating the movement as much as possible.

Keep the lead hand constantly in motion, either extending forwards, tipping over and catching the water or pulling it backwards. Don't pause at any stage!

The drill's mantra is *'reach and roll!'*. Repeat this to yourself to help develop the rolling action. Pull through to your hip on every stroke, emphasising your body roll as you do so.

When you're performing doggy paddle,
emphasise getting over the top of the action,
as if you're reaching over a barrel

Drill Tips

- You can perform the drill either with your head up above the water or down beneath watching your arm strokes. There's a tendency to tense up when performing *Doggy Paddle*, try and relax and breathe!
- Visualise an imaginary rope about 50 cm or 1½ ft underneath you. As you pull-through you are aiming to pull down this rope.
- If you tend to pull very wide in your stroke or pull-through with a straight arm the rope-visualisation will be very powerful. Think of this as if you are normally pulling down two seperate ropes, one for your left arm and one for your right. Merge these ropes together into one single line.
- Once you have a good feel for the drill, experiment with adding a touch more rhythm and tempo to the movements. If you're too gentle with it you will struggle to feel the water properly so lift the tempo a touch to develop the rhythm and timing of a good catch. When *Doggy Paddle* is performed well you can move quite quickly!

Technique Sets

Imaginary rope

As with sculling, transition from *Doggy Paddle* straight into some full-stroke freestyle so as to transfer the catch movement into your swimming:

15 m *Doggy Paddle* into 35 m rhythmical freestyle

Doggy Paddle can be combined with *Scull #1* very nicely – the two drills complement each other very well:

10 m *Scull #1* + 15 m *Doggy Paddle* + 25 m swim

Doggy Paddle is a mainstay of the Swim Smooth drill pack, all swimmers should perform it regularly in their training sessions in order to develop their catch technique and stroke timing.

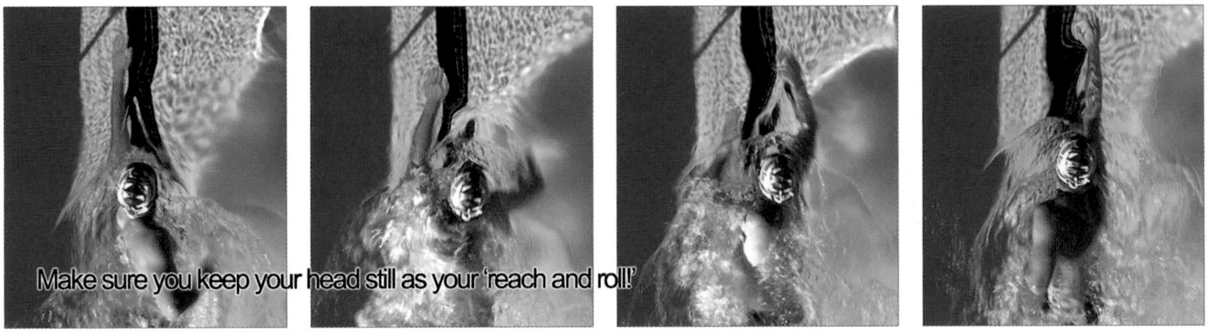
Make sure you keep your head still as your 'reach and roll!'

Scull #1

Sculling is an extremely valuable drill to help you develop your 'feel for the water' – how it feels to position and time the catch and pull movements of the stroke correctly.

The most important of the sculling positions and the one you should practise the most is *Scull #1*. This replicates the point in the stroke out in front of the head where you first latch onto and catch the water. Most swimmers press downward, to the side or even forwards in this position. *Scull #1* teaches you to begin pressing the water backwards at this critical point of the stroke.

If you struggle to perform this drill at first don't be put off, this simply highlights that the catch is a weak point in your stroke and that you will benefit greatly from developing your 'feel for the water' in this position.

Performing the Drill

Always use a pull buoy between your legs when sculling so as not to gain any assistance from your leg kick. Push off and bring your head out of the water, and begin sculling left and right in front of the head. Come slightly wider than your shoulders and bring your hands together so that they nearly touch in front of your head:

Change the angle of your hand slightly so that you are leading the scull with the palm of your hand. You're looking to keep a constant pressure on the palm of the hand from the water. At all times keep your fingertips lower than your wrist and your wrist lower than your elbow – you may be surprised at how low you have to go with your fingers to achieve this position. If you stay too shallow with your hands your forward progress will be slow or non-existent:

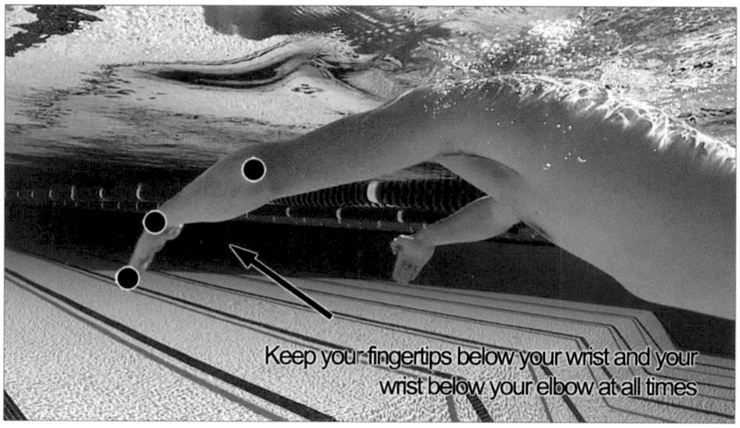

Keep your fingertips below your wrist and your wrist below your elbow at all times

Just like in full-stroke freestyle, by showing the palm of your hand slightly backwards you will be propelled forwards.

Sculling drills move you through the water at a slow pace but get the drill right and you will feel your chest lift up in the water and your pace increase.

Change the angle of the hand so your palm presses outwards
at an angle on the way out and inwards on the way back

Come straight back towards the centre, don't be tempted to
add a breakstroke pull to the action!

The hands should nearly touch at the centre of the scull

When you are getting a good feel for the drill deliberately accentuate this position by drawing your shoulder blades back and lifting your chest high. This introduces good swimming posture into the drill.

Sculling is best performed over short distances of 10–20 m before being immediately transitioned into full-stroke freestyle. For instance, complete the following four times through with 15 seconds recovery in between:

100 m as 15 m *Scull #1* into 85 m freestyle

As you transition into freestyle, think about lightly pressing the water back to the wall behind you. Use the *Smiley Face On The Palm Of Your Hand* visualisation described in Chapter 13 to help reinforce this.

Don't be surprised if your stroke rate picks up slightly when swimming after sculling, that's a good sign that you've improved your catch technique – go with it!

Scull #1 can be used in combination with other drills, for instance:

10 m *Scull #1* + 10 m *Scull #2*
+ 30 m swim
10 m *Scull #1* + 15 m *Doggy Paddle*
+ 25 m swim

Scull #1 is a mainstay of the Swim Smooth drill pack, perform it regularly in your training sessions to develop and maintain your 'feel for the water'.

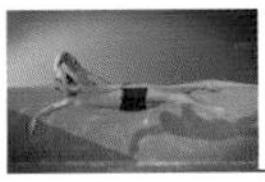

Scull #2

Scull #2 is similar to *Scull #1* but it focuses on an area of the stroke directly under the head as the swimmer transitions from the catch to the pull phase. This drill is very useful if you have a tendency to pull wide with your arm stroke or pull through with a straight arm.

As with *Scull #1*, always use a pull buoy and push off with your head above the surface, looking forwards.

Scull the water directly under the head by keeping the elbows fixed in place, changing the pitch of the hand to keep a light pressure on the palm. Scull from just wider than your body's width into the centre.

This position offers you less support than *Scull #1* and you may feel that you sink a little lower in the water. Don't tense up because of this, relax and breathe smoothly.

Control the position of the elbows and keep them fixed in place. Change the angle at the elbow to generate the sculling action, moving from around 90° elbow bend at the middle of the scull before opening out to around 160° at the widest point.

Complete 10–15 m of the drill and then transition into freestyle with a light focus on bending the elbows and pressing the water backwards under the head.

Scull #1 can be used in combination with *Scull #2*, for instance:

10 m *Scull #1*
into 10 m *Scull #2*
into 30 m freestyle

This sequence helps you 'feel the water' during the catch phase and through into the pull under the body.

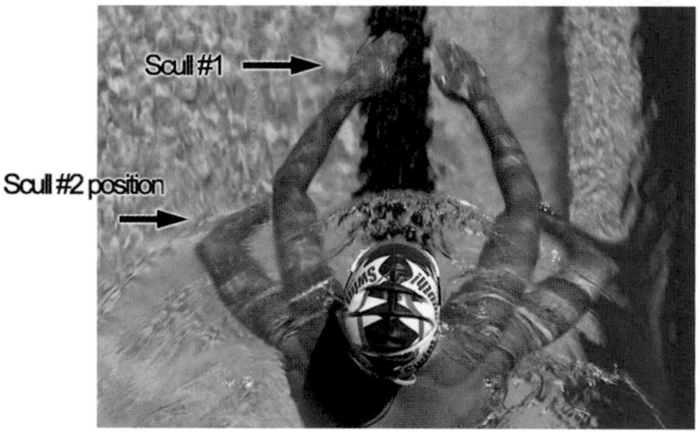

The Unco Drill

Unco is a special drill which helps you to develop the rhythm and timing of your stroke. We love *Unco* at Swim Smooth as it brings so many elements of your stroke together and forces you to time your catch, pull and body rotation correctly. You can even use it to polish up the timing of your breathing.

Australians love to shorten any word and put an 'o' on the end - in this case shortening 'uncoordinated' to make *Unco*. This probably tells you straight away that it is quite a challenging drill! We'd encourage any swimmer to give it a try but it is probably best suited and most beneficial for upper-intermediate and advanced level swimmers.

If you are a bit of an Overglider or have any dead spots or pauses in your stroke then you'll find *Unco* challenging but very useful.

Unless you have an exceptionally propulsive kick, always use fins when performing *Unco*. It's a one-arm drill, performed with one arm by your side whilst the other arm performs a full stroke.

Try 4 × 100 m with each 100 m swum as:

> 25 m left arm *Unco* + 25 m freestyle breathing right + 25 m right arm *Unco* + 25 m freestyle breathing left

How Should It Feel?

Since you are only using one arm with a gap between strokes, *Unco* is always going to have a surge to it: the surge should be forwards with the propulsion coming from the stroking arm. If you feel like you are bobbing up and down a lot then this highlights that you are pressing down on the water at the front of the stroke. This only lifts you up, which doesn't generate any propulsion and acts to sink your legs, creating drag. If you feel like you are bobbing vertically then you need to work on a better catch action, pressing the water backwards, not downward.

The King of Drills

At Swim Smooth we call *Unco* "The King Of Drills". This is because it is beneficial to almost any swimmer, even elite swimmers. *Unco* also helps you to put all the elements of your stroke together, making sure that everything works with the right timing – no other drill does this nearly as well.

You will feel the magic of *Unco* when you swim normal freestyle immediately after performing the drill. We recommend you perform a short swim every time following *Unco*, keeping the fins on and just feeling the easy rhythm and timing of the arm stroke. The improved smoothness and efficiency can be a revelation!

Paddle-Unco: "P-Unco"

Performing *Unco* with a small pair of paddles can be useful as it increases the working area of the hand, which improves your awareness during the catch phase at the front of the stroke. Use a small pair of paddles for this purpose, keeping a small amount of pressure under your fingertips as you use them. We recommend the Finis Freestyler paddles.

Only perform *P-Unco* in small doses as the paddles increase the load on your shoulders. Most of the time we recommend normal *Unco* in your drill sets but the addition of *P-Unco* can make for an interesting and stimulating change.

Breathe on every stroke

Make sure you dip this 'dead' shoulder down into the water

Breathe away from the stroking arm and breathe on every single stroke – even if you don't feel that you need to – this helps to drive your body rotation.

We suggest that you start with your right arm stroking and breathe to your left as shown in the pictures. Once you get the feel of the drill swap sides every 25 m or so.

The key to this drill is to make sure that you rotate your body fully to the dead side as shown in the last picture. There'll be a temptation not to do this, the key is ensuring that you dip your non-stroking arm and shoulder down into the water as shown in the last picture.

The mantra of the drill is *'stroke and dip . . . stroke and dip . . .'*. You will really have to emphasise dipping the 'dead' shoulder into the water as there's no arm stroke on that side to help you.

The body rotation within the drill is critical. Get it right and your stroking arm will recover easily over the top of the water. However, stay flat on that dead side and the arm recovery will be very tough!

If you struggle to coordinate the drill don't worry, that's normal – in fact that's the whole idea and it simply highlights that the timing of your stroke may need some work. When you get it right *Unco* should feel smooth and rhythmical.

Waterpolo Drill

Maintain a focus on bending the elbow under the body

Head-up *Waterpolo* drill is useful for advanced level swimmers as it improves the rhythm and timing of their stroke. The drill is particularly effective for removing dead spots as it's nearly impossible to swim head-up with a pause in the stroke!

Keep your chin on the surface and swim with positive stroke movements and a strong rhythm. Keep the head still and looking forwards, try and relax as much as possible and don't forget to breathe!

The key to this drill is to swim it at near sprint pace over short distances. It's physically demanding so unless you're very adept at the drill, stick to 25 m at a time as a maximum.

Too many swimmers perform *Waterpolo* style drills at the slowest pace they can but for developing stroke rhythm, faster is better as long as good control can be maintained. If 100% is a full sprint then a 90% effort is about right for the drill. If you struggle with *Waterpolo* try it wearing a pair of fins to give you a little assistance, or even a pull buoy.

After performing the drill, transition into a set of short fast efforts swum with a fast stroke rate. For example:

2 × 25 m *Waterpolo* drill at 90% effort
2 × 25 freestyle at 90% effort – emphasise rhythm
2 × 25 m *Waterpolo* drill at 90% effort
2 × 25 freestyle at 90% effort – fast rhythmical stroke

Swimming with Bands

Swimmming with bands is another drill which focuses on delivering better rhythm and timing to your stroke. Wearing a band around your ankles stops you kicking and also adds a little drag to the back of your stroke, which will want to pull your legs downward. For most swimmers we recommend using a pull buoy

between your legs at the same time but if you have good natural buoyancy you can perform the drill without one.

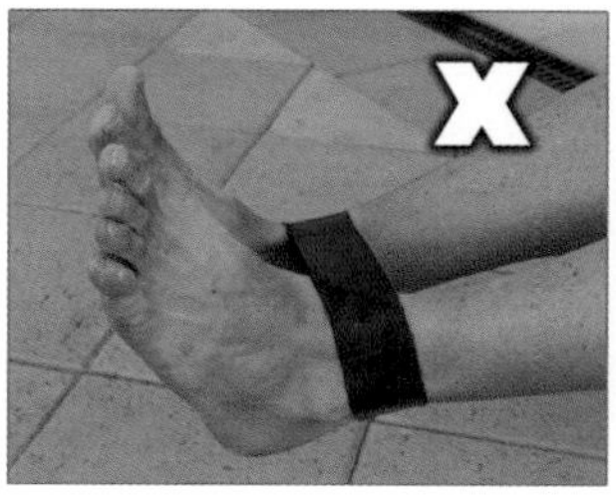

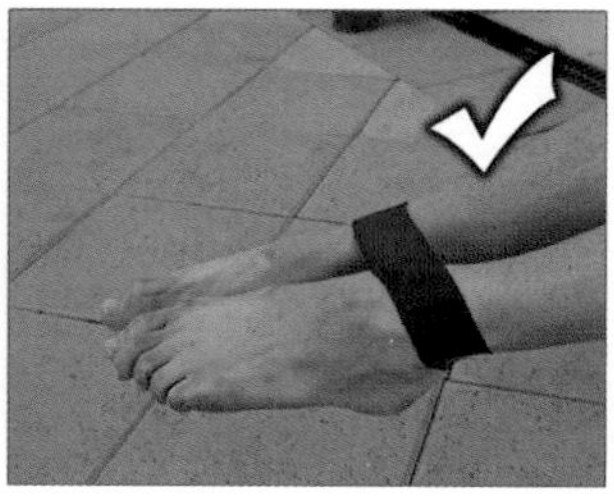

Swim normal freestyle with your upper body and swim with a high stroke rate, getting into your catch quickly. Stretch tall through your core, lifting your rib cage away from your hips as much as possible. Swim short distances at a time such as 25 m or 50 m.

This drill never feels easy as everyone's legs sink to a greater or lesser extent. The key is to keep your legs as high as possible during the drill by using a good stroke rhythm and a stretched core. When you transition back to normal swimming you'll have a heightened awareness of your body position and stroke rate.

You can experiment with your stroke whilst wearing a band to see the effect it has on your body position. Try:

- Pushing down on the water during the catch with a straight arm.
- Pushing the water forwards as if overgliding and putting on the brakes.
- Flexing your ankles to 90° so that your toes point towards the bottom of the pool.

You'll soon experience how much your legs sink if you have any of these flaws in your stroke!

Purchasing Bands

You can purchase bands from swimming retailers or make one by cutting up a car or bike inner tube. The band should hold your ankles lightly together.

Swim Type Stroke Correction Processes

This appendix contains a step-by-step process that each Swim Type can follow in order to correct their stroke, making extensive use of the drills in Appendix A.

If you have not yet identified your Swim Type then first do so in one of the following ways:

- By reading the profiles in Chapters 18–23.
- Using the Swim Type Questionnaire at: www.swimtypes.com/yourtype.
- Using the observation sheet at: www.swimtypes.com/observation.

Arnie Stroke Correction Process

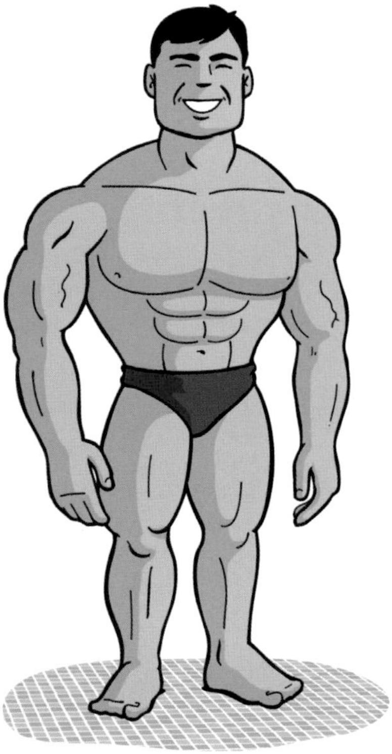

The Arnie: plenty of power, needs more control!

If you are an Arnie, use the process in the order outlined below to develop your swimming, referring to the relevant parts of this book. This process is tailored directly to your specific needs so keep focused on it and don't become distracted by other areas of stroke development which are not relevant or a priority for you right now.

PAUL: *As an Arnie you may feel impatient to become a strong swimmer but ironically that may be one of the things holding you back. You need to slow things down a touch and work on areas of your stroke technique at a slower pace. I often tell swimmers such as yourself to recognise that impatience and to 'Tame The Arnie!'. You won't have a problem speeding things back up in the long run but taking the time and patiently working on your stroke technique is so important for your progress.*

1. **Develop your exhalation technique** using the *Sink Down* and *Breathe - Bubble - Bubble - Breathe* exercises, you are looking to exhale as if sighing into the water – it is not as easy as it sounds to let that air go! Try to relax and develop a real sense of calmness as you perform these exercises and with your swimming in general. You may be surprised at how relaxed you can become whilst swimming.
2. **Improve your breathing technique** by keeping your head lower as you swim using the bow wave, *Popeye Breathing* and *Split Screen* visualisations. Refer to Chapter 7 for more information.
3. **Tune up your kicking technique** using the *Ballet Leg Kick* and *Torpedo Kick and Swim Back* exercises. These may seem overly simple but they can make a huge difference to your body position and so your drag profile in the water. As you swim after these drills become aware of how high your legs are in the water, you are looking to feel your ankles gently breaking the surface but do not do that by bending at the knees! You'll know when you get this right as you will slip much more easily through the water.
4. **Work on your swimming posture** using the YTWL exercise (Chapter 29) and *Kick On Side*, *6-1-6* and *6-3-6* drills. Not only will these drills help you remove crossovers from your stroke they will also improve your body rotation. Becoming straighter and more aligned in the water is critical for your progress as an Arnie and should be a constant focus for you as you continue to develop as a swimmer. Crossovers have a habit of coming back without constant maintenance!
5. **Focus on your initial catch and pull** using the *Doggy Paddle* and *Scull #1* drills. The key goal here is to focus on pressing the water backwards from in front of the head after hand entry and extension rather than pushing it downward. This will give you greater propulsion and act to keep your legs higher in the water.

Remove the crossover from your stroke by drawing your shoulders back and chest forwards whilst performing the side-kicking drills.

6. **Experiment with a straighter arm recovery** to help overcome any restriction in your shoulders or upper back. A classic high elbow recovery requires good flexibility and range of motion in these two areas and does not suit some swimmers with limited range of movement. See Chapter 11.
7. **Try lowering your stroke rate slightly**, ideally using a stroke-rate beeper such as a Wetronome or Tempo Trainer Pro. Lowering your natural stroke rate by 3–5 strokes per minute is not a huge change but gives you time to lengthen out your stroke and develop that body rotation in conjunction with step 4.
8. **Use a regular stretching routine** to loosen off your shoulders, upper back, hip flexors and ankles. These four areas are restricted in many Arnies and making even small improvements in your flexibility will pay real dividends for your swimming. See Chapter 29.

Experiment with a range of head positions to see which works best for you.

Head Position

Many Arnies have been told to look straight down when they swim to help bring their legs up. As discussed in Chapter 8, this is an option for you but we encourage you to keep a more neutral head position if possible as it help you to develop your catch and your navigation in open water. Only look straight down if you cannot lift your body position right up using the process listed above.

Kick Timing

As discussed in Chapter 9 there are two main ways of kicking in swimming, a 6-beat kick or a slower 2-beat kick. You may have heard about the efficiency benefits of using a 2-beat kick but for most Arnies with low-lying legs a light 6-beat kick will suit you much better as it will help to keep your legs higher in the water. Whilst a 2-beat kick uses less kicking effort this will be more than offset by a low-lying body position from the lack of lift created.

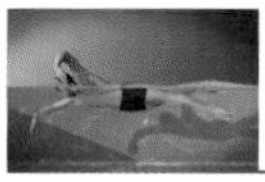

Bambino Stroke Correction Process

If you are a Bambino, use the process below to develop your swimming. Work on one thing at a time, for instance you might start with working through steps 1–3 for a few sessions before moving on to more advanced steps. Sometimes it takes things a while to 'stick' but that's OK, keep practicing and they will come together nicely in your stroke.

ADAM: *Always keep a positive approach to your swimming and enjoy every small improvement made along the way – not only will this keep you motivated but a positive approach will directly result in a more confident and positive stroke style, which will be a great thing for your swimming.*

I love coaching Bambinos as they're swimming for all the right reasons – because they enjoy it and would love to be good at it! A personal plea from me: keep setting yourself small challenges, think of yourself as a proper swimmer and don't be afraid to push yourself. You may be surprised at what you can achieve in the water; most Bambinos are much better swimmers than they allow themselves to believe!

The Bambino: more confidence and a better 'feel for the water' is required!

1. **Develop your exhalation technique** by using the *Sink Down* and *Breathe - Bubble - Bubble - Breathe* exercises listed in Appendix A. This is critical for your stroke because a build-up of CO_2 in your system will make swimming feel much more tense than it needs to be. Exhale smoothly into the water with a relaxed sigh – If you have ever done any yoga you will understand how powerful this can be for your relaxation. As you start swimming use the *breathe-bubble-bubble-breathe* mantra to help coordinate bilateral breathing and exhalation together. Do not worry if the breath itself still feels a struggle, we will come to that later.
2. **Tune up your kicking technique** using the *Ballet Leg Kick* and *Torpedo Kick and Swim Back* exercises. A relaxed flutter kick that comes from the hip (not the knee) will burn less oxygen and bring your legs up higher in the water, creating less drag. You're not looking to kick hard in your swimming so make sure that your kick is just light enough to bring your legs up so that your ankles break the surface.
3. **Tune in to good stroke timing** using the *Kick On Side* and then *6-1-6* drills. These may feel quite strange and hard to coordinate at first but that's OK. A weak point in a Bambino's stroke is that their lead arm slips down in the water when breathing, when in fact it should be out in front of the head offering support. As you perform the *6-1-6* drill you may find that the lead arm wants to collapse down as the top arm comes over during the arm stroke. If this happens practise using a Vitamin tube as a relay baton, as described in Appendix A. Move on to *6-3-6*, all the time catching up for the moment with your arms in front of your head. You should immediately notice more support when breathing.

Developing a good exhalation technique is critical to helping you relax in the water.

4. **Reinforce your stroke timing** by repeating the *1-2-stretch* mantra to yourself as you swim. The *1* and *2* being on normal strokes and the *stretch* on a breathing stroke, this will help to remind you to keep that lead hand out in front of you for support whilst breathing. You should be able to let your breath take care of itself whilst you think about keeping that lead hand stable.
5. **Work on your head position** whilst breathing using the *Popeye Breathing* and *Split Screen* visualisation described in Chapter 7. You are aiming to keep your head low in the water and breathe into the bow-wave trough. If you have tried this before it will be much more achievable now that we have improved your stroke timing in steps 3 and 4.
6. **Develop a basic 'feel for the water'** using the *Scull #1* drill. You may well find sculling quite a challenging exercise at first but that's OK, this is highlighting a bit of a hole in your proprioception (body awareness) at this point in front of your head. Do not be put off by this; you have much to gain by developing this area of your stroke. Make sure that your fingertips are pointing at a downward angle into the water and that your elbows are higher than your wrist – you may have to go a little deeper with your hands than you might expect in order to achieve this.
7. **Further improve your catch mechanics** using the *Doggy Paddle* drill. Perform this drill quite strongly using positive arm movements, focusing on bending your elbow out in front of your head, really exaggerating the movement of 'reaching over the barrel'. Transition into full freestyle and feel yourself being pushed through the water on every arm stroke.
8. **Increase your stroke tempo** by performing some short fast efforts, for instance 4 × 50 m swimming. If you own a stroke beeper such as a Wetronome or Finis Tempo Trainer Pro, set this to 5–10 strokes per minute higher than your normal stroke rate and simply time your strokes to the beep. Even though this is faster than normal it will not necessarily feel harder because the increased sense of rhythm will benefit your stroke.

Kicktastic Stroke Correction Process

If you are a Kicktastic, use the following process to develop your swimming. The main feature is in step 4 where we develop your catch and 'feel for the water'. As you make the shift to upper-body propulsion you should find that the reliance on your leg kick naturally starts to drop away.

The Kicktastic: a better catch and 'feel for the water' will allow them to moderate their kick.

1. **Tune up your exhalation technique** using the *Sink Down* and *Breathe - Bubble - Bubble - Breathe* exercises in Appendix A. Despite being quite experienced swimmers, many Kicktastics hold their breath under the water, which makes swimming much harder than it needs to be. Developing your ability to breathe out smoothly into the water will make swimming feel easier and give you more time when you do go to take a breath as you will only have to inhale, not exhale and inhale in the same short window! Many Kicktastics returning to swimming after years off from the sport feel that they never regain their swimming fitness. However, this can simply be due to poor exhalation technique and essentially turning what should be a very aerobic activity into something much more anaerobic by never releasing the build-up of CO_2 in their system.
2. **Give your kicking technique a once over** using the *Ballet Leg Kick* and *Torpedo Kick and Swim Back* exercises. Despite having powerful leg kicks, many Kicktastics kick hard from the knee rather than kicking with a relatively straight leg from the hip. Developing an improved kicking technique will reduce the oxygen demand from the kick, making breathing much easier.
3. **Work on improving posture and rotation** using the *Kick On Side* and then *6-1-6* and *6-3-6* drills. Poor body rotation is a feature of the Kicktastic's stroke and is often accompanied by a crossover in front of the head. Many other Swim Types would experience a scissor kick as a result of the crossover but Kicktastics normally do not as the strong 6-beat kick smothers this tendency. However, the crossover is still very damaging for a swimmer's catch, which requires good alignment into the water.

   These drills will also improve a Kicktastic's swimming posture, which is often quite poor and results in them swimming quite flat in the water (see Chapter 11). As you perform the side-kicking exercises work on opening up your chest and drawing your shoulder blades together and back. This will help drive body rotation and set up for a propulsive arm stroke.
4. **Develop your catch mechanics** using the *Scull #1* and *Doggy Paddle* drills. As a Kicktastic you can expect these drills to feel quite alien and challenging at first, which simply highlights the catch as a weak point in your stroke. Perform the drills using a pull buoy and resist the temptation to add a little kick to the drill – that is very much cheating!

   Perform *Scull #1* first, focusing on developing a good catch position with the elbows higher than the wrist and the wrist higher than the fingertips. Once you are beginning to feel the water on the palms of your hands, move on and try *Doggy Paddle*. As you perform the drill imagine that there's

The Classic Kicktastic: over-kicking from the knee and pressing down with a straight arm in front of the head.

a rope under your body around 50 cm (1½ ft) beneath you – if you pull through with a straight arm then you will be deeper than the rope so you need to bend your elbow in order to keep your hand on the line of the rope. You can also visualise swimming in a very shallow pool or perhaps over a sharp coral reef in about 50 cm of water! *Doggy Paddle* is a great drill for Kicktastics as it really emphasises their body rotation on every stroke. Exaggerate your body roll during the drill and repeat this mantra to yourself: *'reach and roll!'*

Once you have the hang of sculling and *Doggy Paddle*, try this special progression meant only for Kicktastics. It's a powerful way of helping you shift to upper-body propulsion:

- Use a pull buoy and perform *Scull #1* for around 10 m*, really tuning into the feeling of the water on the palms of your hands.
- Transition straight into *Doggy Paddle* for 10 m*, emphasising your body rotation and pulling through with a nice bent elbow.
- Now start swimming freestyle, using the *Smiley Face On The Palm Of Your Hand* visualisation from Chapter 13, pressing the smiley face back to the wall behind you as you swim.
- After about 15 m* of swimming, part your legs slightly and release the pull buoy (let it float free) but, critically, bring in your leg kick only very slightly, maintaining the propulsion with your upper body.

ADAM: *When coaching a Kicktastic they will often tell me that they can really feel the increase in effort in their upper body as they shift towards arm propulsion. When this happens give yourself a little time to adapt to the workload. At first it will feel quite hard but as the aerobic fitness in your core, back and chest muscles develops it will soon feel easier again. Don't worry, you won't develop bulging muscles – a serious concern for many young women – I very much doubt you'll notice any difference in muscle size!*

*These distances are our best recommendations for completing this exercise in a 50 m pool – if you are swimming in a 25 m or 25 yd pool, try halving the suggested distances or ensure that your turn is quick and does not disrupt your focus on your catch.

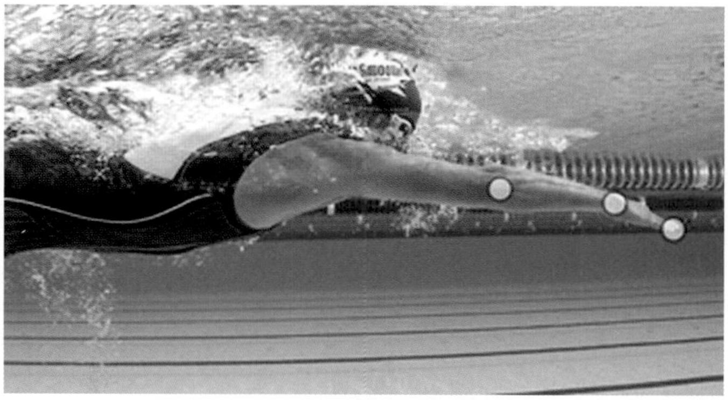

Move from dropping the wrist and showing the palm forwards (left) towards tipping the fingertips down and keeping the elbow higher than the wrist (right).

palm of your hand in this position. Whilst performing *Doggy Paddle* emphasise bending the elbow early in front of your head and keep your lead hand constantly in motion – either extending forwards, catching the water or pressing it backwards but never pausing! Keeping the arms and hands constantly in motion might feel very alien to you at first but this is a critical element to move across into your full stroke.

PAUL: *An interesting experiment to try as an Overglider is the Scull #1 drill but purposefully done incorrectly with the elbows and wrists dropped and the palm of the hand facing forwards. This position is designed to replicate the position that your hand and forearm might be in when trying to overglide. As you attempt to do Scull #1 incorrectly you'll notice that you either stay stationary or you start to actually move backwards in the water! You'll also probably notice your legs sinking at this point, even if using a pull buoy to keep your legs buoyant.*

Pay attention to how much water pressure you feel on the palm of your hand as you scull incorrectly in this position – it's likely to be a lot more than when you do it correctly and are moving forwards. This is one of the key reasons why it's easy to be fooled into the idea that your overglide is preceded by a good catch as you feel significant water pressure on the palm of your hand; the only trouble with this is that the water pressure is actually slowing you down significantly and effectively pushing you backwards! Now transition into doing the drill correctly and regaining forward momentum, taking this same sensation into your freestyle stroke along with your renewed focus on pressing the water behind you, not down and certainly not away from you.

5. **Improve your stroke timing** using the *Unco* drill. *Unco* helps time your arm stroke around your body rotation and makes it nearly impossible to keep a dead spot in your stroke. This will be another challenging drill for you but one that's well worth revisiting and reinforcing as you go forward with your swimming.
   Waterpolo drill and *Swimming With A Band* make excellent additions to your swim programme as you will feel your improved stroke timing coming together.
6. **Experiment with different head positions** to see which works best for you. Many Overgliders have been told to look straight down when they swim but with better exhalation, an improved catch technique and better rhythm and timing you may no longer need to do this to keep your legs high in the water.

Swim 4 × 25 m and on each 25 m try a different head position:

- Bury your head low in the water with your chin coming in towards your chest.
- Look straight down at the bottom of the pool.
- Look slightly ahead, about 1 m in front of you to the bottom of the pool.
- Raise your head further and look about 3–5 m in front of you.

Which feels best and most comfortable? If you can successfully use a higher head position it will give you a much greater proprioception (body awareness) of what's happening out in front of your head, helping you to refine and maintain your catch technique. This is one reason why elite swimmers prefer this head position.

7. **Use a stroke rate beeper** such as a Wetronome or Finis Tempo Trainer Pro to help reinforce the improved rhythm in your stroke. With an improved catch technique you will be pressing the water backwards rather than pressing it downward, this takes less time and helps to lift your stroke rate naturally. Often you will not even be aware that your stroke rate has lifted.

   Set your stroke rate beeper back to what your natural stroke rate was before you started this stroke development process. How does it feel? Uncomfortably slow? Lift your stroke rate upwards with the beeper until you feel your new stroke click back into its rhythm – notice how this does not feel any harder and yet you are moving much quicker and more easily through the water. This is an indication that your swimming is becoming really efficient!

   As you continue forwards from here a stroke rate beeper will be an extremely good investment in your swimming, especially if you train outside of a squad. Use it to control and monitor your stroke rate as you continue to refine your catch technique and stroke timing.

8. **Experiment with a light 6-beat flutter kick** if you do not use one already. Although a 2-beat kick uses less energy it naturally suits a shorter faster stroke style, not a long smooth one. Depending on your natural buoyancy you may find that your body position is higher in the water with a light 6-beat flutter kick. This will create less drag and lower your energy expenditure overall despite the extra kicking.

Swinger Stroke Correction Process

If you are a Swinger follow the process outlined below and refer to the relevant sections of this book to develop your swimming.

The Swinger: experienced swimmer with excellent stroke rhythm who needs a tune-up.

1. **Brush up on your exhalation technique** into the water using the *Sink Down* and *Breathe - Bubble - Bubble - Breathe* exercises listed in Appendix A. Despite being experienced swimmers, Swingers are some of the worst culprits when it comes to holding their breath underwater. It's possible that their fast stroke rate lets them get away with this more than other types since their breathing comes around quicker. However, by improving your breathing technique you'll feel much more relaxed in the water and might be able to move to breathing every five strokes rather than three. Breathing less often is always an advantage as all swimmers lose stroke efficiency when breathing.
2. **Work on improving posture and alignment** in the water using the *Kick On Side* and then *6-1-6* and *6-3-6* drills. After many years of swimming, Swingers often slip into a few bad habits and start to cross over in their strokes both in front of the head and below the body. We'll use the *Doggy Paddle* and *Scull #2* drills later to reinforce pulling down the centre line of the body under the water and not crossing over. The overall effect of these drills may be a slight drop in your stroke rate but a slight lengthening of your stroke, which will offset this. We are not trying to kill your rhythm here, but just to strike the right balance between the length of your stroke and the rate of your stroke.
3. **Pay attention to your hand entry** with the objective of removing a thumb-first entry technique from your stroke. As described in Chapter 12, a thumb-first entry is the most common cause of shoulder pain and injury and should be avoided at all costs. To help remove a thumb-first entry use the *Shoulder Tap* drill and the two visualisations from Chapter 12: *Hide The Palm* and *Briefcase Carry*. Choose the visualisation that feels best for you and return to it when swimming in your normal training to help break the habit. A thumb-first entry can be a difficult habit to break so be persistent here!
4. **Tune up your catch and pull mechanics** by using the *Scull #1*, *Scull #2* and *Doggy Paddle* drills. Working on your catch and 'feel for the water' is a critical area for improvement for you as a Swinger. You may find it best to slow down your stroke a touch to take a little more time over your catch, if you have a Wetronome or Finis Tempo Trainer Pro try lowering your stroke rate by 3–5 strokes per minute. This will help you to develop your 'feel for the water' and give you the time to engage with it properly, increasing your propulsion.

   Doggy Paddle and *Scull #2 drills* are great for removing any crossovers under the body where the hand crosses the centre line. These are common to see with Swingers and will cause you to lose

Work on fixing that tendency to cross the centre line under your body – it will lose you propulsion, put stress on your shoulder and cause you to weave slightly down the lane.

propulsion and weave from side to side slightly as you swim. Visualise a rope under your body and pull down this rope as you swim – focus on not crossing over the centre line!

5. **Reconnect with your rhythm and timing** using the *Unco* drill. After improving your posture and catch mechanics using the above process you will have refined your pull-through technique and will be getting a greater purchase on the water. However, these changes may well have subtly altered the timing of your stroke, which may feel strange at first. To help synchronise these changes to your body rotation use the *Unco* drill, focusing on the mantra *Stroke And Dip* as you do so. Feel how your body rotation drives the stroke, and, when you start swimming, feel that easy rhythm to your stroke. As discussed above, you may end up at a slightly lower stroke rate than you are used to. That is fine if it means better alignment and propulsion in your stroke as you will be swimming quicker overall.
6. **Optional: formalise your 2-beat kick** using the process below. This is an advanced skill and is only suitable for Swingers whose strokes are becoming quite refined. A 2-beat kick only really suits swimmers with fast stroke rates – those with a slower stroke rate are normally much more suited to a light 6-beat flutter kick.
   - Kick on your front with fins on and both arms down by your side. Use a deep vertical scissoring of the legs to kick – we are looking for large movements switching between the two positions: left leg up + right leg down and right leg up + left leg down.

As you kick down with one leg, dip the opposite shoulder into the water.

- As you kick notice how the opposite shoulder naturally dips into the water. Continue this for at least 50 m, becoming used to the sensation, making it feel quite snappy through the hips and core.
- Keep the fins on and move to a lap of freestyle only breathing to the left. As your right hand enters into the water, roll and breathe to the left and simultaneously try the big deep kick down with the left leg. Make this a very positive movement each time the right hand enters into the water.
- Repeat the exercise but this time breathing to the right and kicking down with the right leg as the left hand enters into the water. You are unlikely to be able to think about both sides simultaneously as you swim so just focus on one side and simply mirror the other side of your stroke.
- Progress to swimming using bilateral breathing, timing the leg kick against your hand entry as described.

A 2-beat kick looks easy but is an advanced-level skill. Always practise using fins at first and using big exaggerated movements. Once you feel accustomed to the timing of the kick try integrating it into your normal swimming without using fins and with a much more compact and tidy kicking amplitude.

Smooth Stroke Correction Process

In contrast to the other Swim Type processes, which work on specific weaknesses, these steps are really an all-round once-over on your stroke. As a Smooth there won't be too much amiss but you will notice the benefits from tuning up a few areas of your stroke that have slipped a little.

The Smooth: the envy of the pool but may need to adapt their stroke for high-performance in open water.

1. **Give your exhalation technique a tune-up** using the *Sink Down* exercise in Appendix A. Despite your experience as a swimmer, the chances are that your exhalation is not what it could be. This won't be hard for you to improve but you will need to constantly remind yourself to exhale smoothly and efficiently into the water whilst you develop the habit.
2. **Give your posture and alignment in the water a once-over** using the *Kick On Side* and then *6-1-6* and *6-3-6* drills. As a Smooth this should be a strong area of yours but it is worth becoming aware of the importance of good posture in swimming. As we all get older we lose our natural flexibility so a little on-going maintenance in this area is well advised. If you have only been breathing to one side (see Chapter 7 and steps 4 and 5 below) then this is going to be important to you as you might have become a little lopsided in your stroke from doing so.

   Pay particular attention to your catch set-up position here using a slightly cocked wrist set-up with the fingertips lower than the wrist. This will help you initiate the catch effectively and help you to develop your 'feel for the water'.
3. **Revisit your catch mechanics** using the *Scull #1* and *Doggy Paddle* drills. You are probably familiar with these or similar exercises from your youth but might not have tried them in a while or focused on the right areas when doing so.

   We are looking to reignite your 'feel for the water', which will have already been assisted by an improved catch set-up from step 2. If you feel like your catch is not what it once was then pay attention to bending your elbow early in front of your head – both drills will assist you in doing so.
4. **Introduce bilateral breathing** if you are not already breathing to both sides regularly. With a good exhalation technique into the water and no hint of overgliding in your stroke you will find breathing every three strokes straightforward for the majority of your training. Bilateral breathing helps you to balance out your stroke and gives you practice at breathing to both sides – an important tactical consideration for racing well in the open water.
5. **Check your breathing timing** by visualising turning your head away from your arm as it enters the water and extends forwards on a breathing stroke. Turn your head smoothly away so that you never get a glimpse of it entering the water and you will find that you have more time to inhale, which will make things feel much more relaxed.

Late breathing is shown on the top sequence: the body rotates between (1) and (2) and then the head lifts to breathe (3). Correct timing is shown on the bottom row. The head rotates to breathe in time with the extension of the arm forwards.

6. **Rhythm and timing** is an important component of any great freestyle stroke and after steps 1–5 it is time to revisit it in your stroke. Use the *Unco* drill to help time your arm stroke with your body rotation. You will find that a smooth catch is essential during the drill as well as an emphasis on dipping the 'dead' shoulder down on every stroke. The magic of *Unco* is experienced when you start swimming immediately following the drill – you should feel super-smooth (even for you) and perhaps get some flashbacks to your best days in the water.

   If you feel that you have a tendency to add a slight overglide into your stroke then the *Waterpolo* and *Pull Buoy and Bands* drills are well worth adding to your training routine as they will move you towards a more continuous flowing extension and catch.
7. **Pay attention to your stroke completion at the hip**. The *Unco* drill in step 5 has focused a little on this area already but some additional focus might be useful if you have a tendency to over-emphasise the back of your stroke. A distinct push at the rear is not advisable as it creates a dead spot in its own right and can create a flicking movement into the air. This flick makes for an awkward arm recovery and can cause pain in the elbow known as 'Golfer's Elbow', or more correctly as Medial Epicondylitis. For more information see Chapter 13.

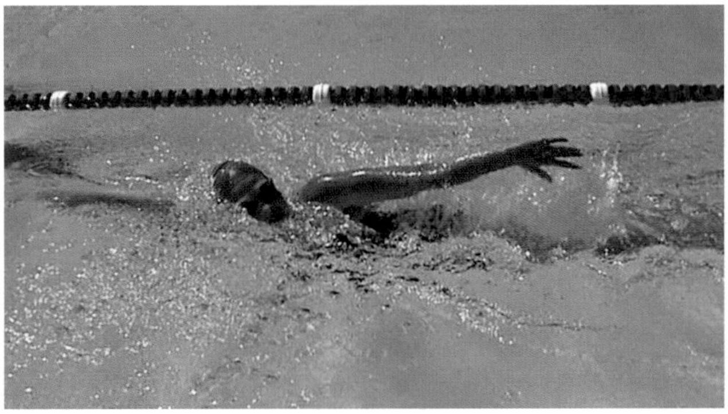

The rear of the stroke should be completed without locking the elbow straight as shown here. It should also finish with a slight inwards turn of the hand towards the top of the thigh to complete the stroke and make for a nice hand exit. Try this the next time you swim and notice how powerful but smooth it feels.

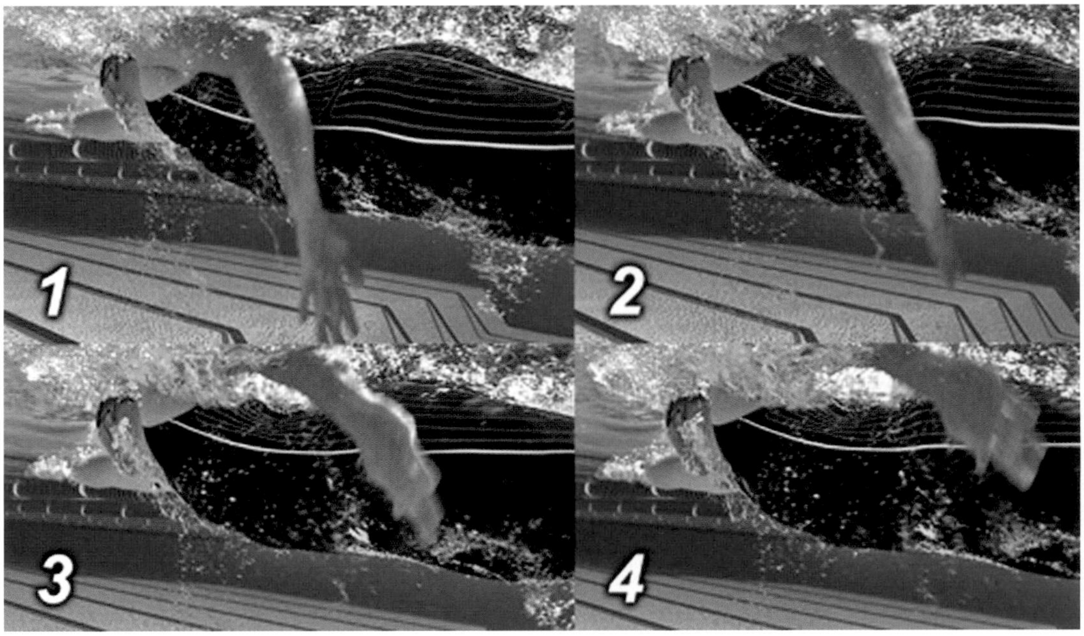

Turn the hand in slightly towards the top of the thigh to complete the stroke and exit cleanly.

8. **Fine tune your stroke rate using a stroke rate beeper** such as a Wetronome. This is a great way to reinforce the good work you have performed on your alignment, catch and timing. You may well find that you can increase your stroke rate slightly after this work, which will help the rhythm of your stroke. If your objective is to perform well in open water races then this is critical. You are not looking to lift your stroke rate by deliberately shortening the stroke – you still start at full extension and finish each stroke at the same point on the hip. Instead you get into your catch a little bit quicker at the front, emphasising stroke length less and focusing on rhythm instead.

9. **Add some new fitness training elements** to mundane interval sessions using our advice on training in Key 2 of this book. If you have a strong sprint background, this type of threshold-based training at CSS pace (Critical Swim Speed) when combined with a lap interval beeper like the Wetronome or Finis Tempo Trainer Pro can really add an exciting and motivating element to your sessions, especially if you find it hard to find anyone to swim with who can push you along at your pace. Set yourself some challenging targets for a set of 200 m intervals for example (e.g. 2:24 / 200 m) and dial in the Wetronome to beep every 18 seconds. Simply aim to be at each 25 m marker each time the beep goes and without realising it you will be half way through a really rewarding hard-fitness set trying to make sure that the little beeper does not get ahead of you! This adds in an element of pace awareness and is very much a technique set in itself – can you survive the entire set holding good form without blowing up? The format for these types of sessions is only limited by your imagination and we have included some of our favourites for you in Appendix C.

APPENDIX C Training Sessions

About These Training Sessions

To create a training session, pick from the training sets in this guide. We've provided six of each type to choose from:

- Warm-up.
- Build sets.
- Technique focused main sets.
- Fresh and fruity (CSS).
- Long endurance sets (suitable for Ironman and long distance open water swimmers).
- Sprint sets.
- Open water skills sets.
- Cool-downs.

Each type of set is available as one of six themes:

1. Something Classically Simple (aimed loosely at Arnies).
2. Something Relaxing (aimed loosely at Bambinos).
3. Something A Little Different (aimed loosely at Kicktastics).
4. Something More Technical (aimed loosely at Overgliders).
5. Something Rhythmical (aimed loosely at Swingers).
6. Something Smooth (aimed loosely at Smooths).

Pick a set that suits your Swim Type or your mood and 'mix and match' with other sets to create a whole session. The endurance sets stand alone as sessions by themselves but for everything else construct your session as a sequence of:

Warm-up set.
Build set.
Main set chosen from: technique, fresh and fruity (CSS), sprint or open water skills.
Cool-down set.

In total there are over 5,000 combinations to experience!

Session Terminology

The following abbreviations are used within the session descriptions:

f/s	Normal freestyle swimming.
m	metres (you may substitute this for yards obviously).
into	Usually suggests an interval which is split into two separate parts but swum continuously, i.e. 25 m drill [straight] into 25 m swim.
PFQ	Pretty Flipping Quick, i.e. fast swimming!
On 1:00 (60 s)	Start every interval after 1 minute (60 seconds) has elapsed since the start of the previous interval, e.g. if you were swimming 50 m intervals and completing each interval in 45 seconds, you would have 15 seconds rest before the next interval.
Build 1–4	Each interval (1–4) gets a little faster than the last, usually so that the last interval is at least at threshold pace.
TT	Time Trial, i.e. a timed swim over a specified distance.
Pull	Pull buoy, using a pull buoy between the legs to focus on arm stroke and / or body rotation exercises. Place the pull buoy up as high as it will go into your crotch. Use of paddles and bands (see below) are optional whenever performing pull sets.
HR	Heart Rate, measured in beats per minute.
Fins	Using a pair of fins / flippers to aid that particular part of the set.
+0:30 R.I.	Rest Interval, i.e. always 30 seconds recovery between each interval regardless of how fast you swam.
Breathe 3 s / 5 s	Breathe after having completed 3 or 5 strokes (where L-R-L is 3 strokes).
CSS Pace	Threshold pace as determined by completing a 400 m and 200 m time trial as described in Chapter 27.
CSS Pace +/−8″	Used to define a slower or faster than CSS goal pace for the set. Time is per 100 m if not otherwise specified.
Torpedo Kick	Streamlined push off wall with arms extended and head between the arms.
3 × (4 × 100 m)	3 sets of 4 times 100 metre intervals, usually where all four intervals in each of the three sets are identical.
↑ / ↓ Up / Down	Swim up the pool performing one thing (e.g. a drill) and after the turn coming back swimming another (e.g. normal f/s).
Straight Swim	Normal continuous freestyle.
I.M.	Individual Medley: butterfly, backstroke, breaststroke, freestyle (in that order).
Kick on Side (left or right specified)	Kicking whilst perfectly on your side, showing your bellybutton to one wall and your back to the other. Keep your top arm by your side and bottom arm reaching forward your ear resting on the shoulder of your leading arm.
Bands	Use of an old bike inner-tube around the ankles to encourage good core control and to work on lifting stroke rate.

Skeleton Structures

suggested outline structure of a training month, see Chapter 26

Swim Smooth's Suggested Weekly Training Structure Based on Frequency of Swimming

Weekly Frequency	Week Number	Monday	Tuesday	Wednesday	Thursday	Friday	Saturday	Sunday
2 times / week	1		Technique			Threshold / CSS		
	2		OW Skills			Endurance		
	3		Technique			Threshold / CSS		
	4		OW Skills			Threshold / CSS		
3 times / week	1		Technique		Threshold / CSS		OW Skills	
	2		Technique		Threshold / CSS		Endurance	
	3		Technique		Threshold / CSS		OW Skills	
	4		Endurance		Speed		Technique	
4 times / week	1	Technique		Endurance		Threshold / CSS	OW Skills	
	2	Technique		Endurance		Threshold / CSS	OW Skills	
	3	Technique		Endurance		Threshold / CSS	OW Skills	
	4	Technique		Endurance		Speed	Technique	
5 times / week	1	Technique	Endurance		Threshold / CSS	Speed	OW Skills	
	2	Technique	Threshold / CSS		Threshold / CSS	Edurance	OW Skills	
	3	Technique	Endurance		Threshold / CSS	Technique	OW Skills	
	4	Threshold / CSS	Technique		Speed or REST	Technique	OW Skills	
6 times / week	1	Technique	Threshold / CSS	Endurance	Technique	Threshold / CSS	OW Skills	
	2	Speed	Endurance	Threshold / CSS	Technique	Endurance or LCS	OW Skills	
	3	Technique	Threshold / CSS	Endurance	Technique	Threshold / CSS	OW Skills or LCS	
	4	Speed or REST	Endurance	Technique	Threshold / CSS	Technique	OW Skills	
7 times / week	1	Technique	Threshold / CSS	Endurance	Technique	Threshold / CSS	OW Skills	Endurance or LCS
	2	Speed	Endurance	Threshold / CSS	Technique	Endurance or LCS	OW Skills	Threshold / CSS
	3	Technique	Threshold / CSS	Endurance	Technique	Threshold / CSS	OW Skills	Endurance or LCS
	4	Speed	Endurance	Technique	Threshold / CSS	Technique or REST	OW Skills	Technique

LCS = Long Continuous Swim   CSS = Critical Swim Speed   OW Skills = Open water skills (pool or open water based on season)

Recommendation is to swim at least three times per week to see improvements. Only ramp up distances by 10% per week or less, having an easier week every fourth week. This easier week is less important if you are training less than four times per week (all sports).

Warm-up Sets

ease into your session and progressively lift your heart rate

Session 1 – Something Classically Simple

Aim: A simple set to get you started on a good note.

Warm-up:

400 m Easy f/s – focus on smooth exhalation and bilateral breathing + 30 sec
300 m Pull Buoy – focus on Good Roll + 20 sec
200 m Fins ↑Broken Arrow ↓f/s steady + 15 sec
100 m Easy f/s – Nice and Smooth

Total distance: 1000 m

Session 2 – Something Relaxing

Aim: Use the fins where possible to start your session in a relaxed and smooth manner.

Warm-up:

repeat 2×:
200 m Fins – long, smooth strokes breathing easily + 20 sec
2 × 100 m Fins ↑6/1/6 ↓f/s + 15 sec
2 × 50 m Normal easy f/s – nice and relaxed + 10 sec

Total distance: 1000 m

Session 3 – Something A Little Different

Aim: Variety is the spice of life!

Warm-up:

		Set 1	Set 2	Set 3
3×	100 m + 10 sec	Easy f/s	Fins breathing 5 s (f/s)	F/s nice and Smooth
	2 × 50 m + 10 sec	Pull Buoy – Good Catch	Torpedo Kick alternating front and back	Fins as 25 m Shoulder Tap + 25 m f/s
	4 × 25 m + 5 sec	f/s as odd # fast(ish) and even # easy	Pull Buoy 1) B3 2) B5 3) B7 4) B3	All f/s getting progressively faster

Total distance: 900 m

Session 4 – Something More Technical

Aim: A great warm-up for establishing rhythm and 'feel for the water'.

Warm-up: 5 × 200 m + 20 sec

1) Normal f/s breathing 25 m Left + 25 m Right + 50 m Bilateral
2) Fins ↑6/3/6 ↓f/s
3) Normal f/s breathing 25 m Left + 25 m Right + 50 m Bilateral
4) Pull Buoy as 15 m Scull #1 + 85 m f/s
5) Normal easy f/s – nice and relaxed

Total distance: 1000 m

Session 5 – Something Rhythmical

Aim: Quite a challenging warm-up designed primarily for more advanced swimmers.

Warm-up: 2 × 500 m + 30 sec

1) Normal – Focus on exhalation and a fluid stroke. Hold a reasonable, consistent pace
2) Pull Buoy – First and last 200 m = pull and bands Middle 100 m = bands only

Total distance: 1000 m

Session 6 – Something Smooth

Aim: A classically smooth warm-up with a focus on the rhythm and timing of your breath.

Warm-up:

200 m Easy f/s – Breathing bilaterally
200 m Pull Buoy – Breathing 5 s
200 m Fins ↑25 m Left Unco + 25 m f/s ↓25 m Right Unco + 25 m f/s
200 m Pull Buoy – Alternating breathing sides per 25 m
200 m Easy f/s – Breathing bilaterally

Total distance: 1000 m

Build Sets

a series of shorter intervals designed to elevate heart rate in preparation for the main set

Session 1 – Something Classically Simple

Aim: A simple way to prepare for a more testing main set.

Build Set: 4, 6 or 8 × 50 m + 15 sec. All done as 25 m fast holding good form + 25 m easy

Total distance: 200 – 400 m

Session 2 – Something Relaxing

Aim: A nice way to prepare for a main set without pushing too hard!

Build Set: 4 × 75 m + 20 sec | *alternating*:
10 fast strokes – nice and positive 'oomph'
10 easy strokes – stretch out and breathe easy!

Total distance: 300 m

Session 3 – Something A Little Different

Aim: A throw-back to your days in swim squad!

Build Set: 8 × 50 m Rolling I.Ms, ie.

2 × *all + 15 sec rest* |
25 m Fly + 25 m Back
25 m Back + 25 m Breast
25 m Breast + 25 m Free
25 m Free + 25 m Fly

Total distance: 400 m

Session 4 – Something More Technical

Aim: Focus on a good catch and feel and maintain this when adding a little 'punch' to your stroke!

Build Set: 6, 8 or 10 × 50 m Pull Buoy + 10 sec

Do each 50 m as:
15 m Scull #1
10 m Doggy Paddle
10 m Fast
15 m Easy!

Total distance: 300 – 500 m

Session 5 – Something Rhythmical

Aim: To gradually elevate your speed and rhythm in readiness for main set.

Build Set: 4 × 100 m + 15 secs | Building each 25 m during each 100 m from very easy to very fast. Adopt a straighter arm recovery to simulate open water swimming in rough conditions and feel really fluid in your stroke

Total distance: 400 m

Session 6 – Something Smooth

Aim: A classic build set over a slightly longer distance to emulate an open water start and finish.

Build Set: 3 × 200 m + 20 sec | *each 200 m as:*
50 m Fast and Smooth
100 m Cruise at moderate intensity
50 m Pick pace back up and finish strong

Total distance: 600 m

Technique Main Sets

develop your stroke technique with these main sets

Session 1 – Something Classically Simple

Aim: Loosen off those shoulders and feel smooth!

Technique Main Set: 4 × 200 m + 20 sec

1) Fins ↑6/1/6 ↓f/s
2) Pull Buoy breathing 3/5/7/3…
3) Fins ↑Broken Arrow ↓f/s
4) Normal f/s – Nice and Smooth

Total distance: 800 m

Session 2 – Something Relaxing

Aim: Focus on the timing of your stroke – don't let the lead arm drop!

Technique Main Set: 5 ×(+15 sec)

100 m Fins as 25 m Left Kick
25 m Right Kick
50 m f/s Swim
100 m Fins as 50 m 6/1/6
50 m f/s

Total distance: 1000 m

Session 3 – Something A Little Different

Aim: Focus on toes pointed and turned in on technique set – long, straight legs.

Technique Main Set: 6 × 75 m + 10 sec as

25 m Pull Buoy
25 m Kick*
25 m Pull Buoy

*use your pull buoy as your kick board

then

6 × 75 m + 10 sec as

25 m Breathing 3 s
25 m Breathing 5 s
25 m Breathing to least favourite side!

Total distance: 900 m

Session 4 – Something More Technical

Aim: A nice technique main set focusing on setting up for a good catch.

Technique Main Set: 30 × 50 m + 10 sec rest

Broken down into blocks of 10 × 50 m with odd numbers = drills and even numbers = 25m fast + 25m easy

Set 1) Focus: Alignment: Fins 25 m Left Side Kick + 25 m Right Side Kick
Set 2) Focus: Rotation: Fins 25 m 6/3/6 + 25 m f/s
Set 3) Focus on Catch: Pull as 10 m Scull #1, 10 m Scull #2, 30 m f/s

Total distance: 1500 m

Session 5 – Something Rhythmical

Aim: Chance to experiment with a range of stroke rates to find a nice optimal point.

Technique Main Set: 4 × 250 m + 20 sec. Focus on stroke rate

1) Basic Rate Stroke Rate
2) Basic Rate Stroke Rate + 5 SPM*
3) Basic Rate Stroke Rate – 5 SPM*
4) Basic Rate Stroke Rate + 3 SPM*

** Requires a Wetronome or Tempo Trainer Pro*

Total distance: 1000 m

Session 6 – Something Smooth

Aim: A great set where time will fly with a simple focus on your stroke.

Technique Main Set: 3 ×

25 m Drill + 25 m f/s
50 m Drill + 50 m f/s
75 m Drill + 75 m f/s
100 m Drill + 100 m f/s

Continuous 500 m with 30 sec between sets

Set 1) Fins – Drill = Shoulder Tap
Set 2) Pull – Drill = Doggy Paddle
Set 3) Fins – Drill = Broken Arrow

Total distance: 1500 m

Fresh and Fruity Threshold Main Sets

testing sets to develop your CSS fitness – perfect for any distance swimmer

All of these sets would benefit from the use of a Wetronome or Tempo Trainer Pro for better pace judgement.

Session 1 – Something Classically Simple

Aim: A classic 'Blue Ribband' main set!

Fresh and Fruity: 14, 16, 18 or 20 × 100 m + 20 sec

- Holding fastest maintainable pace
- If using a wetronome/tempo trainer set this per 25 m @ CSS pace and take 1 beep recovery between 100 m intervals

Total distance: 1400 – 2000 m

Session 2 – Something Relaxing

Aim: A classically simple pyramid set to get your teeth into.

Fresh and Fruity:

100 m
200 m
300 m
300 m
200 m
100 m

All @ CSS pace but take 2 beeps recovery between each interval to make for an easier session.

Total distance: 1200 m

Session 3 – Something A Little Different

Aim: The Goldilocks set – can you hold back to CSS pace on the 100 m ready for the 300 m?

Fresh and Fruity: 2 × (3 × 100 m, 2 × 200 m, 1 × 300 m) All @ CSS pace + 20 sec rest or 1 beep recovery

Total distance: 2000 m

Session 4 – Something More Technical

Aim: Don't be fooled by the 100 m – It's the 400 m at the end that counts!

Fresh and Fruity:

4 × 100 m
1 × 200 m
4 × 100 m
1 × 300 m
4 × 100 m
1 × 400 m

All @ CSS pace + 20 sec rest or 1 beep recovery

Total distance: 2100 m

Session 5 – Something Rhythmical

Aim: The challenge here is to not go out too quick – this is a long fresh and fruity set but rewarding if you hold your pace.

Fresh and Fruity: 8 × 300 m @ CSS Pace + 40 sec rest or 2 beeps recovery
1 – 3 & 5 – 7 = f/s
4 + 8 = Pull and Paddles

Total distance: 2400 m

Session 6 – Something Smooth

Aim: Speed and endurance required here in this challenging but enjoyable main set.

Fresh and Fruity: 40 × 50 m 'Spike Set'
Broken as:

16 × 50 m sprint every 4th, cycle time of CSS + 5 s per 50 m*
12 × 50 m sprint every 3rd, cycle time of CSS + 10 s per 50 m
8 × 50 m sprint every 2nd, cycle time of CSS + 15 s per 50 m
4 × 50 m sprint every one, cycle time of CSS + 20 s per 50 m

*turn-around time is set as CSS pace + 5 s per 100 m, e.g. 45 s including recovery time if your CSS pace is 0:40/50 m
Total distance: 2000 m

Endurance Sessions

these endurance sessions do not require an additional warm-up – they are a session in themselves

Session 1 – Something Classically Simple

Aim: To beat the beeper (or cycle time) to gain rest between intervals. Pacing is key!

Endurance Session:

20 × 50 m	
10 × 100 m	Set your 50 m cycle time to half your 100 m pace
5 × 200 m	for CSS + 5"
2 × 500 m	i.e. If CSS 1'40" – 50m cycle time is 55 secs

Total distance: 4000 m

Session 2 – Something Relaxing

Aim: A very basic endurance set with respite between the longer swims on numbers 2 and 4.

Endurance Session:

5 × 500 m + 60 secs
1) Steady f/s @ CSS + 6" per 100 m
2) Fins as very steady swimming keeping stroke long and smooth
3) Steady f/s @ CSS + 4" per 100 m
4) Pull Buoy breathing 3/2/3/2…
5) Steady f/s @ CSS + 2" per 100 m

Total distance: 2500 m

Session 3 – Something A Little Different

Aim: Stay with the beeper on A sets but get as far in front of beeper on B sets as you feel good for on the day!

Endurance Session:

3 × 200 m A	A – @ CSS pace + 5" per 100 m + 30 secs
3 × 300 m B	rest between intervals
5 × 100 m A	
3 × 400 m B	B – on a cycle time of CSS + 10" per 100 m, but you
6 × 50 m A	must beat the time (beeper) to gain recovery between
3 × 500 m B	intervals – no additional rest on top of cycle time

Total distance: 5000 m

Session 4 – Something More Technical

Aim: A seemingly steady session but one which keeps you focused on pacing and patience!

Endurance Session:

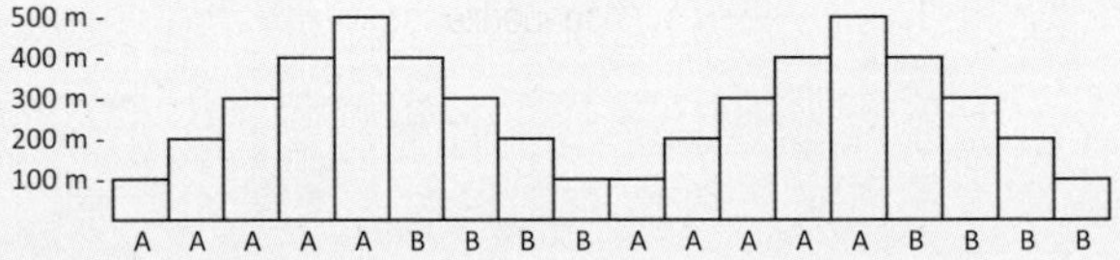

All + 30 secs rest
A = CSS + 6" per 100 m
B = CSS + 3" per 100 m

Total distance: 5000 m

Session 5 – Something Rhythmical

Aim: Can you pace yourself well enough on the 'easy' 500 m in readiness for the 1.5 km?

Endurance Session:

	500 m	@ CSS + 9" per 100 m + 60 secs
2 x	1000 m	@ CSS + 6" per 100 m + 60 secs
	1500 m	@ CSS + 3" per 100 m + 60 secs

Total distance: 6000 m

Session 6 – Something Smooth

Aim: Challenging main set which requires precision pacing!

Endurance Session:

	3 × 100 m	@ CSS pace + 6" per 100 m + 20 secs rest
3 ×	1 × 300 m	All on a cycle time CSS + 10 sec per 100 m
	1 × 500 m	No additional rest: make your recovery
	1 × 700 m	time by beating the beeper!

OPTIONAL: Pull and Paddles on 300 m and 700 m of Set 2

Total distance: 5400 m

Swim Smooth Sprint Main Sets

sprint sets to develop your anaerobic fitness and give you a short-duration turn of pace

Session 1 – Something Classically Simple

Aim: Try breathing every 5 strokes to maintain streamlining.

Sprint Main Session: 10 × 100 m + 60 sec rest
Aim to swim these as fast as possible whilst still being consistent with your pacing

Total distance: 1000 m

Session 2 – Something Relaxing

Aim: Use the easier swims as some active recovery.

Sprint Main Session:
8 × 50 m as 25 m fast + 25 m easy + 20 sec rest
16 × 25 m as odd numbers fast and even numbers easy + 10 sec rest

Total distance: 800 m

Session 3 – Something A Little Different

Aim: Go as fast as you can and deduct the 20 sec rest time from final 200 m time.

Sprint Main Session: 6* × Broken 200 m as
- 100 m P.F.Q. + 10 sec rest
- 50 m P.F.Q. + 10 sec rest
- 50 m P.F.Q. + 90 sec rest

P.F.Q. = Pretty flippin' quick
* Optional fins on last 2 sets

Total distance: 1200 m

Session 4 – Something More Technical

Aim: A pyramid 'fartlek' session to play with your speed.

Sprint Main Session: 3 ×
- 25 m
- **50 m**
- 75 m
- **100 m**
- 100 m
- **75 m**
- 50 m
- **25 m**

Take just 15 secs rest between each interval, but really sprint the intervals in bold.

Total distance: 1500 m

Session 5 – Something Rhythmical

Aim: Where do you feel most rhythmical and powerful in your stroke?

Sprint Main Session: 30 × 50 m + 15 secs

Broken down as:
5 × 50 m @ base rate stroke rate
5 × 50 m @ base rate stroke rate + 3 SPM
5 × 50 m @ base rate stroke rate + 6 SPM
5 × 50 m @ base rate stroke rate + 9 SPM
5 × 50 m @ base rate stroke rate + 12 SPM
5 × 50 m @ base rate stroke rate + 15 SPM
* Requires a Wetronome / Tempo Trainer Pro

Total distance: 1500 m

Session 6 – Something Smooth

Aim: A very tough session for experienced 'smooths' everywhere.

Sprint Main Session: 2 × (take additional 60 s rest between the two sets)
- 3 × 200 m + 45 secs rest between holding your very best pace for each
- 4 × 50 m All flat-out but on 5 secs less rest for each, ie. 55, 50, 45, 40 s cycle time

Total distance: 1600 m

Open Water Skills Sets (in pool)

you don't have to be in the open water to work on your open water skills – in fact the controlled environment of the pool has some distinct advantages

Session 1 – Something Classically Simple

Aim: Practice the essentials of good O/W swimming!

Open Water Session:

4 × 50 m	+ 10 secs	Head-up sighting every 9 strokes
4 × 200 m	+ 20 secs	With a partner practicing inline drafting, swapping every 50 m
4 × 100 m	+ 15 secs	Practicing arrow head drafting at good pace with two friends

* Requires 1–2 mates

Total distance: 1400 m

Session 2 – Something Relaxing

Aim: To get comfortable with the process of sighting and breathing to least favourite side.

Open Water Session: 4 × 300 m + 30 secs

1) Fins – Long and Smooth
2) Fins with head-up sighting every 9 strokes
3) Pull Buoy breathing to least favourite side
4) Normal f/s

If possible do this drafting steadily with a partner

Total distance: 1200 m

Session 3 – Something A Little Different

Aim: Practice close confines drafting and speed.

Open Water Session:

2 × 400 m	+ 30 secs	Inline drafting, swapping every 100 m and holding a really good pace
8 × 50 m	+ 10 secs	Deep water starts with an open water turn at the end of the pool if in a 25 m pool (ie. no touching wall)
4 × 100 m	+ 15 secs	Drafting but trying to drop your partners

* Requires 3–5 friends

Total distance: 1600 m

Session 4 – Something More Technical

Aim: Add a little punch and rhythm to this set by doing it with optional pull and bands.

Open Water Session:

1 × 300 m
2 × 150 m
4 × 75 m
3 × 100 m
6 × 50 m

All at just above CSS pace with only 10 secs rest between each interval. To simulate open water, try a deep water start for each interval and include some head-up sighting too!

Total distance: 1500 m

Session 5 – Something Rhythmical

Aim: 'Funnel' your stroke rate in to an optimal point and experiment with a range of stroke rates applicable for rough O/W swimming.

Open Water Session: 24 × 50 m + 10 secs

Broken down as:

8 × 50 m	4 at base rate stroke rate +12 SPM* 4 at base rate stroke rate −12 SPM*
8 × 50 m	4 at base rate stroke rate +8 SPM* 4 at base rate stroke rate −8 SPM*
8 × 50 m	4 at base rate stroke rate +4 SPM* 4 at base rate stroke rate −4 SPM*

* Requires a Wetronome / Tempo Trainer PRO

Total distance: 1200 m

Session 6 – Something Smooth

Aim: Keep pace high and recovery short to simulate a 1500 m swim.

Open Water Session: 10 × 150 m

Fast efforts – with a climb out and walk to other end of pool to start next interval. Different leader per 150 m who is trying to drop the swimmers behind.*

Total distance: 1500 m

* Requires 2–4 friends

Cool-down Sets

gently bring down your heart rate and flush waste products from your muscles using these cool-down sets

Session 1 – Something Classically Simple

Aim: Great to loosen off the shoulders.

Cool-Down:
100 m Easy f/s
100 m Fins ↑Broken Arrow ↓f/s
100 m Easy Pull Buoy with good body roll

Total distance: 300 m

Session 2 – Something Relaxing

Aim: Love the water, even stop at the deep end for 3 sink downs each time

Cool-Down: 200 m with Fins – long and smooth strokes focusing on exhalation

Total distance: 200 m

Session 3 – Something A Little Different

Aim: Our favourite! A great way to unwind!

Cool-Down: 200 m as 2 × | 50 m easy f/s
50 m 'Leisure Stroke'

Total distance: 200 m

Leisure Stroke = Double Arm Backstroke with Breastroke Legs

Session 4 – Something More Technical

Aim: Try to be precise with your pacing here and maintain good form.

Cool-Down: 6 × 50 m + 10 sec rest, descending speed by 2 sec per 50 m, finishing very slow

Total distance: 300 m

Session 5 – Something Rhythmical

Aim: Reduce Stroke Rate gradually whilst all the while feeling smooth

Cool-Down: 6 × 50 m + 15 sec rest, descending stroke rate by 2 SPM per 50 m, starting @ base rate

Total distance: 300 m

Session 6 – Something Smooth

Aim: To finish off the session smoothly!

Cool-Down:
100 m Easy f/s
100 m Pull Buoy | Try to visualise Jono Van Hazel's stroke www.swimsmooth.com/jono
100 m Fins f/s

Total distance: 300 m

Pace Chart

split times across different distances for the same swimming pace

25 m	50 m	100 m	150 m	200 m	400 m	500 m	1000 m	1500 m	1.9 km	3.8 km	5.0 km	10.0 km
15.00	00:00:30	**00:01:00**	**00:01:30**	02:00.0	00:04:00	00:05:00	00:10:00	00:15:00	00:19:00	00:38:00	00:50:00	01:40:00
15.50	00:00:31	**00:01:02**	**00:01:33**	02:04.0	00:04:08	00:05:10	00:10:20	00:15:30	00:19:38	00:39:16	00:51:40	01:43:20
16.00	00:00:32	**00:01:04**	**00:01:36**	02:08.0	00:04:16	00:05:20	00:10:40	00:16:00	00:20:16	00:40:32	00:53:20	01:46:40
16.50	00:00:33	**00:01:06**	**00:01:39**	02:12.0	00:04:24	00:05:30	00:11:00	00:16:30	00:20:54	00:41:48	00:55:00	01:50:00
17.00	00:00:34	**00:01:08**	**00:01:42**	02:16.0	00:04:32	00:05:40	00:11:20	00:17:00	00:21:32	00:43:04	00:56:40	01:53:20
17.50	00:00:35	**00:01:10**	**00:01:45**	02:20.0	00:04:40	00:05:50	00:11:40	00:17:30	00:22:10	00:44:20	00:58:20	01:56:40
18.00	00:00:36	**00:01:12**	**00:01:48**	02:24.0	00:04:48	00:06:00	00:12:00	00:18:00	00:22:48	00:45:36	01:00:00	02:00:00
18.50	00:00:37	**00:01:14**	**00:01:51**	02:28.0	00:04:56	00:06:10	00:12:20	00:18:30	00:23:26	00:46:52	01:01:40	02:03:20
18.75	00:00:38	**00:01:15**	**00:01:52**	02:30.0	00:05:00	00:06:15	00:12:30	00:18:45	00:23:45	00:47:30	01:02:30	02:05:00
19.00	00:00:38	**00:01:16**	**00:01:54**	02:32.0	00:05:04	00:06:20	00:12:40	00:19:00	00:24:04	00:48:08	01:03:20	02:06:40
19.25	00:00:39	**00:01:17**	**00:01:56**	02:34.0	00:05:08	00:06:25	00:12:50	00:19:15	00:24:23	00:48:46	01:04:10	02:08:20
19.50	00:00:39	**00:01:18**	**00:01:57**	02:36.0	00:05:12	00:06:30	00:13:00	00:19:30	00:24:42	00:49:24	01:05:00	02:10:00
19.75	00:00:40	**00:01:19**	**00:01:58**	02:38.0	00:05:16	00:06:35	00:13:10	00:19:45	00:25:01	00:50:02	01:05:50	02:11:40
20.00	00:00:40	**00:01:21**	**00:02:00**	02:40.0	00:05:20	00:06:40	00:13:20	00:20:00	00:25:20	00:50:40	01:06:40	02:13:20
20.25	00:00:41	**00:01:21**	**00:02:01**	02:42.0	00:05:24	00:06:45	00:13:30	00:20:15	00:25:39	00:51:18	01:07:30	02:15:00
20.50	00:00:41	**00:01:22**	**00:02:03**	02:44.0	00:05:28	00:06:50	00:13:40	00:20:30	00:25:58	00:51:56	01:08:20	02:16:40
20.75	00:00:42	**00:01:23**	**00:02:05**	02:46.0	00:05:32	00:06:55	00:13:50	00:20:45	00:26:17	00:52:34	01:09:10	02:18:20
21.00	00:00:42	**00:01:24**	**00:02:06**	02:48.0	00:05:36	00:07:00	00:14:00	00:21:00	00:26:36	00:53:12	01:10:00	02:20:00
21.25	00:00:42	**00:01:25**	**00:02:07**	02:50.0	00:05:40	00:07:05	00:14:10	00:21:15	00:26:55	00:53:50	01:10:50	02:21:40
21.50	00:00:43	**00:01:26**	**00:02:09**	02:52.0	00:05:44	00:07:10	00:14:20	00:21:30	00:27:14	00:54:28	01:11:40	02:23:20
21.75	00:00:44	**00:01:27**	**00:02:10**	02:54.0	00:05:48	00:07:15	00:14:30	00:21:45	00:27:33	00:55:06	01:12:30	02:25:00
22.00	00:00:44	**00:01:28**	**00:02:12**	02:56.0	00:05:52	00:07:20	00:14:40	00:22:00	00:27:52	00:55:44	01:13:20	02:26:40
22.25	00:00:45	**00:01:29**	**00:02:13**	02:58.0	00:05:56	00:07:25	00:14:50	00:22:15	00:28:11	00:56:22	01:14:10	02:28:20
22.50	00:00:45	**00:01:30**	**00:02:15**	03:00.0	00:06:00	00:07:30	00:15:00	00:22:30	00:28:30	00:57:00	01:15:00	02:30:00
22.75	00:00:46	**00:01:31**	**00:02:16**	03:02.0	00:06:04	00:07:35	00:15:10	00:22:45	00:28:49	00:57:38	01:15:50	02:31:40
23.00	00:00:46	**00:01:32**	**00:02:18**	03:04.0	00:06:08	00:07:40	00:15:20	00:23:00	00:29:08	00:58:16	01:16:40	02:33:20
23.25	00:00:47	**00:01:33**	**00:02:20**	03:06.0	00:06:12	00:07:45	00:15:30	00:23:15	00:29:27	00:58:54	01:17:30	02:35:00
23.50	00:00:47	**00:01:34**	**00:02:21**	03:08.0	00:06:16	00:07:50	00:15:40	00:23:30	00:29:46	00:59:32	01:18:20	02:36:40

23.75	00:00:47	**00:01:35**	**00:02:23**	03:10.0	00:06:20	00:07:55	00:15:50	00:23:45	00:30:05	01:00:10	01:19:10	02:38:20
24.00	00:00:48	**00:01:36**	**00:02:24**	03:12.0	00:06:24	00:08:00	00:16:00	00:24:00	00:30:24	01:00:48	01:20:00	02:40:00
24.25	00:00:48	**00:01:37**	**00:02:25**	03:14.0	00:06:28	00:08:05	00:16:10	00:24:15	00:30:43	01:01:26	01:20:50	02:41:40
24.50	00:00:49	**00:01:38**	**00:02:27**	03:16.0	00:06:32	00:08:10	00:16:20	00:24:30	00:31:02	01:02:04	01:21:40	02:43:20
24.75	00:00:49	**00:01:39**	**00:02:29**	03:18.0	00:06:36	00:08:15	00:16:30	00:24:45	00:31:21	01:02:42	01:22:30	02:45:00
25.00	00:00:50	**00:01:40**	**00:02:30**	03:20.0	00:06:40	00:08:20	00:16:40	00:25:00	00:31:40	01:03:20	01:23:20	02:46:40
25.25	00:00:51	**00:01:41**	**00:02:31**	03:22.0	00:06:44	00:08:25	00:16:50	00:25:15	00:31:59	01:03:58	01:24:10	02:48:20
25.50	00:00:51	**00:01:42**	**00:02:33**	03:24.0	00:06:48	00:08:30	00:17:00	00:25:30	00:32:18	01:04:36	01:25:00	02:50:00
25.75	00:00:51	**00:01:43**	**00:02:35**	03:26.0	00:06:52	00:08:35	00:17:10	00:25:45	00:32:37	01:05:14	01:25:50	02:51:40
26.00	00:00:52	**00:01:44**	**00:02:36**	03:28.0	00:06:56	00:08:40	00:17:20	00:26:00	00:32:56	01:05:52	01:26:40	02:53:20
26.25	00:00:53	**00:01:45**	**00:02:38**	03:30.0	00:07:00	00:08:45	00:17:30	00:26:15	00:33:15	01:06:30	01:27:30	02:55:00
26.50	00:00:53	**00:01:46**	**00:02:39**	03:32.0	00:07:04	00:08:50	00:17:40	00:26:30	00:33:34	01:07:08	01:28:20	02:56:40
26.75	00:00:53	**00:01:47**	**00:02:40**	03:34.0	00:07:08	00:08:55	00:17:50	00:26:45	00:33:53	01:07:46	01:29:10	02:58:20
27.00	00:00:54	**00:01:48**	**00:02:42**	03:36.0	00:07:12	00:09:00	00:18:00	00:27:00	00:34:12	01:08:24	01:30:00	03:00:00
27.25	00:00:54	**00:01:49**	**00:02:44**	03:38.0	00:07:16	00:09:05	00:18:10	00:27:15	00:34:31	01:09:02	01:30:50	03:01:40
27.50	00:00:55	**00:01:50**	**00:02:45**	03:40.0	00:07:20	00:09:10	00:18:20	00:27:30	00:34:50	01:09:40	01:31:40	03:03:20
27.75	00:00:56	**00:01:51**	**00:02:46**	03:42.0	00:07:24	00:09:15	00:18:30	00:27:45	00:35:09	01:10:18	01:32:30	03:05:00
28.00	00:00:56	**00:01:52**	**00:02:48**	03:44.0	00:07:28	00:09:20	00:18:40	00:28:00	00:35:28	01:10:56	01:33:20	03:06:40
28.25	00:00:56	**00:01:53**	**00:02:50**	03:46.0	00:07:32	00:09:25	00:18:50	00:28:15	00:35:47	01:11:34	01:34:10	03:08:20
28.50	00:00:57	**00:01:54**	**00:02:51**	03:48.0	00:07:36	00:09:30	00:19:00	00:28:30	00:36:06	01:12:12	01:35:00	03:10:00
28.75	00:00:58	**00:01:55**	**00:02:53**	03:50.0	00:07:40	00:09:35	00:19:10	00:28:45	00:36:25	01:12:50	01:35:50	03:11:40
29.00	00:00:58	**00:01:56**	**00:02:54**	03:52.0	00:07:44	00:09:40	00:19:20	00:29:00	00:36:44	01:13:28	01:36:40	03:13:20
29.25	00:00:59	**00:01:57**	**00:02:56**	03:54.0	00:07:48	00:09:45	00:19:30	00:29:15	00:37:03	01:14:06	01:37:30	03:15:00
29.50	00:00:59	**00:01:58**	**00:02:57**	03:56.0	00:07:52	00:09:50	00:19:40	00:29:30	00:37:22	01:14:44	01:38:20	03:16:40
29.75	00:00:59	**00:01:59**	**00:02:59**	03:58.0	00:07:56	00:09:55	00:19:50	00:29:45	00:37:41	01:15:22	01:39:10	03:18:20
30.00	00:01:00	**00:02:00**	**00:03:00**	04:00.0	00:08:00	00:10:00	00:20:00	00:30:00	00:38:00	01:16:00	01:40:00	03:20:00
30.50	00:01:01	**00:02:02**	**00:03:03**	04:04.0	00:08:08	00:10:10	00:20:20	00:30:30	00:38:38	01:17:16	01:41:40	03:23:20
31.00	00:01:02	**00:02:04**	**00:03:06**	04:08.0	00:08:16	00:10:20	00:20:40	00:31:00	00:39:16	01:18:32	01:43:20	03:26:40
31.50	00:01:03	**00:02:06**	**00:03:09**	04:12.0	00:08:24	00:10:30	00:21:00	00:31:30	00:39:54	01:19:48	01:45:00	03:30:00
32.00	00:01:04	**00:02:08**	**00:03:12**	04:16.0	00:08:32	00:10:40	00:21:20	00:32:00	00:40:32	01:21:04	01:46:40	03:33:20
33.00	00:01:06	**00:02:12**	**00:03:18**	04:24.0	00:08:48	00:11:00	00:22:00	00:33:00	00:41:48	01:23:36	01:50:00	03:40:00
34.00	00:01:08	**00:02:16**	**00:03:24**	04:32.0	00:09:04	00:11:20	00:22:40	00:34:00	00:43:04	01:26:08	01:53:20	03:46:40
35.00	00:01:10	**00:02:20**	**00:03:30**	04:40.0	00:09:20	00:11:40	00:23:20	00:35:00	00:44:20	01:28:40	01:56:40	03:53:20

Index

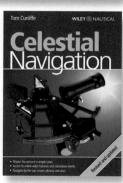

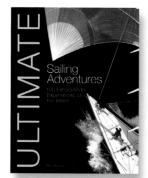

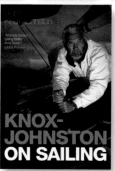